The Irish Diaries
[1994–2003]

The Irish Diaries
[1994–2003]

ALASTAIR CAMPBELL

edited by Kathy Gilfillan

THE LILLIPUT PRESS
DUBLIN

Published 2013 by
THE LILLIPUT PRESS
62–63 Sitric Road, Arbour Hill,
Dublin 7, Ireland
www.lilliputpress.ie

The Alastair Campbell Diaries were originally
published by Hutchinson in Great Britain:
Volume One, *Prelude to Power* (2010)
Volume Two, *Power & the People* (2011)
Volume Three, *Power & Responsibility* (2011)
Volume Four, *The Burden of Power* (2012)
www.randomhouse.co.uk

Copyright © Alastair Campbell, 2013

ISBN 978 1 84351 40 08

1 3 5 7 9 10 8 6 4 2

Set in 11 on 14 pt Garamond by Marsha Swan
Printed by GraphCems in Spain

Contents

Illustrations between pages 168 and 169

Editor's Note

Alastair Campbell's diaries were originally published in extract form and then in four unexpurgated volumes covering the years between 1994 and 2003. They catalogued Tony Blair's leadership of the Labour Party and his premiership through many major foreign and domestic upheavals. The diaries encompassed the wars in Kosovo and Iraq as well as the domestic tragedy of foot-and-mouth disease and the constant sniping between Gordon Brown and Tony Blair for dominance within the Cabinet. Ireland was always on the political agenda and a problem that Tony Blair ached to solve.

Ireland was also a subject that, in Alastair Campbell's own words, 'got into the bones', and that feeling for the place and its politics is what led to this book. He asked Ed Victor, his agent, if an Irish publisher would be interested in an Irish version of the diaries and Ed asked me if The Lilliput Press would publish it. I said yes instinctively, without having read all the diaries, because I knew that Campbell had had unprecedented access to Tony Blair throughout his premiership and that Tony Blair's part in the peace process in Northern Ireland was clearly one of his successes. He was, in my opinion, the first UK prime minister to understand the Irish question and to engage with the politics sympathetically and patiently. I am from Northern Ireland so it was close to me. I understood the detail and the tribal undercurrents.

I like diaries and the best of them, from Boswell to Alan Clark, succeed because of honesty in the recording of events. Cambell reveals temper and tenderness, domestic and political turmoil and humour and hubris.

He writes up his diary either on the day or the next morning. For him I think it was cathartic – a way of defusing the enormous stress of the job. Not only was he working for Tony Blair but also his partner, Fiona Millar, was Cherie Blair's special adviser so there is little separation between home and office. He was also aware, of course, that he was living through extraordinary times – what Roy Hattersley calls being an appendix to history. At the time of the Good Friday Agreement, for example, he wrote that he felt he was recording history.

When I finished reading the four volumes, each over 700 pages long, I realized that I had agreed to a mammoth task. It was not a simple job of distillation. The narrative had to flow as a separate entity. Major events, such as the death of Princess Diana, the conflict in Kosovo and the beginnings of the war in Iraq, I had to cut because they are not of Ireland and they had had a life in the previous volumes. To make sense of the world outside the Irish question without having it intrude too much was a delicate balancing act. I followed the format of the original diaries, extracting and including all Irish references. Additional material to the original text is in the form of expanded footnotes to explain particular incidents in more detail.

Alastair Campbell helped by revisiting the text specifically for this book and providing new bridging commentary on events, which are now history and can be viewed with the perspective that time brings. His fresh comments appear in italics throughout the text.

President Clinton lights up the pages whenever he appears. Campbell is fascinated by the Clinton administration and the modus operandi of a master communicator. When the talks in Belfast reach an impasse, the person to call is always Clinton, who was respected by all shades and sides; sometimes he succeeds in moving events forward. His advice to Tony Blair, at a time when the Monica Lewinsky scandal was raging, was always detailed and considered.

One must not forget – given his public reputation in 2013 – the important role played by former Taoiseach Bertie Ahern. It is obvious from the diaries that he was pivotal in the peace negotiations and valued by Tony Blair for his insight, patience and common sense. The two men, according to Campbell, became close both personally and politically. Their affection for each other along with their respect for Campbell and their admiration of the diaries is clear.

Bertie Ahern and Tony Blair readily agreed to write forewords for this text, for which I am very grateful.

Additional footnotes appear with kind permission from the University of Ulster's Conflict Archive on the Internet (CAIN). My thanks also to Djinn von Noorden for her detailed copy-editing and to John Bowman for his wisdom and kindness.

Kathy Gilfillan
August 2013

Foreword *by* Bertie Ahern

I am delighted to be asked to add a foreword to Alastair Campbell's *Irish Diaries*. To my mind, Alastair's diaries are a hugely significant publication and a primary source for students of Anglo-Irish relations and historians but no mere academic tome. This book is a cracking good read, brilliantly written, and Alastair gives a compelling and exciting first-hand account of a critical period in Irish history when incredible steps were taken to build peace in Ireland and to end decades of violence.

As one of Tony Blair's most trusted aides, Alastair Campbell not only witnessed history, but he also helped to shape events. Alastair had a gift for media management, but I think what Tony valued most was his strategic advice, his searing honesty and his common-sense approach to politics. His advice was often crucial and always to the point.

This diary captures the long and difficult journey towards peace in Ireland. When people ask me how we solved the problems in Northern Ireland and how we brought peace to somewhere that had for so long known only war and killing, my answer is invariably that it was not easy! It took patience – lots of it – and I would say it was 99 per cent perseverance and maybe 1 per cent inspiration. It also took a lot of stamina and reading this diary reminds me again of the late night meetings, the early morning summits and the sheer physical demands of peace-building. I must admit to being amazed when I heard that Alastair actually found the time to keep a detailed diary during his years working with Tony Blair. But then again, considering the amount of drive and energy he possesses, perhaps it is not so surprising.

Oscar Wilde famously once said: 'I never travel without my diary. One should always have something sensational to read in the train.' Alastair's diary is very different. It is not designed to fuel the fires of scandal, but instead it gives an invaluable insight into how politics and diplomacy work at the highest level. It is a warts-and-all account and Alastair, with typical frankness, records his views on the ups and downs of the peace process, the difficulties and triumphs, and his assessment of real people dealing with real challenges under a relentless and often hostile spotlight.

Reading his diaries – especially on the lead-up to the Good Friday Agreement – reminded me of just how much we have achieved and just how often we were so very near, and yet so far from, a resolution. During my address to Westminster in 2007, I was delighted to be able to acknowledge Tony Blair's exceptional contribution to the attainment of peace in Northern Ireland.

Alastair's book documents how closely and intensely Tony Blair and I worked together to achieve peace. We had the closest relationship between any British prime minister and Taoiseach in the history of the Irish state.

We first met in the Gresham Hotel, in Dublin, when we were both in opposition and we developed a friendship that has lasted beyond leaving office. I spent weekends with Tony and his family at Chequers (the prime minister's country residence) when we were in office. I was in and out of Downing Street and he came to see me in Drumcondra and met my friends. I went with him to watch Newcastle United, his favourite team, play. We would have the odd drink together. We always preferred to meet one to one rather than with large groups of officials.

During talks, we liked to go for walks in the grounds, and kick things around. When Peter Mandelson was in the North he would bring his big dog along, and we discussed things as the dog hared off into the bushes. I believe that this friendship between Tony and me was crucial in building an entirely new relationship between our countries. Albert Reynolds had been friendly with John Major for a short time when they were in office, but before that there was no strong bond between Taoisigh and prime ministers.

Alastair gives a good and detailed account of how the Good Friday Agreement unfolded. We were fortunate that in Tony Blair there was a British prime minister blessed in abundance with patience, wisdom and generosity.

The peace process also had many unsung heroes. As Taoiseach, on the journey towards peace, I was remarkably well served by a dedicated core of officials, including my programme manager, the late Gerry Hickey, my adviser Martin Mansergh, my speechwriter Brian Murphy, who could always be relied upon to produce an appropriate quote or phrase, and Alastair's opposite number for so long, my press secretary Joe Lennon.

Tony Blair was equally served by a talented group that included Jonathan Powell, Sally Morgan, David Miliband and Peter Hyman. But at the heart of Tony's team was Alastair Campbell. On one occasion, Tony even went so far as to describe Alastair as the 'Roy Keane of his operation'. Alastair is a convinced Burnley fan so I am not sure he totally appreciated the analogy, but, as a Manchester United supporter, I want to assure him that this is a very high compliment indeed.

Alastair Campbell's *Irish Diaries* is the consummate insider's account of a momentous journey towards peace. If they highlight one thing it is that for any successful process of reconciliation to succeed following a long conflict, it is crucial to remember peace has to be built step by step. It is a gradual, very slow process and no one should think lasting reconciliation will happen instantaneously with the wave of a magic wand. It takes time and it takes courage but it is a prize worthy of perseverance. What, after all, is more important than peace and the prevention of conflict and killing?

Alastair Campbell played a huge role in stopping the murder and mayhem that had defined Northern Ireland for too long. For this, I will always be grateful.

Bertie Ahern
May 2013

Foreword *by* Tony Blair

Many books have already been written by and about the key people of the New Labour era, and doubtless there will be many more. What is remarkable about Alastair's diaries is that they are written without the hindsight usually afforded to authors of political memoirs and biographies, and they offer the closest anyone will get to an actual day-to-day account of life at the centre of the team I led. As such, they are a hugely valuable source to anyone interested in the politics of our generation. They are, as anyone who knows Alastair would expect, full, frank and at times very sharp in their assessment of people and events. They spare nobody, including himself. But they do capture something of the essence of life under pressure in the political hothouse, the ups and downs, the clashes, the things going right, the things going wrong. Nowhere is that more the case than in relation to Northern Ireland. His entire diaries of his time working for me comprised four volumes. That a whole volume can now be made of those parts especially relevant to Ireland perhaps underlines what a priority it was, what a passion it became, and how much time and energy it consumed.

Alastair played a big part in the Northern Ireland peace process on his own account. Together with Jonathan Powell, my indefatigable Chief of Staff, who really was instrumental in the whole thing, Alastair was at my side in all the crucial meetings and negotiations up to his departure in 2003. He provided as he always did not just the media savvy, which was often important for keeping momentum going, but also creativity about the process itself, making suggestions for movement when things were stalled, and developing his own relationships with the central people.

The sheer amount of time devoted to Ireland was indeed remarkable. Rereading the diaries in this form, with Ireland the central focus, it is clear that if anything I underestimated just how often it came to the top of my agenda. We made it a priority very soon after our first election win, with the first big speech there one of the most delicate and significant of my entire Premiership, and it remained a priority throughout my time in Downing Street.

In 1997, the ceasefire had been rudely shattered. Shortly after I took office, two policemen were brutally murdered. Despite that, and despite the natural view of many that we should at that point have binned the whole idea of trying to resurrect the process, we managed to get the ceasefire back in place. We then went through the agonizing days leading up to the Good Friday Agreement, recorded here in minute detail; and that was only a beginning. Then came the truly Byzantine and tortuous process of the years of mini negotiations to clear each obstacle and proceed. There were many times when we thought it was over and the chance for peace was lost. On each occasion, we somehow kept it together and got back on track. Even today, there is fragility. But the benefit of peace is there for all to see. Northern Ireland still faces many challenges but it truly is a different place in so many ways, safer, stronger, more secure, more prosperous.

Even now, with the passage of time, it is hard to look back on the events that led up to the Good Friday Agreement, and the subsequent years, without a profound sense of amazement at how it all came together and how it was sustained. The diary gives the blow-by-blow account, and Alastair rightly says there was something mysterious, almost magical, about how things fell into place. What I want to do here is offer some reflections about the process but also about the broader lessons it revealed about politics.

Firstly, for those of us who in our youth flirted with the somewhat determinist branch of Marxist-oriented left-wing politics, the Northern Ireland peace process is a classic example of how individual people, in a certain place at a certain moment in time, can make the difference. There is little doubt in my mind that with a different cast of individuals, the outcome may well have been different and adverse. We were immensely fortunate to have an Irish leadership – in the form of Bertie Ahern and his key ministers – that was prepared to lay aside the grievances and attitudes of the past in the interests of the future. This is emphatically not to say that they didn't feel those grievances or the pressure to deliver justice for the Irish people. But they rose above the burden of history, consigning it to its proper place – a spur to action, not a chain to anger.

The same was true of the Unionist leadership – at the beginning in the hands of David Trimble – and of course of the SDLP and Sinn Féin. It is easy to forget how simple and superficially alluring wallowing in the feeling of injustice or retribution for past hurt can be. There is a ready audience for it amongst large parts of any party's activist base. The applause lines are familiar and well received. The alternative requires the development of a wholly new narrative, the challenging of

FOREWORD BY TONY BLAIR

old assumptions, the admission from time to time that the other side might have a point. So leaders have to replace a rhetorical formula that involves the statement of grievance and a denouncement of opponents with one that turns that on its head, and starts to speak of the possibility of reconciliation with those with whom the whole of the history up to that point has been about the utter unacceptability of such a reconciliation. This is real political leadership; and it takes real character to do it.

Gerry Adams and Martin McGuiness had spent their entire lives fighting the British and Unionism. They had made the speeches, led the protests, swelled the ranks of the disaffected and the defiant, been dismissed by many as terrorists pure and simple. Now they were speaking about how, despite all of that, arms should be laid down for the hope of peace and the prospect of justice: not for the actuality of either of those things, because that was to come, but for the chance of them. These were not easy steps, but they took them, and I believed in their sincerity. Alastair is on record as saying that he thinks the diaries risk being unfair to David Trimble. David, like many others in the process, could be difficult at times, but often he was merely expressing the huge political pressure he was under from his own side not to take the steps that ultimately he did take. When Ian Paisley finally pulled Unionism over the line, with the current First Minister Peter Robinson, he was obliged to put aside a career spanning half a century based on the notion that peace with Republicans was impossible, and that those who advocated it were naive or betraying the true interests of the people. For the moderates, like Seamus Mallon leading the SDLP, they had to sit there and watch as the party that had always accused him and John Hume of a sell-out then cut the deal to govern with the ancient enemy. And of course we were all of us hugely lucky to have a US administration led by Bill Clinton, and represented by George Mitchell, who were absolutely committed and matched that commitment with political skill of the highest order.

All of this took extraordinary political sacrifice and personal risks. Without the necessary character to do that, peace would not have happened. Different and lesser people would never have accomplished this. We got the right mix at the right time, not just with the big players listed above, but smaller parties and outside groupings too. When it comes to Northern Ireland, Alastair even has kind words to say about the media.

Secondly, the personal relationships that are built during the course of making peace matter enormously. Again this is obvious, but frequently missed. Part of the problem in these situations – which I witness continually in my work in the Middle East today – is that to bring people together you have to understand in a genuine sense why they feel as strongly as they do. This is not a matter of reason, but of emotion. In a conflict, there is suffering of a nature and on a scale that we, from the outside, can scarcely appreciate, because it is not within our experience. Each side has a sense of pain and of cruel consequence from the other side's actions. They need to know that those mediating get this feeling, not at a rational but at an empathetic level. In getting it, the mediator is then able to pass something of the pain of each side to the other. Especially where there has been violence over a prolonged period, and in conflict the violence often either falls or is even directed at the innocent, being able to articulate the sense of hurt and know that the other side has been forced at least to confront it, is a powerful way of opening up the dialogue that can lead to peace.

Many of the hundreds of hours I spent in discussion with the parties were not simply about specific blockages or details of the negotiation, but rather about absorbing and trying to comprehend why they felt as they did, and communicating that feeling to the other side. In this way, they became my friends, because I then had inside me something of the passions they felt inside them. In addition, as the process wound its way, the parties got to know each other, and started to look upon each other as human beings with a different perspective, not as enemies mired in evil and incapable of good. We shouldn't exaggerate, because there was still enormous suspicion and resentment that at times threatened to sink the whole thing. But it was counterbalanced by human interaction and that counterbalance was essential. Seeing Ian Paisley and Martin McGuinness work together, and attract headlines calling them 'The Chuckle Brothers', underlined how far we all came.

Thirdly, there had to be an intellectually credible core framework to govern and shape the process. I always say that at the top, in the leadership of any country, politics is a far more challenging intellectual business than is commonly assumed. People think of politicians making speeches, appearing in the media, engaging in intrigue and naturally taking the decisions that define their leadership. But I found that whatever the major issue being addressed, absolutely of the essence was the ability to frame a way forward in terms that were intellectually coherent. In designing a process for peace, this is especially so. At the heart of what we were doing in Northern Ireland was the idea that in exchange for just and fair treatment of the nationalist and Republican communities, the resolution of the issue of United Ireland vs United Kingdom would be left to the choice of the people of Northern Ireland. What flowed from that was a series of changes and advances; but all referable back to, and consistent with, that core deal. In other words, making peace cannot simply be a trade, even though of course it involves compromise; it must also be an accord based on principle. There has to be a shape and a design that has integrity. A lot of time in Northern Ireland was spent precisely trying to get the shape and design right. It was difficult, slow and frustrating, but it paid off in the end.

Fourthly, I am amazed when I look back on my time as a leader at how much the residue of that leadership is defined by the big things that really matter, and not by the myriad of mini-crises that don't; all those supposedly Government-threatening events, many of which I literally have difficulty remembering now. I know of course that in theory leadership should be defined in this way; but somehow when you're doing the job, the defining work is often being done quietly, sometimes almost insignificantly, whilst all around you is some tumult caused by an event that dominates the news and occasionally your thoughts. This is partly a reflection of the way the modern media operates, but it is also a product of the fact that the best work, the work that lasts, the work that really changes the world, is done by a steady and relentless determination that is often not marked by great bursts of action or punctuated by thunderous rhetoric, but by a patience derived from a sincere belief in the merit of a cause and the consequent will to achieve it.

Finally, never forget the absolute central importance of aligning the reality of life on the ground with the desire to find a formula for peace. The economy matters. Security matters. Giving the ordinary population the sense that they have a stake in the future and that this stake is intimately connected with peace is essential. In the end, a peace process is a curious symbiotic dance between leaders and led. The leaders have to give the hope to the people that change can come. But ultimately, especially as the leaders come under pressure from within their own ranks, they need to feel the support of the people, willing them on, giving them encouragement, empowering them to compromise and move forward. Never forget the people, never under-estimate them and never stop trusting them when finally you put the deal before them, to call it right. They normally do.

Bismarck famously said that there were two things the people should never be allowed to see: the making of sausages and the passing of laws. The spectacle of the process is too off-putting, the laying bare of the assembly of the finished product too unpleasant to delicate sensibilities. But here in Alastair's Irish diaries, the transparency shows politics in the raw, but also at its best: the pursuit of something manifestly in the public interest, that requires leadership and perseverance and teamwork and whose outcome is always in doubt. If politics is, in the final analysis, about changing the world for the better, this is a pretty good example of politics at work. I am very proud of the story this book spells out, as should be so many others who played their part. It is remarkable that Alastair found time to keep such a diary, given the hours he worked, but reading this account of how peace was made, I think history should be grateful that he did.

Tony Blair
May 2013

Who's Who

Alan Milburn	Chief Secretary to the Treasury to October 1999, Health Secretary 2001–03
John Prescott	Shadow Deputy Leader 1994–97, Deputy Prime Minister and Secretary of State to June 2001, then First Secretary of State
George Robertson	Shadow Scotland, Defence Secretary 1997–99, then NATO Secretary General
Clare Short	Shadow Transport 1994–96, Overseas Development 1996–97, International Development Secretary 1997–2003
Andrew Smith	Shadow Chief Secretary to the Treasury 1994–96, Transport 1996–97, Chief Secretary to the Treasury 2001–02, Work and Pensions Secretary from 2002
Jack Straw	Shadow Home Affairs, Home Secretary to June 2001, then Foreign Secretary

LEADER'S OFFICE / 10 DOWNING STREET

Alex Allan	Principal private secretary to August 1997
Tim Allan	Press officer, special adviser
Mark Bennett	AC's researcher
Alison Blackshaw	AC's senior personal assistant
Cherie Blair	Wife of TB
Julian Braithwaite	Press officer, Foreign Affairs
Sir Robin Butler	Cabinet Secretary to 1998
Alastair Campbell	Chief press secretary and Prime Minister's official spokesman, director of communications and strategy
Magi Cleaver	Press officer, overseas visits
Hilary Coffman	Special adviser, Press Office
Robert Hill	Policy adviser, political secretary from June 2001
John Holmes	Principal private secretary and Foreign Affairs adviser 1997–99
Anji Hunter	Head of office 1994–97, presentation and planning 1997–2001, later director of government relations
Peter Hyman	Strategist and speechwriter
Pat McFadden	Policy adviser, later deputy chief of staff
Sir David Manning	Chief foreign policy adviser 2001–03
Fiona Millar	AC's partner, special adviser to CB
Sally Morgan	Political secretary, later director of political and government relations

Jonathan Powell	Chief of staff (JoP)
John Sawers	Foreign Affairs adviser to 2001
Godric Smith	Press officer, deputy press officer from 1998, later Prime Minister's official spokesman (with Tom Kelly)
Sir Andrew Turnbull	Cabinet Secretary from 2002
Sir Richard Wilson	Cabinet secretary to 2002

GORDON BROWN'S OFFICE / HM TREASURY

Ed Balls	Adviser
Geoffrey Robinson	Paymaster General
Charlie Whelan	GB spokesman

IRELAND

Gerry Adams	President Sinn Féin 1983–, MP Belfast West 1983–92, NI Assembly member 1998–2010
Bertie Ahern	Taoiseach 1997–2008
David Andrews	Minister for Foreign Affairs 1997–2000
John Bruton	Taoiseach 1994–97
John Chilcot	Permanent secretary Northern Ireland Office
General John de Chastelain	Chair Independent Commission on Decommissioning
Pat Doherty	Sinn Féin MP West Tyrone, vice president of Sinn Féin 1988–2009, NI Assembly member to 2012
Mark Durkan	Leader SDLP 2001–10, Deputy First Minister 2001–02, NI Assembly member for Foyle to 2010
David Ervine	NI Assembly member for Belfast East 1998–2007, Leader, Progressive Unionist Party 2002–07
Martin Ferris	Sinn Féin negotiator on Good Friday Agreement, TD Kerry North since 2002
Sir Ronnie Flanagan	Chief Constable, RUC
John Hume	Leader, SDLP 1979–2001, NI Assembly member to 2000, Nobel Peace Prize October 1998, retired from politics on 4 February 2004
Tom Kelly	Northern Ireland Office spokesman from 1998, then Prime Minister's official spokesman
Joe Lennon	Irish government press secretary
Martin McGuinness	Sinn Féin chief negotiator, NI Assembly member, Minister of Education 1999–2002, MP Mid Ulster 1997–2013

Andrew MacKay	Shadow Northern Ireland Secretary 1997–2001
Gary McMichael	Leader of the loyalist Ulster Democratic Party 1994–2001
Ken Maginnis	Ulster Unionist MP, Fermanagh and South Tyrone, June 1983–June 2001. Stood down. Created life peer Baron Maginnis of Drumglass 2001
Seamus Mallon	Deputy Leader, SDLP 1979–2001, Deputy First Minister 1998–2001, MP Newry and Armagh 1986–2005, NI Assembly member to 2003
Peter Mandelson	Labour MP for Hartlepool, Minister without Portfolio 1997–98, Trade and Industry Secretary July–December 1998, Northern Ireland Secretary, October 1999–January 2001
Senator George J. Mitchell	US special envoy for Northern Ireland
Mo Mowlam	Shadow Northern Ireland, Northern Ireland Secretary 1997–99, then Chancellor of the Duchy of Lancaster to June 2001. Died 19 August 2005
Paul Murphy	Welsh Secretary, July 1999–2002, Northern Ireland Secretary from October 2002
Siobhán O'Hanlon	Sinn Féin negotiator on Good Friday Agreement, Member, Sinn Féin Executive
Ian Paisley	Leader Democratic Unionist Party to 2008, MP for North Antrim 1970–2010, NI Assembly member to 2011, MEP to 2004
Chris Patten	Conservative peer, chair of the Independent Commission on Policing for Northern Ireland
Ruairí Quinn	Minister for Finance 1994–97, Deputy Leader, Labour Party 1990–97, Leader of the Labour Party 1997–2002
John Reid	Northern Ireland Secretary from January 2001 to October 2002
Peter Robinson	Founding Member of the Democratic Unionist Party, MP Belfast East 1979–2010, NI Assembly member, Minister for Regional Development October 2001–October 2002
Mary Robinson	President of Ireland 1990–97
Dick Spring	Minister for Foreign Affairs, January 1993–November 1994 and December 1994–June 1997 and Tánaiste
Paddy Teahon	Head of the Department of Taoiseach 1993–2000
John Taylor	Deputy Leader, Ulster Unionist Party 1995–2001, MP, Strangford, June 1983–June 2001, NI Assembly member. 2001 created a life peer Baron Kilclooney of Armagh

| David Trimble | MP for Upper Bann 1990–2005, Leader Ulster Unionists 1995–2005, Nobel Peace Prize October 1998, NI Assembly member to 2007, First Minister 1998–2002 |

THE WHITE HOUSE

Sandy Berger	National security adviser to Bill Clinton
George W Bush	43rd President of the United States
Bill Clinton	42nd President of the United States
Hillary Clinton	First Lady, later Senator
Al Gore	Vice President to BC
Joe Lockhart	White House press secretary to BC from 1998
Mike McCurry	White House press secretary to BC to 1998
Colin Powell	Former chairman of the Joint Chiefs of Staff and later Secretary of State to GWB
Condoleezza Rice	National Security Adviser to GWB
Jim Steinberg	Deputy national security adviser to BC

THE LABOUR PARTY

James Callaghan	Labour Prime Minister 1976–79
Lord (Charlie) Falconer	Barrister, close friend of TB, later Cabinet Office Minister and 'Dome Secretary'
Philip Gould	Political pollster, strategist and close friend of TB and AC
David Hill	Director of communications, Labour party spokesman
Glenys Kinnock	MEP, Wife of Neil Kinnock
Neil Kinnock	Labour Leader 1983–92, European Commissioner from 1995
John Smith	Labour Leader 1992–94

PARLIAMENT

Paddy Ashdown	Leader of the Liberal Democrat Party 1989–99
Betty Boothroyd	Speaker of the House of Commons to Oct 2000
Alan Clark	Conservative MP for Kensington and Chelsea, diarist, friend of AC
Robert, Viscount Cranborne	Conservative Leader of the Lords
William Hague	Conservative leader of the Opposition 1997–2001
Michael Howard	Shadow Home Secretary 1994–97, Shadow Foreign Secretary 1997–99

John Major	Conservative Prime Minister 1990–97
Ann Taylor	Leader of the House of Commons 1997–98, Commons Chief Whip 1998–2001
Margaret Thatcher	Conservative Prime Minister 1979–90

THE MEDIA

Adam Boulton	*Sky News* political editor
Michael Brunson	ITN political editor
Michael Cockerell	BBC political documentary maker
Andrew Marr	*Independent* political editor 1992–96, editor 1996–98, BBC political editor from 2000
David Montgomery	Chief Executive, Mirror Group newspapers
Piers Morgan	*News of the World* editor 1994–95, then *Daily Mirror*
Denis Murray	BBC Ireland correspondent
Robin Oakley	BBC political editor
Peter Riddell	*Times* political editor
Paul Routledge	*Mirror* commentator
John Sergeant	BBC chief political correspondent to 2000, then ITN political editor
Richard Stott	*Today* newspaper editor 1993–95
Rebekah Wade	*Sun* deputy editor, *News of the World* editor from 2000
Philip Webster	*Times* political editor
Michael White	*Guardian* political correspondent and later political editor
David Yelland	*Sun* editor

FAMILY AND FRIENDS

Rory, Calum and Grace Campbell	Children of AC and FM
Carole Caplin	Friend and adviser to Cherie Blair
Alex Ferguson	Manager of Manchester United
Gail Rebuck	Publisher, wife of Philip Gouldz

The Irish Diaries
[1994–2003]

[1994]

Tony Blair [Leader of the Opposition] called me and asked me to go and see him in the Shadow Cabinet room. I arrived at 1.30 and into the kind of turmoil you normally associate with moving house. Boxes and crates of John Smith's* papers and possessions on the way out, TB's on the way in, and nobody quite sure where everything should go, and all looking a bit stressed at the scale of the task. Anji Hunter [Head of Leader's office] and Murray Elder [Former chief of staff to John Smith] were in the outer office, and I got the usual greeting from both, Anji all over-the-top kisses and hugs, Murray a rather distant and wary smile. He said Tony was running a bit late. He went in to tell him I was here. A couple of minutes later John Edmonds [general secretary of the GMB union] came out, and looked a bit miffed to see me. Tony's own office was in even greater chaos than the outer office so he was working out of the Shadow Cabinet room. He turned on the full Bunsen burner smile, thanked me for all the help I'd given on his leadership acceptance speech, and then, still standing, perched his foot on a packing case and got to the point, rather more quickly than I'd anticipated. He was going on holiday the next day, and he still had a few key jobs to sort out. He was determined to get the best if he could. He needed a really good press secretary. He

---

* John Smith, Labour Leader 1992–94. His sudden death in May 1994 led to the battle between Tony Blair and Gordon Brown for leadership of the Labour Party.

wanted someone who understood politics and understood the media, including the mass-market media. They don't grow on trees. He said it had to be somebody tough, and confident, someone who could make decisions and stick to them. Historically the Labour Party has not been blessed with really talented people in this area of politics and political strategy but I think we can be different.

Gordon [Brown, Shadow Chancellor of the Exchequer] is exceptional, so is Peter [Mandelson, Labour MP for Hartlepool], so are you, and I really want you to do the job. It's called press secretary but it's much more than that. He'd assumed I didn't want to do it because I was doing so much media now, and really branching out into broadcasting. He'd sounded out Andy Grice at the *Sunday Times*, who had said no. But really, he said, I would like to get the best I can and that has to be you. I know you've got reservations but I just ask you to think about it over the holiday. Even though I expected it, and had thought about it, I didn't quite know how to react. I'd gone in there with a list of names to suggest, and a raft of arguments against the idea. I said I'm not sure I'm suited to it. I've got a big ego of my own and a ferocious temper. I can't stand fools and I don't suffer them. I'm hopeless at biting my tongue. He said, I've thought about that, but I still think you're right for it. I said money might be a problem. I would be earning way into six figures this year, and it's not easy to take a big cut. Also, I could do lots for you from the outside, like I did on your leadership speech. It's not the same, he said. I agreed to think about it. Even as I left the office, though I'd raised all the reasons against, I had a feeling I would end up saying yes.

Ever since John Smith's death, I had effectively become a member of the TB team, even whilst continuing to work as a journalist, including interviewing him, and fellow leadership contenders John Prescott and Margaret Beckett for the BBC. This was the first time TB himself had asked me directly to work for him, previous approaches having come through others. I decided to take the summer holiday to make up my mind, and at one point had my partner Fiona, Neil and Glenys Kinnock in one room trying to talk me out of it while in the other, Tony and Cherie Blair, who had invited themselves as part of his continuing efforts to persuade me, were trying to talk me into it.

Thursday, August 11. On holiday, Flassan, France.

Neil Kinnock [Labour Leader 1983–92, European Commissioner from 1995] arrived with his wife Glenys. Glenys was in a different place to Neil on whether I should do it. She said Neil was totally opposed but she felt that I was dedicated to the Labour cause, we'd got a new leader, he'd asked me to do the job, he was obviously determined that I should do it, and it was hard to say no. Neil kept saying things like – why live your life at the beck and call of a bunch of shits (the press) when you could be the new [Brian] Walden [former Labour MP and TV presenter], the next Jeremy Paxman, the next Michael Parkinson, whatever you want? Cherie Blair's mum [Gale] was due to leave and I had to drive her to Marseille airport. TB came along. Gale was clearly worried about the whole thing. She'd told me a while back she was scared for Cherie and the children. It was just such a big thing, one step from being prime minister, and then the family might as well say goodbye to normality. On the way back, I told Tony in graphic detail about my breakdown. I said I thought it was important he knew, because I had to assume that ultimately I had cracked because of pressure, and the pressure was as nothing compared to what we would face if I did the job. I said I was sure I was a stronger person than ever, but he needed to know there was a risk. He said he was happy to take it. By now, he had also let me know, and sworn me to secrecy, that he was minded to have a review of the constitution and scrap Clause 4.* I have never felt any great ideological attachment to Clause 4 one way or the other. If it made people happy, fine, but it didn't actually set out what the party was about today. It wasn't the politics or the ideology that appealed. It was the boldness. People had talked about it for years. Here was a new leader telling me that he was thinking about doing it in his first conference speech as leader. Bold. I said I hope you do, because it's bold. I will, he said. And he had a real glint in his eye. He knew that in terms of the political substance, it didn't actually mean that much. But as a symbol, as a vehicle to communicate change, and his determination to modernize the party, it was brilliant. He'd first mentioned it in our walk up the hill yesterday. On the drive back from Marseille, a hint became an intention, and he asked me to start thinking about how best to express it, and how best to plan the huge political and communications exercise that would follow. Whether it

---

* This was in essence a rerun of the argument after the 1959 defeat, when Hugh Gaitskell proposed amending Clause 4 of the party's 1918 constitution in a vain bid at modernization. The clause, close enough to Labour's heart and history to be reprinted on membership cards, proclaimed the aim of 'Common ownership of the means of production, distribution and exchange'. Wholesale nationalization, in other words. Gaitskell lost out because questioning Clause 4 was, in the words of one Labour historian, like trying to 'persuade Christian fundamentalists that they need not believe in God'. Gaitskell's attempt at modernization not only failed, but deepened the divisions in the party that by the 1983 election debacle had become a chasm. Effectively Labour had become two parties, one of the centre left, the other hard left. To Blair such a high-risk, resonant symbol was the example he needed. Clause 4 had to go to show a new Labour Party was being forged and it meant business.

was deliberate or not, I don't know, but he had found the way to persuade me, and I told him that I would do the job. I phoned Peter Mandelson in the US. It was obvious that Peter's judgement was largely trusted by Tony and indeed it had been Peter who first sounded me out on his behalf, when he came round for dinner, spent a couple of hours skirting round the issue, finally blurted it out and I said no way. I told him Tony had talked me into it. He said he was pleased. It was the right thing for the party, and he was sure it was the right thing for me. He said I hope we don't fall out, which I thought was a very odd thing to say, but on reflection maybe not. I suppose people working closely together often do end up falling out and there was bound to be tension from time to time in that we would often be advising Tony from different perspectives on the same issues. He said I should consider him as an extra mind I could call on whenever I wanted, but equally I could always tell him to get lost.

Monday, October 17

Finally started full time. Fiona [Millar, AC partner and latterly special adviser to Number 10] drove me in, and I said TB's a lovely bloke, but he is so relentlessly modernizing I feel myself getting more traditional by the day. I didn't feel at all like I was going in for the first day at a new job. Bumped into TB on the stairs as he was leaving for the NEC/general secretary's meeting and he said he was getting worried re Prime Minister's Questions [PMQs]. He rushed off without waiting for Gordon Brown, who I think was hoping for a lift. Office meeting, Jonathan Powell's [chief of staff] appointment confirmed, then a discussion of what we do after Shadow Cabinet elections on Thursday. TB was now going into circular conversation mode re PMQs, and also worrying re Shadow Cabinet. Fiona angry that CB [Cherie Blair] was still so hostile to me over Carole Caplin [friend and adviser to CB].* Can't she see you're just doing your job and trying to protect TB?

Tuesday, October 18

PMQs. TB had decided to go on Europe and the question of a referendum. He decided it should be just two questions if possible. I wondered about him maybe doing something on Ireland at the top, to signal it wouldn't just be gladiatorial combat the whole time. There was a push for him to do something more obviously domestic, but he felt this was where the Tories' main fault line was, it was

---

* AC made Caplin sign a confidentiality agreement after topless pictures of her appeared in the press.

the reality of their conference. PMQs day was obviously going to be stressful. He cleared the diary, and I was like a yo-yo up and down from my office up the stairs from his. 'Can you pop down and see Tony?' and we'd have pretty much the same conversation as before. He said: If you knew how I felt inside you would feel more sympathy. PMQs went fine. Anji was sitting with Cherie in the officials' box. I was up on the Opposition's bench in the press gallery, which was a good view of [John] Major [Conservative Prime Minister 1990–97] but not of Tony, but it seemed to go fine. As I walked out, Jon Craig [political editor, *Daily Express*] said 'Nil-nil', which was about right. I was surrounded by the hacks as we came out. Why Europe? Why Ireland? How did he prepare? Who helped him? Process, all they were really interested in. The reality was there was more interest in Tony than in Major and we had to capitalize on that.

Thursday, October 20

I'd only ever seen reshuffles from the media side of the fence, and could never understand why they always took so long. Surely the PM or Leader of the Opposition just did his list and told people what was what. Er no. First he had to decide what HE wanted. Then he had to find out whether that is what THEY would be prepared to do. And he had to get buy-in from the other big beasts, and if anyone said no to something, or started to negotiate, it was back to the drawing board. Plus there was all the planning going on around the junior jobs, which the Shadow Cabinet people themselves may not want. It was like a big jigsaw puzzle, but the shape of the puzzle kept changing.

Mo Mowlam was really not keen on N Ireland. I couldn't understand why anyone would not jump at NI. It had the potential to be about as interesting, and as important, as any other job. But I think she thought she was in for one of the big domestic jobs. Margaret Beckett eventually agreed to health, which in Labour terms was a big job, but she was clearly disappointed not to be in one of the top four. Robin Cook [foreign affairs] making clear not happy. Phones going all day, like I used to ring, and now I understood why press officers always sounded so irritated.

PMQs. I saw something of the actor in TB, the careful preparation, the rehearsal, the need for time to compose himself, the need for assurance and reassurance. But it paid off. He looked and sounded the part, and the Tories were troubled by him.

TB almost done reshuffle. Kevin McNamara [Labour MP, relieved of the Northern Ireland brief] was almost in tears as he came out and when I went in

TB looked really drained and upset. 'That was a really hard thing to do, telling a decent man doing a job he's really committed to that I didn't want him to do it any more. This reshuffle business is ghastly.

My farewell do at the Reform. Mum said she couldn't believe all those Labour party leaders were there – Tony, Neil [Kinnock], Jim [Callaghan]. Richard [Stott, editor and friend of AC] made a hilarious speech, his basic theme that it was really nice and noble of Tony to give up everything to be my press officer. Said the real reason Fiona had never married me was that, like so many other women, she was waiting to see if Peter M changes his mind. Real mix of my two lives. I had no doubt I was now on the right side of the fence. Mum and Dad enjoyed it.

It is interesting to recall Mo Mowlam's ambivalence to the Shadow Northern Ireland position, given how much subsequently she came to be viewed as one of the great successes of the peace process. Mo was already enjoying a good media profile and popularity in the Party as a fresh, vibrant personality. Just as in government she felt she should have been considered for one of the so-called Big Jobs, so in Opposition she was hoping, not least because of her role in TB's leadership campaign team, for a major position. Northern Ireland was not considered to be such a position. TB's sacking of Kevin McNamara was an early indication that he intended this to be a policy area that he viewed as a strategic priority. He liked Kevin, and clearly did not enjoy sacking him, but he felt Labour's policy was too closely identified with one side of the argument – the nationalist side – and this reshuffle was designed to show he intended to develop a more balanced view between Unionists and nationalists. With his top team appointed, TB's priority at this time was winning the argument for a new Labour Party constitution, key to establishing 'New Labour' as a credible political project.

[1995]

Wednesday, February 1, 1995

Anji was finding it difficult to deal with Peter Mandelson's shenanigans, in particular that he exaggerated our difficulties and problems, but TB was clear we all just had to work together and get on with it. Jonathan [Powell's] arrival had also been difficult for her. Went for a briefing with John Chilcot [permanent secretary, Northern Ireland Office] on the current situation. We were talking about a joint all-Ireland body beneath a Northern Ireland Assembly and the Dáil. The Unionists won't like the substance – all Ireland – or the timing. TB asked what he could helpfully say, and Chilcot said to emphasize there was no deal or sell-out. He said it was like building a house and the walls were up but it was hard to get people to agree to put the roof on.

Thursday, February 2

In to finish work on the NI broadcast responding to Major. It seemed the only thing TB could usefully do was be supportive, look good and sound good and he did all that. He wrote in a section I didn't like about peace being a tender plant we had to cherish and the demons must not blight it. He also wanted a huge amount of detail about the document. It was taking away from PMQs preparation. He'd been planning on education cuts but then interest rates went up which made it easier – worse off under the Tories. Did well. His big worry on N Ireland was that JM hadn't really put the argument, and he thought he should, like he was Major's pressman or something. Clause 4 discussion, with Pat McF [McFadden, policy adviser] and Jon [Cruddas, trade union liaison] feeling we would probably just about win Young Labour, so I started to build the press up to it, with hopefully TB swinging some votes on Friday, and JP doing the same on Saturday. So I started to build it as the first electoral test on Clause 4. Rosie Winterton [Head of John Prescott's office] told me JP not happy with that so I went to see him. He said it was a strategic decision and he should be involved in that, not just asked to turn out as a fucking performing seal at the weekend. I didn't see this as that big a deal, but there was going to be a focus on it and so we may as well shape it on our terms. He seemed fed up with it, asked why he'd not been involved in that decision. I said it wasn't a big decision. I spoke to TB who was on a train to Nottingham. He couldn't see what the fuss was about. GB wanted 'equitable' in the new Clause 4.

Friday, February 3

TB called. He said he reckoned that in our own very different ways, GB, Peter M and I were geniuses, the best in our fields at what we did, and the key to his strategy. But it drove him mad that we couldn't get on. I said I can get on with anyone but it has to be based on an understanding of what we're all doing. He accepted of the three of us, I was trying hardest to make it work. But he said when GB was motivated, he had a superb strategic mind and he would be brilliant come the election. Peter was brilliant at developing medium-term media strategy, and spotting trends and analyzing how to react, and you are second to none at shaping message and driving it through the media. Fine, I said, but we are all flawed in our own way. He said when he was on the way up, the three of them could not have been closer. GB was strategy, he gave it intellectual context, Peter was delivery. They were brilliant together. I said it doesn't mean you can recapture it now.

Saturday, February 4

Spent most of the day locked in the Bedford [Hotel] on the seafront in Brighton working on the speech. I hate noise when I'm trying to write but Peter was talking away, who is talking to the Sundays, have we got pictures sorted with the delegates? I was very short with him. We agreed TB should do a doorstep with some

FEBRUARY '95: TENSIONS IN BRIGHTON

Young Labour activists at 2.30 but he wanted to speak to Peter before we did it. We got him up and immediately had an argument about clothes. I was strongly of the view he should wear a shirt and tie, if not a suit. Peter thought he should wear cords and an open-necked shirt and TB and he were continuing this conversation as we were trying to finish the wretched speech. Even if TB had been the one wanting his advice, I felt it was another instance of Peter winding TB up over total trivia. I could feel myself losing it, said he could not just swan in, upset what we were doing, then waltz out again. TB was like a dad trying to shush two squabbling brothers. 'Cut it out, you two, for heaven's sake.' Then we moved through to my room and Peter was on the edge and eventually tipped over. He said, I'm sick of being rubbished and undermined, I hate it and I want out. 'Get out then and we can finish the speech.' 'That's what you want, isn't it, me out of the whole operation.' I said I just wanted to be able to do a job. He started to leave then came back over, pushed at me, then threw a punch, then another. I grabbed his lapels to disable his arms and TB was by now moving in to separate us and Peter just lunged at him, then looked back at me and shouted: 'I hate this. I'm going back to London.' He went off and he was still shouting at me from the corridor, saying I was undermining him and Tony and I'm thinking who the hell might be out there hearing or watching all this.

Sunday, February 5

The big story of the day was the Unionists talking about election footing and being nice re Labour. TB spoke to Mo to say we should be very statesmanlike about this, the line should be that peace in Northern Ireland was more important than any desire we might have for a snap election.

Thursday, February 9

[Sir] Patrick Mayhew [Northern Ireland Secretary] came over to brief TB on Sinn Féin calling off talks because they'd found a bug in their HQ.

Northern Ireland was one of the few policy areas where there was a genuine sense of bipartisanship between the main parties, and Sir Patrick Mayhew was clearly worried Labour might create difficulties over this. TB could be scathing in his assessment of, and his attacks on, John Major, but he believed the then Prime Minister was genuinely motivated and prepared to take risks for peace in Northern Ireland, so his instinct tended to be to give the government the benefit of any doubt.

Bumped into Peter M and greeted him warmly. He said was that a greeting of friendship or hostility? I said neither, he should stop reading something into everything. He said he was right to read something into everything I did, that he knew he had to look after himself and he couldn't always rely on the people he thought he could rely on. He clearly had a lot of pent-up anger in there and now, very quietly, both of us anxious that the various people passing by shouldn't hear, it was coming out. He said that since I took the job, I had subjected him to 'unrelenting cruelty', undermining him, persecuting him. I said what on earth is the evidence for that? He said you underestimate the effect you have on people when you speak at meetings, when what you think is a humorous aside is taken by others as undermining. I said it's hardly unrelenting cruelty. He said it is if it happens again and again. I have pushed him over the top, he said. He said he had enough enemies without me joining them. I said do you sometimes think of yourself as your own enemy? He did one of his big 'Aaahs' – 'So that's where Tony gets it from, you're your own worst enemy.' I can hear him saying it. I said Peter, I have tried to involve you in a coherent structured way but I've made clear there cannot be two briefing operations. 'You have NOT tried,' he said, 'you have given me the cold shoulder. ' He said he always imagined I would not want him around for the first six months, but the truth was we needed each other and we might as well accept that. I said I was happy to work with anyone but it had to be on a firm basis. I couldn't have him just winding up Tony without me knowing the basis. We should just be open with each other. He said sometimes he wished he wasn't involved at all, and I said it's in your blood, you couldn't live without it. OK, he said, at least I accept I'm schizophrenic about it. This was one of several mental health references, earlier having said my unrelenting cruelty was psychotic. I saw TB later and said Peter had been a friend of mine for a long time. I liked him. I defended him when many others attacked him and I valued both his friendship and his advice and professionalism. I wanted to work with him but only if we agreed and knew the rules and all played by them.

Tuesday, February 21

JM doing well on Ireland. [John Major and John Bruton [Taoiseach] held a press conference in Belfast to launch the Framework Documents: *A New Framework for Agreement* and *A Framework for Accountable Government in Northern Ireland.*]

Spent most of the day on JM's statement on Ireland. When finally we got it, it was clear he was planning to use the line that this form of devolution could only apply to N Ireland. Yet if it could apply here, why were our plans for Scotland and Wales such heresy and such a threat to the Union? He was going to milk Ireland for all it was worth – leadership, patience, attention to detail etc. – and hope nobody made an issue of the devolution read across. But TB felt best simply to support them on NI, show he was on top of the detail and indicate his own interest and commitment. TB was going to a dinner with Eddie George [Governor of the Bank of England], with JP, GB, RC, Alistair Darling [Labour MP and Shadow Treasury spokesman] and Andrew Smith [Chief Secretary to the Treasury]. Bumped into Robin as I was leaving for home. Despite the rain, we stopped to chat. He said 'Do you remember that meeting where you suggested GB might make a speech on Clause 4 and he seemed reluctant?' I said I do. He said 'I'm bound to say GB does not put his head above the parapet. Dare I say it is what people dislike – a lack of courage in the party.' Then he did one of his little nodding 'Mmmmms' and wandered off for his dinner at the Bank.

Further evidence of TB's desire to do nothing to risk the strength of his bipartisan support for the Major government on Northern Ireland. Major was running as one of his big arguments against Labour that our plans for devolution in Scotland and Wales would lead to the break up of the UK, yet proposing a similar approach for Northern Ireland whilst maintaining it would strengthen the Union. It would have been easy to mount an argument of double standards, and one which would have bolstered our position on Scotland and Wales, but TB refused to let us engage with the government on this at all. For the next few months, Northern Ireland slipped down the agenda again, John Major was coming under huge internal pressure over Europe in particular, and eventually announced a 'back me or sack me' Tory leadership election. TB's time was taken up with fighting and winning the Clause 4 debate, but a number of Labour MPs used the summer break to signal discontent over the Party's direction, not least after a controversial visit to address Rupert Murdoch's executives at a conference in Australia, and praise from Margaret Thatcher. But results in local elections and by-elections suggested public support for New Labour was growing. Meanwhile TB used the period between the end of the summer break and the Conference season to make a visit to Ireland, North and South, to get to know some of the main political characters, and signal his commitment to the peace process should he, as seemed increasingly likely, become the next Prime Minister. He was also keen, despite the irritation expressed by Sinn Féin, to underline his support for the government's basic strategy, whatever private misgivings he might have had, not least his view that John Major was staking too much on the idea that the IRA would have to decommission their weapons, something few believed likely, yet which was becoming something of a red-line issue for many Tories. We got an early taste of the ease with which the politics of protest can surround a leader, and TB got a taste for the issue, its complexity and the size of the challenge it represented. And I got a shock when sharing a bathroom with Mo Mowlam.

Thursday, March 2

TB had seen Major to discuss the Prevention of Terrorism Act. TB had written offering a bipartisan approach provided there was a review. JM refused and as they were meeting [Michael] Howard [Shadow Foreign Secretary] was releasing a parliamentary answer renewing the act for twelve months unchanged. JM said he would ask Howard to be restrained so we pulled back from putting out TB's letter to JM, which had the potential to embarrass Major.

Tuesday, September 5

Dublin. Extraordinary start to the day. My bedroom and Mo's [at the UK Ambassador's residence] were joined by a bathroom so I knocked on the bathroom door before going in. 'Come in,' she shouted cheerily. I pushed open the door and there she was in all her glory, lying in the bath with nothing but a big plastic hat on. I brushed my teeth, trying not to look in the mirror, where I could see Mo splashing around, and decided to shave later. She seemed totally unbothered by my seeing her naked in a bath without suds. I hadn't slept at all well. I was unsettled by all the Cherie, Fiona, Anji stuff. Anji was sure CB just wanted her out of the whole operation. We met up with TB for the meeting with John Bruton who seemed in a really bad way. He was twitching, rubbing his eyes, then letting his head fall into his hands. He said the UK government had got themselves caught on the decommissioning hook, it was a mistake, the IRA would never do it and it meant logjam. He said the summit tomorrow was in some difficulty. It was later called off. He didn't doubt JM's good faith but he felt they had handled it badly. TB picked up on the depressive mood. 'God this is difficult politics,' he said. Bruton, to ease the mood a bit, suggested as a joke that we talk about EMU [European economic and monetary union] instead. He said he was absolutely convinced the IRA would not hand over weapons 'as a gesture', that Gerry Adams [President of Sinn Féin and MP for West Belfast] was coming under pressure because he was being told 'told you so' and that we were heading for deadlock. TB emphasized, rather to their disappointment, that our basic position was one of support for the peace process and that meant support for the government. It became clear the longer we were there that Sinn Féin resented this, that they felt we were doing it for electoral reasons, in that we felt there were 'no votes' in Ireland. Bruton agreed if TB were to split from the government it should be over something big. TB agreed privately the government had made a mistake in getting so firmly on to this hook. As Mark Durkan [chair and later leader of the nationalist SDLP] said later, it confirmed nationalist prejudice that all the Brits really thought about or understood was guns. It revealed intransigence and that made it very difficult for anyone else to change their positions. TB was clearly fascinated by the politics of it, and also the scale of the challenge. It was one of those issues where slight nuances could lead to huge progress or massive setback and crisis. Bruton had looked physically ill with it all. You could see the pressure he was under.

At the airport we met John Hume [nationalist SDLP leader] who gave TB a major monologue on how he saw things, how Sinn Féin were serious this time, and TB should use the visit to apply pressure on the government. TB was having none of it, but John got his revenge when we arrived at the Guildhall in Derry. I'd called ahead to TB's car to say there was a Sinn Féin demo and we should get as close as we could, then straight up the steps and in. But John H was in the car with TB and he got the driver to stop early, they got out and had to walk through two demos. TB seemed fine about it but Pat McF and I were furious, not least because Pat had asked for police help which wasn't there. TB and Mo had another chat re Peter in the car. He told me we had to get over the point that it was part of a Tory strategy to take out Peter because they knew he was good. 'He gives very good advice but he's a useless politician when it comes to advising himself,' he said. 'He's not like you; you can be devious and fly but you basically build alliances and make them work for you. He builds enmities.' Hillsborough [Castle] was nice. Lovely gardens. 'You can see why they'll fight hard to keep all of this,' said TB.

Wednesday, September 6

TB said he had been fascinated by yesterday but God, was it complicated and difficult. He was fizzing re JM. 'He's relaunching himself too soon. He's allowing this idea of a "new" Major to develop but there is nothing new in what he's saying or doing.' I called Fiona who said she'd arranged with CB for the four of us to

have dinner on Friday to discuss her role. I could see where this would end up –
CB and FM ganging up on me being a bastard and Carole rearing her head again.
FM said she didn't like the AC/AH axis and also the way we saw the downside of
Cherie. I spoke to Anji later and she sounded crushed.

Thursday, September 7

Feeling really fed up, too much to do and not enough time to do it. Anji was still
very depressed about the CB situation. I was not at all sure about Fiona working
for Cherie. It would help in terms of her being more involved, and hopefully
more understanding of how hard it was, but it would also mean our entire lives
being taken over by the Blairs. I was very ratty all day.

Thursday, September 14

Frank Millar of the *Irish Times* called to ask for my reaction to Kevin McNamara's
resignation [the Labour MP and Shadow Northern Ireland Secretary resigned
from the Labour Party's front bench over an an interview TB had given *The Irish
Times* and which McNamara interpreted as Labour support for Major government policy on Northern Ireland and specifically the Unionist veto over future
developments in the North]. I said I didn't know he'd resigned. Nor, I quickly discovered, did TB. Jonathan got hold of him and he confirmed it, saying he'd faxed
his letter down yesterday, saying it was about N Ireland policy and the approach
to the trade unions. I quickly rang round everyone to try to break it on our terms.

Saturday, November 18

I was speaking to [Tony] Bevins [*Observer* political editor], and was told the
Observer had a full account of Tuesday's Shadow Cabinet meeting. As it was read
to me, TB could sense my mood. He said afterwards 'What am I going to do with
these people? These are not serious people at all. I'll have to tell them that if they
cannot be trusted to have serious discussions in the Shadow Cabinet, we won't have
them.' TB's immediate suspicion was that it came from Mo. Peter M felt that since
she got on to the NEC, she'd got too big for her boots and now saw herself as the
next Edith Summerskill [1901–80, doctor, feminist and Labour Cabinet minister].

President Clinton was in town and unfortunately was going into overdrive in his praise of Major, first at the press conference in Downing Street, then in the address to both Houses, and later at the dinner. He was really pushing out the boat, so much so that only half in jest, I asked his press secretary, Mike McCurry, if he couldn't rein him in a bit. We got the police escort to Wingfield House [US ambassador's residence]. A minute or two after we arrived, Clinton and Hillary appeared and they had a brief chat in the hall before the two of them went out to do a doorstep. It went OK, but it was not going to penetrate the wall-to-wall Major/Clinton coverage, though whether it mattered much at this stage, I wasn't sure. The meeting itself began with a bit of an embarrassment when TB introduced me to BC as a 'legend in his own lifetime', which must have baffled him a bit. The chairs were laid out as for a formal bilateral meeting, TB and BC facing out to the rest as the two sides lined up opposite each other. He was much bigger than I imagined him to be, both taller and fatter. He had enormous strong hands and size 13 feet that looked even bigger. He said that once he and Boris Yeltsin swapped shoes to see who had the biggest feet, and Clinton did.

They went over Ireland, pretty perfunctorily, with Clinton asking TB where it would end, when surely at this stage he was likelier to know the answers. They only really got into their stride when they talked politics. TB went through New Labour, explaining what he was trying to do in general terms, and in all the different policy areas, which Clinton said sounded a lot like what he was trying to do. McCurry said TB's conference speech had been closely studied in the White House. Clinton had an interesting line about how achievement was less important than definition in the information age. He said there is no point saying what you've done, keep saying what you're going to do, have a clear direction. Reagan and Thatcher did it and didn't have to achieve that much. Like TB, he talked a fair bit about the polls and media, and like TB, he was at his best when talking about how to win support and manage change. He said the Congress having gone against him, and with the press more in conflict mode, he was always striving to get his message over to people direct. He was hugely impressive on strategy, especially considering he had just forty-five minutes' sleep on the plane last night. He said it was important to any progressive party of change to have mainstream values, and mainstream economic policies. They got on pretty well, though I thought Jonathan overdid it when he said he could feel a very special chemistry. Clinton did appear very solicitous, and wished us good luck as we left.

JM got a great press for the Clinton visit. There was nothing much we could do about it, and we barely scored on TB's meeting with Clinton, other than pictures of him and CB going to Number 10. CB told me she hadn't much liked Downing Street. In particular, Major had been all over her with false bonhomie, making jokes about tape measures and whether she would want to change the curtains. She also didn't like the feeling of being his guest. But more important, I think it hit her for the first time that it really wasn't a home so much as a stately home, that there would be no real privacy, no escape or freedom from the people who work there round the clock, and it would be very difficult to bring up children there. TB said that although it was perfectly jolly, he didn't really like being there as JM's guest. Also, by the evening we had been getting pretty sick of Bill shoving the boat out for Major.

Visits from world leaders are not easy for Opposition leaders. Particularly when the visitor is as high profile as the US President, these events are self-evidently dominated by the government-to-government, President-to-Prime Minister relations, and the Opposition leader is something of an add on, often purely for form. But even if this meeting attracted little attention, it was an important encounter. Jonathan Powell felt it was the point at which something of a personal chemistry between Clinton and TB began to develop, which would become important once we were in government. I felt that overstated things, but there is no doubt there was an easy warmth between them, and a shared interest and shared agenda on many issues, chief among them the winning of elections. And even if at the time I described the discussion on Northern Ireland as 'perfunctory' it did mean that from the off in their relationship, it was an ever-present on the agenda. TB and I both felt Clinton was overdoing the bonhomie with Major, but it was a perhaps inevitable consequence of the pressures of the so-called special relationship, and the feeling of the US President that he had to signal the closeness of the two countries by being positive about his host. With the US so much more powerful than the UK, successive Prime Ministers have sought to do all they can to maintain the sense of closeness. Major was only doing his job, and Clinton was only doing his in appearing to talk up the Prime Minister. Also, just as TB thought better of Major because of the efforts he was making on Northern Ireland, so did Clinton. I suspect his asking of TB where he felt the process was heading was designed to do two things: to see whether TB would express any criticism of the Major approach; and to see what approach he might take if he became PM which, if the polls at this time were to be believed, was an inevitability.

[1996]

Friday, February 9

The *Mirror* called early evening, said a bomb had gone off at Canary Wharf and would TB do a piece. We had to sort out a TB doorstep and statement.*

Monday, February 19

I stopped by to see JP on the way in to discuss last night's IRA bomb at the Aldwych,† which he narrowly missed on his way back from a meeting with TB at Richmond Crescent, and also to discuss his discussion with TB. But I sensed the discussion had gone well, because he was in a far better mood than in recent weeks, and joking that he still couldn't bring himself to say 'New' before Labour. I said I'd get him there.

---

* The IRA Canary Wharf bomb killed two and marked the end of the IRA ceasefire of over seventeen months. The Taoiseach, John Bruton, announced the following day that the Irish government would as a result cease formal contact with Sinn Féin.
† The bomb being carried by IRA member Edward O'Brien prematurely exploded in a bus on which he was travelling in the vicinity of Aldwych, London. He was killed and several other passengers were injured.

I woke up very depressed, the worst it had been for years. I felt totally dead inside and knew it was going to be a struggle to get through the day. I don't think most people, who say they're depressed when they mean they are a bit fed up, really get how bad it can be. TB, who is never down for long, doesn't. I don't think Fiona does and of course for her, like me, there is the nagging fear that it leads on to what it led to before, a cycle of depression and hyper-ness that ends in mental meltdown. On days like today, dead days, every single thing, getting into bed, getting dressed, putting on a sock, brushing teeth, starting the car, answering a phone, saying hello, becomes a huge challenge. You have to summon the energy and strength to do it and when it's done you wonder if it was worth it. Then I see Fiona and the kids being normal, having normal conversations, and you know you should take part, or at least be civil, but you're dead inside and you can't do it. Only the kids can get me out of this, so I took them to Regent's Park and we played football, and Rory got into a match with some kids and won 4–3.

Pat McFadden and I went through the speech for Scotland tomorrow with TB and he suddenly piped up that he had plans for major change to our devolution policy. He wanted to limit the tax-raising powers. He wanted to promise a referendum before the Parliament is established. And he wanted to be explicit that power devolved is power retained at Westminster. That, he said, is the answer to the West Lothian Question. He said it in that way he has of making clear he has thought and it will be very hard to dissuade him.

He said he had been reading Roy Jenkins' book on Gladstone, and the reason he didn't do home rule was because these same kinds of arguments were being put to him, and they were nonsense. He said he was absolutely clear about this. He intended at some point in the not-too-distant future to make a big speech on it, then stay for a few days and take all the shit that was flying, and win the argument. 'We would fall ten points in the polls because of all the noise and then do you know what will happen? The party will breathe a sigh of relief and the public will think we have seen sense and we will finally have a defensible position.' He was terrific when he was like this. I could forgive him all the circular conversations and the weakness with some of his key relationships when he was like this: clear, principled, determined and set to lead from the front.

TB had agreed with Matthew d'Ancona to do a piece on his religious beliefs for the Easter edition of the *Sunday Telegraph*. People knew he believed in God, if not perhaps how important it all was to him, but I could see nothing but trouble in talking about it. British people are not like Americans, who seem to want their politicians banging the Bible the whole time. They hated it, I was sure of that. The ones who didn't believe didn't want to hear it; and the ones who did felt the politicians who went on about it were doing it for the wrong reasons.

TB, Jonathan and I were due to have lunch at the US Embassy with the ambassador [Admiral William Crowe], Mike Habib and Jim Young [embassy officials]. TB emphasized how hopeful he was about Northern Ireland, and how important it was the US stayed engaged in Bosnia. It was clear they wanted to pull out but it would be very difficult. They were very keen to stress that we would get a good reception in the States.

Mo was giving the Sundays a statement saying the government had made an error of judgement in part of the handling of the [Northern Ireland] peace talks. She had told Anna Healy [Labour press officer] she had cleared it with TB, but I doubted that very much and said I'm sure TB will be furious. Indeed he was and said we should pull it. I called Mo and said it couldn't go out. She sounded angry then said if that was an order, fine, but I wish you people would make up your minds. I told her she had misread signals. I had told her that I thought TB thought it was OK to be a bit more distant from the government. That didn't mean distancing herself from TB.

This was my first recorded example of Mo's frustration at bipartisanship, and the limitations it put both on her profile, and her ability to 'own' the brief. TB did not want to give the government a blank cheque on Northern Ireland, but his instinct was that politically it was not sensible to second guess, or to criticize, or even to apply the same rules of political engagement that would apply to any other policy area. Partly, this was about laying the foundations for a reciprocal approach by the Tories if and when he was Prime Minister, when there would be considerable opposition in Tory circles to some of the steps that might have to be taken. Mo was uncomfortable from time to time with an approach that she saw more as blank cheque than trying to think ahead. TB had been impressed by the point John Bruton had made – that if we were going to desert the government, it should be over something big. This was not big enough, and TB's anger with Mo was that he felt her gambit was more about her profile than the policy.

Wednesday, April 3

We had a good turnout for my briefing on TB's US trip, and it was clear from the questioning the tabloids were trying to build up to present it as a snub situation. Jonathan had been warned by Peter Westmacott, the number two in our embassy in Washington, that there was concern that the hype was being overdone. But I went ahead and continued to hype. Mo came to see me to say next Tuesday she wanted to put out a statement, laying down what the government should do with the Northern Ireland election planning.* She said they would then not do it and we could say we disagreed with the bill. I couldn't readily see the logic. Jonathan joined us and we agreed she should be cautious. She was beginning to feel the heat of TB's desire to be too close to the US government on this.

Saturday, April 6

The *Sunday Telegraph* were splashing on the row engendered by TB's piece on God. I felt fully vindicated. As I said to TB: 1. never believe journalists when they say they are doing you a favour or giving you a free hit; 2. never do an interview without someone else in the room, and 3. never talk about God. Hilary [Coffman, press officer] and David [Hill, Chief spokesman for the Labour Party] felt it wouldn't play too badly but I sensed a mini disaster, as it was Easter, and they were trying to spin this as Blair allying Labour to God. When you looked at the words, he didn't say that, but he said enough to let them do the story and get Tories piling in saying he was using his faith for politics, and saying you couldn't be a Tory and a Christian. This was the permanent risk with UK politicians talking about God.

---

* The elections were designed to select which parties would be eligible for the all-party negotiations on June 10, 1996. The Forum delegates would also be chosen. 110 delegates would make up the Forum. The SDLP and Sinn Féin were critical of the planning proposals.

Monday, April 8

GB called and we agreed God was a disaster area. TB had called him from Spain because he had not been able to get hold of me. We joked about TB going to Tamworth [in Staffordshire, for a by-election] tomorrow to say he had been resurrected. The papers were pretty mega on TB and God, the splash almost everywhere with several bad editorials saying he was playing politics with God. Fiona and David H were still of the view that it was basically OK. When I spoke to TB he admitted it was an own goal, totally unnecessary. 'I should never have agreed to do it and I won't do it again.'

Tuesday, April 9

The US build-up was going well, *People* mag was out, *US News & World Report*. Jonathan called to ask what we wanted Mike McCurry to say. I said our media would judge things on the length of the meeting, and the way he was treated, not least the media arrangements. He suggested a joint press call, which might be too optimistic but that was what we should aim for. I said they should also say that TB's stance had been helpful on Ireland.

Thursday, April 11

On arrival, TB disappeared off with the ambassador in the Rolls-Royce to see Alan Greenspan [chairman of the US Federal Reserve], while I left to find the bar where Mike McCurry was coming to meet me and our press. It was a really nice thing for him to do and an excellent meeting. He talked up TB while lowering expectations. He said it had been very odd in the November meeting, because someone in the room had said it was almost as if TB was the senior figure at times. He said Clinton wanted to carry on basically where it left off last time. Mike and I had a chat about how to handle things. He said Clinton wanted to do a walk through the garden, but they were coming under pressure from the embassy not to do anything that would wind up the story that Major was being punished. Mike and I agreed he would give a very positive readout. They would talk up TB on Northern Ireland, and TB's role in left-of-centre politics. He was clever and funny and had a light touch. He was obviously going to help us make it a success. TB said earlier that we should underline after the by-election that the Tories had no friends at home and no friends abroad. Some of our press assumed the White House was pushing the boat out because of Major's lot helping Bush.

TB was really motoring, winning everyone over. The reception was fine, they had put together a good list of people. I was surprised that Colin Powell [former chairman of the Joint Chiefs of Staff] remembered me from the last meeting in London. I was seated between Tina Brown [editor of the *New Yorker*] and [former *Washington Post* editor] Ben Bradlee's wife but I was like a cat on a hot tin roof waiting for Tamworth by-election result. I had an interesting chat with Tina and Harry Evans [former editor of *The Times*] about how awful the modern press was. It was almost 3am when I finally got the result from Fiona Gordon. 13,700 majority. I felt like bursting into tears. In fact I almost did and later, in the privacy of my room, I did.

Friday, April 12

We left for the White House. TB was more nervous than I'd seen in a long time. Several times he took me to the corner of the waiting room to ask about minor details, some not so minor. 'Do I call him Bill or Mr President?' Clinton was waiting just inside the door and greeted everyone individually, then introduced TB to the rest of the US side. There was a fair bit of small talk, Clinton explaining some of the paintings and artefacts, asking about New York, putting people at ease. I was surprised at the level of turnout on their side. Clinton, Warren Christopher [Secretary of State], [Robert] Rubin [Treasury Secretary], [Tony] Lake, [Leon] Panatta [chief of staff], Nancy Soderberg [US policy official on Ireland], [Mike] McCurry.

The American pool came in and threw one or two domestic questions, and then the next pool, with lots of eager Brits. Peter Riddell from the *Times* broke the silence. 'Do you think you're sitting next to the next prime minister?' There was a pause, both smiled and you could feel Clinton's mind whirring, thinking carefully what to say. 'I just hope he's sitting next to the next president,' he said. TB looked nervous, though he got into it. Clinton praised our statesmanlike stance on Ireland, as Mike said he would. The last time I was in this room was as part of the press pool and I can remember thinking how little time you had to ask questions or absorb the atmosphere, and how quickly they bundled you out. It was strange to see them being parcelled out, much the same people I used to be with, and I stayed behind, and then listened to and took part in discussions about the big issues of the day. Clinton surprised me in several regards. His enormous feet were all the more noticeable because his shoes were even shinier than TB's. His suit and tie were immaculate, as was his hair. He had huge hands, long thin fingers, nails clearly manicured and he used his hands a great deal as he spoke, usually to emphasize the point just before he made it. I was also struck at the amount of detail he carried in his head. Like TB, he was good on the big picture, but he backed it up with phenomenal detail. He was a people person, terrific at illustrating policy points by talking about real people, real places. He was also tremendous at working a room. He was more relaxed than at the meeting in London, presumably because this was his territory and he was less tired, but if he made a long intervention, he found a way of addressing part of it to all the different people in the room. It's a great talent in a politician, and in his manner and his speaking style, he engages you, makes you feel warmly disposed towards him. I guess that wasn't a surprise, and it shouldn't have been a surprise that he was so big on detail, but it was. Also like TB, he came alive talking about strategy, campaigns, message. He got it instinctively, more than probably any political leader in the world. There was one revealing moment when Clinton said of our stance on Northern Ireland, 'It's smart,' then a pause, then he added, 'and morally right.' You felt he saw it in that order.

TB said straight out: how do you win support for more equity and justice without it meaning more tax? Clinton said the private sector was the key, that we must not be defined simply as a public-sector government, but bind in the private sector, emphasize their role in wealth creation. There was a clock just to Clinton's left by the door and after twenty-five minutes a tall young blonde woman, beautifully dressed all in black, came in, gave him a nod, smiled at the room and then closed the door behind her. It was time to go, but Clinton kept talking, more talking and eventually got up and he carried on talking. Mike and I disappeared into the corner to agree we would say they met for thirty-five minutes, more than scheduled, very friendly, useful, productive, go over the issues they ranged over. Mike then took us through to the Cabinet room, TB included, and he said he would say it was a forty-minute meeting which covered Bosnia, Ireland, world economy, Europe, mad cow, etc. He had been a terrific help. We then collected our thoughts and went through what TB should say at the stakeout spot. Again, I found myself thinking of previous visits here, on the other side of the fence. In particular when Neil [Kinnock] was stitched up by a combination of the White House, Number 10 and our disgusting right-wing press. I got a certain satisfaction from seeing them straining to hear TB's every word, and knowing that this time, because the White House had been so helpful, there was no way they could write this as anything but a success. Before the press conference TB said he wanted a chat with me alone. 'Am I doing OK?' I said yes, but you are letting your nerves show, just be yourself.

To CNN where Anji and I watched from the control room, where a huge guy was barking orders and laughing at the fact that there had been an Easter Bunny Party in the by-election. Towards the end we could see TB was getting a nosebleed. The big guy started shouting 'Cut the talk, cut the talk, the guest has a nosebleed situation.' I said to him if he had been in Britain, they'd have carried on so they could have a TB nosebleed live on TV. We then went for a meeting with Al Gore [US Vice President], which was fine. I was surprised how heavy he was and how much he relied on cue cards to speak. I was sitting next to someone who was literally ticking off the lines as Gore delivered them. It was interesting that whenever TB was away from GB, JP, Peter, all the nonsense, things went a lot smoother.

The Clinton relationship was well sealed on a visit that in almost every detail could not have gone better. Even within the confines of diplomacy, which puts limits on how far a government can push out the boat for a visiting Opposition leader, the impression left was that the Americans did indeed think they were dealing with the next Prime Minister, and they seemed pleased to be doing so. Again, what they called TB's states-manlike position on Ireland figured both publicly, and in the private discussions. The last point in the entry above, about our operation running more smoothly when we were away from the 'nonsense' of difficult top-table relationships at home, was perhaps borne out in the subsequent weeks, with the diaries full of references to TB's difficul-ties in getting his key people to work together, particularly Gordon Brown and Peter Mandelson. There were policy clashes too with John Prescott and Robin Cook, and complaints in the Shadow Cabinet about GB's modus operandi, and TB's seeming tolerance of it. Meanwhile John Major appeared to be getting something of a lift via his so-called 'beef war' in Europe, and I was distracted by a court case brought against me by Tory MP Rupert Allason from my journalist days. Ireland had slipped down the agenda. Not for the first or last time, it was put back on it by an IRA bomb.

Saturday, June 15

Manchester bomb.* We had to organize TB's reaction on TV. I took the kids' football class and then we set off for Wembley [for England vs Scotland in Euro 96]. We had good seats, but apart from [England midfielder Paul Gascoigne] Gazza's goal and [Scotland midfielder Gary] McAllister's missed penalty, it was all a bit flat and anticlimactic. However, on the way out, you got a sense of just how much of a feel-good factor you could get going on the back of all this [England

---

* An IRA bomb had devastated the shopping centre of Manchester, injuring 200 people. The bomb was estimated to have contained one-and-a-half tonnes of home-made explosives. In response to the Manchester bomb the UFF announced that it was putting its members 'on alert'.

beat Scotland 2–0]. The Manchester bomb was massive across all the media and yet there was no sense of fear in London, which was odd, and again presumably an effect of the football.

Friday, June 28

TB was going through his mail, including a letter from [Cardinal] Basil Hume [Archbishop of Westminster], saying that he would have to stop taking Communion in a Catholic church.* TB wrote back 'I wonder what Our Lord will make of this.'

Monday, July 1

I got home and was going to bed when there was a rash of late calls about a story that TB had taken Catholic Communion, which was likely to cause a bit of upset here and there.

Wednesday, July 3

TB was worried about the Catholic Mass story, fearing it was doing us damage, but I honestly felt people would by and large not get the fuss. He was sitting there, in his dressing gown and underpants, his hair all over the place, with a slight look of the mad professor, and I knew it was going to be a long day.

Wednesday, July 10

Major was on the news four times at lunchtime: pay, the meeting with [Nelson] Mandela, Wales, and Northern Ireland.† He was looking good and motoring. We could not really go on as we were. We were not at the races in the last few days.

---

* Although an Anglican, Blair often took Communion at a Catholic church in Islington. Cherie Blair was Catholic. Hume later conceded that it was permissible for him to attend a Catholic church while on holiday in Tuscany.
† All-party talks began in Stormont chaired by former US Senator George Mitchell. John Major and John Bruton announced at a joint press conference their support for Senator Mitchell as chair of the Forum. As they had broken the ceasefire, Sinn Féin were excluded from the talks.

Ireland was massive in the press. Mo was trying to move from the government a bit, presumably with the Shadow Cabinet elections in mind.

The Manchester bombsite visit was fascinating. I was really impressed by the cops and the council people and they were determined they were going to build something special out of what had happened.

TB was doing an interview with Mary Riddell [journalist] and we discussed beforehand how he should try to open up a bit more on the personal front. People wanted to know more about what he was, where he came from as a person, who and what shaped him. He said, I hate doing all that stuff, people hanging their lives out for others to stare at. I said it was important because some people out there would only connect with us through him and his personality, and until they had got that they would not even get near the whole policy area. He did his usual policy stuff with Mary, and was on good form and when she started to push him on the personal front, he started hesitantly on the kids. Then she asked him if he ever felt stalked by tragedy – dad's stroke, mother's death, John Smith's death, and he went through each of them and how he felt and when he talked about his mum he really opened up, and I found it quite moving. I had never really heard him talk about his mother in such detail before and there was a real naturalness and warmth in his words, and a look in his eyes that was half fond, half sad and when he had finished talking about her, he just did a little nod and a sigh and then looked out of the window. I said to him afterwards I'd never realized he was so close to his mum because he had never really opened up like that before, even in private. He said she was a wonderful woman and he still felt guided by her. What would she make of where you are now? I asked. Heaven knows, he said. I think she would be anxious for me, but proud. Dad is always saying I wish she was here to see this, she would be so proud. He said he hated talking about this kind of thing in interviews, because there were things he felt should stay personal. He said the thing that his mother's death had given him above all was a sense of urgency, the feeling that life is short, it can be cut even shorter, and you should pack in as much as you can while you're here, and try to make a difference.

TB said the Shadow Cabinet was more friendly and productive, but he was a bit alarmed there appeared to be so little support for doing anything to Jeremy Corbyn [Labour MP] for inviting Gerry Adams to launch his book at the Commons.*

Carole Walker [BBC] called and read me an *Everyman* interview with Cardinal [Thomas] Winning in which he said our handling of the pro-life conference stall issue two years ago was 'fascist' and that TB's refusal to condemn abortion meant his Christian faith was a sham. The guy was unbelievable. My instinct was really to go for him, but TB calmed me down and was instead blathering on about why the BBC were running it. I said it was a perfectly legitimate story if Scotland's top Catholic Church man was calling the would-be Labour prime minister fascist and saying his religious beliefs were fake. We agreed a statement in which we simply said he disagreed with Winning on abortion and it had always been a matter of conscience for MPs. It was a good measured statement, which we hoped people would contrast with the over-the-top way in which Winning had expressed himself.

TB told me that Donald Dewar [Labour Chief Whip] had told him of a complaint from Betty [Boothroyd, Speaker of the House of Commons] that one of our MPs had shown a group around the House that included two IRA people. TB asked DD to get written assurances it wouldn't happen again. He was also ruminating on how he must surely be a bit of a security risk. I'm sure he was and we sometimes felt a bit exposed travelling around with no security at all.

Fiona and CB were seeing the Home Office and intelligence people who said that if we won, TB, JS, RC and Mo would be properly protected, but not CB and the kids. They felt there was no security need. They felt the house in Sedgefield was not safe and would need a lot of work done to make it safe. Fiona said CB was getting more and more anxious re what would happen to the kids.

---

* *Before the Dawn: An Autobiography.*

We arrived in Dublin and straight out to meet President Mary Robinson, a really impressive woman who seemed to mix a genuine warmth with a hard-headed assessment of issues. I got a message that JP did not want to do tax at PMQs and I had to get TB to talk to him as we drove from the president to lunch with Dick Spring [minister for foreign affairs and Tánaiste]. Neil had said he was one of the loveliest men in politics and he was, but he gave a very gloomy prognosis of the peace process, and he was pretty sure violence would resume before the election. He was gloomy on Europe too. His finance guy, Ruairí Quinn [minister for finance 1994–97], came up with the quote of the day at lunch. 'Every Labour government has foundered on the issue of a sterling crisis – so why not just get rid of sterling?' TB said he was determined to be pro single currency but they had to understand just how awful our press were. JP having been sorted then got angry because someone was putting it round that he had to be forced to do tax. I asked Spring how we dealt with the 'waiting for Blair' and he said the best line was that Europe wanted a British government with strength and a clear position. At the press conference, TB had to deal with the charge that Northern Ireland was not a priority for him, and also an attack on him for marrying a Catholic.

We set off for the [Northern Ireland] border. We met up with Jonathan Powell and Mo who although she could be a bit OTT was incredibly good at the touchy-feely, chatty, meeting and greeting. To Portadown to meet the troops and a briefing from the RUC [Royal Ulster Constabulary] deputy chief constable [Colin Cramphorn], who was very gloomy and said he expected a major IRA bomb before Christmas. Then to meet David Trimble [Ulster Unionist leader] on a farm. There was huge media interest and they did a joint doorstep standing in front of the cows. TB drove with him to his office and said afterwards he was a difficult guy to talk to, very internalized and hard to probe. We had a rather more rumbustious meeting with Peter Robinson [Democratic Unionist MP] in Belfast. Lunch, then to TB's speech at Queen's [University]. It was striking how few women there were wherever we went compared with audiences in England. We were promising support and continuation re the peace process. I was briefing hard against the 'waiting for Blair' line saying that what they were waiting for was clarity, coherence and leadership, the qualities sadly lacking with the current lot.

Peter M called from the States. He said the big difference between the Clinton operation and ours was (a) cohesion and (b) attention to detail. He said before a big interview Clinton would video rehearse four or five times. The people at the top got on together in a way that ours didn't. I spoke to Ed Balls [adviser] as Fiona and I were driving to Philip [Gould, political pollster and close friend of AC and TB]'s for a drink with George Stephanopolous [ex-Clinton spokesman]. George was less than flattering re Peter, who he had met in the States. He said he was surprised how insecure he was. PG made the same point Peter did, re the greater cohesion of the US team. I said the problem was we all had big egos and sometimes competing interests. I got the sense the US people were much more subservient. George thought Peter was a particular problem because he was seen neither as politician nor as spin doctor. James Carville [pollster, Clinton adviser] had told PG that TB was clearly our biggest asset and we had to play the leadership line for all it was worth. On the way out, a scene that would have made a great story had it been filmed. I was walking down the stairs behind GS, tripped, landed on his back and flattened him to the floor. He was not much more than half my weight and yet got up and was almost apologetic, as if he had landed on me. I liked George. He was sharp, clever, engaging and he later sent PG a message saying he got the sense TB's campaign was in very safe hands.

I put in the changes to the New Year message, which TB had phoned through from Ireland. TB was spending the Christmas Holiday in Ireland in Skibbereen at David Puttnam's house.

As 1997 arrived, we knew we were in election year, and with the Tories in continuing difficulty – at one point we had a poll lead close to 40 points – we were most of the time in full-on campaign mode, finalizing policy detail, trying to get the campaign structures we had put in place to work effectively, travelling all over Britain. Of course the Tories too now had their thinking and actions much more dominated by the pending election. It meant that despite the good work Major had been doing, Northern Ireland went back down the agenda again. There are strong arguments for and against Tory and Labour representation in Northern Ireland, but one of the arguments for is surely to try to reverse the sense that Parliamentary elections in the Province are almost like a separate event. Major did visit the Province, but primarily to show frenetic activity at a time he knew the election was slipping away. By the time polling day came, and the votes were counted, we had a majority far bigger than any of us had dreamed possible.

[1997]

The *Sun* didn't run the piece we did for them yesterday. Mo Mowlam was on *Today* re party reform and was absolutely dire. TB had been driving his kids somewhere and said he almost pulled the car off the road. She was all over the place. He said the problem was there were people who still felt happier talking to a few activists than to the public. Mo's basic message was that nothing much was changing. We agreed that TB would have to do the interviews on this.

Tuesday, April 8

Anna Healy took me to one side and said she needed to speak to me about Mo. She explained that Mo had a brain tumour, which had required radiotherapy, and steroids that were making her put on weight. She had managed to keep it quiet for around three months but she thought people were beginning to notice and wonder. Mo wanted to talk to me about it. I spoke to her for ages, and she was really worried about the whole thing, not just for obvious reasons. She said she was worried if it got out, the Ulster Unionists would somehow use it against her. I said I was sure she was best to get the whole story out there, on her own terms, rather than wait for it to dribble out and she be forced to react. It reflected nothing but good on her and even the UUs [Ulster Unionists] would be forced

APRIL '97: MO HAS BRAIN TUMOUR   33 to express some sympathy. Also, if we briefed it, we could accompany it with a statement of absolute support and approval from TB. She said she was fine but it had been a bit of an ordeal.

Friday, April 11

I was working on briefing lines for the Sundays, and also a note on Mo, which I got Anna Healy to fill in re the facts. Mo had agreed it was best if I make it part of the Sunday briefing. It was a human interest story but also in me briefing it, it would be clear TB saw no reason why it should affect her future politically.

Saturday, April 12

I did my briefing to the Sundays, big on education and also the Mo story, which straight away became the source of rumours around the place. We decided we would have to put it all round, before which point the *Sunday Mirror*, who had been at my briefing, put it out as their own press release, claiming it to be a big exclusive. What vile unscrupulous people they are. The late news was a lot better, TB on law and order, and the Mo story done straight and sympathetically.

Friday, April 18

The IRA let off some bombs [in the UK] and TB did a doorstep. His words were fine but he was worrying about his hair, which was having a real flyaway day. He was really capable of focusing on the trivial from time to time. He was also pushing for three days off next week, which was ridiculous.

Monday, April 21

I'd really pushed to get the broadcasters to lead overnight on TB's leadership speech. The speech was strong but then IRA bomb alerts shut down Gatwick, King's Cross and Charing Cross and that was clearly going to be the big story of the day.

Thursday, May 1. Election Day.

It was a weird feeling. It was as if we had been fighting a fifteen-round fight and as the bell rang for the last round, the other guy just didn't show. I had barely slept, even though for the first time in months, there was no reason to get up early. I gave up trying to sleep just after 6, got up and read through the papers. They could hardly have been better. CB had said she wanted the kids to go with them to vote, which was great, but getting everyone ready was all a bit stress-y, like going to a wedding or something, but they looked good walking across the field at the back of the house to the polling station. Carole had clearly chosen all the clothes. Hilary had got them all lined up, good pictures, then TB set out to do a tour of polling stations. The weather was good, the mood was good. I started to get word of the early exit polls during the afternoon and it looked like it was going to be big. TB didn't believe the figures and nor did I. When he came back from his tour, he said 'Do you really think we're going to win?' I said it looked like it.

Fiona arrived with lots of TB and CB's family, and the house was filled with noise. Fiona said the journey was pretty chaotic. TB was locked away in his office. All around us, everyone was incredibly jolly but TB and I were feeling flat. We kept getting updates on exit polls and we still didn't believe them. It wasn't until we got the call from Number 10 later saying JM wanted to speak to him that we dared to believe it for sure. TB sat in the armchair by the fireplace, was very quiet and polite, as Major conceded, said it was clear there would be a considerable Labour majority and congratulations. Jonathan and I were watching him from the chairs by the door, and I think we both had a sense of the history of the moment, despite the cluttered setting and TB's clothes – he was wearing a rugby shirt, dark blue tracksuit bottoms and his ridiculous granddad slippers. TB paused, thanked JM for the call, said he had been a strong opponent and history would be kinder to him. In truth there was little love lost between them and I could only imagine how much JM hated making that call.

TB got a huge cheer as he arrived at the count. He was meant to be doing some interviews but he said he didn't want to. I did them instead and wished I hadn't. I was still doing no complacency when the votes were already in. I couldn't explain why I felt flat. I'd called David Hill earlier and said TB felt they were being too exuberant when the cameras were on them. David said it is very hard to persuade people that a landslide victory is a reason not to be cheerful. TB said we probably felt flat because we had to start all over again tomorrow. Imagine preparing for a new job by working flat out travelling the country for six weeks and then go a few nights without sleep. There was a TV in the bar and we stood together at one point as more and more Tories were falling. 'What on earth have we done?' TB said. 'This is unbelievable.'

We were driven out to the airport and listened to the radio and the fantastic news that after a series of recounts Rupert Allason had lost. Even that didn't lift me out of my flat mood though. Fiona asked what was wrong. I said it was probably the anticlimax and the worries about the future. We got on the plane, TB and CB across from me and Fiona, the cops, John Burton. Tom Stoddart was snapping away and we also had a TV camera for ITN. It was a really comfortable plane, better than the ones we had used for the campaign. There were bottles of champagne there but TB was still not really in celebratory mood. Just after take-off, he and CB had a very private chat across their little table. This was him telling her how important she had been and her saying how proud she was, what a great prime minister he would be, she would always support him, etc. I said to Fiona, it may be tough at times but it's quite something to be here, on the plane flying a new PM to London, to know we helped.

We landed and I sought out Terry [Rayner, TB's driver] to give him a big hug. How many times had I sat in the back of the car and asked him if he thought we were going to win, and now we had. We headed into London, all quiet really, and then the Special Branch had a nightmare as we got to the Festival Hall. Somehow they ended up down a wrong road and we got stuck, the whole convoy. We could hear them playing 'Things Can Only Get Better', again and again, and on the radio they were saying TB is only moments away, but what they didn't realize was we were stuck, and the whole convoy was having to do three-point turns and get TB's car up ahead of all the rest. Eventually, we got there, stopped briefly at the bottom of the ramp to get TB miked up, then up the ramp to a wall of noise as the cars pulled up. Fiona and I were in the car behind the police backup and I suddenly realized I had his speech notes in my inside pocket. I jumped out while the car was still moving and the wheel went right over my foot.

Friday, May 2

I had an hour's sleep, a shower then to Richmond Crescent. Just a short sleep had bucked me up, and I had a session with some of the hacks in the street before going in. It was another lovely sunny day, and there was a good crowd outside. Inside, the usual frantic activity. Carole was there fussing around Cherie. TB was up in the bedroom working on the speech for the street. 'Practical measures in pursuit of noble causes.' Not sure about that. He got dressed and Jonathan and I went out to be met by Trevor Butler, who I knew from my *Mirror* days when he was looking after Thatcher and Major, and who would be taking over protection. He talked us through what was going to happen, the drive to the Palace, what Jonathan and I would do while TB saw the Queen, the drive back to Number 10. TB came out, did a little walkabout and then off we went. Jonathan and I were in the car behind the backup and the whole journey was fantastic, people coming out of houses and offices to wave and cheer. Going down Gower Street, it was almost like watching a cascade. We were looking down the street and people following the car on TV were coming out to cheer. I had a surge of emotion almost on a par with the one in Sedgefield on Wednesday night. I said to JoP 'This is unbelievable.' We agreed that expectations were going to be way too high. There were big crowds outside the Palace, huge cheer as he went through. Then TB was taken off to see the Queen while JoP and I were taken into a room with Alex Allan [principal private secretary], Robin Janvrin [deputy private secretary to the Queen] and Geoff Crawford [press secretary to the Queen]. It was all very friendly and relaxed, and I couldn't quite take in that it was all happening. Alex Allan seemed a really nice bloke. It was odd to see people who didn't look exhausted. I was talking about how hard it had been to be away from the kids so much and then Janvrin said oh, look at those children at Number 10, and I turned round to the TV to see Calum and Grace sitting on the steps of Number 10, looking bemused, Calum playing with some sunglasses. I called Mum to get her to watch, and she already was.

TB was in for half an hour or so, came out and we set off for Downing Street. As we turned into Whitehall, we could hear the crowds. The cars stopped at the bottom of the street and we got out and the noise was deafening. Ton-ee, Ton-ee, Ton-ee. Labour's coming home, Labour's coming home. TB and CB got out, started the walk up. JP and I followed on behind. The noise was almost like a sporting event. I caught sight of Fiona holding Grace up the street, and Rory and Calum standing there near the door. Tim [Allan, press officer] was in tears in the crowd. It was fantastic to see the party people and the people from the office who had all worked their rocks off and were now able to enjoy this. David Bradshaw [special adviser] and Kerry [his wife], Liz Lloyd [policy adviser], Peter Hayman [speechwriter]. It was brilliant. We got to the top and TB went to the lectern, did his speech, a few more pictures and then inside to meet the staff. Jonathan and I, Sally Morgan [political secretary] and David Miliband [head of Policy Unit], followed. I'd been through that door so many times as a journalist. I'd stood in that hall dozens, hundreds of times, waiting to be called through with the rest of the hacks to [Margaret Thatcher's press secretary] Bernard Ingham's briefings. But this time it felt very different, walking in behind the new prime minister, knowing that for some years I would be spending more working hours here than virtually anywhere else. I felt a mix of confidence, but uncertainty too.

TB went off with [Sir] Robin Butler [Cabinet Secretary] to the Cabinet Room for a security briefing. I was introduced to Alison [Blackshaw], my new PA, who seemed a bit dizzy, told me how much she had liked Major and every time I wandered off, she said she had to know where I was and she was worried I would be too 'independent' for her to be able to do her job.

TB seemed to be in his element. We were in the Cabinet Room, working through the Cabinet and some of the junior jobs, and he was clear and decisive, had found new reserves of energy. Butler and Alex Allan seemed to take to him. Butler said later all the machine wanted was clear direction. I told him I had not been too impressed with the way the government media machine worked, and nor had TB. I asked if I was within my rights to get them all in and emphasize the need for change and he said no problem. That was what they expected.

Once lunch was out of the way, TB started to see everyone to appoint the Cabinet. JP [John Prescott, Deputy Prime Minister] came in first and was really happy with his lot. Robin [Cook, Foreign Secretary] went straight out and did a doorstep and TB said we had to keep a very wary eye on him. 'He is playing the old games.' Derry [Irvine, Lord Chancellor] was happy enough. [David] Blunkett [Education and Employment Secretary] came in and I introduced him to [Jonathan] Haslam, who was going to be his top press man. It was interesting how quickly the idea settled that they were now in government and off to do real jobs as opposed to all the Shadow stuff we had been doing for years; listening to TB set out priorities, and then talk about detail of policies, which were now going to be put into practice.

Margaret [Beckett, Trade and Industry Secretary] and Jack S [Straw, Home Secretary] in particular made the point they just couldn't wait to get started.

Saturday, May 3

We got through the appointments quicker than any of us thought possible. Mo and I had a very friendly chat before she headed straight for Northern Ireland. I did a briefing for the broadcasters on the appointments, and then for the Sundays. I gave them the story about TB and family living in Number 11 not 10, which had them going on for ages. Also, re the official residences – RC Chevening, GB [Gordon Brown, Chancellor of the Exchequer] Dorneywood, JP access to both plus Admiralty House. Jack S wanted to stay at home so Mo was using South Eaton Place.

Sunday, May 4

TB was at home working on more appointments. Peter M did a photocall at the Cabinet Office without clearing it with us, which pissed me off, particularly as he was simultaneously saying that people should not be doing things without clearance through Number 10. We had to establish quickly, even with Peter, that things had to be routed through Number 10. It was going to be more important in government than in opposition, because there are so many different places that can make news.

Tuesday, May 6

There were loads of CB moving-in pictures. Charlie [Whelan] was tipping off people from 7.55 that the Governor of the Bank was seeing GB at 8. The BBC were pretty slow off the mark. The assumption was interest-rate rise full stop. I listened to the news in the office. John Holmes [principal private secretary and foreign affairs adviser] came in to say he was worried the news was overblowing TB's Irish visit. It was unlikely to produce much at this stage. He wanted me to play it down.

Wednesday, May 7

TB was worrying about Ireland, wanting quickly to take an initiative but worrying whether he could do it without upsetting too many parts of the equation. TB met the Northern Ireland Office people for a briefing, and then [Sir] David English [chairman, Associated Newspapers] with [Lord] Rothermere [chairman, *Daily Mail* and General Trust]. English popped round for a chat and said what a brilliant campaign it had been.

Thursday, May 8

Today was unbelievably busy, with relentless interest in every detail of the Cabinet, Queen's Speech, plus the John Bruton meeting. The Cabinet started arriving fairly early and there was a good mood around the place. They gathered outside and were drinking tea and chatting. TB said the last government had been a shambles and we had to learn from that. He said we will sink or swim together. There was too much chattering to the media going on. It was a bit like first day at school. TB was on great form but he looked tired. He said 'Good morning everyone,' sat down and then said he had been thinking what they should call each other at these meetings; that they had been together so long that it would be odd suddenly to start using titles, so we should carry on calling each other by our Christian names. Hear, hears.

I asked whether anyone had thought about sacking the people at the top. I did a note for the four o'clock [lobby briefing], and was fairly downbeat, covered Cabinet, twenty-two bills, pay, meeting with Bruton. On most of the bulletins, we had the first three stories. The Bruton meeting was fine, and TB was clearly up for a big push on it. He didn't want to do media and so we left it all to Bruton and Mo.

Friday, May 9

We got good coverage out of Cabinet – 'Call me Tony' – and on Ireland. TB was heading off to Chequers [Prime Minister's official country residence]. We had a chat before he left and he said I had to try to get some rest. He said we had had a good first week and we had to keep on establishing grip and competence. I was missing PG's [Philip Gould] notes but he sent one through today saying the mood was overwhelmingly positive and the first week had been great. He had played an absolute blinder during the campaign. There had been times when it felt like he and I had held the thing together. He had a lot of the qualities needed for a long campaign like that – work ethic, perseverance, enthusiasm and not getting too fussed when things went a bit wrong. It annoyed me that he was virtually written out of the post-election script, partly because he was not in the government, but also because Peter was so busy taking credit.

Monday, May 12

Things had settled down fairly quickly and I was missing the intensity of the campaign. I had a lot of challenges and problems but many of them were dull, administrative kind of things, making change that should have been made yonks ago. TB was seeing Ian Paisley [Democratic Unionist leader], John Hume [nationalist SDLP leader] and David Trimble and it was interesting to watch them put their own spin not just on the meetings, but the bigger picture. TB said he reckoned he could see a way of sorting the Northern Ireland problem. I loved the way he said it, like nobody had thought of it before. I said what makes you think you can do it when nobody else could? I had a long session with him and John Holmes, who looked after Ireland as well as Europe and all the big foreign policy stuff. He was not your typical Foreign Office man. He was from Preston, had a very dry sense of humour and had been totally grown up about the main changes. He worked fantastically hard and quickly established a rapport with Tony, and an ability to speak his mind without bullshit. I could tell he was a bit quizzical about TB's optimism, but willing to give it a good go. TB was thinking of going to NI at the end of the week, making a basically pro-Union speech but at the same time saying that officials could talk to Sinn Féin. John said it was not guaranteed to produce a ceasefire but it was probably the best way to try. I could see TB getting really seized of it. Every time I saw him today, whatever the issue, he would say something about Ireland. 'I can see a way on this.'

I had a look round the Number 11 flat with Fiona and Roz [Preston, assistant to CB]. It was a bit musty and not terribly homely. The main living room felt more like an overpriced hotel than a home. The pictures were pretty dire. The kitchen was awful. I felt a bit sorry for them, having to move in, but the kids seemed fine enough with it. I was beginning to work on the planning of the Bill Clinton visit, which clearly had to go well.

'TB said he reckoned he could see a way of sorting the Northern Ireland problem.' This was one of my favourite lines in the entire diary. When I was transcribing the diaries, it was rare that I came across a line that took me aback, but this one did. It showed not only that TB had been thinking a lot about Northern Ireland in the early days of government, but also that he had worked out the strategy that would inform our approach, starting with the first big speech on the issue. Principle of consent to satisfy the Unionists, commitment to equality for the nationalists, the rest all negotiation; and with the need for bold steps to get the process moving with his popularity and political momentum high.

The role of Jonathan Powell has rightly been highlighted in the analysis of how the peace process became the success story that it did, but senior civil servant John Holmes' role, particularly in these early days, was crucial. He knew most of the main players, having been alongside John Major in his attempts to make progress. His insights into them, and what they would take by way of change, were important judgements. He sometimes found TB's boundless optimism wearing, but he became an integral member of the team. The fact that he was also the main civil servant dealing with foreign policy, with a huge in-tray covering Europe, the US et al, explains why, whenever I am asked if the cliché about a Rolls-Royce civil service is true, I say, No, but there are some civil servants who were truly exceptional, and John Holmes was one of them.

Tuesday, May 13

Fiona, Anji, Magi [Cleaver, press officer] and I met the Clinton visit pre-advance team. This was the team that would set up the visit before the real advance team came in. Talk about overmanning. There were about fifteen of them to our four.

We agreed Clinton would go to Cabinet, and speak, and that we should have coverage of that. There would be a TB/BC lunch. They were also keen for what they called a 'fun event', but they were totally divided on what it should be. Someone suggested a big crowd in the street. I said it would look too much like TB after the election. The Foreign Office wanted a visit to the Globe theatre. Fiona said CB would be doing a separate programme when TB/BC were doing the talks etc. We went round in circles, and I sensed there would be lots of planning that came to nothing. But we had the main bits in place.

I had a meeting with Jonathan and John Holmes re the NI visit. John felt it was important we set the visit up as an act of reassurance to the Unionists, maybe TB say he didn't expect a united Ireland in our lifetime, but give the go-ahead for talks with Sinn Féin. I said, so we want the spin for the Unionists; the substance for the nationalists. I said come the day, the move to talks would be the bigger thing. He said the last government didn't do it because of the fear of the reaction, and because of their tiny majority, but we had a chance. He said this was a big step, and the spin operation would be very difficult. I said I would need to immerse myself in this. It was important we did the two main lines together and avoid any briefing before it was ready; and make sure it came from here.

Wednesday, May 14

There was lots of toing and froing on the visit to Belfast on Friday. I put to TB the idea of walking to the House and the Special Branch said fine and planned it out. He and CB set off and we got terrific pictures out of it, very good mood in the crowds, and then to his new office in the House. How many times had I walked past the outer office, seen the secretaries and the security people hanging around, and wondered whether we would ever make it? Now we had. TB's new office was similar in style to the one down the corridor, but a bit grander, with a full Cabinet-sized table in there, bigger paintings and mirrors.

We had a meeting in the Cabinet Room on Ireland – TB, Jonathan, John H, Robin Butler, Alex Allan and me. JH had done a draft and it was in tone very Unionist but I felt the offer of talks with Sinn Féin was sufficiently big and bold for that to be the main story out of it, and so it was OK. TB said he was sure we had only a brief window of opportunity and we had to take it. He said he intended to sleep on it before making a final decision to do it. He was seeing Paddy Ashdown [leader of the Liberal Democratic Party] in the morning and he would speak to JM tomorrow night, and tell him he intended to get officials to talk to SF [Sinn Féin]. He admitted that the effect of what we were proposing was that SF would get into talks without a ceasefire. It was hard to see how the Unionists would do anything other than go mad at that, which is why the tone had to be heavily weighted in their favour.

I spoke to Anji about setting up the visit without actually pressing the button. We really had to think about mood, tone, backdrop, pictures. My hunch was he was definitely going to do it and go for another bold move early on.

Thursday, May 15

On Ireland, Mo emphasized that TB would make the UUs feel secure. Magi Cleaver was meeting trouble at the NIO [Northern Ireland Office], with Andy Wood [head of press] seemingly briefing already that it was on. We then had another meeting on Ireland. I had written a few passages trying to distil the whole thing. TB was clear that if he was saying, basically, 'I am a Unionist,' then he had to do the other side. The feedback from the NIO on the draft was OK, up to a point. TB said he was aware of the objections but he instinctively felt he had a very brief window of opportunity, that the election was the only change in the land-scape, and we had to do it now. He knew the talks would end up as the main thing out of it, and it was tricky without the ceasefire, but he felt it was a risk worth taking. He clearly liked John Holmes, who had a really good manner with him.

He clearly knew the issue inside out, and was not afraid to say when he thought one or other of us was talking crap. He strikes me as a very good bloke, straight and trustworthy, and very clever. Having read the latest draft, TB looked up at him and said 'You're not the Master of the Grand Orange Order, are you?' JH said needs must. TB spoke to John Major who was supportive and said he would say so publicly. The US, the Irish and SF would also be supportive. The problem, despite the warm words, would be the Unionists.

Friday, May 16

I really enjoyed today, for all sorts of reasons. Northern Ireland was a big story, announcing government officials talking to SF without delivering a ceasefire. A bold move, full of risks which by and large we handled pretty well. We spent a lot of time getting the words right, the details of the visits; there was a lot of sophis-ticated spinning had to be done, and it paid off. The Northern Ireland Office had been far too gabby about the visit, but nobody had a sniff of the scale of what TB would say. Terry collected me at half six and I got in to hear the visit leading the news, but without much detail. I wrote a briefing note and Q&A based on the conversations with TB, JH and Jonathan. The difficult balancing act would be to reassure the Unionists while signalling a major change. Before we left, he spoke to Trimble and he was pretty candid with him, but he seemed OK-ish. In the car to Northolt, he spoke to Hume, who was fine. We got driven to the RAF plane, which was more comfortable than I expected, and the four of us went through the last-minute changes and the difficult questions. I was picking JH's brains in order to be sure I would be able to handle any question at a briefing. I was pretty clear that no matter how warm the words for the Unionists, there was only one story in it come the end of the day. We agreed TB would let his words speak for themselves, I would brief, Mo would do all the interviews.

We landed, then flew by helicopter to Armagh. TB met what Mo called 'the holies', namely the Protestant and Catholic top guys, then did a fantastic walkabout, really good mood, really friendly and warm. I called Denis Murray [BBC Ireland correspondent] on his mobile just before the lunchtimes and briefed him fully on the speech. 'Bloody hell,' he said. He was impressed. He said it was a great story. I liked Denis, had always liked his reporting, and I felt I could trust him to put both parts of the equation. He did. The first reports were important, and they were word-perfect for us when I listened down the phone a bit later. TB felt buoyed up after the walkabout. He said those people are desperate for something good to happen. He did the troops, then back into the helicopters to head for the agriculture show where he was doing the speech. By now there was an enormous media presence to match the expectations. We were as happy as we were ever going to be with the text. I was a bit alarmed hearing Trimble's overwhelmingly enthusiastic response, so briefed Denis again, who emphasized at the end of the lunchtime bulletin that the big thing here was the offer of talks, and Mo would be writing to Gerry Adams. Again, we were getting credit for being big and bold and ballsy.

TB did another walkabout on the way out. It was a very rural, very Ulster event, but he seemed to have a natural empathy. As he walked along shaking hands I told him Hume and Trimble had been fine, Paisley very hostile. TB put his foot in an enormous cowpat but just carried on till we got to the car. None of the media seemed to have noticed. Bill Lloyd [protection officer] gave him a packet of tissues and I said what a glamorous life I led, sitting alongside the prime minister as he cleaned bullshit off his shoes. He was worried that the over-positive Trimble reaction would make SF hostile and unable to play along. Martin McGuinness [Sinn Féin] reacted with a very churlish response but did at least say they would enter the talks. TB was waxing lyrical about his team again. He said he was always amazed to learn how much we had to do behind the scenes to keep the show on the road. It had gone pretty much perfectly.

The dangers of getting out of touch were all too apparent as we headed to Chequers, through beautiful scenery, up the long driveway, that unique sound of wheel on gravel. It was a lovely building but didn't feel very homely. TB and I chatted away as we waited for CB, FM and the kids to arrive. The food was terrific and one or two of the staff said it was nice having children around. We were taken upstairs and told we were sleeping in Winston Churchill's bed. TB said he was getting exasperated at GB's refusal to move into Number 10 after they had agreed he, CB and the kids would take the bigger flat in Number 11. We talked over the Clintons' visit and what we might do on the social/ private front. TB was really on a bit of a high after the success of the Irish trip. Fiona said we would have to work really hard to keep our feet on the ground. Peter M was getting loads of publicity out of an interview he'd done with a psychiatrist, in which he started crying. The attention-seeking was becoming absurd.

Saturday, May 17

I weighed myself – fifteen stone five. Bloody hell. It didn't stop me eating an enormous breakfast served up by the Wrens. The *Sun* had a poll saying we were the most popular government ever! Even the *Telegraph* praised the 'sure-footed' Ulster initiative.

Monday, May 19

TB was seeing minor Irish party leaders.*

Wednesday, May 21

I got back for a meeting with the next Clinton advance team. It was hard to make progress because Clinton had apparently said he wanted to go shopping, eating and didn't know whether he wanted to make a speech or not. They're all very nice, but very vague and didn't really know what they wanted. They thought Clinton wanted to go for an Indian meal. We were still completely dominating the news. Northern Ireland talks between SF and NIO were under way, the first PMQs. Maybe there was too much but we had to keep the momentum going.

---

* Gerry Adams, president of Sinn Féin, and Martin McGuinness, vice president, went to Westminster to press their case for office facilities within the House of Commons. The two abstentionist SF Members of Parliament were denied access to the House when they refused to take their seats, which would have involved taking an oath of allegiance to the Queen.

I got back for the end of TB's meeting with [Margaret] Thatcher. Nobody saw her go in though there were people – e.g. GB – who saw her inside the building. I doubted it would stay quiet. I had real doubts about the need for it but he was adamant it made sense to involve her, make her feel her advice was valued. She struck me as a bit unhinged, over-hamming it all a bit, reminiscing loudly. Then the two of them went off for a session on their own, where he picked her brains on foreign affairs. He said afterwards she was still very sharp, though sometimes her determination to make a point got in the way of a broader understanding. I went in at the end to move him on for the next meeting and she was in full flow, warning him to keep an eye on the Foreign Office, saying Germany will follow if TB gives a real lead. The French cannot be trusted, and the Italians make nice clothes. Then a long lecture on single parents, illegitimacy etc. They were sitting on the sofas in the Green Room and she was complaining at the way loose threads were hanging off. To be fair, they did look a bit shabby. She told him he should do lots of receptions for the voluntary sector, then paused as if she was about to make a huge point, looked him in the eye and said, 'And don't forget to invite the Lord-Lieutenants.' We agreed that if we had press enquiries we should simply say he wanted to talk to her re foreign affairs. 'Quite so,' she said, and off she went.

'God, she is so strong,' he said as she went. I was more struck by how obvious it was that she missed the place. Her reminiscences had been less about the big things than the little routines that she got into. There was a group of party people waiting to see TB and their eyes almost dropped out when they saw her walking past the Cabinet Room with TB.

When Margaret Thatcher died on April 8, 2013, David Cameron and the right-wing media went into overdrive with what felt like a canonization plan. There was much talk of legacy, of claims that she had saved the nation economically – arguable when you actually look at a few facts and figures, and frankly an insult to large parts of the county left economically and socially devastated by her -ism. Of course she did achieve a huge amount that she set out to do. But when it comes to the peace process, John Major is the Tory Prime Minister who rightly takes plaudits for having taken risks and moved things forward. Given that Margaret Thatcher spent much of her career under active threat of assassination, lost her friends and colleagues Airey Neave and Ian Gow to separate bomb blasts, and came close to losing her own life in the Brighton bomb in 1984, one can perhaps understand why she was not naturally disposed to putting too much effort into helping those who were trying to kill her. She had a considerable legacy, even her opponents would concede, but it is hard to put Northern Ireland high up the list.

She was in her own way a hardliner. So long as an organization was involved in terrorism, or close to those who were, she would have nothing to do with them. She would not let their voices be heard on television, let alone invite them into talks, as Major did, or into Downing Street, as TB did. Not long after she became Prime Minister, she had to deal with the IRA and INLA hunger strikes, and she took a hard line then too, resisting any step towards seeing Bobby Sands and Co as political prisoners.

It is true that she set up the Anglo-Irish Inter-Governmental Council with then Taoiseach Garret FitzGerald in 1981 and four years later, at some political risk among the Unionist community, and her own party, signed the Hillsborough Agreement with FitzGerald, which granted an advisory role to the Irish government in relation to Northern Ireland. But these were not the breakthrough moments. Those came later, notably the opening of talks between government officials and the IRA after Major became PM – a huge risk at the time, the Downing Street Declaration signed with Albert Reynolds (the IRA ceasefire followed the next year, 1994) and of course the Good Friday Agreement.

The right wing of her Party was at times a difficulty for both of her successors, yet Major and TB have been proven right in taking the risks they did. The progress in Northern Ireland from the violence and hatreds of the Thatcher era, to the relative peace and democracy of today, stands as a piece of 'legacy' as significant and as hard fought as any claimed for the Iron Lady. Major was made a Companion of Honour in 1999 for his work on Northern Ireland.

I cannot recall Mrs Thatcher ever discussing Ireland with TB and – I have checked – nor can he. At the time of her death, Peter Mandelson recalled his one meeting with the Iron Lady. It was the day he was appointed Northern Ireland Secretary. He was at a drinks party and suddenly felt a finger jabbing into his back … it was she. 'I have one thing to say to you, dear boy. You can't believe a thing the Irish say, nothing, nothing, they're all liars.' The French and the Germans were not the only ones to suffer her sweeping generalizations.

Thursday, May 29

The Clinton visit was well set up, with papers and broadcasts pretty much set according to the overnight briefing. In truth, we were getting such a good press at the moment that the Americans stood to gain far more than we did, especially as Bill C was being done in by the Paula Jones sexual harassment case again.* TB

---

* Jones, a former Arkansas civil servant, filed a sexual harassment case against Clinton in 1994.

wanted it to be a day of definition so we went through the various areas where we could say a new politics was being forged, neither old left nor new right. The weather was terrific so my idea of an open-air press conference in the garden was on. The lecterns were a bit second rate and shabby so we got two better ones sent down from the US Embassy.

There was a real sense of anticipation at the idea of Clinton speaking to the Cabinet in the Cabinet Room. We waited for him to arrive and got word he was a few minutes away. Cherie came down, looking great. She was on good form at the moment and had got a good press in the run-up, largely because of comparisons with Hillary. Fiona had to get a lot of the credit for the advice and for the outcome in the press. TB was nervous, fussing about tiny details, like where on the step to stand when he arrived, should he kiss Hillary – we decided not – whether he and BC should stand in the middle or put the wives in the middle. He was talking very quickly, a sure sign of nerves. I had a brief chat with JP re the choreography for Cabinet, and we agreed they should applaud but stay seated. Then the car pulled up. It was a lovely sunny day, there were hundreds of photographers there and the mood between them was great. The pictures went straight on to the front of the *Standard* – 'Best of pals' – which BC loved when he saw it and later he asked if he could get a copy. By then we were at Le Pont de la Tour restaurant and Hilary Coffman had to go and buy one from a punter for ten quid!

TB's kids had come down to say hello just inside the door and he chatted to them as the rest of the American party piled in. There were too many of them and it was a bit crowded and hard to manage. BC's operation was overmanned and there were too many people claiming to have his ear who didn't. We had had the nonsense about the Indian. Now we were reliably informed he wanted the four of them to go to a pub. Anji had even got Jon Mendelsohn and Ben Lucas [Labour staff] to stay in the Anchor Tap pub literally all day, and when TB mentioned it to BC, just as when we had mentioned the Indian, he looked at us like we were mad. He sparkled at the Cabinet. 'I'm so thrilled to be here. It is very exciting for an American president to be in this room.' He spotted Mo and said he had seen her speeches on TV, and you could see her melt. He said he had read the policy handbook and went into the mantra – many not the few, future not the past, leadership not drift, education the number one priority. I said to him afterwards I wish our own people could express it as fluently. His main point was that we had faced up to change, been professional, seized the future. We could show the world that it was possible to have an advanced economy and a humane society. Upstairs, GB muscled in for a few minutes to talk about the G7 jobs idea. I liked Clinton. He had a great sense of humour, was clever, very political in almost everything he said and did. He was a master of the pause in public speaking. I'd noticed that watching him on TV but it was even more powerful in meetings. He could hold a room with a pause and a nod, and so control events. He had enormous, beautifully manicured hands and he used these too to powerful communications effect. TB was very nice about me in public again. I don't know whether this was just flattery or whether it was a way of sending a signal to the Civil Service machine. He said to BC that I was 'something of a political legend', who scared our opponents.

The main bilateral was in the White Room. As they settled down to talk TB said he wanted no officials in there at all for the first bit, so I went to the street to brief for the lunchtimes. They stayed in there together for ages, mainly doing Bosnia, Ireland and politics. Afterwards I said to TB I was surprised how formal it was at times, Mr President, Mr Prime Minister. He said if it had been any less formal, it would have seemed gimmicky. But at both the meetings and the press conference he felt there were times when what they said was interchangeable. He really felt he was someone on his wavelength. Jobs, welfare, education, citizenship, that whole agenda he felt was shared by a kindred spirit.

We left for Le Pont de la Tour at 6.15, having finally cancelled the pub plan. A small crowd had gathered because word had got out. I wanted good clean shots out of it and my experience of the way the US pools fucked up pictures led me to get Mike McCurry to buy into us doing one outside their system. I tipped off one TV crew and three stills to be there and called them in one by one, with the agreement their stuff went everywhere. BC noticed it was not a full pool and asked what was going on. When I explained he said to TB 'This man's worse than McCurry.' TB said 'He's mad, bad and dangerous but he's mine so it's fine by me.' BC said he felt the whole visit had been handled well and he was grateful. Hillary said she had really enjoyed meeting Fiona. 'She is quality,' she said. I then left them, joined some of his people further down the restaurant and they embarked on what quickly became known as the dinner that doesn't end. I interrupted them when we got a front-page proof from the *Sun* sent through, which had the restaurant picture splashed all over the paper. He said he was impressed we got the papers before the public. TB said afterwards that Hillary was more into strategy than he had expected. BC was much more political. They went out at one point for a little walk down towards the bridge and a whole lot of people gathered at the windows of the yuppie flats, waving and cheering. BC said these are your people and you must make sure they stay bound in. He also advised him to get out and about with real people at least once a week, because it would stand him in good stead when the harder times came. TB called after BC and HC had left and he was on his way back to Chequers. He felt today had been really important, and a great success whichever way you looked at it. BC had said to him that he – TB – would be the real leader of the left in many ways because he [BC] could not win again; he would be history by the time of the next election in 2000. TB said he [BC] had blazed the trail and now they had to set a new agenda for the left and centre left that made progressive politics dominant in the way conservative politics had been. I also felt we had shown them a thing or two about media management and I was more convinced than ever that it can only work if you are clear you are working for the politician, not for the press.

From the perfect weather, to the mood music between President and the Prime Minister, the substance of the discussions and the positive media reaction, the visit could hardly have gone better. The personal warmth developing between TB and Clinton, allied to a shared agenda on so many issues, including Northern Ireland, would stand both in good stead.

Sunday, June 1

TB called early, saying he did not like the *Mail on Sunday's* story that the Queen was not happy about lack of consultation over the Clinton visit. I said they were going to do this kind of thing the whole time. He said he wanted it dealt with. Geoff Crawford was a great help, privately in saying I could assure him on her behalf it was nonsense; and publicly by killing it early.

Tuesday, June 10

TB was seeing the Queen, then called Clinton re Northern Ireland. He thought he might have upset the Queen who was wearing a green dress. She said she was going to Northern Ireland tomorrow. 'I hope you're not wearing that dress,' he said, and for a moment she thought it was a comment on the dress, not Irish politics. 'I think she got the point,' he said. 'But I couldn't be too sure.'

Monday, June 16

[During the Amsterdam summit] the media were running with TB as peacemaker between France and Germany, which was a real surprise to him when I raised it at the breakfast meeting. The European media was very much on the theme of TB as a real power in the land. Then news came through that two RUC officers had been killed in Lurgan [County Armagh].*

---

* The IRA admitted responsibility for the killings. The RUC officers were the first to be killed by the IRA since the ending of its ceasefire on 9 February 1996.

JUNE '97: RUC OFFICERS MURDERED

TB looked sick at the lunch. He said it was clearly a deliberate sabotage, that they knew the plan we had to get them into talks with a date next week and this was the signal that they intended to scupper it. It was pretty grim. John Holmes and I put some words together, while we tried to contact the Americans, John Hume etc., to get them on the same line. I saw TB just after lunch, and he really was in a grim mood about the killing of the policemen. He was keen to go straight out, really go for the IRA, reveal that they were close to getting something, but we persuaded him against. We organized a joint doorstep with John Bruton, who was at his last summit. They had a brief meeting, then did the doorstep together. Bruton was really powerful, particularly in his attack on Gerry Adams and weasel words. TB was quite strong too, but the impact was all the more powerful coming from the Irish PM. Afterwards, in the car, TB said 'What on earth do you do? We do everything we can. Clearly they don't want to know.'

Tuesday, June 17

TB was preoccupied by Ireland and the shooting and wondering whether to reveal the exchange of letters he had with Sinn Féin, to show that they were beyond the pale and also that they were acting in bad faith.

Thursday, June 19

We started the day thinking TB was going to make a statement on Northern Ireland, announcing that Sinn Féin had a timetable for coming into talks. We ended it saving the Millennium Exhibition. TB was now against an NI statement, not least because there was a possibility it would clash horribly with yesterday's funeral of the policemen, one of whose sons was absolutely heartbroken on the TV news last night. On the Dome, he had pretty much decided to go ahead.

Friday, June 20

We were due to leave for the G8 in Denver and I was up much of the night working on the briefing. The Clinton bilaterals were falling into place and the Northern Ireland story was coming together. Mo had wanted to do an article for the *Belfast Telegraph*, revealing that Sinn Féin had the chance to come into talks six weeks after a ceasefire, and they sabotaged it with the killing of the policemen. TB, JH, Jonathan and I had a conference call and agreed he would be wrong to do it in that way. Better to do it with Clinton tomorrow, and get his support for our approach. I briefed in the Denver briefing how important Ireland would be to the Clinton talks. Then John Holmes came through. We had a problem. The draft *Belfast Telegraph* article had gone through, allegedly for production purposes. It meant they had the information even though we had decided to pull the article. It was classic Mo – give them the article before it was finished, or before it had been decided. I spoke to Mo and agreed we would speak to the editor, to see if they would do it in a way to cause least trouble, e.g. we were seeing Clinton to tell him there had been progress, what we had done to get it, and to say we were looking at new ways of taking it forward. He was terrific, and agreed only to speculate on the fact that the timetable idea was on the table.

TB chatted to Hume on the way to the airport. We were getting Concorde to New York before flying to Denver. TB did a session with the press, and the main focus was Ireland. He was looking forward to seeing BC again, and was hoping for some time to continue their political discussions. I went to the press centre and did a briefing on the whole summit agenda, but again our lot were focusing on Ireland. I pretty much confirmed that three weeks before the shootings they were offered a place in the talks after six weeks. This was OK but I gave the impression it was not equivocal, and the story was rather running away. I had to ring round to try to calm them down. Meanwhile the mood with Clinton was great. He was looking for more time with TB, ditto Hillary and CB, and Hillary clearly took to Fiona as well.

Saturday, June 21

We had the bilateral planned for 11 with Clinton, and I was trying to fix up a picture and joint doorstep. We left the hotel after doing the Sundays and then to Denver library. TB had a few minutes with Clinton on arrival and John Holmes saw [Sandy] Berger [Clinton's national security adviser], and news came back that there would be no press. Eventually they agreed there could be a pool at the end, but it was not what we needed. [Michael] Brunson [ITN] was hanging around outside with Godric [Smith, press officer] on the off chance I got him in. I briefed him, [Robin] Oakley [BBC], [Adam] Boulton [Sky News political editor] and Phil Murphy [Press Association] with the details of the aide-memoire, in particular that before the Lurgan killings, Sinn Féin were offered a place in the talks after six weeks. They ran big with the story but to hammer home the message that SF were in the wrong, it needed TB and BC side by side saying the same thing.

The main G8 discussions were leaders plus sherpas, so I hung around for the meeting to break. TB and Bill C were talking about the aide-memoire and what Bill C called Adams' 'stupid response' to the killings. Jonathan and John Holmes joined us and Clinton said to me 'OK, what do you want me to do?' I said what would be great from our point of view, as the aide-memoire is now public, is if you and TB stand side by side, say the same message, and that you in particular say 'The ball is now in Sinn Féin's court.' He said that sounded right to him. By now, a rather nervous-looking Mike McCurry had joined us. He said 'Mr President, don't you think you should discuss this with your policy advisers first?' BC said get them down here then, and someone went to get Berger and Jim Steinberg [senior Clinton aide]. They went into a little huddle, but I think I had won the argument with Clinton that this was the right thing to do. He came back and said OK, where are we doing this? I got word to Godric to bring Brunson and his lot in, and we did a little pooled doorstep. Mike was almost hyperventilating by the time we got there. Clinton asked one more time 'Right, what do I say? Ball in their court. OK.' He did it brilliantly, looked the part, sounded the part, and it led our news all day. I could tell that Sandy was pissed off that we'd got Clinton to do it, but if it was the right thing to do, and the president thought so, I couldn't quite see the problem.

Then we heard David Trimble had gone mad because far from hearing an attack on Sinn Féin, he just heard the offer of a place at the talks. I was acutely conscious of the fact we were dealing with issues so sensitive that life and death sometimes depended on what we were saying. It was always a difficult balance we were trying to strike. I called Mo and she said it was coming over fine; the main impression was TB was trying hard to make it work, but one side was always upset, and often both sides were. At my next briefing, I was a bit more low-key about the offer [to Sinn Féin] and did not go into detail.

Afterwards Fiona and I, JH and Jonathan went for dinner with Mike McCurry, Dee Dee Myers [press secretary], Jim Steinberg and a few others from the White House. McCurry was very funny, had everyone in hysterics describing how he came into the meeting room to find the American president being kidnapped by the UK delegation.

It was further evidence of the extent to which Northern Ireland was a priority for Clinton that, whilst chairing the G8, he found as much time as he did to discuss the issue with TB and team, and that he went against the advice of his own advisers in getting out there publicly to put pressure on Sinn Féin. Though TB busied himself with the summit agenda, and a series of bilaterals with the other leaders, Ireland was dominant in his thinking, and while there we fixed a series of meetings with NI leaders as soon as we got back to London, with negotiations between the parties about to move to greater detail.

I was up at 6 to prepare for ABC. TB was full of himself again, especially having met Chuck Berry [musician] with Clinton. He was also full of how much BC and [Helmut] Kohl liked him. Kohl clearly saw him as a kind of successor in Europe. So did Chirac, which is presumably why he had not taken to him. We went over some of the tough questions then left for the interview. I saw the questions by accident, knew they were going straight in on Northern Ireland. He was relaxed, competent, no real story but he talked about a letter he got from a young Northern Irish girl, and I knew the press would be on to it so we were tearing the Garden Rooms* apart trying to find it. I then went to Gordon's press conference, where I inadvertently turned the lights out leaning on the wall. GB was still very much doing his own thing. He didn't like these big foreign events, and he especially didn't like them when TB was the main man. I felt he tried too hard to be making news separate from TB. He'd do better to be part of a team. I went back to the library where our private office was based to work on the environment speech for the Earth Summit at the UN tomorrow. BC asked me how I thought yesterday went on Ireland. I said it went well. Media-wise, could not have been better. I said he had carried the thing. He said TB was all over the US networks. I said he was all over the British ones. Of all of them, he was the warmest and the friendliest. Mike McCurry told me he had been really appreciative of how we handled his visit to London, and managed to blow the Paula stuff away. Maybe the stuff yesterday was a bit of a payback. TB pointed out it was interesting how Bill asked my view on media stuff. I really liked him. Clinton was clearly a great politician and communicator, but had not been that impressive chairing the meeting.

TB did fine at the press conference, and then we walked back to the hotel. He was presented with a photo album of himself at the summit then he went for a brief kip. He was thinking more and more about Ireland, trying to find a way forward. We eventually found the letter mentioned in the interview, which was actually sent to CB, from the young girl in Northern Ireland. We arrived in New York, and Cherie changed in the loo. UN ambassador John Weston came on and from then on, he was never more than six inches behind TB.

TB woke me up and asked me to go to see him. He wasn't happy with the clips he had done on the environment late last night and wanted to redo them. He

---

* Downing Street home of the prime minister's secretarial staff.

thought both on the environment and Ireland, the story was running away from us. I assured him it was fine, there was no point redoing it because events would overtake what he said anyway.

TB had a brief bilateral with John Bruton, which didn't go into much detail but would come back to hit us later. We went into the chamber at the UN with JP, RC, Clare [Short]. TB's speech went fine. Then we heard Bruton was doing a big doorstep. Magi came and told me that the media were saying Bruton had said we had reached an agreement on decommissioning. The impression some of them had was that this was an agreement with Sinn Féin. We had a few days to go and were saying this was a big breakthrough. I had the twenty-five minutes of the Al Gore bilateral to think it through and then talked to Jonathan, John and TB. TB said we should play it down. They had a long session on Ireland and again Gore was fairly impressive in his knowledge. Bill C seemed to have talked to him about who was who.

He and TB had a private session while I was bounced by the press re Bruton. He said there had been agreement reached. I said there was not. An agreement was something all the parties signed up to and this was not the case because Sinn Féin were not there and it was vital the Unionists were totally on board. I was basically suggesting Bruton was overstating things. It was very irritating. We had agreed we should play down the significance of the meeting, and here we were with all hell breaking loose. We went over to meet TB. UN Ambassador John Weston was really getting on my nerves, now inserting himself into the discussions on Northern Ireland. He really was joined to TB's shoulder. TB did a doorstep to get it in a better place, emphasizing no agreement reached etc., and what the issues were, namely the governments were close to agreement on the way forward on decommissioning but we needed Unionist support. We were getting a big hit from his green speech, but I was really tired and starting to feel depressed. At the airport I couldn't be bothered with all the false bonhomie and the joshing and joking that always happens when we bump into the media at airports.

Tuesday, June 24

We were back in the office just after 8 and the day was mainly given over to Northern Ireland. Both the briefings were almost exclusively about that, even though TB had a Commons statement on the G8, [William] Hague's first as leader [of the Opposition], after which he met TB to get briefed on Ireland. The main meetings were with Trimble, John Taylor [deputy leader, Ulster Unionist Party] and Ken Maginnis [Ulster Unionist MP] – not great but outside they were not as bad as they were in the meeting – and John Hume. In between briefing that it was positive and upbeat, I was fixing up for the twelve-year-old girl TB had mentioned in the ABC interview to come in tomorrow. Trimble was pretty difficult though, at one and the same time said he did not like the document, whilst claiming he had not been allowed to see it, and said we were conceding too much to the IRA because there was no mechanism to throw them out. The UUs were overemotional and saw conspiracies everywhere. 'It's all a pattern, always the same pattern,' said DT. TB said it was a moment of decision. He wanted to make a statement saying it was time to get substantial negotiations under way, leading to a devolved Assembly plus North-South dialogue. He said the mood in the US vis-à-vis SF had changed. It was time they got a move on. TB said they had to recognize there had always been the prospect of them getting into talks without giving up actual weapons. He talked up the independence of the commission on decommissioning under de Chastelain*, which would review the situation every eight weeks. He had always felt the Tories bound themselves in too hard on decommissioning, and DT kept coming back to it, again and again, saying the mechanics were not strong enough. TB said there had to be inclusive talks with SF, and meanwhile build from the centre with the SDLP. He said there was a brief window of opportunity with the Irish and US governments together with us on this now.

Trimble said the paper gave the IRA most of what they wanted and they would now push for more. There is no real pressure on them to pursue only peaceful means. TB said there was an emergency brake. Maginnis said they would not be thrown off once they were in because the pressures would be to keep them on board. DT said they needed 1. a firm commitment to decommissioning happening alongside talks, 2. machinery put in place to prevent SDLP and the Irish government putting a spanner in the works, 3. no 'guns for concessions'. Once we got on to 'confidence-building measures', they were all 'another sop to the IRA'. Prisoners, plastic bullets, changes to policing, they saw them all as a sop to the IRA. Any change must have the acceptance of both traditions. DT said we cannot survive in the same room unless SF are in parallel building confidence through decommissioning. Maginnis said Paisley would be able to create mayhem with this. TB said there would be sanctions on SF. DT said they were too weak. TB said if we didn't go for this now, we would miss the opportunity that was there. He knew it was a risk. He knew that SF had acted in bad faith. He knew all the obstacles, but he felt they had to move it forward now. Ken Maginnis kept underlining just how deep the mutual suspicions were. The IRA had infiltrated

---

* General John de Chastelain. Canadian former soldier and diplomat, head of the Independent International Commission on Decommissioning in Northern Ireland. Born a British subject and, like Blair, educated at Fettes College, a private boarding school in Edinburgh.

many parts of their national life. This proposal would let them infiltrate top-level political life without any real demand being made on them. DT said Hume would never cut his links with Adams and McGuinness.

On one level, it was a terrible meeting in that every time TB made a specific point, they had strong arguments against it, and put them very emotionally. On another level, they were positive in public and TB felt they wanted to do something. Some of the civil servants found the UUs a pain to deal with, but TB said he thought Trimble was fair. He said it makes quite a powerful impact when Maginnis tells you he has personally met people who he knows had plotted to kill him. Taylor was keen to have the documents and in the end we gave them, and they did a pretty positive doorstep in the street. Hume came in, was just as emotional, said he was authorized to say he could set up a meeting between Martin McGuinness and Quentin Thomas [senior Northern Ireland Office official]. TB said that was not possible and he had to say that if SF did not come on board as a result of the decommissioning paper, and the IRA declare a ceasefire, he would acknowledge that we had to move on without them.

Hume felt we were close to something, though John Holmes warned me he always said that. But he had seen Adams and McGuinness and they had not dismissed the decommissioning paper out of hand. The prisoners issue was important. He said one meeting between him, Quentin Thomas and McGuinness would lead to a ceasefire. 'The prize is enormous but so is the danger.' TB felt he had gone as far as he could in pushing the UUs. He would tip them over the edge if he went much further. 'I'd get torn limb from limb.' It was again, on one level, a good meeting, on another it was not. They were miles apart, but the one thing TB took out that was positive was a shared desire to make progress, even if both sides were basically saying the other would make it impossible.

Wednesday, June 25

Ireland statement day. We had agreed yesterday to get in the twelve-year-old girl TB mentioned in America, so that was the focus early on. I was in late, having taken the boys to school for once, and worked on Ireland most of the day. TB was worrying both about Northern Ireland and Hague. Then a Clare Short fiasco to deal with. She had 'accidentally' invited Adams and McGuinness to a reception at Lancaster House [mansion in St James's used for government functions]. This only came to light when Adams called to say he could not make it and could he send someone else? I told TB, who said he needed an explanation. I said we should announce what she had done, and how, and at such a sensitive time, and he should sack her. He said no. My view of Clare was that she was nothing but trouble, had virtually no redeeming features and would give him more grief than any upside from her merited. But he had a more favourable view. [The next few days were taken up with the handover of Hong Kong to the Chinese, and the Budget.]

Thursday, July 3

The main event of TB's day was his meeting with Bertie Ahern [BA succeeded John Bruton as Taoiseach on June 26]. TB had a private session first, and then the broader meeting with a clear difference in mood between Bruton and Ahern. BA was a nice enough bloke, and very affable, but TB felt he was basically putting the Sinn Féin line most of the time. Bruton had basically been hostile to SF. Ahern was not. TB said after they went he was worried the peace process had taken a setback. I bumped into GB in the Commons after my briefing on the Ahern meeting and he gave me a lift back. He was a lot friendlier than usual, obviously felt yesterday had gone well, and that we had helped.

Another surprising entry, given how crucial Bertie Ahern became to the process, and given some of the disputes he would have with Sinn Féin in the future. TB and Ahern became close, personally and politically in terms of their handling of the issues, which is why it is all the more surprising that his first impression seems to have been one of concern that the new Taoiseach would be too close to one side of the argument.

Saturday, July 5

TB called after I'd gone to bed to say that the Drumcree march was going ahead on strict conditions and if they were not met it would be banned next year.* He said it could be a bloodbath but the overwhelming advice of the army and the RUC was that it would be worse if it was called off. I spoke to Mo who said she thought it was the wrong decision; that it showed Unionism would win these arguments by being more vocal in complaining. This would set us right back with

---

* The troubled annual parade by Orangemen from Drumcree Parish Church, Portadown (County Armagh) through the Catholic Garvaghy Road area. The parade was a key event in the Protestant marching season, marking the victory of William of Orange over the Catholic James II at the Battle of the Boyne, culminating on July 12 each year. In 1998 the Northern Ireland Parades Commission banned the Drumcree march because of the Protestant/Catholic clashes. In following years the march was prevented from using Garvaghy Road as a route.

the nationalists who would feel they were never listened to in dialogue, a mindset that fuelled a belief in terrorism. She said Ronnie Flanagan [chief constable of the RUC] had been dithering all day but the plan was to move to Garvaghy Road at 4am, make it secure, let the marchers go down with no music, a few flags, then wait for riots around the province, and SF saying we were the same as the Tories, always kowtowing to Unionism. She said she really believed it was a crazy decision but if this was the army and RUC advice she would go along with it.

Sunday, July 6

The violence overnight [in Northern Ireland following the Drumcree decision] was bad though as yet there were no deaths. I got next to no sleep as I was speaking to TB, Mo and others. Mo was really fed up with things, but she accepted not to have gone along with the overwhelming security advice would have been a very big step to take, especially if things then went wrong in a different direction.

Monday, July 7

Mo was taking a few knocks, but in briefings all day I stressed support and how she was doing well in very difficult circumstances. As ever when Northern Ireland was in the news, the papers were desperate to splash on something else. TB did a doorstep, first on schools, and also on Drumcree, saying the search for peace goes on.

I started to brief myself on Madrid and the NATO summit. We got there and TB headed off for the dinner. We hung around for ages waiting for it to finish and then got a call from the cops saying he had gone off for an unscheduled bilateral with Clinton, which looked like it would go on for a while. They had gone back to Bill's hotel and asked for some beers to be sent up. Godric worked out we had now gone round the world in forty-eight days, having topped 25,000 miles. The press was straight on to the special relationship story, with TB and Clinton off together again till the early hours. Mo called me at midnight, said there was no violence on the streets, but Denis Murray had produced a leaked document in which an official said that forcing the march through would be the least worst option. She was obviously worried it would lead to renewed attacks on her from people saying the deal had been stitched up, but I said she should be robust, say of course we looked at all the options. The real worry was that now there was leaking going on from inside.

Yesterday ended at 2.30 this morning, when we were debriefing TB re his session with Bill. He was wearing nothing but underpants and a wide-open dressing gown, and telling us cheerfully he had forgotten to raise Ireland. He was worried Clinton was wobbling on Slovenia and Romania and saying we could end up being more Catholic than the Pope in holding out firmly re NATO entrants. He said it had been mainly social, drinking beer together, talking politics. He thought Clinton was basically a dealmaker and was going to make a deal on NATO enlargement.

Unbelievably gorgeous hostesses. During the break, it became clear that Clinton and TB felt exactly the same. There was a bizarre scene during a break, in the Gents. Several leaders, including Clinton, TB, Prodi, [Wim] Kok and Kohl, were all having a pee in a row of stand-up urinals. Clinton turned around and said 'Isn't this the greatest picture that was never taken?' TB told him the story of the time Churchill moved away from Attlee while they were peeing together. Attlee looked hurt. Churchill explained: 'Every time you see something big you want to nationalize it.'

The hard NATO work was all done, just a little clearing up left, plus the Ukraine signing ceremony. I briefed on Clinton backing us on Ireland. TB was raving about the palace in which they had dinner last night and said again that we needed a more clearly thought-through approach to foreign policy. We prepared for PMQs on the plane home. At the four o'clock I was getting irritated about the line of questioning on Drumcree. The leaked memo had suddenly taken off and Mo was under attack from all sides on the grounds that it suggested the decision on the march to go ahead was taken three weeks ago. I defended her strongly, as had TB in the House. Then TB met Hume, Seamus Mallon [deputy leader, SDLP] and Eddie McGrady [SDLP MP] in his office at the House. He was very firm re Mo, said he felt for her but he was sure the right decision was taken – you cannot ignore the head of the police and the army. They were more reasonable today, though Mallon made the point that those who made threats the loudest tended to be the ones who got their way, and it was neither fair nor sensible. Hume said we were sitting on a tinderbox. McGrady said it was always the nationalists who were not listened to. TB said that was not fair. He was downcast afterwards, said some days it was impossible to see the way forward.

Friday, July 11

We had a policy awayday at Chequers but were late leaving and then we stopped for a cup of tea at a takeaway near Paddington, people gobsmacked to see us walking in to get a cup of tea. Chequers was a good place for these kinds of meetings. Very quiet. Mobiles didn't work. Good food. Long walks and all that. Lunch was interrupted by a call with Bertie Ahern. The news that the Orange Order had agreed to reroute the Drumcree march vindicated Mo and gave a real sense of lift and hope. The big disagreement with Bertie was still decommissioning. Bertie did not think [George] Mitchell [independent chairman of the negotiations that led to the Good Friday Agreement] meant decommissioning during talks. TB did.

Sunday, July 13

We had a very nice lunch at Derry Irvine's. Peter M and I had our first proper conversation in ages. He felt that I had been deliberately excluding him, not seeking his views and ignoring them if he volunteered them. I felt he had slightly lost the plot and was too grand and hoity-toity. We were able to speak very frankly to each other and agreed that TB relied on both of us in different ways, and wanted us to work together, which we had to do. It cleared the air, but he had got more out of touch, and more concerned about his own profile than the effectiveness of the government.

Monday, July 14

The *Irish Times* had the story of resumed contact with the IRA, which put me on the spot, and I had to confirm it. It was difficult not to.

Tuesday, July 15

TB, Jonathan and I all complained of feeling tired today. We were bound to make mistakes when we all felt like this. The problem dominating the eleven o'clock briefing was the DUP [Democratic Unionist Party] attacking Mo over the revelation that we were engaged in contact with Sinn Féin. Peter M and I had a meeting with heads of information, at which we stressed the need to get a strategic message around stories, so they did not just pop up out of the blue. It was a really moribund event.

We got back for a meeting with the UDA/PUP [Ulster Defence Association, Progressive Unionist Party]. I asked John Holmes to do me a left-to-right. He scribbled David Ervine, John White, Hugh Smyth and Gary McMichael [elected peace-talks delegates, PUP and UDA]. When I put a question mark over John White's name, JH scribbled back 'double murderer'.* TB did a long spiel about why he was so engaged in it, why he made the speech he did, emphasized consent and no entry to the political process without giving up violence. If they didn't come in, he would move ahead with SF. He said he was determined on it. They were suspicious – as were the press – re us claiming the SF contacts were about clarification. They said it made it difficult for them, and gave Paisley etc. another stick with which to beat everyone.

Thursday, July 17

I went in for the end of the Trimble meeting, which had clearly gone badly. Trimble was in a foul mood and the atmosphere was terrible. TB was really tired.

Friday, July 18

As we arrived in Wales, Jonathan called to say overnight intelligence was suggesting a Northern Ireland ceasefire was imminent. This was clearly going to dominate the agenda for a while. The only glitch was that it was following attacks from Trimble about us conceding too much to the nationalists so it was bound to prompt the charge that we had done some kind of deal, even though we hadn't. It was difficult. This was clearly going to be seen as tactical. On the way to the Q&A, TB was worrying the Unionists would respond the wrong way to a ceasefire. 'It will be seen as positive, won't it?' I said of course it will. He was dead serious about this stuff.

John Holmes called and said [Belfast] Downtown Radio were reporting Hume and Mallon saying the prospects for a ceasefire were good, so it was moving in the right direction. TB did a series of interviews, stressing the positive case for devolution in Wales, almost convincingly. I got home in time for the news and there was fourteen minutes on the BBC re Northern Ireland. The ceasefire was clearly coming, which was good news, but I agreed with Mo we should say nothing until it was announced.

---

* White had confessed to the 1973 murders of Catholic councillor Paddy Wilson and his friend, Irene Andrews, and he was sentenced to life imprisonment in 1978. Released in 1992, he joined the Ulster Defence Association. Following an internal feud, he was expelled from the UDA in 2002.

The ceasefire was the main story. It finally came at 9.30 and I called TB, who was unaware of it. He was worried about the line being run at us that we were giving too much to IRA/SF. He asked me to emphasize that the approach on decommissioning had not changed, that we were clear there must be some decommissioning during negotiations. John [Holmes] told me John de Chastelain, the Canadian general, was probably going to chair the independent decommissioning body. I talked that up as something that should reassure the Unionists, but the noises coming from their briefings all day were not good. TB said Trimble was not good at standing up to his own people. But he had to be kept onside. We fixed a pooled TB doorstep at 2pm, which we agreed should be with fields rather than Chequers in the background. TB did it in an open-necked shirt, which was just about OK. His statement was fine. He said we should not appear overly euphoric because our main problem in this was going to be the UUs in advance of Monday's meeting with Trimble before Wednesday's vote on the decommissioning paper. TB was worried. He called on and off all day to ask how it was going, and to keep emphasizing the points he wanted me to emphasize.

TB called early, worried about Ireland. He felt the way the coverage was leaning could add to the pressure on Trimble to pull out. There was a sense that the IRA ceasefire was a tactic to secure exactly that, so that the Unionists would be the ones blamed for screwing it up. TB suggested that I sprinkle around references to the UUs surely not wanting to be seen to throw away the best prospect of peace for years. He wanted it made clear that we had not changed the line on decommissioning, and there was far too much of that around in the Sundays. We had both to reassure the Unionists, but also make clear how much was at stake if they pulled out now.

We went down to Robert Harris' [novelist, columnist and friend of Mandelson] for the day. He was in very good form, clearly enjoying life. I was probably a bit too down on Peter, as they were good friends, but I explained Peter was not really doing the job TB asked him to do. Robert said Peter felt frustrated because he was not really being allowed to be a politician. I understood that but he had been given a job and I felt I ended up doing a lot of the work he was meant to be doing, while he swanned around pretending to be in the same league as GB or JP. We got home at 9.30 to discover that we had been burgled. The video and some cash had gone. Very upsetting all round.

Ireland was leading the news in the morning because of the Trimble meeting. I briefed very hard on him not wanting to be the man who scuppered the peace talks. But we were in a difficult position. You have the sense that DT brings his own enemies with him, meaning John Taylor and Ken Maginnis. TB was worried about the whole thing, but said that at the eleven o'clock briefing I should be robust, making clear that we resented the suggestion by Trimble that we had done a deal with the IRA. I stressed that decommissioning meant during the negotiations. TB was becoming more and more preoccupied with Northern Ireland. He felt that if Trimble showed more strength, he could blow out Paisley. The mood was cautious and realistic. The problem was that the Irish government probably did tell Sinn Féin there would be no need for actual decommissioning, and we were saying the opposite to the Unionists. I didn't flam up but I didn't flam it down either. I spoke to Mo to suggest a doorstep hitting back at Trimble over the 'deal with the IRA' suggestion. We should stress that two weeks ago we were being accused of betrayal by the other side, because of Drumcree.

The meeting with Trimble and Co was friendlier than the noises around suggested it would be. Maginnis was the only one who lost it really. The problem was that Trimble was not really in charge of the show, and you sensed he was constantly worrying what they were thinking. He had a naturally red face which turned redder and redder as the meeting wore on. He had a mildly priggish smile which got more priggish the more nervous he got. Jeffrey Donaldson [UUP MP] was the quietest but he spoke with considerable force. Taylor was quite languid. Maginnis was the ranter today. But he too could be subtle while being tough. When we were discussing the decommissioning line, he said very nicely, but menacingly, 'I'm very worried that if we take that approach, it will be very damaging to you personally, David.' TB was pretty firm, admitting he could not deliver the Irish government to say what we understood by decommissioning happening. He started the meeting by saying it was 'high noon' and laughing. He said the problem was they wanted a guarantee that SF would be kicked out after a certain period if there was no actual decommissioning and he could not get the Irish signed up to that. They said that it was intolerable for them to have to sit round a table with these people, knowing that they would not give up a bomb or a bullet and yet there would be no way of kicking them out. Trimble said SF were making it clear they had a guarantee they would not be kicked out. They do not believe they need to decommission. TB said there had to be some acceptance of good faith. Maginnis scoffed. DT said you can be acting in good faith and not reach an agreement. TB said the principle of consent was paramount. The greatest difficulty for SF will come when it is clear this is not necessarily going to lead to a united Ireland. He said decommissioning had become symbolic. He said he wanted a timetable, September to May. He did not want this dragging on forever. He said it felt like swimming through blancmange. We went round and round in circles over the various problems. TB was looking exasperated at points and explained that two weeks ago he had the SDLP telling him he was guilty of the most monstrous betrayal, and now *they* were saying it. In the end we felt it might be better if Wednesday's vote on decommissioning did not take place and we got more time. Donaldson said it was always the Unionists being asked to help out, and there was nothing to show for it. He said he had lost members of his family to the IRA. 'We understand these people. They will go back to violence any time they feel like it.'

Mo was getting fed up with them, pulling faces etc. Eventually we agreed that there were some points of clarification we could try to meet in relation to the issue of arms being given over, how and when. I sensed Trimble was trying to be helpful, but it was clear he had to watch his back the whole time. TB said it had to be worth trying. He said he could not promise but he would try to get 1. clarification that Mitchell means decommissioning during negotiations, 2. UK and Irish governments to agree words on decommissioning, 3. schemes in place by the time we talk on September 15, and 4. agreement that consent is the fundamental principle. DT said there was an operation to build confidence in the nationalist community. The government needed an equivalent process with the Unionist population. He said he would not be able to support the decommissioning paper this side of the summer.

'DT brings his own enemies with him.' There was such a difference in the meeting styles of the UUs and Sinn Féin. Whatever private differences existed among Sinn Féin leaders, they hid them well. TB described dealing with Sinn Féin as like watching 'unity in motion'. But the meetings with the Ulster Unionists tended to put internal differences on display, and the pressures David Trimble was under from his colleagues were all too clear. TB was broadly sympathetic to Trimble, feeling he was doing his best with a difficult, fractious Party and bunch of colleagues. At least he committed to stay engaged in the talks, even if the vote in the Party was lost. But a lack of mutual respect between Mo and the UUs was also becoming apparent.

TB was preoccupied with Ireland while I was working on the Cabinet committee announcement re the Libs, and also preparing for devolution. He spoke to Trimble before the eleven o'clock and they agreed that the vote on the decommissioning paper would go ahead, that the Unionists would vote against but stay in the talks. We agreed to use the eleven o'clock briefing, which I would be doing as TB saw Paisley, to make it clear the vote would be lost, but to stress that we would continue to try to find a way forward, keep on talking. It was a straightforward news management operation and worked fine so that on Wednesday when the vote was lost, the BBC said it had been so well trailed it was virtually an anticlimax.

I got home and had a terrible scene with the boys, who were really angry and shouting and generally misbehaving. It was pretty grim at the moment. Fairly bored at work, depressed at home, and we were desperately in need of a holiday.

I was getting depressed, worried that the boys were unhappy because I was at work so much, travelling too much, and bringing too much work home with me. The campaign had been bad enough, but it had been just as intense since. Hague's office called to say he would be doing Ireland at PMQs. JH told me I had worked miracles on the press on Ireland, and it definitely helped shape the outcome of the meeting yesterday. TB was in a foul mood and it took me ages to get him to agree to a simple 'thumbs up' picture for the *Daily Record*. I got a nice picture sent through by the White House, with a handwritten message from Clinton, suggesting I do a job swap with Mike McCurry. I told TB I intended to take it unless he snapped out of his mood. PMQs was OK but in general we were not handling Hague terribly well. TB called as I was coming back from the afternoon briefing and agreed we didn't get Hague right, we had to think more deeply about it. He said he didn't fear Hague at all, except in the chamber, where he was good. He didn't feel he was making an impact anywhere apart from the House, and that is where we had to weaken him. He was a debating-point merchant, not a strategist.

The summer holidays came as a welcome respite, though for the first few days I was dealing with the fallout from the News of the World *revealing Robin Cook's affair with his secretary.*

Over breakfast, TB said he sometimes despaired at the quality of some of his ministers. Even the ones we thought were good were not that good. GB and Peter M were the only ones who fully understood the way the media was changing politics. We spent the morning planning out the speech and interview programme for the next few weeks. He was going to get back into Ireland. I spoke to Mo who wanted to do the announcement on Sinn Féin talks tomorrow and wanted TB involved. TB was adamant that it was a no. He went to play tennis and I headed to the office.

We were slowly getting a grip. Mo was at the end of her tether with the UUs, who were being really vile about her. She came into a meeting with TB and filled him in. TB was not too downbeat. After the Trimble meeting, TB said after Sinn Féin came into the talks we had to get more positive stories published for the Unionists.

The MI5 situation was taking up a fair bit of time. I had long chat with Jack Straw who was putting the case for being quite heavy. TB was not keen to make [David] Shayler* a martyr but Jack said damage had already been done. We agreed I would speak to Jonathan Holborow [editor, *Mail on Sunday*]. He kept saying he would do nothing to damage national security. I said he was not in a position to know whether it did or not. I said, for example, there were concerns that Shayler knew stuff re Libya and the IRA and could do considerable damage. He said he would try to be sensible and came back to me to say there was nothing about the IRA or Libya.

People can say what they like about 'spin', but such was the emphasis the main parties in the peace process placed upon how they were being perceived that orders like this [getting more positive stories published for the Unionists] were fairly common from TB. Some of the worst crisis moments came when one of the parties felt the other was doing too well within the public debate. It was like a zero sum game at times. If the UUs were thought to have 'won' something, it meant SF had lost, and vice versa. So the significant step of SF entering the talks meant that the UUs had to be compensated with positive media profiling elsewhere, the planning of which is clear from the next

---

* David Shayler, a former MI5 officer, whose 'revelations' to the *Mail on Sunday* led to the government seeking an injunction to prevent publication.

entry, September 11. The intervening period included the death of Princess Diana, and the remarkable global response.

TB saw Trimble and we agreed to a media strategy that would involve one or two announcements of confidence-building measures, TB article in the [Unionist] *News Letter* on Saturday stressing the principle of consent, then over the weekend a story on the BBC about new language on consent agreed by the two governments, which we would put out in part through Trimble on *Frost*. But *An Phoblacht*, the Republican newspaper, had a piece saying they had trouble with the Mitchell principles.* This struck me as a real problem but TB felt it could help Trimble, because they could say it was all the more important that they were there to hold Sinn Féin to what they were saying. It was tricky and TB asked me to speak to Trimble direct and make sure we were on the same page re the media plan. We spoke a couple of times.

Friday, September 12

TB spoke to Trimble again [from Scotland, where we were celebrating the successful referendum campaign for a Scottish Parliament] to say he would go hard on consent, decommissioning and the links between IRA/SF. The interview was fine, stressing to the UUs the need to stay in the talks. We spoke to Trimble again and agreed he would go on *Frost* and call for further concessions and then be seen to get them. TB said fine. 'He is such a mercurial character.'

Saturday, September 13

TB called early. 'What will the English make of this Parliament?' The same scepticism you've got, I said. His main worry today was Northern Ireland and Monday's resumed talks. I took the boys to York vs Burnley.

---

* The Mitchell principles called upon all partners to affirm total and absolute commitment to the peaceful resolution of political issues, total disarmament of paramilitary organizations, opposition to force that would influence negotiations and effective steps to prevent punishment killings and beatings.

TB called a couple of times, worried about pay. He felt there was trouble coming with a pay freeze allied to Cabinet ministers taking their full salaries. The other issue today was Northern Ireland, with talks due to start tomorrow. Part of the plan was that we put out a statement early tomorrow, agreed by the Irish and British governments, on consent and decommissioning. TB had persuaded Trimble we would present it as a concession to him, that we had forced Ahern into it because DT wanted it. TB had spoken to Bertie, who was such a good bloke that he was just about happy with going along with it. TB said the trouble with Trimble is that he is so bloody mercurial it was impossible to know what he was really up to. The statement was finally agreed at 9.30. I gave it embargoed to [Robin] Oakley and Alison Little at PA. Oakley was excellent. I said we would really appreciate it if he made clear that we were bending over backwards to woo the Unionists, and he called to read me his script, which was nice of him. He said, I realize that sometimes the national interest is potentially affected by what we say, and I'm perfectly happy to go through it with you. There was definitely something about Northern Ireland that brought out the better side of the media.

Monday, September 15

Oakley's report was leading the news and Trimble came on to make broadly welcoming noises and later in the day he announced he would be joining the talks, which was seen as a real breakthrough. It had been balls-aching getting there but got there we had. The 11 o'clock briefing was mainly Ireland, Royals, Lib-Labbery, Hague and the week ahead.

Wednesday, September 17

Today's main problem was Ireland, Trimble enjoying being the one needing to be courted and looking for excuses not to go to the talks. He was vitriolic about Hague.

Tuesday, September 23

The UUP going to talks with Sinn Féin in Belfast was the main story.

TB was calling fairly regularly and I could sense he was getting more and more nervy [about the Labour Party conference next week]. We had a breakthrough in NI in that the UUs were staying at the talks. 'It really is an amazing achievement,' he said, 'I hope you know that.'*

I was feeling very down, possibly depressed. It was in part tiredness but also I felt I was having to do too much and carry too much on my own. Peter M and I just weren't working together and though I felt it would work out, it was a strain because I felt I was picking up a lot of the load he should be carrying. I stayed at home and went for a long walk on the heath. TB called before his meeting at Chequers with Trimble and Donaldson.

Kenny Macintyre [BBC Scotland] called to warn me of the scale of the furore re Jason Campbell, a convicted Rangers thug who knifed a young Celtic fan to death. Campbell had been granted a transfer application from a Scottish to Northern Irish jail and the Scottish Office had said that the peace process – helping Protestants – had been part of the reasoning. This was viciously attacked in the press and Donald Dewar [Scottish Secretary] and others wanted to reverse it. On the way to the airport, we couldn't raise DD so TB spoke to Henry McLeish, the minister responsible, who was unclear about the facts or even who made the decision. TB asked Butler to sort it out and Butler came back with the suggestion that we could change tack because a review had been set up to change procedures. But TB spoke to DD later who felt the only grounds to justify the decision were indeed that he had been told it would harm the peace process if the decision was not taken, and that was not a good enough reason. So we agreed he would go on the radio tomorrow and say he intended to review it, and we would brief he was likely to come to a different decision. It had been woefully handled.

---

* There was agreement over procedures for the conduct of the negotiations. It had taken sixteen months to achieve. This was the first time in seventy years that Unionist parties had sat around a table with Republicans and agreed to discuss 'substantive issues', a blanket term for decommissioning.

TB kept emphasizing the only thing that mattered was whether the criteria had been properly applied, and that it was nothing to do with the peace process. The press were in full cry up there.

The Times ran a story that we were planning to apologize over Bloody Sunday, which I played down. Back in Number 10, I listened in to a conversation with DD, who had still not sorted out the Jason Campbell case. He'd done *Good Morning Scotland,* said there would be a review but he could not see the point that it had to be announced that it was going to be reversed, and also that we had to admit it had been badly handled and had not been related to the peace process. In the end, I had to go over to the Scottish Office and write the press release for him. I read it to TB and to Mo, who was fine about it, even though she was going to get a bit of stick.

Mo called and we agreed it was best to say nothing about TB's visit [to Northern Ireland] yet.

TB was due to go [to Belfast] tomorrow and meet Adams and, again, the focus was on whether they would shake hands and whether we would see that. The NIO called to say SF were making clear it would be unacceptable if TB was photographed with the other leaders but not Adams. I spoke to TB, who said he wanted us to get it sorted as it would be bad if the meeting now didn't go ahead. Mo called to say that she feared if we got on to them it will become a story straight away, that we were promising another meeting. TB had been against a filmed handshake so the earlier plan of meeting Adams in a line of people fell. Now he was saying he would meet all the participants privately. There was massive interest in it and we had very little to say.

I was up really early and in with Jonathan to Number 10 to pick up TB and head off to Northolt for the flight to Ulster. Football violence was still the main story, with some pick-up on the Adams handshake situation. On the plane we went over how to handle the Sinn Féin meeting. As we arrived, it was still not clear it was definitely happening because SF were so pissed off there was to be no camera present. They were big on visuals these guys. We did a brief doorstep so TB could say why he was meeting Adams, the importance of trying to move from violence to dialogue.

We then had a short helicopter flight to Trimble territory. DT was his usual self, veering between smug and downtrodden, which was an odd combination. At the main meeting he sat on the sofa with TB and just whispered to him, making sure nobody else could hear, and he was clearly contemptuous of Mo, and was trying to signal that she didn't matter, that only TB did. She just looked over at me, smiled and shook her head as if to say it happened all the time. DT gave him a little lecture on the history of the handshake – it was to show you had no arms, which could not be said of Mr Adams and Co. 'I'm sure my hand will be tainted,' said TB. TB also had a couple of little speeches to do and we had to do some careful footwork to avoid a meeting with a group of SF councillors who were clearly trying to ambush us.

We flew to Stormont, where he had maybe ten meetings with different groupings. In most of them, we were just going through the motions and everyone knew that. He had a good session with [Senator George] Mitchell and his colleagues. He said they had one of the most difficult and thankless tasks and we were incredibly grateful to them. George M said that SF were skilful and articulate and worked the process well. The SDLP were hurt. DT was getting hit every day by Paisley. DT took TB to meet his staff. Seamus Mallon complained that TB was letting Trimble control the negotiations. He said every time DT went running to him for special favours, it undermined the whole process. We kept TB in there longer than planned because Adams was due to come down the corridor and for now we were avoiding him. As TB worked his way through all the parties, I could see they were impressed at his grasp but also the determination. He was basically saying he wouldn't stop till they sorted it. As Gary McMichael [leader of the Ulster Democratic Party] left and shook TB by the hand, he said 'Is this the one that will shake Gerry Adams by the hand?' TB smiled at him and shrugged. TB was with the [non-sectarian] Women's Coalition and said it would all be fine if they were running it.

Then, after a brief interlude to go over what he would say, we went in to the talks administration office, Adams, McGuinness, Pat Doherty [vice president of

Sinn Féin], Siobhán O'Hanlon [Sinn Féin negotiator], TB, Mo, Paul Murphy [Northern Ireland Office minister], John [Holmes], Jonathan, myself. They all shook hands with TB, who was steely but welcoming and warm at the same time. He said it was good they were in the process. He believed in equality of treatment. He knew there had to be change. The question was what kind of change? He emphasized there could be no return to violence and no change that does not carry the consent of the people. It will all require goodwill. 'I understand history better than you think. We have an opportunity which, if we do not seize it, will not come again in our lifetime. I feel a deep commitment to make it work. All the energy and dynamism I have will go into this if need be. It is a very rare thing for humanity to make sense of history but that is what we must try to do.' It was powerful stuff. They hung on every word, but very steely-eyed with it.

GA and McGuinness were both impressive in different ways, Adams more prone to philosophizing, McG always sizing things up, with a smile that veered from charm to menace. He said to TB he [TB] was the only man who could take this forward but he had to understand they had taken more risks than anyone. TB said he wanted to make this happen but it meant he had to get inside their minds. GA gave him a gift of a small harp. He said he acknowledged we had moved the process forward. But it is hard to build peace when the playing field is not level. The biggest cause of conflict is British involvement in Ireland. 'I want you to be the last British prime minister in this jurisdiction. Do you have any idea what it is like to live in your own country without proper rights?' He said he was still stopped by police the whole time, and asked what his name was. I was trying to gauge their sense of TB. They were impressed. GA said he would like to meet him often and talk more. 'I think you can be the person that brings peace to Northern Ireland.' TB said both sides had to try to see the other side's perspective. It's pointless to go back to the old ways. You need to unlock the better side of humanity among your people. He made a joke about how he was attacked by the Orange Order for marrying a Catholic. These things don't stop you. There is no point just going into all the old feelings. McG put in a stack of complaints re the NIO, the RUC. Doherty spoke a little, O'Hanlon not at all. They felt John Major messed up because he listened too much to the Unionists. They still felt TB's statements were the statements of a British PM looking from a Unionist perspective. The security agenda has dominated for thirty years. We need a political agenda, said GA. TB asked if the ceasefire would hold. GA said as far as he was concerned the last one was genuine. McG stressed the risks they were taking, said he saw no reason why there should be any more lives lost. He struck me as more pragmatic than GA, which surprised me. 'I know we won't get everything we want.' They pushed on Bloody Sunday, said it needed an international investigation. It was a running sore. GA said, I know British people have died at the hands of the IRA and I regret it but we have people who were shot by Soldier A and Soldier B. TB said he could not stress enough how unique was the opportunity we now had. The political will is there from us, but it has to be matched. TB exuded a sense of confidence and authority on this. Even some of the NIO sceptics were beginning to shift, I sensed, and think it might be doable. I did a press briefing then GA did an OK doorstep. They had to go through a few ritual attacks, but the overall sense was that they were engaging in a way they had not done before. Then I heard that TB had met a lot of trouble on a walkabout in a shopping centre. I called Anji who said I had better get down there. He had basically been set up by the DUP who had tipped off a few friends to get down there and hurl abuse at him, and the policing was a bit loose. He was a bit shaken up by it, but above all angry that he had been set up. It was a total pain in the arse. I half blamed myself because Trevor Butler [protection officer] said when we were at the RUC earlier that they were worried about it. My alarm bells were ringing and if I had followed my instincts I would have got it called off, but I didn't because all the focus and forethought was on Adams. I was really pissed off and so was TB. We laughed about it later, but it left a nasty taste.

Tuesday, October 14

There was an inquest going on into the shambles of the [Belfast] walkabout, and whether anyone from inside the RUC was involved in tipping off the protestors. 'The big PR disaster' was one of the Irish headlines. But the substance of the event cut through as well, and there was plenty of focus on GA etc.

Though the [DUP] ambushing at the shopping centre was irritating, and produced a few unfavourable headlines, in substance terms, the meeting with Sinn Féin leaders was a significant moment. It was the moment when some of the barriers and suspicions began to break down; when Sinn Féin believed TB was serious about delivering peace, and understood the importance of the equality agenda within that process; and when TB began to firm up on his hunch that Adams and McGuinness were serious about opting for democracy over violence. After all the hype, the handshake seemed the most natural thing in the world, whatever the rubber-glove-wearers* might think. As often happened after a big symbolic moment, other priorities then took over for a while, including a Commonwealth Summit in Scotland, and a near crisis over policy

---

* TB was proffered a rubber glove filled with blood to shake, to indicate that he had 'blood on his hands' in talking to Sinn Féin.

on the single currency, which laid bare the divisions at the top of government and led TB to read the riot act, warning GB, Peter M and AC that if we did not work out differences, we were 'dead'.

Alan Clark [Tory MP for Kensington and Chelsea] was on great form at lunch. He came in, swished through and said very loudly before he had even sat down 'You lot are just tooooo brilliant.' He was longing for it to get out we were having lunch. 'Are there any journalists in here? Can't see any. Shit.' Robert Fellowes [Private secretary to HM Queen Elizabeth II] and Tony O'Reilly [Irish businessman] were at the next table. 'O'Reilly will tell someone.'

Friday, November 21

We had a working breakfast, then set off for the [jobs] summit. TB and Bertie Ahern had a bilateral, BA briefing on his meeting with Trimble, which he felt went well. He felt we should be removing more troops [from Northern Ireland]. TB said he was agitating on that the whole time but he had to listen to what the security people were saying. When the summit wound up, TB's press conference was attended by a fifth of what we normally get. We were all a bit tired at the moment and not firing.

Friday, November 28

I drafted a briefing note on the latest Sinn Féin delegation coming on December 11, and went through it with Mo as soon as we landed. TB said I must have a rest this weekend. I said don't phone me then. I was feeling really stressed out at the moment and at home Fiona and I had a dreadful row. It started on hunting, but it could have been anything.

Saturday, November 29

Fiona and I weren't speaking. It was a quiet day work-wise, apart from briefing on the December 11 Adams meeting. I briefed my SF note in two separate conference calls, one for the press, one for the broadcasters. It was pretty rich and was leading the news within minutes. And that was without even getting reaction from the

NOVEMBER '97: BUILDING UP TO SF DELEGATION COMING TO NUMBER 10   75

Unionists, which duly came – anger, fury, outrage etc. The Tories piled in as well, said it was provocative. But TB was clear we had to press on and maintain momentum, and that he did not want to be in a position, if the talks collapsed, where the IRA could say they were never given the chance to come in. I had a bad cold but went out most of the afternoon with Calum on the heath. The phone went mainly re Ireland.

Sunday, November 30

I said to TB he should speak to Hague because Andrew MacKay [Shadow Northern Ireland Secretary] was very anti the Adams meeting, and we should try to defuse the politics on it. He said he had to speak to him on a security matter anyway, so would also raise Adams.

Monday, December 8

TB was looking tired. Fiona thought he was ill, and CB told her he had a bit of a turn on the tennis court, and that he hadn't slept at all well. We were also preparing the way for [Gerry] Adams' visit, with TB on Thursday planning to table the UK Heads of Agreement, with the Irish doing it separately, despite their being opposed to doing it that way. I ran into Alan Clark, who said [Nicholas] Soames [Conservative MP] would give up his seat if we could get him the Paris embassy. Couldn't tell if he was joking.

Wednesday, December 10

We had been hoping to publish the Heads of Agreement on the NI talks, but couldn't in the end because of various difficulties with the Irish and the UUP, but there was growing interest in Adams' visit. Then to cap it all, there was an IRA breakout from the Maze [prison]. TB called to ask whether I thought it meant we should cancel the Adams visit. I said no, don't be daft.

Thursday, December 11

I drafted a statement to be read out at the 11 o'clock, on the meeting with Adams, which was likely to take over as the main story later in the day, defending TB for seeing him despite the risks. Adams and his team arrived fifteen minutes early, and he did a little number in the street, where the media numbers were huge. This was a big moment, potentially historic in the progress it could lead to. They came inside and we kept them waiting while we went over what TB was due to say. Mo and Paul Murphy were both there and Mo was pretty fed up, feeling she was getting shit from all sides. They were hovering around the lifts and were summoned down to the Cabinet Room. We had agreed TB should be positive but firm. He actually came over as friendly, welcoming them individually as they came in. I shook McGuinness by the hand, who as he sat down said, fairly loudly, 'So this is the room where all the damage was done.' It was a classic moment where the different histories played out. Everyone on our side thought he was referring to the mortar attack on Major, and we were shocked. Yet it became obvious from their surprise at our shock that he was referring to policymaking down the years, and Britain's involvement in Ireland. 'No, no, I meant 1921,' he said.

I found McGuinness more impressive than Adams, who did the big statesman bit, and talked in grand historical sweeps, but McGuinness just made a point and battered it, and forced you to take it on board. Martin Ferris [Sinn Féin negotiator] was the most cold-eyed of the lot. He really did emanate a sense of menace. Mo slipped me a note saying he had a very bad history. Of the women, I could not work out whether they really mattered, or whether they just took them round with them to look a bit less hard. They were tough as boots all three of them. TB was good in the use of language and captured well the sense of history and occasion. He said we faced a choice of history – violence and despair, or peace and progress. We were all taking risks, but they are risks worth taking. He said to Adams he wanted to be able to look him in the eye, hear him say he was committed to peaceful means, and he wanted to believe him. I was eyeing their reaction to TB the whole time, and both Adams and McG regularly let a little smile cross their lips. Ferris was the one who just stared. Mo got pissed off, volubly, when they said she wasn't doing enough. TB was maybe not as firm as we had planned, but he did ask – which I decided not to brief, and knew they wouldn't – whether they would be able to sign up to a settlement that did not explicitly commit to a united Ireland. Adams was OK, but McGuinness was not. Adams said the prize of a lasting peace justifies the risks. Lloyd George, Balfour, Gladstone, Cromwell, they all thought they had answers of sorts. We want our answers to be the endgame. A cobbled-together agreement will not stand the test of time. He pushed hard on prisoners being released, and the aim of total demilitarization, and TB just listened.

TB said he would not be a persuader for a united Ireland. The principle of consent was central to the process. Adams said if TB could not be a persuader, he could be a facilitator. He said we would be dead in forty years, but in the meantime this was the biggest test of TB's time in office, how he deals with the displaced citizens in a divided territory. A lot of people believed the armed struggle was legitimate. They have to be shown a different route to the same goal. There are two blocks – British policy, and the Unionist veto. He gave a series of history lessons on the way, including the industrial carve-up against the nationalists. McG was the more aggressive of the two, inside and outside. He said this was the most important meeting in seventy-five years, but it would pass quickly.

There were things in our power we could do now, if we stopped the securocrats from stopping us. He said the next meeting has to be with Trimble and TB must encourage it. Mo mentioned an escaped prisoner. Adams said 'Good luck to him.' Mo snapped back 'That is not a very helpful comment.' But there were flashes of humour. Mo slipped me a note saying she found GA sexier than McG.

On the way out GA took TB to one side, and clearly wanted to be able to brief they had had a one-on-one session. All he said was 'Merry Christmas.' I said we needed to agree a briefing line. He said why don't we say we've agreed to withdrawal of all troops by February and a united Ireland by spring? Fine, I said, I like a good clear line. TB roared with laughter. They were clearly trying to hang around and, added to their early arrival, exaggerate the length of the talks. I'd already learned how much these things mattered in relation to their impact on the other side. The three women went to the loo, and our security people were getting antsy at how long they were in there, while Jonathan and I chatted to GA and McG re holidays and Christmas and kids and stuff. Vera Doyle [Irish messenger at Number 10] was on duty and came over to chat to them, and within seconds McG was charm itself, checking out where she came from and where she went on holiday. Vera was clearly a fan, but said to them as they left 'Now you two just behave, and help out our man here.'

TB had gone back to his office, and I saw them off as they went out to see the press in the street. It had gone pretty well, and TB was pleased. I got the press in straight away and had to strike the right balance between being positive, and going over the top. They wanted as much detail as possible, seating plans, who spoke first, who said what. I could see them all scribbling when I did the line about TB looking him in the eye. They all sensed it had been a big moment, which of course it was. TB said later McG might have had a point when he said the securocrats did not really want to bring about a settlement. TB did a series of clips on the SF meeting for UTV, BBC and RTE. He was a bit too pro SF on RTE so I arranged for UTV to be the pool. Meanwhile Adams was doing the Millbank [Labour Party HQ] rounds with a bodyguard. Some of our security people were clearly horrified that they were in here, and that we were being civil to them.

The Adams coverage was OK. Papers you'd expect to be hostile were hostile, but the others were OK. It was also huge throughout Europe.

Another huge moment, followed by another lull. In all of TB's time as Prime Minister, he had very few meetings that were preceded by a two-week media build up. My office in our first term looked out onto the street where the media gathered, and I think the Adams-McGuinness visit to Number 10 had even more media than for Clinton's visit. It was also an area of policy where I sensed the media willing us to succeed whereas, even in this honeymoon period, in other policy areas, and whenever personal or political scandal hit, their desire was to cause us as much trouble as possible. The media always love a big story, and Adams and McGuinness walking into Downing Street, a building their supporters had tried to demolish in the past, was certainly that. But apart from a small rump of right-wingers who felt anything that risked Unionist dominance was wrong, the media were broadly supportive.

The day had drama, but it also had substance, and TB's statements in particular laid out the central tenets of the strategy he would pursue thereafter. His emphasis on the principle of consent, and his statement that he would not be a persuader for a united Ireland, reminded me of why he had chosen to sack Kevin McNamara, as a signal of a changed approach by Labour. For me, the most dramatic moments were these: when McGuinness made his crack about damage being done, and the Number 10 team all thought he was referring to the mortar attack; TB looking Adams in the eye and saying he wanted to believe him when he said he was committed to peaceful means; his asking them whether they could sign up to a deal that did not commit to a united Ireland; and Adams saying this was the biggest test of TB's time in office (something TB himself said from time to time). The other impression confirmed to me that day was that Sinn Féin took their public presentation seriously, and they did it well. How long they were in there mattered to them – a bit like us when we went to the White House in opposition. What they said before and after the meeting was carefully prepared. We did at least have a shared interest – we wanted the meeting to be seen as historic, we wanted the discussions to be substantive and significant, and we wanted to be able to give a sense of momentum to the process, sufficient to blow away any opposition to the fact of the meeting, clearly upsetting to some in the Unionist and Conservative parties. I think both we and they felt we had succeeded in meeting those objectives. The day after the Sinn Féin meeting, we headed to an important European summit on the euro.

The visit to Belfast went fine, Waterfront [Hall], school Q&A, which was quite emotive. We talked to the driver, who was a self-effacing kind of guy, but had a quiet authority about him, and said to TB there had never been a better chance of making peace happen.

The news was dominated by Northern Ireland, Billy Wright having been murdered in the Maze.* There were a few ritual calls for Mo's resignation, easily dismissed, and between them Mo and Adam Ingram [junior Northern Ireland minister] were handling it fine.

---

* Billy Wright, the imprisoned commander of the Loyalist Volunteer Force, had been killed by three nationalist prisoners, Christopher McWilliams, John Glennon and John Kennaway, members of the Irish National Liberation Army. The three issued a statement: 'Billy Wright was executed for one reason and one reason only, and that was for directing and waging his campaign of terror against the nationalist people from his prison cell.'

[1998]

We had a fairly quiet New Year's Eve, then set off early for Paris. My New Year resolutions were to stop swearing, stop eating chocolate and try to go home earlier in the evenings. The first two bit the dust fairly early on. Tim Allan [special adviser, press office] did a good job of keeping most calls from me but even so I felt under stress and generally overworked. I managed a couple of days which were genuinely days off. But I had done very little thinking over the holiday period, unlike TB, as was clear when he came back from the Seychelles brimming with energy and ideas.

Ireland was a major problem with the talks in danger of collapse. TB agreed to see Trimble and John Taylor, hopefully privately but it leaked. TB was determined to get a Heads of Agreement tabled by Monday, preferably with the two governments, UUP and SDLP, but it looked pretty remote. Taylor went through the problem areas – the Billy Wright killing, documents being given late, prisoner release, and the feeling that the nationalists are getting too many concessions. TB was pretty strong on the idea that you cannot allow murderers to dictate the flow of the process. 'It would be crazy, if the extremists start to kill each other, for the moderates then to say the process is at an end. It gives them a permanent veto on progress.' When TB said that Sinn Féin had to be able to point to progress on their terms, Taylor raised his eyebrows very ostentatiously and coughed loudly. DT said it was impossible to engage [John] Hume in a serious discussion about an Assembly. TB said what would Hume do if you showed him a draft Heads of Agreement? 'He would certainly pick his nose,' said Taylor. 'No, he doesn't pick, he rubs it,' said Trimble and there followed a discussion between them about whether he was a nose picker or nose rubber. John [Holmes] and I exchanged looks of bewilderment. I could tell TB was avoiding looking at me in case he got the giggles. 'I'll speak to Hume,' he said. 'I'm determined to do this this week.' He was totally gobsmacked when Taylor said that Maze prison officers have to go through metal detectors but prison visitors don't. Taylor said it was good to see scales falling from eyes.

Tuesday, January 6

The Maze was the main focus of any news today, because UUs and others were going inside to see some of the paramilitary leaders, and came out having failed to persuade them it was the right thing to stay in the talks. TB was busy on the phone, to Ahern and Hume. Adams came out and said the whole thing was a ploy to stop any further engagement from the Unionists.

Wednesday, January 7

TB saw Mo to assess where we were – not in a good place – and go over a few options to move it to a better place. None of the options included the one that was leading the news at six o'clock – namely that she was going to go to the Maze to talk to the Loyalist paramilitaries. TB was totally unaware of it, and genuinely taken aback that she could just announce something like that without thinking and talking it through. I spoke to her and she said it was something Gary McMichael had suggested to her at her meeting with the UDA and she went straight out and announced it. 'Sorry,' she said. Actually, I felt OK about it. It was big and it was bold, though of course the Tory press would say she was pandering to criminals. I said I thought it was fine, but she should not have done it without getting TB's agreement. After we talked it through, he also saw the potential upside. I briefed very firmly that TB backed what she was doing, and didn't let on we didn't know.

Mo was just about getting away with the Maze idea. Only she could really have done it, though even so there was a lot of unease around the place. There was a tense mood at Cabinet. Mo said her gut feeling was the ceasefires were holding. TB said it sometimes looked terrible when it wasn't and sometimes looked good when it was terrible. At the moment it didn't look good but he was still hopeful. He was fulsome re Mo.

The diary entry fails to capture TB's surprise at Mo's unilateral decision. As I said earlier, he always knew that big bold steps were going to have their place in the process, but he preferred to plan them than have them sprung upon him. When Jonathan Powell and I went into his office to tell him, he reacted as he often did when something unexpected was revealed to him: with a loud, open-mouthed 'what?' followed by laughter, followed by, 'you're kidding me?' But though all of us could immediately see the risks, not to mention the undesirability of seeming to hand over the keys to success or failure to men in prison for terrorist offences, equally we could all see the potential upside if, as indeed happened, the boldness of the move was matched by a response that kept things moving forward. It was classic Mo – instinctive, dramatic, slightly flying by the seat of her pants, but confident it would come off, and content that if it didn't, no lasting harm would be done. She was often frustrated by the feeling that all the main moves were being orchestrated from the centre. This was a big, bold move that was all her own handiwork, and to some degree made the strong reputation she enjoyed. And whatever doubts TB had about what she did, he was determined the Cabinet did not know about them, and could not have praised her any more highly. But if her gambit kept things moving forward, within days, on a trip to Japan, a fresh setback quickly followed. The visit was already tightly scheduled, and with plenty of risk and controversy attached to it. Yet like so many foreign trips during this time, Northern Ireland was never far from the top of the agenda.

The time zones were playing a bit of havoc in Tokyo and having spent hours trying to sleep, I finally did and slept in. Ireland was a problem again. Someone had leaked to the *Telegraph* the details of the negotiations between Trimble, us and the Irish over the latest paper, which included proportional representation for Assembly elections and a new idea, the Council of the Isles. Worse, he had done it to the one paper more hostile than any other to what we were doing. They featured the idea of keeping Mo out of it because TB had to take over and they also said, rightly, that the SDLP and SF would be unhappy. This was all very irritating and John Holmes was deeply pissed off. TB was fairly calm about it. I feared Trimble was trying to scupper it. It meant that from 8am London time, with Jonathan negotiating there, and John H here, every spare minute was going into trying to fix it. If ever peace is secured in Northern Ireland, and a film is made, then one of the key scenes will see TB in a posh Japanese restaurant, cross-legged and barefoot, with our hosts serving course after course as he tried to talk to Mo, DT and others and get it back on track. Even now, he was very optimistic. John thought he was overly so. He did a doorstep on Ireland, FEPoWs,* Japan generally. Siobhan [Kenny, press officer] in London said the pictures were fantastic.

Sunday, January 11

TB did Japanese TV, which showed loads of pictures of him being mobbed, then he went to church, where annoyingly Sky turned up. I waited in the car and worked on lines for his *Frost* interview, including getting up the welfare tour. 'I'm going to the heart of the country to debate the heart of the matter.' Maybe.

The vicar made a big fuss of him during the service and as he came out, and then we set off for *Frost*. He was strong and clear and there were four or five good news lines out of it, Ireland, welfare, Lords reform, PFI [private finance initiative], RC. I took the tape back to play to the hacks and by the end of it they were pretty breathless, with Ireland and welfare the strongest lines. The general feeling was the trip was going well and so did the interview on *Frost*. TB made a stack of calls on Ireland, Mo, Bertie, Trimble and later, as a private call, to Adams.

Monday, January 12

TB had been up till 3, arguing with various people in the Irish situation, the main stumbling block being the UUs on the wording for the cross-border bodies. As soon as he was up, in between the meetings in Tokyo, he was on the phone again, first with Ahern.

At the briefing I was asked if TB had spoken to Adams, and said no, and then had to go and correct myself because he just had. The Japan coverage was

---

* 'Far East Prisoners of War' and former civilian internees objected to the planned visit to London by Emperor Akihito, son of Hirohito, and demanded an apology for their treatment during World War Two.

terrific. TB said of GB that on reflection he would not like the way it had all played. He would not like all these headlines. I said I would be surprised if you didn't end up having to sack him some time down the road. He looked sad about the whole thing, then said every Labour government has perished on division, tax and spend or ego. The worst thing about this situation is that it's ego. He was also annoyed at RC at the way he was handling things and felt recent events showed up flaws in both him and GB. Peter was all about ego too, he said. At least JP being difficult was usually about policy or direction.

Wednesday, January 14

Mo called, wanting to push for a Bloody Sunday announcement and trying to deter TB from going to Ireland next week 'because it would be bandwagoning'.

Monday, January 19

I had a real sense of foreboding about the week ahead. As I was preparing for the 11, I was dreading the straight question whether I had done the Rawnsley briefing [which led to headlines about GB being 'psychologically flawed']. Though I could deny 'psychological flaws', if they then pushed on other parts of it, it would be hard. I'd used some heavy language and, as TB saw several times, I gave them licence. The lobby turned out not to be as bad as I feared. I made clear irritation at [Ed] Balls and [Charlie] Whelan [GB spokesman], stressed TB's admiration for GB and said that had not been changed by the events of the last few days. Ministers were calling in, both to say it had to be calmed down, but clearly some of them also thought it was about time he got a taste of his own methods. Mo said it was bad on one level, but it had to happen. His people did us in all the time, she said.

There was a meeting with Sinn Féin at 4, and Mo insisted it was in the Cabinet Room because that was where we met Trimble. TB gave her his agreement to a Bloody Sunday apology and the handing over of new evidence to the police. She was very happy with it. TB said the recent killings meant the situation was 'very grim indeed'. But we have to make progress despite that. Adams did most of the talking early on, then McGuinness with Pat Doherty chipping in from time to time. They all made the point that the Orange card was being played. They want to minimize change. We want to maximize change. Adams said nobody envisaged the Billy Wright killing but it was almost inevitable in this climate of destabilization. Adams was not angry with TB, indeed kept saying he didn't blame him, but felt the 'gap' over Bloody Sunday and the way they were shafted by Trimble made it very difficult.

TB said he understood their situation. Nobody should have a veto. He said he had hoped that a single document, covering NI itself, North-South and East-West, would be the way forward. As ever the one who got their story out first causes difficulties for the others. McGuinness said the document was a mistake. Trimble had gone out of the door and told the world 'I've got my Assembly', as if that was all there was. Presentationally it was a 'disaster' for SF. The bottom line was that the most reluctant participant in the talks was being allowed to dictate the pace. TB felt the killings were an attempt to derail the process.

Adams gave a detailed statistical picture of where the nationalists were and where they had majorities but said their political agenda was nowhere near being met. He said Trimble was 'playing a blinder internally', but he had created space for the LVF [Loyalist Volunteer Force] to operate. TB thanked them for the measured way they put the case. They were certainly calmer than usual though McG was seething away quietly. TB said the most important thing was they contribute positively to the detail on the North-South discussions. I know these guys get up to bad stuff but I found them nicer and more intelligent than the other side.

Wednesday, January 21

The GB story had died in the press. Murdoch told Anji last night that it had been a quite brilliant operation to enflame it and extinguish it in two days.

The big political story for the TV was [Stephen] Byers getting his sums wrong [he had said 8×7 was 54 in a BBC interview promoting numeracy], plus Ireland, with more killings*, and the IRA put out a statement saying the talks were in crisis and they rejected the blueprint. Mo and I met up to work out the best way to respond. I spoke to Siobhán O'Hanlon but she just recited the mantra at me. The four o'clock was partly about that.

Thursday, January 22

The peace process was looking in more trouble and all we could do was keep talking it up as best we could. But just before Cabinet Mo told me Ronnie Flanagan was about to say that the recent killings involved the UFF [Ulster Freedom

---

* Benedict Hughes (55), a Catholic civilian, was shot dead by the Ulster Freedom Fighters (UFF) in Utility Street, south Belfast. Hughes was shot as he left work in Sandy Row, a Protestant part of Belfast.

Fighters], linked to the UDA in the talks. It meant we were going to be under pressure to kick the UDA out of the talks. Cabinet itself was OK, Iraq, Bosnia, Ireland, with both TB and Mo pretty gloomy. Clare surpassed even her ludicrous self on interventions. 'It's very important we try to catch the killers.' JP just sat shaking his head. Clinton was in a lot of trouble on the [Monica Lewinsky]* sex scandal cover-up front and I put out TB words of support at the four o'clock.

Friday, January 23

Clinton's problems were getting worse. The problem was not his affairs so much as the fact he asked Monica Lewinsky to lie. Philip had spoken to George Stephanopoulos who said they all felt totally betrayed, that he had promised once he got to the White House, all this kind of stuff would stop. We were being pressed to say we were rethinking the visit, but on the contrary we were expressing strong support for him despite his difficulties. TB said he intended to be very supportive when we went there and maybe say he thought it was ridiculous to have this system where someone like Starr† was appointed at massive public expense to go fishing for dirt on the president.

Saturday, January 24

Ireland and above all Clinton would dominate the weekend. TB had asked me to find a way of signalling TB/GB back together again. I said we should brief that GB and Peter were working together on specific areas and Peter M and I drew up a briefing note. GB didn't like it and did not want any reference to TB taking an interest in the Budget. He said it would produce 'Blair takes over' headlines. 'Do you want to undermine your Chancellor?' he said. I said no. He said that's the effect. I disagreed, felt it was just him wanting to present the economy solely as a GB issue. It felt like though he said he wanted a truce, he didn't want to do anything to signal there had been one. TB said it was not worth pushing but I should talk to the commentators and get them to reflect things were working better. GB didn't raise the weekend briefings at all, and though he seemed hurt, he was in some ways more consensual.

---

* White House intern who had an affair with Clinton.
† Kenneth Starr, American lawyer and former judge, appointed as Independent Counsel in 1994. His investigations led to the impeachment of President Clinton.

Clinton was mega in the press and it was looking pretty bad for him. Clinton, Hillary and Gore did a press event on childcare, at the end of which BC said he did not have an affair with Lewinsky. He did a pretty good job. Then the UDP walked out of the NI talks in London, which were now in their latest stage of collapse.* I spoke to Mo to get myself briefed before the four o'clock.

TB took a call from Clinton. He said he and CB were thinking of them and anything we could do to support him, we would. They talked over MEPP [Middle East peace process] and NI [Northern Ireland] but the purpose was clearly to get us focused on bombing of Iraq. He said it was vital we were together, got the French onside and the Chinese and Russians to abstain. TB said afterwards that the last time they spoke, BC was less hawkish than TB, but that had definitely shifted. They were preparing for an attack, no doubt, and we had to be out there setting the ground for that, because there is no doubt we were going to take a political hit on this.

Mo called re the North-South structures document. TB felt betrayed, that they had agreed the document with David Andrews [Irish foreign minister] and now squared Trimble, who was going mad because it put back in the framework document that the UUs hated. Trimble was screaming abuse at John Holmes as though it was all his handiwork. I had to meet TB at Lambeth Palace, where he was seeing the Archbishop [of Canterbury], before heading to Lancaster House for the NI talks, where TB had to have separate meetings with all the parties, large and small. It was clear from the mood in the SDLP team – upbeat and happy – that the document went way too far for the UUs, who were walking round with faces like thunder. They were incredibly rude to TB, who seemed to laugh it off, but I said at one point I was surprised they felt they could talk to the prime minister like he was a taxi driver who had taken them on a route they didn't much like.

---

* The multi-party talks switched venue from Stormont in Belfast to Lancaster House in London in an attempt to inject impetus to the search for a political settlement. However, following the revelation that the Ulster Freedom Fighters (UFF), a pseudonym used by the Ulster Defence Association (UDA), had been involved in the killing of (at least) three Catholics in the recent weeks there were calls for the expulsion of the Ulster Democratic Party (UDP), which was politically associated with the UDA/UFF. The British and Irish governments, at the insistence of some of the other parties, took the final decision to expel the UDP. By this time the UDP had already absented themselves from the talks venue. [CAIN]

Ken Maginnis said the NIO were treacherous and disloyal as well as totally incompetent. They just played the Irish game. David Ervine [PUP] was calmer and more sensible than a lot of them, but started by saying 'We are not happy campers' and told TB he should stop making it so obvious he has to give special treatment to Trimble. He said DT was like a big girl's blouse, constantly running to TB to whinge when the slightest thing went wrong. 'A good swift kick up the arse would do him no harm at all.' There was a similar black-humour feel to the SF meeting. TB said 'It's a great life. How is it for you?' 'The earth didn't move,' said Adams. He too felt Trimble was overreacting and losing the plot. They are not really negotiating. He said that if right-wing groups with links to the Tories were killing Hindus, you'd all be outraged and doing something about it. That is how Catholics feel at the moment. That people linked to a party in the process are killing them. I saw John Holmes raise an eyebrow and a smile and it was extraordinary how they could present themselves as innocents in the killing game when the killings were on the other side. McG told TB he had to stand up to Trimble and the Loyalist death squads. The nettle of Unionism must be grasped. TB said nobody was more frustrated than he was.

The SDLP said we needed a few days away on this, without the media. TB felt on Strand 1,* we were close, but the North-South issues were difficult. DT told him he had to get rid of Mo. TB said he would not, and told DT he had to understand how this was all perceived – that the UUs called the shots. He was pretty firm with them, and really fed up after taking all the rubbish being spouted at him all day but as we went to the reception he said he was furious with Mo. He felt we had been bounced into a position that wasn't sensible. She had to understand that DT needed the extra support because the SDLP have the Irish batting for them, and they need a sense of us batting for the Unionists because they feel isolated and beleaguered.

Wednesday, January 28

We were working on the wording of the Bloody Sunday Inquiry announcement. We were going down the 'inquiry but no apology' route. TB was not totally convinced but the arguments from the NIO were fairly strong. It was a running sore. There were a lot of people we would have to tell, political and military, and TB was due to speak to [Sir Edward] Heath [Conservative Prime Minister when

---

* The peace talks would focus on three 'strands': Strand 1 related to exclusively Northern Ireland matters; Strand 2 to relations between Northern Ireland and the Republic of Ireland (North/South); and Strand 3 to relations between Ireland and the UK (East/West).

'Bloody Sunday' happened in 1972] and Hague. I was keen to brief nothing overnight but as the circle widened, it started to leak out in all directions. By the time I was at home, I was into full Bloody Sunday mode. PA had put out a story based on an SDLP briefing which had a few serious inaccuracies – e.g. there would be an apology and an American judge – so I briefed them and Denis Murray on the right lines. There were potential problems with Betty [Boothroyd] but it was one of those we had to get in the right place as it started. John H felt Mo would be offside. TB was growing a bit fed up with the NIO, felt they didn't handle the UUs well and lacked subtlety.

Thursday, January 29

I'd been up till 2 dealing with the Bloody Sunday briefings, and first thing I got a message to Betty explaining that I had had to brief in advance to stop adverse reaction, which could have got out of control. For example, as soon as PA did their story on the SDLP line, Ian Paisley Jr [DUP] was straight out of the traps saying there would be trouble. Denis M was great, checking the emphasis with me the whole time. If only there were a few more like him – knows the subject inside out, cares about it but always wants to get the balance right. Cabinet was largely Iraq, which was all pretty worrying; Ireland, and a discussion on Bloody Sunday; pay and welfare reform. Mo thanked George R [Robertson, Defence Secretary] re agreeing to the Bloody Sunday Inquiry, said he would take a lot of flak in the military. I went over with TB for the Bloody Sunday statement, which went fine, as did the briefing afterwards. Even though some of the Irish experts were in there, I felt on top of all the detail. I had a long chat with Chris Meyer [UK ambassador to Washington] about the US trip.

An interesting few days, not least as a reminder of how often crunch moments on Northern Ireland coincided with a clutch of big, difficult issues. So controversial did the 2003 military action in Iraq become that even the most vehement TB critics sometimes forget it was not the first time we took action against Iraq. The growing personal and political crisis for Clinton over his private-life misdemeanours was part of the backdrop for both Iraq and Ireland. And with the Lancaster House talks once again showing how hard it was to keep one side from going overboard if the other side was 'happy', the decision finally to hold an inquiry into Bloody Sunday added another piece to the ever-changing jigsaw. TB was always reluctant to hold the inquiry, and as its costs mounted over the years, had felt his reluctance justified. But a combination of Sinn Féin, Bertie Ahern, Mo and the NIO persuaded him it had to be done. Only when it concluded, and David Cameron issued an apology in the Commons on June 15, 2010, were sceptics like TB finally persuaded of the merits.

Monday, February 2

We had a brief meeting with the US ambassador [Philip Lader], who had a weird, and very American, over-firm and over-friendly handshake. Then we started the rounds of US interviews, with Diane Sawyer [US broadcast journalist, former press aide to Richard Nixon]. I really didn't take to her. The worst type of TV blonde confection, gushing smile. She was obsessed with questions on marital fidelity, which TB non-answered. When they changed tapes, the producer started asking her to do more on Clinton/fidelity and I stepped in and said please stop wasting your time. They did Clinton, Iraq, Ireland, Diana. TB liked her a lot more than I did.

As we left TB did a kind of swooning look and we had an argument about whether she was sexy or not. He had been worrying how best to express support for Clinton but in the end it was fairly easy. It was all about emphasizing the big picture, the importance of the transatlantic relationship, the leadership BC had given to the centre left. The ABC producer told me there was massive interest in TB's visit, more than he could remember for any leader.

Wednesday, February 4

On the plane, we took TB through the detail on the trip, but he was worried about PG's recent groups. He kept asking me 'How much trouble do you think we're in?' I felt it was win-backable but we had to see it as a warning signal if we wandered off too much. We were on Concorde so taking TB up the back of the plane was a bit more crowded than usual. Some of them [the media] were a bit too excited for my taste and the feeling was more school trip than important visit. After our briefing I got back to find Jon Craig [reporter] talking to CB and Fiona down the front, with all sorts of papers on Iraq lying around. I told him to go back to the press bit and lost it a bit with Fiona for letting him stay down there in the first place when TB had just left his papers on his seat. Jack Straw was also up chatting to the press. Helen Liddell [Treasury minister] and Alan Milburn were with us. TB said GB was livid he was not coming with us, but that would have given us a JP problem. I had a chat with Gavyn Davies [chief UK economist at Goldman Sachs, husband of Sue Nye] about the IMF.

We arrived and there had been heavy rain, almost flood-like. We were driven to Blair House [official guest house], a stone's throw from the White House. It was like a very homely five-star hotel, but without too many flunkeys going round ringing bells. The shorter flight meant we still had a stack of work to do and after TB did *GMTV* – not pushed too hard on Lewinsky – he set off for the IMF dinner while I stayed back to work on the three speeches we had planned, one for the arrivals ceremony, then the others re Ireland, education at the centre of our politics. It was nice having Fiona on the trip but I was working till 4am UK time and was knackered but unable to sleep. They'd also put us in a room with single beds, which I hate.

Thursday, February 5

TB was really quite nervous as we left for the White House, wanting to go over every detail again. I was a bit pissed off to discover me, Jonathan etc. were meant to be part of the reception ceremony. I couldn't stand all that stuff, felt it should be down to the principals. Anne Edwards [White House staff] found me and took me away thank God. Bill and Hillary looked a little bit pinched and the body language between them was cool to non-existent, except when Bill tried to be warm, and she sort of responded because she knew she had to, for the sake of form, but there was none of the chemistry that was normally there. He seemed a bit diminished by it. He was still phenomenally charismatic and I could see the impact he was having on people who had met him for the first time, but I also sensed that slight diminution. The mood between the four of them was excellent. Bill was clearly grateful for the support. They went off for a private session, then came back and as we settled down in the Oval Office, the two pools came through. The American pool was half on Monica, half Iraq. The British were three-quarters Iraq and the rest Monica. Boris Johnson [*Telegraph*] annoyed TB with a question asking if he was jealous of Clinton. The news came in that Lewinsky was to get immunity. Clinton was starting to get a bit more steamed up. He, TB and I started talking about how we would deal with it all at the full press conference they were going to have to do. He was steamed up about some of the commentators, going on about stuff in *their* private lives. I said he was crazy to engage on the detail. He is so much bigger than them. Keep going on the big picture. He said there has to be a change in the way the media operates, that politics will become impossible if media trends carry on as they are, into this stuff the whole time. They went off for lunch, mainly Iraq, Iran, N Ireland. Mike and I did a joint briefing off camera in the White House press room. The hacks enjoyed it, felt the visit was producing strong copy, not least on the 'shoulder to shoulder' message.

BC was definitely more relaxed when HC was off with CB and again that was totally understandable. I asked him what it was like having the whole world thinking and talking about your sex life. He said as long as he couldn't hear them all at the same time, he could get by. He said Hillary had been great, considering. There was still an awful lot that bound them together and she knew he was no saint, but somehow they kept going. I got the impression he was quite pleased to be talking about it in a very normal, human kind of way. His staff were close, and supportive, but I had picked up a lot of anger against him. Also, they were far more deferential to him as president, and I'm not sure any of them had the kind of really personal conversation that I could have with TB. I think TB was worried I was being a bit forward even raising it, but the fact BC kept coming over for little chats made me think he welcomed it. He said I can't tell you how good it is to have you guys in town right now.

The only time during the trip I felt Hillary was really looking at BC was when, during one of the wonkathon* sessions, he appeared to be nodding off, and she really stared into him. He opened his eyes, nodded forward, saw she was looking at him, and smiled weakly, then she just looked away. There was a real strength and dignity to her, but the hurt was there.

Friday, February 6

TB and I were going over how to handle the press conference. It was going to get massive coverage and we decided there was no way to finesse, we just had to be shoulder to shoulder. The tough question was whether he thought BC was telling the truth, and we agreed the best answer was to say Bill Clinton had always been a man he could trust and do business with. Clinton came down with Sandy Berger, Mike and one or two others and we started to go through difficult questions. The breaking story was about a secretary being told to lie. He said he would deal with it, no need to bother Tony on the detail. The others went away to take their seats with the press, leaving the four of us there for five minutes or so. BC was in a fairly vulnerable position. This had built up and up and up and he was more nervous than TB. TB took me to one side before they went through, as he often did, just to restate everything we had agreed, and get that final reassurance he was on the right lines. Total support. Big picture. Important relationship between our countries. I told TB which of our hacks to call, and in what order. BC took a few deep breaths, cracked a joke about asking how many of the press could claim hand on heart to be faithful, then off they went.

---

* Policy debates of policy thinkers known as 'policy wonks', hence 'wonkathon'.

Mike and I went in on the side, and got there just as TB and BC got up to the lecterns. There was an explosion of camera clicks, then they waited till everyone was settled. Both did good introductory words and closed down the Monica stuff well. TB could not have been clearer, nor BC more grateful. There was the odd flash of humour, as when Phil Murphy asked whether Bill appreciated TB's support and he said no. TB was even more warm and supportive than we planned, and Bill really appreciated it. As theatre, it was virtuoso. As they came out, Bill said TB would increase his standing because of what he did and was effusive in his thanks. He and TB walked down the red carpet and met us in the room where we had done the briefing. BC took us to one side and said I'm going to make sure you will always be proud of what you did out there. 'It was a noble thing to do.' He was on a bit of an adrenaline rush, realized it had gone well, and was glad it was over. The others came through, Berger etc., and everyone was pleased. There had been a real sense of foreboding, that the whole thing was going to be humiliating for him, and it was fine, in fact better than fine, though the reality remained.

As we left, I asked Clinton if he had any thoughts for the briefing I had to do, and he said what about Northern Ireland? Tell them I've told Tony I'll do whatever he wants to help, that I'm going to reopen all the channels, push them hard, including with Trimble, but say if there is any return to violence, that's it. I said what about you make a visit to NI at the time of G8. 'Say we're looking at it.' What a pro. Fiona had been up in their flat with Hillary and CB and said it was really nice compared with Number 10, very homely but really smart. Alison [Blackshaw] was hanging around waiting to give me some papers and BC spotted her. I introduced them and he really turned on the charm. She was a bit embarrassed but what was interesting was how he just could not help himself.

Saturday, February 7

The Sundays were doing tons on the trip. I wrote up a stack of background notes, on the visit, Iraq, Ireland, Lewinsky, so that they could share some of the briefing back there. Fiona and I went for a long walk around the back of the White House. We agreed BC was feeling really vulnerable, and that if he was anything but president, it's hard to see how Hillary would stay with him. She said Hillary was much softer and nicer when she was away from him, but in his presence he was softer, and she was harder. I had picked up from Mike and from Berger that they really didn't think he was through the worst yet.

Monday, February 9

After the success of the US trip, we were straight back into the grunge of trying to get some kind of cohesion and energy going. GB was impossible at the moment, just didn't want to know. At the strategy meeting he reminded me of the kids when they don't want to go somewhere.

Tuesday, February 10

TB did *Larry King Live* [US talk show] on Iraq and NI but we were still struggling to dominate the agenda. Mo came to see me, a bit upset because Maginnis had called her a liar. I said she had to understand their game was partly to undermine her the whole time so they could feel they could run to TB whenever they wanted.

Wednesday, February 11

Northern Ireland was getting trickier. [Ronnie] Flanagan had told Mo they believed the recent killings [of Brendan Campbell, a Catholic drug dealer and Robert Dougan, a prominent Loyalist] were the work of the IRA. If this was right, it meant SF would have to leave the talks. We agreed Mo should speak to Adams, and JH should speak to the US to get them to put pressure on to condemn. Flanagan did not give Mo all the intelligence that led him to the conclusion that Adams knew. TB said we had to know it was kosher. If we had to throw out SF we were pretty much dead, as the UUs were going to walk if we didn't kick them out anyway, so we were pretty much dead either way. He looked unbelievably fed up and angry. John Holmes was cautioning, saying that strange though it may sound, the IRA would not want to say something that was not true. TB had to leave for the New Deal reception, saying 'You guys work on it.' All we could really do was try to buy some time.

Thursday, February 12

The Clare [Short] film* arrived and was totally nauseating. It was trivial at one level but revealed an ego the size of an elephant's arse, and of course I had to go through all the bollocks of pretending we were relaxed about it. TB took a

---

* In the BBC documentary, *Clare's New World,* Short accused an unnamed colleague of maliciously and untruthfully leaking details of a Cabinet discussion in which she allegedly likened Ulster Unionists to the Ku Klux Klan.

meeting on PIRA [Provisional IRA] with Richard Wilson [Cabinet Secretary], Mo, Quentin Thomas, John Holmes, Jonathan, AC. Mo had seen the transcripts of the calls that showed beyond doubt the killings were the work of the IRA. She was now 95 per cent sure and felt we couldn't really do anything but go along with it. TB and I were arguing we didn't have to go so hard, and we needed more time. TB felt Irish and US opinion would push them back in if we could keep the temperature down a bit. John H, Mo and I worked on a statement but it was at best ambiguous and she said Flanagan would not wear it. TB was desperate to keep the thing going. He said there were times when you had to do things that might seem unprincipled to others, in order to give yourself the time you need to make positive change happen, and this was one of them. He was really fed up about the whole thing. Mo said Flanagan had been very tough with them and resented her wanting evidence to back up what he had said. The police believed that they were doing it first, as a warning to show they could always go back to it (as if anyone doubted it) and second, to push the UUs towards the exit door if the blame game had to be played. They didn't want to be caught out but they fucked up. It was going to be difficult to buy much time at all.

TB spoke to Bertie and Clinton, Bertie being helpful and Bill less so. Despite the pressures, Bertie was brilliant, said he was totally with us on it. TB felt that if the two governments stuck together Sinn Féin would then have to come back in through a ceasefire. He said there will be a lot of ups and downs and this was a big down. He felt let down by Adams and McGuinness. Otherwise things were a bit grim, Ireland grim. Clare grim.

One of those issues where the morality of decision-making is not always clear. One of the principles of the process was that if any of the participants went back to violence, they could not be involved in the talks. But this was not the first time that the logic of that became clear – it gave the men of violence an effective veto on progress. It explains why TB, once he was presented with the evidence of IRA involvement, was nonetheless desperate to get Sinn Féin back inside the process as soon as possible.

Friday, February 13

TB was seeing GB first thing on the Budget, but his big worry was NI. I briefed Denis Murray overnight on condition he waited till after 6.30am. As ever, he played straight and did the business. He was really good, totally on-message, put where we were in a proper context. It is an incredible help having someone you can actually level with, explain why certain things have to be said in a certain way, without them bleating about me trying to do their job. The thing about Denis is he understands the sensitivities he is dealing with.

The Clare story was effectively killed by the niceness of my briefing. I wrote a note to TB nonetheless saying he should rein her in. He said it was pointless because she will never change. On Ireland, TB felt Bertie was fine but we needed more people coming in behind this, especially Bill Clinton. Sinn Féin were saying that they should not be pushed out and denying that there was incontrovertible evidence it was them.

Monday, February 16

The Northern Ireland talks in Dublin, and the possible expulsion of Sinn Féin, were the main thing for the day.

Tuesday, February 17

TB was pretty fed up by the time we left for lunch at the *Guardian*. He also spoke to Bertie in the car and things were rocky there. The *Guardian* was the usual conspiracy theorists and leftists, and one or two voices of sanity. TB did fine on Iraq, Ireland, welfare, but didn't really shine until the lunch itself. Peter Preston [editor] was obsessed with the idea that the security services were lying to us all the time, because that's what they did to Labour governments. It was reasonably friendly and TB probably overdid the attacks on the *Guardian* but Mike White thought it went fine. He'd been looking a bit fed up throughout.

Wednesday, February 18

TB came out after PMQs and had a meeting with Hague and [Michael] Howard on Iraq. Last night he had seen Hague and [Andrew] MacKay on Ireland, where he sensed they were moving to ditch bipartisanship if we let Sinn Féin back into the talks. On Iraq, he said Howard was clearly of the view that if it worked they would support us, and if not they would kick us all over the place.

Thursday, February 19

The Iraq meeting was quite bad-tempered. Cabinet was mainly Iraq and Ireland. There was a comical moment when Mo suggested Clare do an article about it all

[Iraq]. Yes, said TB, you could get some coverage if you were out batting for the government. TB was working mainly on Ireland. Bertie still wanted to be able to say that Sinn Féin could be back in by March 2, less than two weeks away. TB said it was not possible. He was worried both about the Tories and public opinion. March 9 was their next offer. He said, as he left for the theatre, that he felt between a rock and a hard place on this. He said, I don't suppose it's possible to get them in too soon, is it? I said no, not really.

Friday, February 20

We had real problems on Ireland. Bertie was still pushing for Sinn Féin to be back in the fold by March 2 as a condition for expulsion. TB said it was not possible and we finally settled on March 9. That in itself will be difficult, as was clear from a very difficult call with Trimble, though at least he did not say he was walking. He asked TB to start pushing for the talks to wrap up earlier than May, something I started to hint at to the Sunday lobby. Sinéad Cusack [actress] came in for a cup of tea and said that the arts really were fed up with us. The Irish and Mo put out statements on the Sinn Féin expulsion.

Saturday, February 21

In media terms, [with Iraq the dominant issue at the moment] Ireland was not nearly as bad as it might have been, but an overnight bombing made life difficult again.* TB called to say that the early intelligence suggested it was some renegade Republican outfit. The main calls of the day were on whether TB would accept Adams' suggestion of a meeting before Sinn Féin came back to the talks. TB was more confident the Budget was going to be a success. He said yesterday's meeting went OK, and part of the story around it had to be TB and GB coming together again, and he wanted me to make another effort to work closely with GB and his people. I had probably gone a bit too far with Sarah [Brown] and should never have said I thought Ed Balls should go as well as Charlie. TB said that was not a very wise thing to say, because GB believed now I was doing him in on a daily basis, systematically. I said that was ridiculous, and showed how off-balance GB was. He said that was no longer the point. He also said the problem with 'psychological flaws' was its brutal truth, which is why it hurt him so much. Then he

---

* The CIRA (Continuity Irish Republican Army) exploded a 500-pound car bomb outside the RUC station in Moira, County Down. Eleven people, mostly RUC officers, suffered minor injuries. Extensive damage was done to premises in the village centre.

said 'But I'm worried, Ali.' He was the one person who called me Ali when he was being serious. He said there had to be a sense of the two of them coming together after a difficult phase.

Thursday, February 26

The UDP meeting was fairly positive despite all the difficulties. They raised several times the point TB must not see Adams and if he did they would have to review the position. Yet they were still giving us the impression it could be OK by May.

Bertie Ahern arrived and Joe Lennon [Ahern's press secretary] and I had agreed there should be pooled statements by the two of them from armchairs, as if the cameras just wandered in and found them. It was a bit Saddamesque but it went OK. They were both determined that we can get there by May. It was a good meeting. TB said he feared if we did not keep working towards a deal, and get one by May, we were sunk. Bertie spoke of evil criminal elements who were trying to derail the whole thing. He said he had told Adams and McGuinness that TB had been generous with his time but could not wait around forever. We were at least back into real detail on the North-South council and the ministerial bodies. Bertie said the UUs believe you can leave all the North-South bodies in a grey area and you can't. We have to be specific.

Friday, February 27

TB was seeing Trimble, otherwise it was a fairly quiet day. I went to the *What the Papers Say* lunch, which had all the Fleet Street great and good, so-called, and was fairly jolly. But it was at these kinds of media events that it always got home to me that I had left journalism for a very different world, and felt more comfortable in the new one than the old. It was nice to dip back in for an hour or two, but that was it.

Wednesday, March 4

At the briefing after PMQs, all the press were interested in was the PA story that TB had been seen in Westminster Cathedral, on his own, and was he converting to Catholicism? I was pretty brutal, saying even prime ministers were entitled to some privacy. We ran around the block on that for ages.

Cabinet was Ireland, agreeing to see Adams next week, Iraq, BSE and the Lords. TB mildly read the riot act with them all, said he was fed up with leaks and the like, that there was not enough discipline. MPs were complaining that ministers and special advisers were out of control so why should they be so well behaved? Ivor Richard [Leader of the House of Lords} said he could not work out if the Tories wanted a deal on the Lords or not, but they have accepted the hereditary peerage has to go. TB was not so sure, felt they were engaged in a stalling exercise. They were trying to get us into a box. I was dealing with Mo re Adams and also the various Lords competing forces.

John Holmes asked me to start thinking about how we could best present delaying the May deadline on the NI talks. It was clear from his phone call with Trimble later that it was getting very difficult.

TB was very funny, joking about all the little gifts that he got. He said he loved Chirac's watch. He liked the pen from Germany, so Helmut [Kohl] was a top bloke. Japan gave him a kite. So he could still make us all laugh, but I was finding life a pain in the arse at the moment. I felt I was running around putting out fires, stopping fires, managing things OK, but that we were not really driving through a strategy. And despite the recent chats, I felt the GB situation getting worse not better.

We announced the Adams meeting for Thursday, which went fine.

I was getting really tired and had to be up early to get in and prepare for the Adams meeting. McGuinness was away. The visit was leading the news all day. I was working on a Budget article but despite the conversation with GB last week, and the plan to meet and agree a communications plan tying TB and GB together, nothing had come of it, and he was clearly ploughing his own furrow. Inevitably, there was a lower media turnout for Adams, and a diminished sense of excitement or expectation, but in substance it was a good meeting, more positive than we had felt in advance. Adams was a good talker, maybe talked a bit too much, but he had a rich voice, usually stopped to think before speaking and didn't let up till his point was made. He struck me as less emotional than McGuinness, whose absence maybe took a bit of tension out of the meeting.

Adams said he did not have control of the IRA, but we have influence and we have tried to use it. He was adamant the crisis of confidence came before the killings, though he accepted they had not helped. But he felt there were double standards applying. We got down into some real detail and Adams sensed TB and Mo didn't exactly know the constitutional implications of some of this, and said he found it odd. TB said Jonathan [Stephens, NIO] could work it out with them afterwards. TB said if they could embrace consent, they would get greater US support. TB had to leave for the EU conference at Lancaster House. Adams and I had a little session at the end and agreed he would say he wanted back in the talks as soon as possible, which was good, and the press were picking up positive vibes.

Saturday, March 14

I allowed myself to let David Wastell [*Sunday Telegraph*] talk me into a splash on TB taking over the Northern Ireland talks, which as a result went too big on the news, and with no real strategic gain. I should have just told him there was no story. These Sunday guys were so fucking desperate the whole time, whining that we had to feed them or they would have to write shit that would cause us trouble.

Sunday, March 15

Jonathan and Sarah [Helm, partner] came round for a drink, in a real state. Jonathan looked tired, like he had not been sleeping. He felt badly undermined. Sarah was really angry that he could work so hard, and be so loyal, and be made to feel like trash. I said he shouldn't worry. TB was forever pushing us all harder, was not great at compliments or thanks, and could criticize all of us from time to time, but I had heard not the remotest hint he was thinking of getting rid of him. He should also ask TB what he actually wanted him to do. But also, let's not pretend that things were working very well, because they weren't. Anji was just one of the problems. The big one was GB. Peter M was another. I guess I was another, because TB's constant complaint to me was that his key people were just not working together, and he didn't think I made the effort I should with GB and Peter. Jonathan was very down, and very down on TB. He said he wasted so much time and energy, duplicated so much work. 'If he wants me to be a glorified diary secretary, then no thanks, I'm off.'

The main thing today was getting lines out from last night's dinner with Bertie Ahern, which had been three hours' pretty tough talking.

I saw TB re Ireland first thing, just before he spoke to Trimble. He complained that the Irish were making it more difficult by briefing so hard. We left for the [China] summit and I had a nice chat with Bertie as TB was meeting and greeting. He said he didn't know how we coped with our newspapers, both the number and the way they were. Chirac brightened things up a bit, singing happy birthday to Kohl. TB had to persuade the PM of Vietnam [Phan Van Khai] not to walk out in protest that all the speeches and opening ceremony were not being translated into all languages. There was worse to come, when it became clear Kohl did not have a headset, and he was clearly getting into a rage, with people flapping around. Then it emerged there was no German on the translation, which was ridiculous.

The conference centre looked good, very modern and minimalist, but I found these set-piece summits really annoying. Bertie told me during one of the breaks he hated them too, with everyone on show and very little business actually done, particularly one like this, ASEM [Asia-Europe Meeting], where most of the work was done bilaterally in the margins. TB's speech went OK but I made sure afterwards he sought out Kohl and apologized. He had not even been able to get translation of the statement on the economic crisis. He had to follow it all with his own interpreters rather than through the headsets. I did a briefing on the morning session while all the leaders went to Derry's residence for lunch. Kohl was very grumpy, probably in part because the chairs were quite small, and he then started raging at the air conditioning. But of all the set speeches in the summit, his was the only one I found inspiring, as he did a big number of his vision of the new Europe. He said no country needed to give up its national identity as Europe became one. But the euro would bring us closer. Chirac made similar points but let himself down with his sly attacks on Leon Brittan and his little digs at the US. He said the world was not trilateral but multilateral. Asia was a power, the US was a power, Europe was a power, South America would become a power. '*L'Union fait la force, une force politique, une force économique.*' ['The Union is a force, a political force, an economic force.']

The enlargement discussion was fascinating though, as the different leaders put slightly different slants on what they were pretending were the same points. Kohl said German unity and European unity were two sides of the same coin.

Hashimoto was the most dominant of the Asian leaders, some of whom I never heard speak once. TB said it had been fascinating. He said enlargement was an ambitious project but the history of Europe was the triumph of ambition over cynicism. We can do it because the world is opening up. I did a briefing at the end of the afternoon, mainly on the economic statement, the Japanese economy and dealing with currency speculators. I also did a number about how TB made a fuss of Kohl on his birthday, giving him a bottle of his favourite port.

In between times we were working on getting an agreed statement with the Irish. John Holmes and Paddy Teahon [senior adviser to Ahern] had pretty much done the business, but [George] Mitchell wanted us to put it down at 8pm. But we felt TB would have to square Trimble first. He was worried it would not take much to push DT off the ship. Trimble called after the Channel 4 news and said this was all looking like a UK-Irish stitch-up and he was not happy. TB and BA agreed it would be better if they had a bit more time and tabled the text at Stormont not here. I got Mitchell to do a conference call with them, agreed that was the way forward and then did a joint statement to that effect, mentioning the Mitchell call, indicating progress without going too far. TB said on the way back to Number 10 that it was ridiculous he was expected to deal with complicated negotiations like this while he was meant to be chairing a summit.

Saturday, April 4

TB was totally consumed re Ireland, but he was still fretting about my set-up, and the need to get in a strong deputy to lift some of the load. I drafted clips for TB and Bertie to do, just to keep the Ireland story freshened up on the bulletins, and fill what was becoming a vacuum. At the Sunday lobby, there was an insatiable demand for Irish stuff. All we could do was give the sense of incessant pressure.

Monday, April 6

Ireland was the big story again. [The deadline for the Stormont talks was April 9, so the papers were busy with conjecture.]

Tuesday, April 7

Mitchell finally tabled his paper around midnight and though it didn't leak, it was clear there were going to be problems. TB was furious when he came down from the flat because he felt both Mitchell and the NIO had not handled the

UUs properly. He said they didn't understand how, because the Irish government had such a close relationship to the SDLP, we had to give the UUs the sense that we were there for them, at least keeping an eye on things from their perspective, even when we were pushing them in a certain direction. By 10, we had basically decided we were going to have to go there but TB had to chair the PES [Party of European Socialists] at the FCO, which was a pain. He was worried about being associated with failure, but I said he would be anyway and if he could make a difference by going, then we should go. By 3, we were set to go.

We left around 3.30 and I briefed Denis Murray and John Irvine [ITV Ireland correspondent] from the car. On the plane we went through the paper in some detail and it was obvious what Trimble's problem was. The areas for cooperation were too numerous and too all-encompassing. TB was a bit fed up with it because he and Bertie had not actually negotiated all this, but Mitchell insisted it was all in there. He had been angry with DT before, but felt he had a point here. He discussed plans for a doorstep on arrival at Hillsborough [Castle, Northern Ireland Secretary's official residence], and I drafted a few lines. But he pretty much did his own thing. This is not a time for sound bites but I feel the hand of history upon my shoulder. Hell of a sound bite. The press loved it.

Given our reputation for so-called spin, and the determination always to try to find the right words for every occasion, it was immediately assumed – and has been since – that the 'hand of history' soundbite was a deliberate and carefully planned attempt to set the scene for a big breakthrough. In truth, it was an accident. In the discussions beforehand we had agreed not to raise expectations too high. Jonathan Powell and I were standing a few yards from TB, and were close to laughing out loud when the now famous words left his lips. Also, as is clear from recent entries, though Mitchell had finally tabled the paper, there were more reasons to believe we would not reach an agreement than reasons to believe we would. Despite the hand of history rhetoric, TB was actually in quite a pessimistic mood, and felt the gap between the UUs and Sinn Féin was too wide, both in terms of policy and, just as importantly, psychology.

DT arrived at Hillsborough and was perfectly friendly but a bit detached, as though this was all happening around him but was not directly in his control or even relevant to him. It was his coping mechanism, one I had noticed before, that he was almost like a commentator, but then something would spark him into seeing the total absolute relevance to himself and his situation, and his temper would go, and the face would go puce. Tonight he was calm and lucid, and said simply – and repeatedly – that he could not do a deal on this basis. TB said effectively that he would negotiate for him. I organized the departure, TB in shirtsleeves, chatting at length to DT as he left, giving the sense he was in there and able to get his point across. A lot of this was just going to be about balancing the sense of treating the parties well, but at this stage DT better than the rest. Mitchell himself looked tired, as did Mo. We were not going to get the UUs signed up to this as it was. George [Mitchell] was less concerned, saying we would only get one bite of the cherry and they would not want to negotiate. TB said he feared they would want to negotiate every last point. He said DT was not grandstanding. He had genuine points of concern that had to be met, and we had to try to meet them.

Mo seemed a little peeved that TB and Bertie were taking it over, but this was inevitable. I went in to see TB as he was getting ready for bed. He said his gut feeling was very negative. He couldn't see how to fill the gaps. Adams had been pushing for another meeting. The SDLP had been on, saying we must not give in to blackmail. TB said if we were dealing with reasonable people, this would be fairly straightforward, but we're not, and the historical hatreds are just too deep.

Wednesday, April 8

I got a message to go and see TB before I was even up. He was in the bath, and said he was worried. I knew he was worried anyway because he was playing the fool the whole time, putting on a thick Irish accent, pretending he was a newsreader announcing that Cherie was going to become a Protestant and he was going to speak with an Irish accent as part of a deal to secure peace in NI. Bertie's mum had died and he was coming up for breakfast before then going back for the funeral. TB said what was important was to get Trimble pointing in a more positive direction. He said my task for the day was to get DT out there being more positive than the Neanderthals, by which I think he meant Maginnis and Taylor, who were doing most of the media and pushing the worst-case scenario for the UUs. Paddy Teahon said Trimble was asking for the Holy Trinity to be replaced by the Almighty God in the Irish Constitution. Even Bertie managed a laugh. Bertie said if he was exposed to either of them too much today, he would be worried he would end up thumping them.

We left by helicopter for Stormont and after a brief doorstep we were taken up to the office that had been picked as our base. It was not a nice building, and the room was too hot. The furniture was not nice either. A plain brown table, a dozen or so not very comfortable green-backed chairs, three easy chairs. We were going to be spending a lot of time in here and it was a depressing start. Then came meeting after meeting, with occasional pauses to take stock and indulge in black humour. The most important were with the UUs, and they were also the most difficult. Even Reg Empey [UUP vice president], who could normally be called upon to be reasonable, was being more Maginnis/Taylor than his usual self. Trimble was trying hard, but he just had too many people at him. He would say something, and then find the others translating it into something harder. Then Trimble would nod his agreement to the revised version. TB was getting frustrated and angry as the day wore on. He was emphasizing the two main points – principle of consent at the heart of it, and proper recognition of different traditions.

TB was having to see all the parties regularly just to keep them on board but the focus was DT. He came in on his own just after lunch and this time TB really tried all the charm and the cajoling and DT was moving, but then moved right back again. [Jeffrey] Donaldson was being difficult, said it was all a charade being run by the Anglo-Irish secretariat. We were also a bit stuck without Bertie but he came back around 6.30, looking even more knackered than before. I felt really sorry for him. It was obvious the way he talked about her that he was close to his mother, and she was barely buried and he was back taking a whole load of grief from the UUs. They talked to him, and about him, with something close to contempt, and it was terrific the way he took it. TB was now getting very irritable and the surroundings were beginning to drive us all a bit crazy. The idea of being stuck in here for a day or two was not terribly appetizing.

I did a reasonably optimistic briefing and then afterwards came the key meeting of the day, with TB, BA and the UUs, at which Trimble and, more implausibly, John Taylor suddenly signalled they were ready to do a deal.

Bertie started, speaking very quietly, said it would be a great tragedy if we could not reach a deal now. Joe Lennon scribbled me a note saying DT had too many enemies for this to work, but the mood was fine. It was when Taylor suddenly piped up – 'There is room for manoeuvre here' – that we thought there was a sign of change. Bertie had said before he would walk out if he started up on his usual record. He said he couldn't be arsed listening to it all again. But this time Taylor was significantly different. It was the first time he had ever been anything remotely approaching positive. It was a big turnaround and they agreed to go away and sort it with their people. It cheered us up no end, because we had been half expecting the opposite, but something had clearly happened in their discussions to trigger a switch.

After the main trilateral, we had a long session with Adams and McGuinness and later with Adams alone. They were both very charming in their own way, also very clever, and always making points at various levels. I liked McG better of the two. Whatever he had done in the past, there was a directness to him that I liked and he was driven by a genuine sense of grievance about the way people were forced to live. I guess Adams is too, but he also strikes me as more interested in his own place in the firmament, more a politician than a people's person.

TB and I went for a walk out in the freezing cold. We didn't want to be seen so just found this little garden and walked round for a few minutes. 'This is like prison exercise,' said TB. But he had perked up. 'Do you think we can do this? It would be amazing if we pull this off. I think we can pull it off, I really do.' It was the Taylor shift that had put some fresh wind in our sails. The problem remained the implementation bodies. But as the evening wore on, Bertie was getting more and more depressed and felt it was all sliding back. Bertie met Trimble for hours, during which time we were either hanging around or seeing the other parties, who were spending more time hanging around than we were. The press pack was growing and I was doing fairly regular briefings just to keep them busy and stop them taking too many negative lines elsewhere. [Denis] Murray and [John] Irvine were terrific.

DT came to see us again, and said he had a UU solution that he thought would do the trick. We went down to the Irish office and TB tried it on Bertie, who was very gloomy. We bumped into Mitchell on the way back and he looked pretty fed up too. He said he felt we were living through a Greek tragedy. Maybe the UU shift had been bollocks. Also, TB was a bit spooked by Adams saying the shift on policing wasn't enough. TB said there was still the basis of a deal and he felt we should go through the night. Jonathan and I felt it was too early and the mood wasn't right. He was very pissed off. We had a last effort with BA and DT and the sticking point was the powers of the North-South bodies. 'They don't really want these implementation bodies at all,' said BA, who was really tired and gloomy by now. They want consent principle enshrined, an Assembly, the Irish constitutional claim on the North gone, and they want to give fuck all in return. TB said if we don't break it down tonight, we are in trouble, and suggested we get DT back in. He was getting tired too. 'I'll go fucking spare if he brings in Maginnis and the rest again.' DT was a bit more hopeful. TB said we should not leave the building until we have Strand 2 tied up and agreed. But we did, about 1am, exhausted and not there yet. On the helicopter back to Hillsborough TB just looked out of the window, his face tired and angry, occasionally shaking his head. We had been up and down all day, but were ending it very much down.

The indication of a new approach by John Taylor was a defining moment. We had got so used to Trimble doing his best to indicate a planned direction of travel, only for his colleagues to signal he was moving too fast. So to have Taylor sending the signal of a possible deal was a breakthrough, seized upon by TB and BA.

It saddens me that Bertie Ahern's reputation has taken such a hit as a result of the financial crisis and the impact on Irish business and families. My most powerful memory of him was his return to the talks, still in black tie, putting his public duties ahead of his private grief, and doing so with a commitment, and tolerance of abuse and criticism from some of the participants, that was beyond the call of duty. One of the reasons the Good Friday Agreement came about was because of the teamwork of the different collections of individuals and groups of people involved. By now, TB and Bertie were established as an effective double act in these negotiations, their teams also working together well despite occasional differences of emphasis and opinion. The last time I was in Ireland, a woman staying at my hotel said 'all Bertie will be remembered for is the financial mess he left us.' I don't accept that. His role in the peace process was hugely important, not least on the day he was dealing with his mother's burial. People should never forget that.

Thursday, April 9

Writing this on Saturday, back at home, just random thoughts really, with the main notes done as the discussions happened, and a real sense I was recording history. It was an extraordinary time, and felt like it. It showed TB at his infuriating best. Once he got the bit between the teeth, and decided to go for it, he always knew best, there was no one else could put a counter-view, he was like a man possessed. He would ask to see someone and then ten seconds later shout out 'Where the fuck are they? I need them here NOW.' He would pace up and down, go over all the various parts of the analysis, work out who was likely to be saying what next, work out our own next move. We had room for the usual black humour in there. Jonathan was putting on weight and I christened him 'Five Bellies'* which stuck, and whenever TB was in need of a laugh he would put on a Geordie accent and ask 'Five Bellies' to get him a cup of tea and some pork scratchings. Nick Matthews [duty clerk] was fantastic, just kept the tea and the food and the laughs flowing. Claire [Harrington] and Lizzie [McCrossan] from the Garden Rooms were doing a brilliant job, having to record an endless succession of meetings, with poor old John Holmes having to take part, and record, and transcribe as we went. As the days wore on, he started to take on a grey-green tinge, and looked exhausted, but he was brilliant throughout. Thursday had started for me with a wrestle with a fucking bath. Not only was the plug stuck in, but the taps wouldn't turn off, and I had to get the cops up to sort it. Great start.

---

* A reference to footballer Paul Gascoigne's rotund friend Jimmy 'Five Bellies' Gardner.

We had breakfast in the Throne Room, and started without Bertie who was on his way up. We agreed they should arrive together. Bertie was in OK mood considering and we had a load of small talk re Burnley and Man U.

TB had been worried last night that BA was actually depressed but he seemed a lot better today. The plan on arrival was just for some nice clear pictures of TB and Bertie, with a few words, but David Andrews bounded in and buggered it up, interrupting the doorstep. TB did a couple of answers then cut it short and was livid when we got up to the office. I said DA ballsing it up wasn't worth bothering with. There would be a lot worse to come during the day.

It was the start of a long and emotional day. Mo did a great job keeping people's spirits up. She and I took it on ourselves to keep a bit of humour going through the proceedings. Even though it got on her nerves that she was largely kept out of the TB discussions with Trimble, because DT didn't really want her involved, she didn't allow it to get her down.

We had the benefit of a media who basically wanted this to work. One of the cameramen said he picked up Mo saying something she shouldn't – Maginnis and the Irish being in 'a paddy' – so he suggested we do it again and wiped the tape. He had also caught her belching on tape, something she did rather too often for most people's taste. I seem to have been taken up by SF as their point man, just as Jonathan was clearly seen by the UUs as their man in the Number 10 team. John Holmes and I were both finding the UUs very hard work. So was Bertie and at one of the joint meetings, I don't know how he didn't end up lamping one of them. They talked about him like he was a piece of dirt at times. I did three big briefings during the day, just really pushing the same basic messages and trying to give a sense of momentum. But by far the most important briefings were the one-on-ones with Denis Murray and Mike Brunson who did a fantastic job getting the balance right and reflecting a lot of the nuances. We all knew that whilst we were in the talks, the parties outside the talks were just watching the telly and following it that way, and by giving Murray and Brunson special treatment we definitely got the media as a whole in a better place.

The midnight deadline we had set just came and went without people really being bothered. Mo was sitting in our office, under the clock. It's gone past midnight, I said. Oh, she said. Oh well. TB said how bad is this if we fail? I did the 'better to have tried' bollocks, but truth be told it would be bad to come this far and fall at what now felt like the last. Come the early hours we started to feel that it was going to fall into place, but none of us quite knew how. There were lots of ups and downs but the mood most of the time felt doable. Nonetheless he asked me to sit down and work out an exit strategy. It would have to be based on the idea of returning for intensive talks. Mo came in and had us falling about with the story of Plum Smith [of the Progressive Unionist Party] asking whether he would get out in two years if he went in and wiped out Trimble. So the black humour was all around us.

TB at breakfast not very optimistic, and convinced maybe we should have kept going last night to get the thing done. When Bertie arrived we were straight back to could we get Strand 2 agreed or not? Trimble had said he was ready to compromise and do a deal but Bertie was pretty sceptical, said I'm not sure I trust these guys. North-South bodies, police and decommissioning were going to be the toughest areas.

1.05pm TB ranting and raving because he wanted to see BA, who was locked in discussions in the SDLP office. There is not one clever person outside this fucking room. His problem was he wanted everyone to work at our pace and to our agenda. E.g. there were times he was suspicious of Joe Lennon giving Bertie the wrong advice, but I pointed out the BBC ran a dire package for the Irish, full of vox pops saying they had to keep Articles 2 and 3 of the Constitution. When the Irish came in, I suggested to TB that he 'turn off the charm tap' and he start to get a bit heavier. The problem was they wanted clear Westminster legislation to set up implementation bodies; otherwise, said Paddy Teahon, it would be just like Sunningdale, built on sand, all too easily collapsible.* Bertie said on the one hand they are expected to change their Constitution – to give up the claim to the North effectively – and yet there is no 'on the other hand' of equal clarity. Bertie said he saw them last night and he knows they will use every trick in the book to stop the N-S bodies happening. We went round in circles. By prior arrangement, TB asked me what the reaction would be if we didn't do a deal. I said Bertie would be crucified. 'They think the other lot are mad anyway, but they think you guys are sane so it would be you that gets crucified if we fall apart over this.' Teahon laughed his head off, but Bertie nodded quietly, and got the point. TB said we had them in the right place on Articles 2 and 3.

Decommissioning was still a problem. Next meeting was DT and Taylor and we had an interminable discussion about N-S bodies, what areas, what they would actually do. TB called up Bertie for a meeting, during which Siobhán O'H came round for a chat. More gallows humour, Jonathan said we'd better get rid of the Taoiseach (meaning finish the meeting). SO'H: 'You don't need to get rid of him.' Jonathan: 'I didn't mean it in your sense of the word.' George Mitchell came in and said he had a document ready for tabling pretty quickly but now Trimble was away with his executive for two hours. Mitchell wanted to give them

---

* The historic agreement signed in 1973 at Sunningdale between the UK, the Republic of Ireland, the UUP, SDLP and Alliance Party of Northern Ireland to set up the ill-fated power-sharing executive which collapsed in May 1974.

half an hour to read it and then have a plenary. He said to TB the difference he had made was in forcing the pace through deadlines. Major would never put a deadline, which meant they would keep us here for ten years if they could.

5.55 Adams, McGuinness, O'Hanlon. In to do some more chiselling. They were not happy. All the big concessions had gone to the Unionists.

A changed Irish Constitution. NI Assembly. Right to veto implementation bodies. McGuinness said what can we point to? TB said changes to UK Constitution, nationalist identity recognized, implementation bodies, changes to policing, prisoners, equality agenda. And he said everything was protected by mutually assured destruction. If the Assembly failed, the whole thing failed. If the implementation bodies didn't happen, the Assembly falls. Adams said the UUs were the perceived winners and them the perceived losers. TB said they had to get over this thing with the spin on it, as if it was a zero-sum game. Everyone could win, but everyone had to compromise. He said 'I've got blood out of a stone from the Unionists, and the points you're making are not persuasive.' Paddy Teahon put his head round the door and said the SDLP were going wobbly. TB said in the past forty-eight hours I've been wondering whether I understand politics at all. Sinn Féin went away then came back, no doubt influenced by *Channel 4 News,* which had too much of the pro-UU spin, and said they would not be able to sell the document as it was. They could not accept the Unionist veto on the implementation bodies. Policing was also a problem. TB said 'I don't accept you can't sell this. This is a programme for change and a lot of the change is to the benefit of your community.' GA said he was a British prime minister speaking. Their audience didn't listen to British prime ministers. TB said this was the best framework for a united Ireland they had ever had – if people wanted it. His voice was rising as Adams' was getting softer. We have dealt with decommissioning on your terms. We did Bloody Sunday – Mo: 'And we applauded you.' TB: 'I appreciate the pressures on you, believe me I do, but this is fundamental change and you would be mad to turn away from it – N–S bodies, consent, new policing, prisoners, equality.' GA said we want to do the best for our people, to end the conflict with hope. TB: 'I cannot tell you how difficult this has been. If you pull out of this now, I don't know where that leaves us.' After they left, Jonathan, optimistic as ever, said it was just a good-cop-bad-cop routine to drag a bit more out of us. TB was downcast, said he felt they weren't able to get it through their heavies and they were going to fall off the end. 'You have to remember they are negotiating with at least a modicum of worry someone will come along and blow their brains out if they go too far.'

7.30 SDLP, Hume worried about the feasibility studies re N-S bodies. No, no, said TB, it means the six bodies will be set up by the time of the Assembly. He gave them the same line re mutually assured destruction but they were not convinced. TB asked me to get out a briefing for the later bulletins that there is a battle between an irresistible force and an immovable object. 'The irresistible force is the legacy and the baggage. The immovable object is me.' Seamus Mallon had a good line. 'Enough is never enough for those who think that enough is too little.' I said get Clinton engaged. TB – To say what? To tell them nobody will understand if they walk away over this. TB said we weren't cooked enough yet. 'They're deciding everything according to the spin of the others. It's pathetic. Yesterday the nationalists' tails were up. Why? Because the UUs were going round with long faces and saying everyone was against them. Today, one good headline in the *Belfast Telegraph* for Trimble and the other lot are going round like the world has ended. It's ludicrous.'

8pm I drafted an exit strategy, two notes, one from TB, one from Mitchell, saying how far we had come and how we would come back to it soon.

8.10 Trimble, Taylor, Reg Empey. They were in better mood, which John [Holmes] rightly took as a bad sign, because the other lot would be falling off the end. Rumours started of another DT triumph – Assembly to decide the implementation bodies, and it was running far too much in their favour. I got in Mike Brunson and Denis Murray and for the third time in a day did a very greenified briefing, stressing the implementation bodies could be up and running at the same time as the Assembly itself. I also reduced them to hysterics by saying, with a straight face, that they had to ignore the spin and just listen to me. All our problems today were really started by the headline in the *Belfast Telegraph*. The UUs reacted too positively and SF too negatively. It was just another fucking story in the end, I said to McGuinness. He said at one point to TB 'Believe me, this is not a threat, but they could return to violence.' Murray's reports were brilliant today, got the balance and the nuances and the little shifts. Bertie went off to a Mass, during which Paddy T came in with some more changes on Strand 2. 'No, no, I can't,' said TB. Bertie said he had to be sure SF were going to be on board. TB was worried Bertie was not getting enough out of the media stuff so I tried to correct it with Brunson, re the point about Westminster legislation, but he went OTT and said the UUs had made a massive concession to the Irish, so then we had a counter-problem with DT. I called Joe Lennon to make sure he had seen it, and make sure he understood we were trying to push the boat out for Bertie. He said SF were trying to persuade them the point about legislation was a concession TO the UUs, not by them. It was like walking a connecting web of tightropes. I called Siobhán O'H and said we were trying our best to get the spin in the right place for them to do what they had to do.

10.30 TB very down again because they were all off doing their own thing. John Holmes had come back with a whole load more Strand 2 changes from the

Irish. He had a list of twenty implementation bodies they wanted. John lay down on the sofa, just shaking his head. TB: 'I've been wasting my time.' John said it has all been about keeping SF on board. TB said they will push the UUs off board again.

10.40 Bertie and Mo came in to go through the list. TB just listened, pretty stony-faced. Again, we had the odd light moment to help us through. An Irish official called Wally [Wally Kieran, deputy secretary in the Dept. of the Taoiseach] came in and said we should remove food safety from the list 'because the Irish government is not quite ready for it.' Bertie: 'We are going to poison everyone instead.' TB sat shaking his head with his arms folded as we went through them one by one. Arts. It's out. Language. They won't wear that. Paddy suddenly piped up. 'It's all quite simple. 1. Get Strand 1 sorted. 2. Do the deal with Trimble on Strand 2. 3. Get Clinton to force Sinn Féin into line.' TB just sighed and looked like he wanted to curl up into a ball. John H was almost asleep on the sofa. Jonathan was still smiling. Nick Matthews was in and out with food and drink. After they left, TB just said 'Fuck, fuck, fuck.'

11.28 DT came back. John Taylor was with him and rather cheerily announced there was a new death threat out against him. They had had a good meeting with the SDLP and felt we could make progress. Again we had to listen to the minutest detail of the smallest ideas for the bodies we were talking about. But at least the mood was better. They left at 11.50 and TB and I fell into hysterics again, putting on our best Irish accents and wondering what new bodies we could come up with – the waste-paper bin emptying body, the screwing tops off bottles body. They had been banging on about closing the Maryfield office block*, and I set TB off, saying why has Scotland's rugby ground suddenly become a crucial part of the negotiations? It was all designed just to keep us going through the low moments, of which we sensed there were more to come as we got tired. Mo's private secretary, Ken Lindsay, called me and Jonathan out to tell us [Ian] Paisley and 400 of his friends were in the grounds and marching to the press tent to be there at midnight. It would actually serve as a good media distraction for a while as the deadline passed. We called Clinton and asked him to be on standby to make calls to Adams and Hume and maybe DT.

Friday, April 10

12.15 John H and Jonathan met with Dermot Gallagher [Irish diplomat] and Paddy Teahon and the Irish were saying they couldn't change a word of Strand 3.

---

* Maryfield, location of the Irish Secretariat in Belfast, became an issue in the talks. AC thereafter referred to it as Murrayfield, Scotland's rugby ground.

They were spooked by Sinn Féin. I said they could not possibly do a deal on prisoners if SF were not part of the deal. People just would not understand it. TB suggested a four-way meeting with Bertie, DT and Hume. He now believed SF were pulling the plug because they didn't want a deal at all. Nothing had changed on Strand 2, but they were holding the whole thing to ransom. Mo was trying to calm him down, but he was really aerated. GA has gone right down in my estimation.

12.30 TB spoke to Bertie. SF were stuck on three years for prisoner release. There was no way we could do a deal on prisoner release without SF being on board for the rest of it all. I suggested we make it clear prisoner release only applies to groups who are fully signed up to the deal.

1.10 DT and Taylor in to argue about the size of the Assembly.

1.45 Bertie plus his key officials, to discuss the weight of voting in Assembly. Mo said 18 x 6 plus a civic forum was fair and just. TB: 'We'd better reject it then.' Laughter. Joe Lennon: 'He's learning.' We were still arguing re Irish language.

2.15 Hume and Mallon re the size of the Assembly. I asked Hume to see DT and appeal directly re the Irish language. TB asked Hume what SF were up to. He said it was all about prisoners. They basically want them out in one year, and think they will end up with two. TB said this can only be sold as a meaningful agreement if they are signed up to all of it.

2.30 David Ervine et al. UUP were saying voting weight 18 x 5, Ervine 18 x 6. TB was suddenly worried that we had told Hume we were prepared to offer one year for prisoners. When he told Bertie he had done it, he panicked a bit and got Hume back to say he was worried and, for now, forget he had said it. Mo was also of the view that we were giving away too much too soon. [Jeffrey] Donaldson was being pretty difficult about everything. TB asked me to go with him to see their people, and said I should interject at the right moment that they will be crucified if they suddenly throw in new problems now. George Mitchell said even for these guys, they were being ridiculous. I asked him if he intended to write a book about the talks. 'No, the truth would be too awful for words.'

3.10 TB finally said get Clinton.

3.15 UDP. Gary McMichael said they wanted 18 x 5 plus a top-up.

3.25 TB and DT, Trimble for once without his other people. TB had another go at getting the Irish-language promotion [body] in and equality of treatment out. We had a long lecture about the history of Ullans, the Ulster-Scots language.

3.37 TB spoke to Clinton. 'Where are we?' asked Bill. TB said we had been going non-stop for three days. We were close to a deal, and had been for some time. The problem is every time we get close to a bottom line, a new one comes up. SF have an issue on prisoners, and on language. They want their prisoners out in a year. They want to put together a long list, which they just want to throw in at the last minute. They are playing silly buggers. They have suddenly come up with a new list of amendments days and days into the negotiations. He said he was worried they were getting nervous about doing a deal at all. Nothing has changed except the UUs are on board and when they're on board, SF feel they can't be. BC asked about the [Irish] language issue and as TB tried to explain it to him, it was clear there was no way we could let this be a stumbling block. It was crazy. Bill asked if TB wanted him to call. TB suggested he call Bertie and emphasize the big changes they have won here. There is no way we can do the deal on prisoners unless SF sign up to the whole agreement. Our public opinion would rightly say what the hell is going on if we gave them that, and still they were not recommending the whole package. TB said the Irish and SDLP were happy. It was now about putting the pressure on SF. TB ran through the areas we had conceded on and it was a long list. But he still felt best to hold BC back from SF for now. Bill said there is nothing more important to me right now than this. Call me whenever, even if it means waking me up.

3.50 Clinton was ready to call Bertie. Paddy T was still pushing on language. For the first time, I detected Mo being pretty down, when she said she wasn't convinced they were serious. Adams was still holding out on some of the stuff they put in at the last minute. TB asked Mo to go and see him and tell GA he was 'staggered' at the way he was behaving. Paddy said there was no need, it was better we left the Taioseach to deal with him.

4.10 John H called Sandy Berger and briefed him for the Clinton calls. John was worried that if the side letter to DT on decommissioning was leaked we would be accused of playing the Orange card.

TB decided not to see Adams. Nick Matthews came in with a huge plateload of bacon sandwiches. Mo was doing the toing and froing between GA, who was clearly pissed off TB was not doing it himself. Mo had six issues they were still concerned with. They wanted a department of equality. TB was eating bacon sandwiches and bananas, and beginning to look a bit grey.

4.18 TB/BC. Bill had made some calls and said it was time to move for it. He said Adams was nervous about being blamed for collapse. He was trying to squeeze down to six months. TB said we were always at two years. BC said DT was 'really tight-assed'. He had slept so was rational. He had more energy. He was looking for something because he felt Adams had done better.

4.30 Another Clinton call: 'Hell, I'd rather be on holiday with Kenneth Starr than hanging out with these guys.' He said SF were moving to the deal, thought TB had done a great job, but we had to watch the UUs running away once GA said yes. TB called DT and said we have to do this now, otherwise it is going away. DT was in one of his distant modes, not really engaging. We had a problem when it seemed Donaldson was trying to engineer some kind of vote against DT but Trimble called and said he was going for it.

5am John Hume in for a chat. He makes TB nervous re prisoners. After he's left, TB says he's worried how DT and [Lord] Alderdice will react. Mo, now looking exhausted, said her officials were saying the prisoners deal would be really hard to get.

5.35 We agreed BC should call Adams, and we briefed he should set out how difficult the prisoners issue was, unless they signed up to the whole deal. Bill got the point straight away and was on the phone to him immediately. It felt, finally, like it was falling into place. We were now working with Bertie on Adams and McGuinness with the officials kept out. They finally left at 7.30. Mitchell McLaughlin [general secretary of Sinn Féin] was being a bit more positive at the press briefing, and again the press got a sense we were going the right way. TB just about persuaded them on prisoners. Then Gerry read out another list of demands and TB laughed and said he was not prepared to negotiate any more. 'You are a compulsive negotiator, Gerry. This is a balanced package and you know it.' We then sat down to try and pin him down re his public reaction, which was going to be important. He was fine, if tricky. They said it was important I do my best to spin it positively for them, and said several times they would have to get it through their conference. McG was not saying much and I detected a little bit of anger directed at Bertie, but BA was brilliant at taking flak from the lot of them.

8.10 If you had to pin me down and ask me to explain how it suddenly came together, I couldn't, but by 8.10 I was in the press tent briefing that basically we had a done deal, that it was huge, historic, ginormous, all that stuff. I felt really quite emotional and had to hold myself together. I could see in some of the NI hacks too a real deep emotion, and a desire for this to be true. Even some of the real cynics from London who had managed to stay awake all night were almost wholly positive. Ted Oliver [ex-*Mirror* colleague] was there, [Donald] Macintyre [*Independent* political commentator], [Mike] Brunson seemed genuinely quite moved too. Jonathan paged me to say it had all gone through the plenary.

Amazing, unbelievable. I actually felt like crying but held it together. The final TB, BA, GA, MMcG meetings were crucial and I did my best to spin for the Shinners without pushing the other lot too far off the other side. The whole thing nearly came unstuck over a fuck-up over the wretched implementation bodies, because by mistake the Irish-language promotion (Trimble's staff's fault) and export promotion (our fault) were back in the fucking list. We then had another history lesson from DT on the importance of Ullans. TB could not believe what he was hearing. I said why can't we just say it is promotion of Celtic languages? Because Ullans is not a Celtic tongue, said DT. We had effectively announced the deal was done, give or take a bit or two at the edges and here we were, with DT ready to unpick the whole thing over this. TB said at one point 'We are dealing with the Afrikaner mentality. They're tired, they're scared and they're panicking.'

We then had to sort out access for the ceremony at the end. I was so desperate for us to get away that I said no filming, but Denis Murray rightly persuaded me that would be a mistake, that something as big as this had to be on film. I said we would allow cameras in for the main speeches. We crafted a couple of strong sound bites for TB, though truth be told we were knackered and desperate to get away. TB and Bertie did the signing ceremony, and the closeness between them in their farewells was obvious. In the car out I asked TB if he was tired. He just shrugged and said he needed a break. He said Gale [mother-in-law] would probably have given away Gibraltar by now.*

As we got into the helicopter Jonathan said the Queen wanted to talk to TB but we couldn't make the call pre take-off. TB thanked his staff for once, said everyone had been terrific and should be proud of what we had done. He was on a bit of a high now. I worked on a briefing note for the Sundays which I'd just about done by the time we got dropped at Northolt and then TB headed on to Spain. He talked to the Queen from the tarmac. Brunson called me and said thanks for all the help I'd given him. He said we did a great job and he found the whole thing really quite moving. I got home, wired and exhausted, and still trying to remember how it all came together at the end.

I have often been asked what were the low points and high points of my time with TB. The feeling on that plane as we flew out from Belfast was probably the high point. It had barely seemed possible just a few days earlier. There have been plenty of accounts of these crucial days written, but just as at the time I could not really work out how it all came together as it did, so I can't now. Most of the participants have been asked what lessons might be applied to other peace processes — indeed Jonathan Powell runs a charity dedicated to just such work. But one clear lesson is the need for absolute and determined focus by those in direct charge — in this case the two governments and Senator Mitchell. Rarely, for example, has the Middle East peace process had such commitment from those who have the greatest power to make a difference. The other lesson is the power of deadlines, and sleep deprivation. Many deadlines have been missed along the way, and yet they nonetheless concentrated minds, and once it was clear TB and BA were planning on staying in that awful building for as long as it took, the other parties' sense of urgency increased.

---

* The Blair family were in Spain at the holiday home of the Spanish prime minister, José Maria Aznar.

There are lessons too in understanding the role of the media to help or hinder progress. It was terrifying at times the extent to which the main parties, particularly the UUs and Sinn Féin, would allow their mood and indeed their tactics to be driven by the last news bulletin or the last headline. It meant that the briefing of what was going on inside the talks could have a direct impact on the next steps for the talks. But the other crucial ingredient, surely, was luck. Hard work, yes, never giving up, certainly, clever people having the wit and inventiveness to create the words and situations that would unblock the seemingly unblockable.

But none of that was ever going to be enough. The luck, I believe, came in the extraordinary collection of personalities who happened to be in the most relevant positions at the time. TB and Bertie, and their respective teams, Mo and David Andrews, Adams and McGuinness, Trimble and the often discordant group he travelled with, John Hume and Seamus Mallon, the leaders of the smaller parties, and crucially the 'leader of the Western world'. Any American president is always likely to carry a certain weight and authority in any situation. But the peace process was lucky to have Bill Clinton in office at the time of these talks. Lucky to have someone with a passion for the cause, who understood the detail as well as anyone, and who was clear from the word go that when push came to shove, he was up for doing whatever it took. When push came to shove, he did a fair bit of the shoving, and helped take the deal over the line.

Saturday, April 11

I felt totally shagged out, that awful mix of being completely wired whilst still having to work on to make sure the thing came out in the right place, so though I wanted just to be with the kids, it was hard because the phone never stopped. TB called just before 8, and sounded exhausted. He said we did something bloody good there, but we have to keep on the case. By which he meant I had to keep on the case. He said Aznar's place was fantastic, and the family were having a great time.

We felt the need to keep TB's voice in there today, so I got Peter Wilkinson [Downing Street press officer] to fix an interview with the local [Spain] BBC guy. There was a lot of scope for talking up the others, e.g. Bertie and the role BC played as it fell together. I said to TB, can you remember how it all fell into place? Not really, he said, but it did, I always felt it would. Bill came in at the right time, no doubt. I took one of the lines BC used in his phone calls for TB's words – time for the men of vision to defeat the men of history.

The Sundays were all after every spit and fart so I organized to do a conference call – seemed to go on for ages, but I could tell from their tone, even the total wankers, that they realized they were dealing with a pretty special story. They wanted loads of stuff – low points, high points, how we ate, who took notes, all the colour stuff. I did a bit extra with a couple of the broadsheets and wanted to give a real plug to John H and Jonathan. Jonathan was at his best in these types of situations. He never seemed to get down like TB and I did, and strangely the thing that people criticized him for – a lack of feel for politics – was sometimes what was needed, because he had a way of cutting through crap and when we said you can't do that, he would just say why not, and we would start thinking.

I took the boys to a birthday party where news came through the UUs had backed it two to one. Fantastic. The FCO sent through a digest of some of the coverage and reaction around the world, which was enormous and positive. PG called and said TB had moved up several notches on the world scene. I was starting to feel a bit more human but still exhausted. TB called before and after his interview, which went fine. He sounded revived already. His capacity to revive on a few hours' rest was a real asset, which I wish I had. He spoke to Bill C and also to Major, which helped stand up the line in my briefing that we didn't rule out TB and JM campaigning together to sell the deal.

I was so consumed with NI I had not quite realized how bad the floods in the Midlands were, and how the image of TB sunning himself in Spain contrasted with the misery there. I spoke to JP, who was having a weekend in Chester. I said I was worried this would move quickly to what was the government doing about it? He got the point straight away and got on to his office to get them to organize a visit tomorrow.

Sunday, April 12

The papers were good, still heavily focused on Ireland and the briefing of yesterday came out well. TB called from Cordoba, said there were a lot of photographers around and should he be pictured playing a guitar? No. He spoke to Kofi Annan and also to [William] Hague, who did a pretty good interview. JP's visit went well and he was pleased he had done it.

Tuesday, April 14

TB called re whether he should do a doorstep in Madrid tomorrow. I wasn't convinced, but his constant refrain at the moment was how big he was out there, so he was bound to do it. The press were starting to pick over the NI deal much more aggressively.

Paisley was dominating the news all day with the launch of his No campaign. He still has the capacity to put over a point with real force, and he was not to be underestimated. At the moment he was on big picture, but there was detail he would get into as we went along. David Kerr from Trimble's office called, said they were getting real grief re prisoner release. I got a note through to TB to address prisoners in his doorstep, to the effect that they would be out on licence, straight back in if they reoffend.

TB back, and was doing a visit in Croydon. He called and said he was confident re NI. It actually helped that Adams was keeping his counsel, because it helped DT say to the Unionist community there was something here the other side didn't feel happy with. It was dreadful that was how we had to operate, but the reality. He was worried that the *Telegraph* and the *Mail* were straight on to what was undoubtedly the weak point of all this – decommissioning. We had danced around it for now but it would come back. Re the briefings I was doing, he wanted me to keep going with bolstering DT even if it meant pandering a little.

For most of the day, I was reading up on the upcoming TB visit to the Middle East, and getting an agreed briefing line written. The breakthrough in NI was a great backdrop, though we had to watch 'Blair peacemaker' stuff, which was bound to set the bar too high.

I fixed up for TB to do three NI interviews, just to keep the pot boiling. TB was worried the see-saw was dipping too far the other way. But Donaldson was making reasonably encouraging noises and DT seemed OK. TB also spoke to Adams on the way to the airport, and he seemed OK, though Mo had told me that TB – or 'Blair' as she called him – had to be careful not to look like he was only worried about keeping the UUs on board, because GA was more vulnerable than he liked to admit. The Middle East briefing had gone fine, and the visit was fairly well set up.

In Cairo news came through of a shooting in Belfast.* The media were

---

* Mark McNeill (32), a former member of the Irish National Liberation Army (INLA), was shot dead by two gunmen as he got out of a taxi on Shaw's Road in west Belfast. McNeill was a father of five. (It was believed that the attack was a 'grudge killing'

desperate for TB to react, but we refused. No point. I called Mo, who said it may have been a punishment beating that went wrong. A week on from NI, the reverberations were still being felt.

We went to see the press on the plane to Saudi Arabia. I was being vile to Rachel Sylvester about the *Telegraph's* coverage of the Northern Ireland agreement. They were determined to do whatever they could to unpick it. TB did a doorstep on the UUP successful vote [David Trimble secured the critical support of his party]. In talks with the Saudis they went over MEPP, trade, Ireland, defence.

Sunday, April 19

[In Israel] TB, Netanyahu [Prime Minister], me and my opposite number went through to BN's inner office. TB was trying to pin him down re saying he would engage on the US proposals. We got him to agree he would say he would be willing to come to London within a month to discuss, but the mood we got was that he would not agree to them. So it was progress but only of sorts. They both did fine at the press conference, and certainly our lot felt it was a big story, but the experts knew better, including one who tried to wind me up at the briefing afterwards.

TB was back into superman mode. He said if I had three days with these people all in a room, I reckon I could crack this [the Middle East situation]. John H and I both laughed. He also felt there was a lot more to Bibi [familiar name for Netanyahu] than met the eye. I failed to see it. I called home and Fiona said everyone seemed to be saying TB had solved the Middle East. It was going a bit too far all this, and I felt we were walking the high wire. The dinner was pretty dire, both the food and the conversation. I didn't find Netanyahu impressive, but he definitely had the best-looking secretary I had ever seen in a leader's office.

Wednesday, April 22

TB spoke to, and later wrote to, [Sir] Alistair Graham [chairman] of the Parades Commission [for Northern Ireland] to say he felt he should postpone their preliminary report of the Commission. Though technically we didn't know what it

involving former INLA members and there was speculation that the killing may have been drugs-related.) [CAIN]

APRIL '98: TB IN 'SUPERMAN MODE' ON MIDDLE EAST TRIP   121 was going to say, in practice we did. We knew it was going to upset the Unionists, not least re Drumcree, and he didn't want that right now. I spoke to Graham and drafted a statement and we just about got it under control. Graham wanted to publish TB's letter and we could not really object to that. Hague did beef on the bone and Ireland at PMQs.

Thursday, April 23

Cabinet was mainly Ireland and then a political discussion. TB was very nice re Mo, said it took a very special personality to absorb what she did from all the various parties and she had been heroic. Re the Agreement, he said we have a design for the building, but now we have to build it and there will be a lot of difficulties along the way. He said every time one side is on board, the other starts to get flaky. GB was doing an economic package for the province. Mo lavished praise on TB and, more surprisingly, on Trimble, said he had finally shown real leadership. TB reported on his Middle East trip, said it was altogether more tricky.

I went to the [Labour Party fund-raising] gala dinner at the Hilton. There were not that many ministers but there was a good turnout generally and TB spoke well. I chatted to [David] Montgomery [chief executive, Mirror Group newspapers] re N Ireland. He thought we had made a mistake interfering in the parades but also felt media-wise we were getting away with it.

Friday, April 24

I was feeling exhausted and a bit depressed and called in to say I was staying at home. Mo called late. She said she was due to speak to TB in the morning and she wanted to alert me to what it was about as it could become a big problem. Someone had leaked to Peter Robinson the fact that Sinn Féin, after being tipped off, had discovered a bug inside [Sinn Féin negotiator for Good Friday Agreement] Gerry Kelly's home.

Saturday, April 25

TB and Mo spoke on a secure line and we agreed we should just say we didn't comment on intelligence matters, which everyone would basically take as confirmation. But there was not much else we could do. I took the boys to Bournemouth vs Burnley but had too many interruptions.

I felt totally deadened. I'm writing this on Wednesday because I have had so little energy in the last few days. The only good thing today was when Rory came in [to Downing Street] at 6 and I took him to Crystal Palace 0 Man U 3. We saw Alex before and he picked up on my mood too, said I looked pressured and down. I said I was. I had barely spoken in the morning strategy meeting. PG was briefing us on the local elections polling. TB said the problem remained that we do not have a big-picture economic narrative that binds the government.

TB had a long meeting with Adams and McGuinness. The bugging row was a difficult backdrop but they didn't seem that bothered. We did schools, language, troop levels, 'signs of occupation' on the ground, plastic bullets, access to the House, prisoners. Mo, Adams and McGuinness came to my office afterwards to agree a line, which was easy enough and as ever they were a mix of charm, friendliness with the occasional hint of menace. McG and I talked about football. I found him more straightforward to deal with than Gerry.

I told TB that Fiona and I were having a bad time together, and I was really worried where it was heading. I said whether it was true or not, she felt the job was responsible and it was kind of hard to disagree with that. He said there was no greater priority than sorting it out. We were a great couple and I would be totally lost without her, he said. I said I was fully aware of that but it was really difficult just now. The *Telegraph* had the story of [Chris] Patten getting the policing commission job [chair of the Independent Commission on Policing for Northern Ireland]. The story was right but it was irritating it was out there. We had to confirm it without confirming it. TB saw a few hacks and did an interview with a very irritating Roy Hattersley [Deputy Leader of the Labour Party], who seemed dreadfully upset that TB had said he was moved by [the Steven Spielberg film] *Schindler's List*. I'd long thought Hattersley was fairly superficial. I asked Godric [Smith] to do the four o'clock, partly as a test for him, but in truth because I was feeling really depressed now. I struggled through the day then left early for home, and Fiona was pretty down too.

I was feeling better. I went in with Jonathan and felt myself coming back into gear. I told Godric he'd got the job as my deputy. Tim [Allan] spoke very well at his farewell, said that Peter M was still a friend of his, which was quite something because Tim wasn't even a minor member of the Royal Family. John H called and said the IRA were putting out a statement which would sound worse than it was.

Thursday, April 30

I stayed home a bit late to be with Grace opening her presents. I was conscious of the fact I was home with her a lot less than when the boys were little. We were still trying to decode the IRA statement. It was coming over as very negative in the media, but those who know about these things reckoned it was possible they were trying to signal they would sign up to most of the Agreement. Mo came over and we drafted a line for her to put out as a press release and then a doorstep post-Cabinet. We presented it as a very clear message to the IRA they had to give up violence for good, but also making clear we should not link decommissioning directly to release of prisoners. TB was angry that GA had allowed decommissioning to become the issue for both sides and he was worried the Tories might start to pull the plug. He asked Mo to speak to Gerry A. She said she had already spoken to McG and when he said they had not been aware the IRA statement was coming, she just said 'Oh fuck off Martin.' Adams is in danger of fucking this up. TB was still pretty steamed up when we left for Northolt.

Friday, May 1

The one-year-on review pieces had if anything got better as the week went on. The *Express* did four pages, and pretty positive. Even the *Guardian* had a pretty good leader. We had done an article in there which we used as the basic message for TB's *GMTV* and IRN [Independent Radio News] interviews – lot of good progress, lots more to do, values. We went back to the flat and he made some eggs on toast and we just sat about chewing the fat for a while. He was worried the economy might tip. He was worried the NI situation was really unstable. The *Telegraph* was at it again, saying TB had said no decommissioning meant no seat in the Assembly, the very hook we did not want to get caught on.

Sunday, May 3

TB repeatedly compared the ECB [this weekend saw the often brutal EU summit, chaired by TB, to decide who should head the new European Central Bank] with the Good Friday Agreement, saying that just when you thought you were there, someone came in with a new problem to fuck it up. The whole thing was pretty unedifying and it was definitely the end of the 'Blair walks on water in Europe' phase.

The main story of the day was going to be Ireland, with TB and John Major doing a joint Q&A tonight. PMQs was largely local elections stuff, but Hague went on the decommissioning point re NI, and TB thanked him 'for his support'. He was furious afterwards, felt Hague was just dicking around under a bit of internal pressure. We left for Northolt and on the plane over did an interview with Des McCartan [*Belfast Telegraph*]. He felt the No campaign was stepping up and the Yes campaign going largely by default. TB was good on the vision thing, had a good whack at Paisley and tried to send reassuring signals re consent, prisoners etc. Major was already at the Waterfront Hall and had earlier made a good speech. JM was a bit nervy, unfailingly polite as ever, though there was always an edge when I was around. 'He really hates you,' said TB. 'He prefers to blame you for doing him in than face the fact that we beat him fair and square.' But they both did well, and the interaction was pretty good with the kids. I could never take JM too seriously but he had a good manner, and was clearly on top of the issues. The sight of them together was a powerful one and I sensed it would have the desired effect in terms of impact.

TB met the Parades Commission and had to do a big number to reassure them of their independence. Then to the RUC where Ronnie Flanagan was very friendly in private but where TB walked in in total silence, and I sensed a bit of antagonism. It was a little better as we left, but warm it was not. Back at Mo's office, we had a meeting with [Jeffrey] Donaldson* and six young anti-Good Friday Agreement voters. TB was alarmed afterwards – they were clearly bright and reasonable and if we couldn't get people like them behind it, we had a problem. As they filed out, I asked Donaldson if there were any circumstances in which they might vote yes. He said maybe but it was hard to see what they were. I said would they not respond to leadership? He smiled.

On the way to the airport, TB was worried. He said he was worried the NIO and Mo found the Unionists such a pain in the arse they didn't show enough sensitivity to legitimate concerns. He had been shocked to be told more compensation

---

* Donaldson was one of the Ulster Unionist negotiating team for the Good Friday Agreement, but was now part of the faction within the party campaigning against it, arguing there was no link between proposed Sinn Féin representation in government and IRA decommissioning.

went to prisoners than victims and he wanted a victims' fund launched. He was going to have to get more involved than we originally envisaged in the campaign. So was Clinton, even if the UUs said they were opposed. Idiotic. He was the best campaigner there was and would definitely shift votes towards us. TB felt we had to target people like the young people we met today. They were not bad people. They were also potential Assembly members. They were not unreasonable, yet they were intending to vote with Paisley. We had to win them round.

He said he would not be happy unless we had a majority of nationalists and a majority of Unionists. Their main beef was that they didn't really believe the IRA would give up violence and they saw Adams and McGuinness as central to that. They could not stomach seeing them in government, no matter what they said. The prisoners issue was really tough and as TB tried to reassure them, I could tell he was recalling in his mind the phone call with Gerry A earlier, who reminded him he had said they would all be out within one year. Aaaargh. TB said they would never have got an agreement without a deal on prisoners but it was not easy to persuade them.

Donaldson said they had to say the war is over. Those words. And mean it. And be seen to mean it. He said the lines between violent and non-violent were too blurred. Prison officers, police officers, witnesses, magistrates, everyone who knew their ways felt physically sick at the thought of these people in power. TB said he had to show some leadership, take on the Paisleyites. He said it was the one thing he woke up in the night about, the thought that we get the Agreement passed but Paisley wins enough support to undo it.

Remarkably quickly, the excitement and hope from Good Friday had been replaced by anxiety. The visit with John Major went well, but some of the fundamentals – in particular from this entry Unionist suspicion of a sell-out to the nationalists, their wariness re Mo and the NIO, Tory fixation upon decommissioning, ambiguity about prisoner release – made us realize that the campaign for widespread support for the Good Friday Agreement would not be easily won. TB believed from the outset that there had to be majority support from both the nationalist and Unionist communities, and he worried a combination of Paisley's campaigning skills, basic Unionist anxiety and NIO insensitivity could lead to an erosion of the widespread support for the Agreement when it was first struck. It meant that we went onto a campaign war footing, run along similar lines to an election campaign. Good Friday may have been a high point, but it was far from the end point of a process with many ups and downs to come.

Today was the first of the daily conference calls with the key NIO people, me, John H and Jonathan to try to keep pushing on an agreed strategy to win the arguments and votes on the GFA [Good Friday Agreement]. Today, following the meeting with Donaldson, we were going to focus on the new government fund for victims.

Cabinet was fairly brief. Afterwards GB and I went through to Number 11 and agreed we had to move quickly re the economic package for Northern Ireland, and maybe do the Sundays on it. He also agreed I could go straight out and do the victims' package, which I briefed directly as a response to the concerns of the Donaldson group last night. The DUP came out instantly, saying it was a bribe, which helped give it legs on the lunchtimes. The media bit straight away. We were going to have to make this a news-driven campaign. The overall narrative had to become about TB persuading and winning over the Unionists.

TB was seeing the Orange Order, who were difficult but I sensed even some of them were persuadable. He was very good at presenting the arguments and some left a lot less hostile than they arrived. The crunch point was coming around prisoners, decommissioning and the right to sit in the Assembly. They were looking for legislative expression of the links between them so that GA could not take a seat until it was clear there had been decommissioning and an end to violence, and that there could be no release of prisoners without it either. I kept thinking of, and shuddering about, GA's reminder on the phone of what TB said in the early hours of Good Friday – that they could be all out in a year.

I tried to have a day off but the calls started just after 7, and carried on most of the day, mainly on the local elections. We did reasonably well and TB did a good doorstep. Out of the NI conference call, we agreed I would call Trimble and get up the line that Paisley was the man who would say no to anything that brought progress, which the media would pick up and run with as Dr No. I was also keen we start putting the US into the equation. I saw the [US] ambassador last night and explained the UUs were being resistant to Clinton being involved, but was confident we would win them round. Getting up the economic package was the best first start. We told the Treasury they had to improve the economic plan presented yesterday, and we asked NIO to plan for another TB visit next Thursday.

We were also getting into trouble over the TB/Hague/Paddy Ashdown visit to NI. Everyone seemed to think it was a bad idea but we had no idea how to get out of it. The UUs felt Paddy might shift a bit of support but they didn't think Hague would. They worried the overall image was of Westminster telling them what to do.

GB was on *Frost*. I suggested he really push to get up the NI economic package as a broadcast story. GB said it would be more than £100m. He was also asked about the [Paul] Routledge [journalist, *Daily Mirror*] book* and for the first time he said there was no deal and we reached the right decision when TB became leader. It was a good strong interview for all kinds of reasons – good on general message, good on personal, and he did the NI stuff really well.

Sinn Féin had their special conference on the Agreement and the positive vote – 95 per cent – was even bigger than we anticipated. It made TB more determined than ever that we had to get a majority of the Unionist population. I wanted to get Clinton's response to be that SF would never be welcome again if there was a return to violence, but could not track down McCurry. The vote was so big it was likely to set us back with the Unionists for a while. In our reaction, we were cautious but emphasized they had now signed up to the principle of consent.

The Irish government had let out the Balcombe Street Gang[†] for forty-eight hours and they got a heroes' welcome, while Mo had let out four as well, including the IRA leader in the Maze. The sight of Adams and McGuinness out with the Balcombe St Gang [Adams described the four as 'our Nelson Mandelas'] was awful, even if the overall effect was 'The war is over'. But their refusal to say the words clearly was a continuing problem. I went round to PG's. Peter M came over too. PG said that I was a lot less popular with the press than a year ago, that a lot of them thought I was arrogant and dismissive. I suppose the problem was I found it hard to hide contempt.

Ireland was a disaster area. A combination of the Balcombe Street Gang plus the IRA leaders out of the Maze was about as bad as it could get for the strategy we were trying to pursue. Mo had let the Maze guys out without us knowing,

---

* *Mandy: The Unauthorised Biography of Peter Mandelson*
† Eddie Butler, Hugh Doherty, Harry Duggan and Joe O'Connell were part of an IRA Active Service Unit involved in the bombing of London in the mid 1970s. After a six-day siege in Balcombe Street, Marylebone, the four released two hostages they had taken, surrendered and were imprisoned in 1977.

which was ridiculous. It was a side favour Mo did for Adams, I suspect, but it was disasterville for the Unionist votes we were after. David Kerr called from Trimble's office. Even though DT could be very old-womany, he had a point when he said this was as bad a move as we could have made. It had prisoners, past outrages, SF confidence and two fingers to the rest of you all wrapped up in one. Mo was not nearly sensitive enough to the UU side of things, because she found DT irritating. But this showed a lack of judgement, also evident on the *Today* programme when she made a crack about how people were let out if their granny died, and that this had been necessary to get the vote up for the Agreement. TB was livid all round.

He asked John H to do a note to the NIO both on the substance but also why we had not been properly consulted. I said we had to be careful about leaks, and people would be appalled at the fact we had not even known this was happening. Mo had gone up to the North-East with TB on the train on Friday and had not even mentioned it – unbelievable.

We did our conference call with the NIO, and were pushing the economic package. I finally got hold of Mike McCurry and Jim Steinberg to get out the line that Clinton was making clear that he saw this as an irreversible moment, that there could be no going back to violence and if they did, he was through with them. Mike got Steinberg out of a meeting and as ever he wanted to tone down what I was saying but we got pretty much what we wanted. Godric was doing the 11 and I drafted lines on NI.

TB had a [Belfast] Downtown Radio phone-in, which Eamonn Mallie [journalist] did very well. There was a good balance of tough but fair questions and TB hit all the right Unionist buttons. Definitely worth doing. He was very reassuring on prisoners, decommissioning and seats in the Assembly. It wouldn't take long for the other lot to complain, but TB felt we really had to push the boat out at the moment. The four o'clock was hard work. I did Northern Ireland up front, which went fine.

Whereas TB had been pretty tolerant of Mo's visit to the Maze a few weeks earlier, her decision to release a group of prisoners provoked real fury from him. He had been developing the opinion that neither she, nor some of her NIO advisers, paid sufficient attention to Unionist concerns, and that this had the potential to do real damage to the Unionist support for the Agreement. Mo would not have been human had the near contempt some of the UUs showed for her at times not got to her, but he felt this revealed poor judgement. It was also, in all likelihood, another expression of Mo's frustration at TB's dominance in the process, a desire to do something that was her decision alone, not dictated by Downing Street. TB had been clear that we had to operate as though during an election campaign, with proper central coordination, and thought given to every word and action.

I started the day in a foul mood and it got worse as the day went on. Ireland was still a real problem as we were trying to get off the decommissioning hook while trying to give the UUs the legislative expression they wanted. I was working on TB's Ireland speech with John H, and every word had to be weighed carefully now. I was getting more tired and irritable and although everyone in the office told me not to lose it at the 4, I gave them another whack.

Don Macintyre took me for a cup of tea and said I had to calm down. I said I was sick of dealing with wankers. Why should I pretend to respect them when I didn't? There were only half a dozen I would give the time of day to if I didn't have to see them every day. I told him the politicians were getting on my nerves too, and I was thinking of quitting. It was the first time I had articulated that. I had a cup of tea with Betty Boothroyd up in her residence. She was really nice, said she was very pro me, and not to worry about all the MPs who were having a go, they were basically doing it because I was good at my job. She advised me to play a very straight bat when I appeared at the PASC [Public Administration Select Committee]. Her Yorkshire accent was back in full flow as she went over some of the MPs on the committee. Her general take on the Opposition was that they were useless, but TB would be wise not to underestimate Hague. I said he thought he was a good debater, and clever, but he had a judgement problem and he was listening to too many of the wrong people.

I couldn't really get a feel for her take on TB. I got the sense she was being as nice to me as she was because she basically thought I was more Old Labour than TB. It was a really nice meeting though, and I felt my batteries a bit recharged. She had been very nice about what she saw as my role in getting us elected and I suppose I should always hang on to that when the press and the politicians were getting me down. We were still doing good things, and TB was still the only show in town.

I woke up tired and fed up, and wishing I could just stay in bed and tell the whole lot of them to fuck off. I knew I had screwed up yesterday. I had gone totally over the top and was now beating myself up. I did real damage to my own relations with the media yesterday. Most of them I didn't care about, but I actually lost it with some of the good guys too, which was just daft. I knew I could recover it, but it would take time and it would take energy I could be putting elsewhere. I hated making daft mistakes like that, and letting my mood drive me to make them. I went to see TB in the flat. He said he was worried I was exhausted and I would make mistakes and I had to get more support, and have the odd day off. I said every time I tried to take a day off, he created a stack of work.

After the NIO conference call, I put together a briefing note starting to trail the outlines of TB's Ireland speech, indicating a shift on legislative expression to make clear what had to be done re prisoners, decommissioning etc. John H was really worried Sinn Féin would go off board if we went too far, and emphasized I had to be really careful on the balancing act. I was getting used to it. We didn't want SF to be happy with what we were saying. But nor did we want them to be too unhappy. 'What are you saying, we want them mildly pissed off?' Yes, he said.

TB spoke to Bertie who was more relaxed than we thought he would be, said provided we were not reopening the Agreement, it was fine. He said the Balcombe St pictures were too much, and they were made worse today by the temporary release of Michael Stone, the cemetery killer.* Mo said it couldn't have been avoided, it just happened to be the time for it to happen.

The mood in the lobby was bad, the overhang from my ranting at them yesterday. Some didn't turn up. For half a second, I thought about apologizing, but then imagined the satisfaction it would give them, and instead just decided to be less unpleasant than yesterday. I didn't speak to [Robin] Oakley. He and Patrick [Wintour, *Guardian*] were the ones I had gone way OTT with, and I would probably have to apologize eventually but I couldn't face it for now. Later George Jones [*Telegraph*] called about something and I did apologize, whilst emphasizing I thought they were all take and no give.

John [Holmes] did a fantastic rewrite of the Ireland speech. Of all the civil servants he was top drawer, real quality. TB spoke to Donaldson from the car on the way to the airport. John had read him a few relevant extracts from the speech and he was quite positive. He was pretty nervy about the next twenty-four hours. We took Mo with us, as well as Adam Ingram [NIO minister] and Kate Hoey [Belfast-born Labour MP], who was seen as one of theirs by the Unionists. Mo said she understood that Kate had to be in the picture.

On arrival we went straight to the Balmoral Show [agricultural show in Belfast] and as we walked in front of the stand, you could feel the coolness. This

---

* Stone, killer of three mourners at an IRA funeral, was sentenced to thirty years, but released after serving twelve under the terms of the Good Friday Agreement.

was real UU country. After talking around a bit, I reckoned sixty-forty against, but these were maybe more the activist end of the market. We did a meeting with prison officers, and then victims of violence, which was really moving. There were some dreadful stories of brutality and hatred and with effects that would outlive the victims. TB left more confident than I was that we could win the majority of Unionists we wanted. He was certainly the key to that, because the UU politicians were not shifting the arguments hard enough.

I complained to the BBC and ITN about them putting Michael Stone ahead of TB's speech and we got better coverage later on. On the plane home, I was tired and stressed, but TB was more up about things and said he was sure we could do it. I said we would need to take the campaign over even more. They were not capable of driving a strategic message and their continuing opposition to Clinton getting involved just underlined they didn't understand campaigning.

Friday, May 15

The Irish coverage was totally dominated by Michael Stone so the impact of TB's speech was pretty limited. Several times during the day, TB, me, Jonathan and John H variously said we could kill the NIO sometimes. They really had fucked up and we had to work extra hard to rein it in. It was going to be hard to keep on top of this while he had the G8 to chair as well. On the train up to Birmingham TB was trying to work out how to sustain momentum. We agreed we should go for the prison service medal idea,* as mooted by the prison people yesterday, but ran into one of those infuriating blocks straight away as it was a matter of the ceremonials committee and Buckingham Palace who would need time to look into it. TB, Jonathan and I also spoke at various points of the day to Donaldson, whose support we had to keep going for. He knew what he was up to, and we were happy to play along, provided he came out for it clearly in the end. But when TB spoke to him from the hotel he ended the call pessimistic. Donaldson said the speech didn't go far enough, which was code for no. TB asked me to call him and ask him direct. I said Jeffrey, we have to think about the PM's authority here, and how much time and energy he can expend on this, and I did not want him with egg all over his face. We need to know, in your gut, is it yes or no? He said I'm afraid I think it's no. I dropped in a hint that the press were beginning to see this as being about him and Trimble, rather than yes or no, to indicate we could move it into that if he milked it, but he didn't really budge.

---

* A medal was to be issued to recognize the services of the officers of the Northern Ireland Prison Service.

Meanwhile we were having to work out a response to India's nuclear tests and get fully briefed pre G7–8, though all TB was really focused on was NI. He said it was criminal the way they had let the Balcombe St Gang and Stone do what they did. On arrival in Birmingham, he did a doorstep on India and Ireland, and a clip about Frank Sinatra's death. It was a beautiful sunny day and Birmingham had put on a good face for the whole event.

Jeffrey Donaldson sent through his words and although they tried a bit of fence-sitting, I said to him they would basically be seen as a no. I said I needed to know if he was going to make clear it was a no in briefings and interviews. He said he would probably, that it was better to do it now than have it drag out over a few days.

When Bill C arrived, he was full of the usual bonhomie. He asked if he could do anything to help on Ireland. I said a doorstep pushing the general line, and being a bit more pro Unionist and raising the pressure on SF would be good. Let's do it, he said. I got Anji to organize but of course the Secret Service made such a palaver of it that within a few minutes, Sandy Berger came panting in, clearly pissed off we were getting Bill to do stuff without his own people around him. He said they would have a riot if they did not get the US pool in too, which made it an altogether bigger event. I had another go at trying to persuade McCurry to change their pooling arrangements but he said they were all too set in their ways.

After the first G7 meeting wound up, we had a brief huddle then Bill went out to do it. Berger and Steinberg were not happy, but I couldn't establish if it was the process or the message they didn't like. Mike [McCurry] was a bit more relaxed but even he did a barbed 'Mr President, I wonder if you shouldn't speak to your own foreign policy team before making major public statements.' BC made light of it and said he was doing what I told him to do, because that guaranteed a quiet life. He asked what the line was – I said it was the best chance of peace for a generation; he sided with those who sided with peace; and if any of the protagonists went back to violence, they would get no welcome in the US. He did it brilliantly and it would go straight to the top of the news in NI and probably here too, after [Frank] Sinatra's death probably. He was a total pro. Later he did a photocall drinking a pint on the balcony of a pub by the canal, which would make big time. TB was happier now but still felt we needed more time to turn things round. The next story was the LVF issuing a ceasefire and a No vote call.

I had another briefing to do, both on Ireland and the summit, then back for the Heads' dinner. The row over dinner was whether to 'deplore' or 'condemn' the nuclear tests. Yeltsin and Chirac – the latter loudly, and the former barely making sense – were arguing for a softer line. Clinton's people were worried he would take a big hit if they were too soft. The dinner was almost comic though. Chirac was at his most Chiracian, grand gestures, saying *'la France'* when he meant 'I', generally huffy if anyone disagreed. Boris Yeltsin was laughing loudly when nothing had been said, making loud gestures to the waitresses. Bill was laughing at the pair of them. TB looked over at one point and mouthed the word 'madhouse'. TB and Bill hung round at the end and we ended up chatting about which world leaders were fanciable. Benazir Bhutto [former Pakistani Prime Minister] was probably tops. Tansu Çiller [former Turkish Prime Minister] got fairly high marks all round. One of the advance people told me that some poor sod had removed the stamens out of two and a half tons of flowers because of Clinton's allergy. I told Bill, who said it was bullshit. 'Everywhere I go this happens and it's bullshit. It's got into one of those State Department notes and it's wrong.'

TB was totally obsessing re Ireland, said we had to have story after story after story to keep the momentum going our way. I asked BC if he would do *Frost* with TB. He said he would do anything we thought would help. I said it would. 'You decide,' he said, 'I'll do whatever you want.' Jim Steinberg again looked a bit antsy at my just asking BC straight up to do stuff, but I said a big joint interview on Ireland would help ease his worry about BC being whacked too hard on India [nuclear tests]. I called to tell [David] Frost [broadcaster] and Barney Jones [editor, *Breakfast with Frost*], who were orgasmic at the thought. Back at the hotel I put together a briefing note on India, Indonesia, MEPP and Kosovo, taking in the main points out of the dinner. I suddenly felt tired, deflated and depressed again. It was probably just overwork. Clinton cheered me up a lot, because he was such a laugh just to chat with, and a real pro to work with. Mo threw a wobbly because we were pursuing the prison medal from Number 10 not NIO.

Saturday, May 16

TB's main concern was Ireland again. We'd agreed to get a summit statement, which John and I drafted, purely to keep NI at the top of the news agenda over there, and on our terms. The aim was to get over the message that the world was watching, and willing them to embrace change. We did a *GMTV* pre-record where again he was mainly hitting the reassurance buttons for the UUs. TB was having to chair all the summit meetings, manage the outcome, as well as deal with NI and fairness at work, which was going a bit wobbly because the unions had finally woken up to the idea they could spin it as being good for them.

TB and I were working up a script for *Frost* and settled on fear and emotion vs hope and reason, which was the kind of thing BC would do well. I saw Bill when he got back and we had a chat about it. He wanted to say it was time for a leap of faith, and that the risks of a No vote are greater than the risks of a Yes vote. It was a good line. He was worrying that Frost would ask about his personal life and I pinned David down to an absolute assurance. We did it as a pre-record in the gardens. It looked great and Frost helped us get the message up. We had agreed he would ask straight out what could you do to reassure the Unionists and TB just went through the points one by one. BC was awesomely on-message. His use of a pause, his hand movements, the cadence of his voice, he was a remarkable communicator in so many ways. He was particularly strong at the end. After it ended he said how was that? I said awesome. We had agreed in advance he should push the message on US inward investment, and also that any return to violence meant no welcome in the US, and he did both really powerfully. We agreed Mike King of CNN could piggyback on the end for a special he was doing on Ireland, but it led to a huge row later when they decided they were going to use some of it as news footage in advance of *Frost*. McCurry complained. Bill had been true to his word in helping but was now worrying whether he was too involved. It was odd how even people like him worried, maybe especially people like him, so needed reassurance the whole time. As he left, he came over again and said was it helpful, because this situation really mattered to him and he really wanted to help. I said it had been a masterful performance, which it had, and if I knew anything about anything, I was sure he would swing votes on the back of it. I said I wished to God we had sent him to NI to campaign because I am convinced it would have shifted votes galore. But the UUs had been adamant. I said we were in his debt. Not at all, he said.

It was evidence perhaps of the cultural gap between the UUs and us that they expressed constant concern at the idea of President Clinton taking an active part in the campaign. Deep down, though they did not express it this way, I think their concern was that the controversy over his private life was seen as such a negative among God-fearing Unionists that it would overwhelm any positive impact his campaign contributions might have. But Clinton was – still is, as President Obama recognized in giving him a key role in his re-election year convention – one of the world's greatest campaigners and communicators. These interviews were strong events in themselves, but the power of the message resonated for some time afterwards too.

A hell of a lot of people had come out to wave at the convoys on the road into Birmingham, and although there was a big demo in town, the mood generally was great. Fiona and I went out for dinner with Mike McCurry and some of his media favourites. Mike had them rolling about when he told the story of how we got BC to do media without any of his people knowing. He had a friendlier relationship with his media but when we discussed it later, he said the difference was that the press basically saw me as a politician not a spokesman. That was what gave me authority, but it also made me fairer game in a way maybe he wasn't. He also felt he benefited from being quoted by name because he could then be more dismissive of anonymous stuff.

Sunday, May 17

It was interesting to watch BC around the place. Of all of them, he was the one with the most natural empathy with e.g. the stewards and waiters etc., and it was that basic human touch allied to his intellect and communications skills that made him the ultimate modern politician in many ways. I started to wind up TB about how much better BC was as a communicator.

The farewells were fascinating. Yeltsin was going round doing great bear hugs. Chirac told TB that the food had been better than any of the summits he had been at, which I suspect he said at the end of every summit, and he said he thought Birmingham was a beautiful place to hold it. Bill C was saying how he would like to go up in a hot-air balloon fuelled by all the discussions at summits. 'Hey, we could stay up there for days.'

We had a meeting with Colin Parry [father of twelve-year-old IRA bomb victim Tim] who was a lot nicer than I thought he would be. I don't know why but I had formed a bit of a negative view, but his genuineness came through in person in a way that was maybe diluted by TV and I ended up feeling bad at having thought ill of him. God knows what I would be like if anything happened to the kids. He was due to go to Belfast to campaign for the Yes vote which had the potential to make a strong impact. Parry gave me a couple of his books, one for TB, one for Clinton who seemed genuinely moved by it when I showed it to him later, just before they left.

On the way out of the hotel one of the hotel staff had asked if I could help her to meet Clinton. I arranged for her to be in the lift. She was a little old West Indian woman and by the time we hit the ground floor, he had her whole life story out of her. She practically collapsed as he left the lift and later we heard she had been in tears for hours, moved to bits. Back in London, TB and BC headed off for their Chequers wonkathon. I was tired and hot but felt things had gone as well as they might have done.

The BBC were leading on Ireland, last week pre-campaign etc. On the NIO morning call we agreed TB should go on Wednesday and try to drive up support. TB was late back from Chequers where he had been with Bill who had been swimming and bike riding with the kids. He had also gone to play golf and TB, who had never played, went along for the ride and apparently hit the ball really well, so would be unbearable for a while. It also meant he was underprepared for the EU-US summit, which actually had a lot of tricky stuff attached to it and he had basically spent the weekend schmoozing with Bill. We ran through the things he had to get on top of.

Both BC and TB had been worrying re Ireland and BC said he felt the problem was Trimble's failure to rise to the occasion. He exudes problem not opportunity. [Jacques] Santer arrived for the summit and again I had a sense of the absurdity of the position where the US president was meant to think a rotating prime minister from one of the smallest countries in the world [Luxembourg] was the person you deal with in Europe. It just wasn't serious and nor was Santer. TB was yawning the whole way through so clearly Bill had kept him up yacking.

I briefed at 11 – mainly Ireland, the summit, also golf. John Hipwood [Wolverhampton *Express & Star*] asked why Peter M had been at Chequers. 'He's the caddy,' said Oakley. For the press conference with Bill, trade was going to be the difficult issue. We got an FCO official in to brief TB and he was like a gibbering wreck. He had a two-page note, which we thought was for public consumption, but then as we went through it, he would say 'Oh no, can't say that,' till eventually TB said what can I say? Finally, he realized the guy was falling apart, said OK, I think I know what to say, and off he went. It was almost comic.

Santer came in then we went up to the White Room where Bill was preparing with his guys. The trade stuff is fine, he said. Very fine, said Santer. I had one more thing I wanted BC to do. The *Mirror* had asked for an article on Ireland, which was a good idea. I asked them to draft something, and after I reordered it a bit, I showed it to Bill who thought it was fine. Jim Steinberg went ape though. He had not liked me dealing direct with BC, and he didn't like the doorstep operation we did in Birmingham. He said 'We will write the president's words, not you.' I said he seemed fine with it. Jim said they would have to look at it.

The press conference was fine and they were both strong on Ireland, which would hopefully carry. Afterwards they did a joint call to the Pakistan PM [Nawaz Sharif] re nuclear tests. Bill didn't want much said publicly, simply that the call took place and we were urging restraint. In the call they had both been clear re the economic benefits of restraint for Pakistan. Jim [Steinberg] had another go re the *Mirror*. He was really pissed off with me now.

The golf got the biggest coverage out of yesterday, but Ireland was ticking over media-wise and there was a feeling on the ground that the Unionist vote was slipping away from us a bit. We were sending PG to do some groups to help sharpen the last few days' message, but without DT really motoring, we were going to struggle a bit. I said to TB we were going to have to try to use his visit as the big shifter, and we began to build it up as an event.

Geneva, for the WTO [World Trade Organization] meeting when Stuart Higgins [*Sun* editor] called and reminded me they had asked for a Clinton piece. It had gone completely out of my mind and I said so, and added he was doing something for the *Mirror.* I had to weigh up quickly which one to piss off most. The revised BC version had come through and as I was unable to reach Jim [Steinberg] or Mike [McCurry], I took it upon myself to give it to the *Sun,* with my earlier revisions, on condition they splash it. The *Mirror* would go mental but I would just have to deal with it. In the Unionist context we were going to get more out of the *Sun.* TB did a phone-in before we left, which was OK but he was worried about the slippage. I told Piers Morgan [*Daily Mirror*] about the *Sun* and not surprisingly he went berserk, and I just let him sound off and needs must. But it would do lasting damage to our relations with the *Mirror.*

PG called after his first group. He didn't know that much re NI politics but he got a pretty good grasp quickly. He said that they were worried the IRA would use politics to get into power, then TB would leave them to their fate. They needed a lot of reassurance. Even though it didn't really fit the conference theme, we put in a section re NI and organized applause after directing the broadcasters to it. We also had the briefest of meetings with [Cuban leader, Fidel] Castro. TB just bumped into him, literally, and they found themselves standing toe to toe, shaking hands, and not a photographer in sight. He was taller than I imagined, also looked older but had a wicked smile. He said he admired TB and he had read all the Third Way speeches.

As we landed [in the UK], PG called again and said we really had to get a strong TB message out there. As things stood we were not going to get a majority among the Protestants and he was the only one who could turn that round. It would be hard but this was urgent.

Piers called a couple of times to vent his spleen, said he had wound up Kelvin [MacKenzie] and Monty [David Montgomery] and they agreed we always favoured the *Sun* and they were all fed up with it. Higgins called and said it was the right thing to do, for the peace process. But I hated the double-dealing I had to do at times like this.

I went up to the flat where TB was preparing for PMQs. He was tired and irritable and worrying re the vote. PG had done a note which was pretty relentlessly negative re where the Unionist community was. But he did say that TB, trust, connection, conviction, still had the capacity to turn things.

I had the idea of a series of handwritten pledges, which we would put up as a poster backdrop when he spoke in Northern Ireland. I called the NIO to get an ad van and agency on standby while John [Holmes] and I worked on the wordings. TB was not totally sure about it, and said the wordings had to be very, very careful. I said it was the best way of doing what we had to do – link him explicitly to reassurance. Charles Moore [editor, *Telegraph*] came in for a chat. He was impossibly hostile on Ireland and wouldn't listen to another side, but he was more friendly than before. He said I was doing a very good job and the reason I was becoming the story was because of that. People know that you are behind a lot of the things that happen, he said. You are not a press officer, you are a politician effectively so the media will treat you as such.

PMQs was fine, with the Tories attacking on waiting lists, and TB dealt with it fine. At the briefing I started to talk up the NI pledges and the poster and they latched straight on. I could always tell when a story was going to work, because [Phil] Webster [*Times*] and [Michael] White [*Guardian*] would both have a little smile, then scribble earnestly. TB sat with Hague on the plane and they mainly talked Ireland, Europe, Chirac. Hague was very proper in these circumstances, always called him Prime Minister, didn't push too hard, listened and then spoke briefly. TB thought he was likeable enough and a very good debater, but he felt he lacked judgement on the big-picture stuff. John H warned me there was a chance of more NI prisoner day releases. I said we had to make sure there were none before Saturday.

We landed and were flown to Coleraine. The backdrop looked good though as ever TB was a bit awkward. I don't know why he found posters so difficult. It looked good, there was substance to it and it would connect big time. He did a really strong emotional speech, without notes, and did a strong tribute to Trimble who was a lot more relaxed and malleable than usual. We did some strong pictures during which a little guy came up to me and said 'All he needs to say is "Trust me and trust yourselves."' It was a terrific line and we used it later in the day.

We left for dinner at Stormont and after I watched the news I felt things were better than before, and Mo said she felt things were turning a bit. The NIO officials were advising us not to do too much because they felt it would look like TB lecturing them. I called PG and we agreed that was balls, that we needed more not less. I got the news extended to get more time to keep the momentum going.

We did a visit at Knock Golf Club then to the BBC for a fairly tough panel but again he hit the right buttons. There was a good *Irish Times* poll out so finally, at the right time, we had a sense of momentum. TB was knackered by the time we got to Hillsborough.

Thursday, May 21

Bill C said to me the other day that we wake up every day with fear and hope, and one is always heavier than the other. Today it was hope, and we all sensed things were turning our way. I don't know why but we did. Everyone's instincts were saying yes. Maybe it was the weather but things just felt better. The pledge poster had certainly worked and in Antrim TB met a guy who said he had seen him on the TV panel last night and he had swung him from no to yes, so again that cheered us up a bit. We had limited time in which to pack in as many interviews as we could. First up was Eamonn Mallie on Downtown Radio, and it was tough because he focused totally on decommissioning and TB went further than ever in linking to prisoner release. Both John H and I winced a little, worrying he was making too many promises.

The next four interviews were better and as he got into his stride I felt we were back on a roll again. We were taken up by helicopter to Dunadry [County Antrim], to a hotel. Trimble was again more relaxed and confident. He was due to take on [Bob] McCartney [leader of the UK Unionist Party] and I gave him a few lines he might deploy. He was dismissive of [Jeffrey] Donaldson. But TB said my advice would be to be magnanimous in public but never forget. We did more pictures, then the poster signing and the media were taking it all in. We left for the Royal Irish Regiment, who were not exactly warm. But TB's walkabout went fine and among some of them there was genuine warmth. There was a bit of abuse from some of them, but not much and when McCartney had a go at TB at the end, members of the crowd turned on him. When he called them 'rentamob' they got angry with him and the stunt backfired.

TB did an emotional little speech, again using the line trust me, trust yourselves. I got a joint article placed in the *News Letter* and the *Irish News,* and both editors were happy to go with it. We had had a good run-up to the voting and TB said he was not sure we could have done much more. Our lines were running strong and even DT was getting good coverage. We did an economic meeting in Antrim and that part of the message had definitely got through. TB said he was beginning to hope as high as 77 per cent, no lower than 68. I felt it would be better still, that we were peaking at the right time.

On the plane home TB was really tired. He, Anji and I talked over the political operation in the office. He was down on Jonathan at the moment but that was because he was expecting him to do things he was never expected to. He was not the solution to a problem re politics, but he did a lot of other good things. TB was also thinking of a small reshuffle next week. Back at Number 10 I had to decide who to give the spare press job to and went for Lucie McNeil who was bright and had a bit of drive. I was feeling confident about the vote now. Today felt better than last time which felt better than the time before that.

Friday, May 22

Referendum day and with most of the media just waiting for that, I had a quiet day.

Saturday, May 23

The referendum results [71.1 per cent in favour of Belfast Agreement] came through earlier than expected and I spoke to TB from Wembley where I was watching England vs Saudi Arabia. I sent Hilary Coffman to Chequers to help organize his doorstep. The line was fairly straightforward – the beginning not the end, now make it work etc. It pretty much ran itself. We were also starting early on talking up voting not just in the referendum but the elections when they came on June 25. I didn't do much briefing because it was a big story pretty much on autopilot. The football was dire [0–0]. TB did his doorstep and statements came flooding in from overseas.

Sunday, May 24

Ireland was running fine though as ever after a big moment the media were wanting something to move it on.

Monday, May 25

The story in NI was focusing too much on decommissioning.

The main media event, going from sublime to ridiculous or vice versa, was recording the Des O'Connor [comedian and talk-show host] interview at Teddington [Studios]. He was worried the stories we had planned weren't funny enough, but it all worked fine. TB was relaxed and on form and afterwards had a chat with Elton John who was going to Belfast for a concert and was interested in the whole NI thing.

We went out for dinner with Philip [Gould], Gail [Rebuck, PG's wife] and Lindsay [Nicholson], ostensibly for my birthday, but I was definitely going into another dip. I felt overworked, felt I was firefighting too much, and doing too much that others ought to be doing. The office meeting earlier was hopeless, TB at his worst, meandering, unfocused, moaning.

TB called a couple of times from Chequers. He felt [Robert, Viscount] Cranborne [Conservative Leader of the Lords] was up to no good on decommissioning in the Lords.

Mo was on *Frost,* and was a bit ropey re decommissioning, and why Adams and McGuinness were invited to the Hillsborough garden party with Prince Charles. She lacked the finesse needed for tricky questions.

TB was installed in his new office, which was bigger and better and lighter. I did the eleven o'clock early and it was mainly Ireland and Prince Charles. I denied outright the claim reportedly being made by Charles' people that they had not been consulted [about garden party invitations]. TB said later he felt they could have been more sympathetic to the idea of Adams being there. He felt we were going to have running problems with Charles because on many issues he was more traditional than the Queen. We left for Northolt and the flight to Spain for the start of the pre-summit tour of capitals. [José Maria] Aznar, like [Bertie] Ahern later when we arrived in Dublin, was totally opposed to some big initiative on the future of Europe, and was worried we were going to be bounced by the French and Germans.

We arrived half an hour late in Dublin. We'd been working on a new state-ment to relaunch Anglo-Irish relations. Bertie asked TB to address a joint session of the Parliament. They did Ireland mainly tête-à-tête then over dinner, where they served quite the best meat I had ever tasted, they did the European summit stuff. TB was confident we could make economic reform fly, but I felt it was all a bit too dry and technical.

I liked Bertie a lot, and I think he shared my general unease about European summitry. He and Aznar were both adamant that we could not be signalling a big shift or another grand design for Europe. Bertie said the public would not thank us if we came out with a stack of more institutional reform. He supported Europe but he felt the remoteness of it all was becoming a problem.

Tuesday, June 2

We were staying at the Westbury [Hotel, Dublin] and I had breakfast with TB in his suite, where he was wound up re Sinn Féin and decommissioning. He said we had to watch Cranborne like a hawk; when it came to NI politics he could do a lot of damage inside the Tory Party. We left for Belfast in the smallest and most uncomfortable plane the RAF could provide, the 146 having been taken off us to take Prince Charles somewhere. It was noisy, both of us did our necks trying to get in and drinking without spilling was virtually impossible. We headed for Parliament Buildings, did a big doorstep, where it became apparent there was no clear narrative for the day. As the meetings went on, the marching season was the main concern for most of them. Sinn Féin turned up with a couple we had not seen before, introduced by Adams as from a residents' association. One of the security guys told me they were in fact fairly high up the IRA ladder, so do not be taken in by the label.

TB seemed to have the measure of them early on. John Hume had made the point SF could pretty much turn the violence on and off like a tap, and Adams virtually admitted as much when he said he thought they could calm it if TB managed to get them a meeting with Trimble. They also reminded TB of his exact words on one year and prisoners, and he had to dissemble on it. DT was much more confident. He had Donaldson with him but was not deferring at all. He said the Parades Commission was damaged goods. Ian Paisley was missing from the DUP line-up because he was in Scotland, and there was a very funny moment when the fire alarm went off as TB was trying to persuade them re the principle of consent. 'It's a lie detector,' said Peter Robinson.

TB laughed, glad to be able to stop talking under pressure when they clearly weren't buying it. [Sir Bernard] Ingham was at the select committee inquiry into the GIS [Government Information Service] and really laid into me but he was so over the top it got very little coverage. The nine o'clock news had GB on spending, TB on NI, JP on the Channel Tunnel rail link, DB on schools, Jack Straw on football violence so it was no wonder the Tories were getting frustrated.

Peter M was in a sulk about not yet being in the Cabinet and didn't come to the morning meeting. At PMQs TB went a bit beyond the line on the two guardsmen and whether they could be released.* I had to calm it down a bit afterwards when I was huddled. The problem with the guardsmen was that it wasn't clear whether Mo was reviewing the sentence or the case as a whole. I had the first of my pared down heads of information meetings, a smaller group of the people from key departments, which was a lot better but the real problem was one of quality. Some of them seemed not to know what their departments were doing, and some appeared to have no relationship with ministers at all. I think they were intimidated by me but in fact I was trying to involve them more not less.

We set off for Holland for the latest pre-summit round. Along with Bertie, I'd say [Wim] Kok was the most likeable of the leaders, but he could also be very tough in negotiation and we had a lot on the Dutch contribution. Jaap van der Ploeg [Dutch government communications director] told me that every Friday the Dutch Cabinet did fitness training together! Christ knows what would happen if we tried the same.

Kosovo was definitely moving fast. TB was worrying re NI again. Far from moving to decommission, SF–IRA were looking for new arms the whole time. Publication of the Prisoners Bill went fine, with both Trimble and Adams onside, DT because it contained the Balmoral pledges, Adams because there were no preconditions. So far so good.

---

* Blair raised hopes that Scots Guardsmen James Fisher and Mark Wright, serving life sentences for shooting dead a teenager in Northern Ireland in 1992, could soon be freed. They would be released under the terms of the Good Friday Agreement in September 1998.

Saturday, June 13

The Tories were stirring it and this, allied to them attacking us over the presidency, and saying they might vote against us on Northern Ireland, got TB really irate. He said Hague just wasn't serious when it came to it.

Wednesday, June 17

It was becoming clear Andrew MacKay was pushing to break bipartisanship. He is a total idiot that man. I spoke to [Peter] Temple-Morris [now sitting as an 'Independent One-Nation Conservative'] and said he might do his final step to defection [joining the Labour Party] on *Frost* on Sunday, and say MacKay doing this was the final straw in the way he was behaving on the Prisoners Bill.

Thursday, June 18

I put together a briefing note on Temple-Morris, twisting the knife on Ireland as they were about to vote against us on the third reading of the Prisoners Bill. When I got back I called Barney Jones to get Temple-Morris on *Frost*.

Sunday, June 21

Temple-Morris did the business on *Frost* and was leading the news by lunchtime. There was a bit too much build up to my select committee appearance on Tuesday.

Friday, June 26

There was a bit of gloom re the NI elections. As the first results came in, Trimble was not doing as well as expected. TB was blaming himself and the NIO, feeling that he should have followed his instincts to be more involved, but the NIO were insisting Trimble's position would be fine. He was very down about the government as a whole. If only people knew, he said, that we have to do virtually every significant thing this government does.

TB sounded a bit dispirited by the NI elections and was worrying that Drumcree [planned Orange march] was just a week away. He was cursing the Tories and MacKay, feeling their diddling had done a fair bit of damage. The Sundays didn't follow through very hard on the select committee stuff, though [Bernard] Ingham had a piece whacking me in the *Mail on Sunday*.

TB spent much of the morning on the phone to NI politicians – Trimble, Hume, Adams, Alderdice. We briefed on the calls with the message that he was confident the future was strong, and was pleased more than 75 per cent of the votes went to pro-GFA parties. We had a conference call, TB, AC, John Holmes, and agreed it would be odd to exclude Paisley so he should try to speak to him too. When he did so, it was a very difficult call and TB sensed Paisley was feeling emboldened to go harder against.

Paisley accused TB of going back on his word when he hadn't, but it was becoming a given that he had said there would be no seat on the executive without actual decommissioning. TB never actually said it but of course for us to do a big number saying he never said it would look like a retreat. Keeping the balance right on these connecting issues was bloody difficult at the best of times, but harder than ever if Paisley was able to drive public opinion. TB sounded really fed up after the call and said he felt we would probably have to go there this week. We went to [daughter of Neil and Glenys] Rachel Kinnock's for lunch and Neil was a lot more relaxed than usual and we had a good time.

The 11 was all about Drumcree and EMU. The moment I said TB was making a speech tomorrow, it was obvious they were going to overwrite. I told them not to get overexcited but I could tell they would. Lord Alderdice quit [as leader of the Northern Ireland Alliance Party] to become Speaker of the Assembly. I went home to watch Holland vs Yugoslavia [2–1 win for Holland].

I was up early to get out to go to Frankfurt. TB's speech [at the European Central Bank] was fine and he had a useful meeting with Bertie Ahern. TB felt we had to pull off something dramatic re Drumcree. He felt Trimble, to his credit, had crossed a Rubicon and was now fatalistic. TB said it was Unionism though, not nationalism, that was in crisis. We were back in London in good time and TB went off to make the party broadcast on the NHS. I did the four o'clock which was pretty desultory because really people were only interested in the football.

I got home to watch England vs Argentina. TB and I spoke several times during the match. He was watching it on his own and as well as us having to prepare a response because of the demand there would be, I think he also just wanted someone to watch it with. At the end we agreed words based on how well they played, and how the courage of their game did not deserve the cruelty of their exit.* Rory was not as upset as he might have been. I tried to explain how stupid Beckham's kick had been, how he had let down the whole team, and all the supporters, and how [Michael] Owen was a better role model for aspiring sportsmen.

Wednesday, July 1

Today was the first day of the NI Assembly, which was a fantastic achievement, but with a tough backdrop now. Trimble became first minister, [Seamus] Mallon Number 2. TB then did two interviews on England going out of the World Cup, BBC then Sky, and came out with one of the worst sound bites in history – 'a mountain of courage and a molehill of luck'. Yuk. I was almost tempted to start a coughing fit in the hope they would have to do it again.

Thursday, July 2

We were discussing again whether TB should go to Northern Ireland or not. He spoke to Mo on the phone. She was not keen, but then she always resented the notion only he could sort things. Bertie was really keen for him to go and it was obvious he would. What was extraordinary re Mo was her inability to make a series of points simply, so by the end of the conversation he sort of knew she didn't want him to go but he was hard pressed to explain why.

We left at 3 for Northolt, TB not exactly sure what he would do when he got there. Mo and I were both worried he would get trapped into negotiation and never get out of there. We arrived at Aldergrove and were driven to a burnt-out church [there had been overnight arson attacks on ten Catholic churches]. Fairly big crowds had gathered and they were reserved. There was a real feeling

---

* England lost to Argentina on penalties in the World Cup second-round match after a 2–2 draw. David Beckham had been sent off after one minute of the second half.

of sadness, and a muteness that went with it. They were not disrespectful, just distant and sad and, when they did get close, clearly longing that he could do something for them. He did a strong doorstep saying this was exactly why we had to choose the path of democracy and dialogue. This was the past and we had to embrace the future.

We left for Castle Buildings. The last time we were there TB and Bertie hailed a great success. Now we were back with another great drama on our hands. Trimble and Mallon seemed to be getting on fine but were both very gloomy. Drumcree was a disaster area. The Orange Order were adamant they would march. The nationalists were adamant the Parades Commission decision should stand. [Brendan] McKenna of the [Garvaghy Road] residents' association was milking it for all it was worth. Adams was not contactable, probably because he was seeing IRA people and he would not want his mobile being tracked. We left for Parliament Buildings to see the churchmen, who were frankly pretty useless, really disappointing, lots of hand-wringing and rather needy looks in their eyes. They said they would support us if we had a plan, and they were praying for TB, but they lacked any sense of leadership quality. [Ronnie] Flanagan was full of foreboding. He feared the Loyalists would indiscriminately kill Catholics if the march was stopped. When you heard him say that, you just thought will these people ever ever be able to get on? Were we wasting our bloody time? Adams came up at 8.45 and TB wanted to see him on his own. GA was clearly ready to work towards some kind of compromise. TB felt maybe the march could go down, but with a commission to review re future routes, or a civic forum idea. Then John Hume who was very rambling and repetitive, and said he was anxious.

After the meetings ended, we had a stocktake and agreed it was a risk for TB to get trapped into being an active negotiator, and that we should get back. John Hume felt TB's presence hyped it too much as it was. Mo was really pissed off at the idea she could not just be left to do it on her own. She also feared Flanagan lacked balls. TB had a couple of Scotches and unwound on the flight home a bit. He told a very funny story about a guy at the NHS reception who said that when Thatcher was PM, most Alzheimer's patients could name her as PM, and most still did.

Friday, July 3

TB sent Jonathan to Belfast, and Mo was even more pissed off. Major was on the *Today* programme, and proving yet again what a silly little man he is. How he ever became PM is one of the great mysteries. He had done a speech attacking TB for doing interviews on football and being more interested in the Spice Girls than serious issues. It was an odd thing to say on the day TB did a major speech re the future of the NHS, which got very good coverage today, and was also dealing with Northern Ireland, but it didn't stop him.

The media picked up on Jonathan being in Belfast. It was an irritant but of course the real downside was it would send Mo into a mini meltdown. Trouble was TB just didn't think she had the skills needed to hold all the different sides of this together. He felt she just didn't understand how you had to deal with the UUs, and that to call the NIO civil servants 'a bunch of clods' – in front of some of them – was not very clever.

Saturday, July 4

We had absolutely no chance of a quiet weekend with the Drumcree march tomorrow, and a whole new load of Blair/Brown rubbish in the Sundays. TB, Jonathan, John Holmes and I had eight conference calls at various points in the day, most of which led to us then having to do something we had agreed, so we might as well have been in the office. Neither the Irish nor Adams seemed to have any control of [Brendan] McKenna at all, and he was very good at looking and sounding reasonable as he stirred away. TB believed the only way out was to allow a symbolic march, officials only, but John H was sure it would not be possible while McKenna was part of the equation. Jonathan had done a good job talking to the Unionists, and laying the ground, so that we did not have the feared backlash as the reinforcements went in to block the road and make clear the march was not going down. There had to be a real effort to get this sorted for next year. Our basic line was it had to be sorted, and only local entrenchment was stopping us from doing so.

Sunday, July 5

The Sundays were full of even more shite than usual, most of it TB/GB related. Reshuffle, Geoffrey R, Peter M, endlessly stories about the government that were all personality driven. TB said he was actually getting on better with GB than for ages, but the rift was in danger of becoming the driving theme for the whole government. TB was on the whole time, trying to push for local accommodation [re Drumcree] but every time Jonathan came on, even he sounded pessimistic. TB felt if we could get it sorted by the national leaders and churchmen we could do it, but locally it was proving the hatreds were so deep it was impossible. The only story that really bothered me out of the Sundays was the *Observer*, which had claims of their influence by [Derek] Draper, [Ben] Lucas, [Neal] Lawson [lobbyists, former Labour advisers].* Also it was reported that Roger Liddle [Downing Street policy adviser] had told the journo who had posed as a businessman that he would help get access. It was probably bollocks but was one of those stories that would fly a bit.

We had three situations on the go – Drumcree, which had the potential to be an absolute disaster area; the *Observer* stuff on lobbying, which we had to grip quickly; TB/GB, which was running through the whole of the Sundays, and after speaking to TB, GB and CW we put out a statement simply saying it was the usual summer party, Sunday made-up nonsense. Peter M called re Derek Draper, said he was a young impressionable working-class boy who felt he had money and influence and didn't know how to handle it. TB, Jonathan, John Holmes and I had a series of calls through the day just trying to keep the Drumcree show on the road, but it was really difficult. There were so few rational people seemingly able to get into the situation and exert influence for the good.

Jonathan was speaking to the Orange Order, John Holmes to the SDLP, and we were just trying to work round McKenna. McKenna had next to nothing to do with the area yet had got in there and was now spoiling for a fight. I watched the start of the march on Sky. They came out of the church, walked peacefully down to the barricades, then back again. It was perfectly good-natured, then up popped McKenna to say that the government and the RUC were not doing enough to stop the march. I called TB and said it was time really to go for him. I called Joe Lennon and we agreed a joint TB/Bertie line welcoming the peaceful nature of the protest, and condemning the provocative and inflammatory language, wherever it came from. We named no names but I briefed PA it was aimed at McKenna.

TB wanted Jonathan to get even more deeply involved in the negotiations, which pissed Mo off even more. TB was getting really fed up with her. She was more worried about how she was seen in the equation than actually solving the fucking problem. Lance [Price, special adviser, press office] was dealing with the *Observer* [lobbyists] story and said he felt a head of steam building on it. I was so consumed re Drumcree all weekend that I had probably let my eye wander off the ball on that one.

---

* Claims of favoured access to ministers and advisers by lobbyists Draper, Lucas and Lawson had been reported in the *Observer*. One comment from Draper would come to sum up 'Lobbygate': 'There are seventeen people who count, and to say I am intimate with every one of them is the understatement of the century.'

The marching season was an annual reminder of just how different, and difficult, some of the cultural and historical differences between GB and NI really were. As for McKenna, he may be pleased to know that TB once said he would win any 'global pain in the arse' contest.

Thursday, July 9

TB had a meeting with the Orange Order, which was particularly difficult. When TB said we could not possibly break our own law, [Revd William] Bingham [Orange Order chaplain] said it was a bad law that said you cannot protest and then started to compare it to a Hitler and the Jews situation. TB took it, but I could tell he was getting angry beneath it all. TB pushed hard to get them to reroute, or wait till September, or limit the numbers. But we were dealing with a very thick brick wall. It was bloody hard work. He emphasized how much he supported their right to march, but they did not share his reasonableness. Cabinet was mainly Northern Ireland, the Comprehensive Spending Review, and a desultory conversation re the lobbying row.

Friday, July 10

There had been some bad violence against the police in NI overnight and we got TB to do a clip with [Robin] Oakley which led the news at lunchtime. Jonathan and John Holmes were working flat out trying to get a plan for indirect contact talks between the Orange Order and the Garvaghy Road residents' association. Eventually we were in a state to send letters to both. We thought we had real progress; the sign of engagement, a venue etc. I called a 4.30 briefing to go through it and it was leading the news straight away. It was a case of taking the initiative and going with it. It was high risk though because it was so capable of being rejected. It became more and more clear that McKenna was the problem. He just didn't want to be co-operative. He said a venue for a meeting had to be Portadown as he would not be safe in their areas. He was basically giving us the runaround. I lined up [Clinton's Mike] McCurry and [Ahern's Joe] Lennon to be positive in response to what we were doing. I was knackered by the end of the day. I hated Fridays because I had the going into the weekend feeling but knew the weekend would probably be consumed with work too. I was enjoying the NI stuff but was juggling too many things at once.

We went round for dinner at Philip [Gould] and Gail's. Peter was also there, full of his usual paranoid obsessiveness re GB. He basically presented GB as the root of all evil, with no redeeming features. I said it had to stop, that until one of them took the lead in just stopping it, it would be permanently destabilizing.

Saturday, July 11

And so to one of those dreadful weekends that drive me mad. Drumcree was again dominating our lives, a never-ending round of calls that led pretty much nowhere. Jonathan was there and was trying to get the talks moving. McKenna was a total pain in the neck, but eventually we got things under way. TB, Jonathan, John Holmes and I had a series of conference calls to work out at every stage where to take it. It was really tough. Anyone landing from Mars would wonder how on earth we could be arguing about this so intensely but it was about as hard as anything we had to deal with. You were dealing with something that looked simple but beneath the surface was really complex. Jonathan said the Orange Order were happy to talk up to midnight but then we would be into the Sabbath and they would have to stop. Then it would be on to the march on Monday. TB was getting really worried we would be into major violence and political crisis fairly soon. The best we could say was that we were pleased dialogue had opened.

McKenna was pretty much driving the media agenda, with the Orange Order making their usual noises. I listened in to a couple of TB calls where he was being pushed for the march to go down, but stood firm. Jonathan was doing a good job keeping things ticking over but it was hard there. I wanted to go on the attack against McKenna who was a nasty piece of work but TB was keen to keep the pressure on the Orange Order, which we did. The last call I took was just after midnight and meanwhile I was dealing with the Sundays over the wretched lobbying stuff too.

Sunday, July 12

Jonathan called to tell me three young children had been killed in Ballymoney [County Antrim].* It was a terrible thing to think, but it was true, that this would

---

* Three Catholic boys, Richard (11), Mark (10) and Jason (9) Quinn, were burnt to death after their home was petrol-bombed in a sectarian attack carried out by Loyalists. (It was later disclosed that members of the Ulster Volunteer Force had been involved in the attack.) Christine Quinn, the boys' mother, her partner, Raymond Craig and a family friend, Christina Archibald (18) escaped from the house but they and neighbours were unable to reach the three boys. Another brother, Lee Quinn (13), the oldest son, was staying with his grandmother when the incident occurred. There was a general sense

turn the mood, and the reality was we had to help it in that direction. People would think this had all gone too far and hopefully want to pull back. I spoke to TB and we agreed he would do words of condemnation. Then Jonathan called again and said the Revd Bingham, the Orange Order chaplain, was going to say in his sermon that people should get off the hill and go to their homes. It was crazy that it took these deaths to move people.

I called [Mike] McCurry to get another Clinton statement out. TB called and said we should put out fresh words saying people really needed to look at themselves and the consequences of their words and actions. The four of us had half a dozen conference calls through the day. Jonathan said Trimble and Mallon were meeting the Orange Order and were going to go up there to try to persuade people off the hill. The death of three children had become the catalyst for a major change of mood. Flanagan was excellent, in private and in his public statements.

TB was thinking he might need to go there tomorrow. He felt we had to move to build on this change of mood. He was worried some of them were so mad that they would go back fairly quickly. He spoke to DT, Adams and Mo, and took soundings. Bingham's words were excellent, Trimble did well and we had to keep the momentum now. The media had totally changed tack. The Unionists were spreading a rumour that the murders were domestic, not sectarian. What a jerk. In between it all I tried to watch the World Cup Final [France beat Brazil 3–0]. Chirac was milking it for all it was worth.

Saturday, July 18

Jonathan called from Belfast and said the talks were back on. We agreed a statement which I put out straight away. Otherwise it was a fairly quiet day.*

Sunday, July 19

Jonathan was on a few times re Drumcree, which he seemed to think was in a better place.

---

of shock when the news of the deaths broke and in the following days the incident was to have a major impact on the Orange Order protest at Drumcree. Although senior representatives of the Order tried to distance the organization from the violence that had been almost continuous since 5 July 1998, many commentators argued that the Orange Order had to accept some responsibility for the violence of its followers. [CAIN]
* The British government introduced the Northern Ireland Bill into the House of Commons. The Bill was designed to implement the provisions of the Good Friday Agreement.

Clinton announced his NI visit, which ran pretty big. We had decided to ignore the Unionist objections.

Jonathan was off to Drumcree again.*

TB had a bad cold and was losing his voice, which was a big problem. People hate politicians with colds, there is no sympathy at all, so we had to see what we could do to cut his diary down. Then Joe Lockhart, who was to be McCurry's successor [as Clinton's spokesman], came in for a chat. He was a nice guy but different to Mike, a bit more static maybe, but I could easily imagine working with him.

I was on the phone to Peter M [recently promoted to the Cabinet as Trade Secretary] in the States when Wendy Abbs [Downing Street duty clerk] came through on the other line to say there had been a huge explosion in Omagh [County Tyrone],† twelve thought to be dead, the PM was just being told, having just arrived at the house in France. I asked her to fix a conference call with him and Philip Barton, who was manning the office as duty private secretary. PB had already done the basics you'd expect, but the details were all a bit patchy. As we spoke, reports were coming in that the death toll may be higher and all the holiday ease that had been in TB's voice at the start was gone. I said he would have to do

---

* The Northern Ireland Office estimated that the disturbances surrounding the Drumcree parade had resulted in damage to property of £3 million. (The estimate for 1997 had been £10 million and for 1996 it had been £20 million.) There was a demonstration in London on 23 July as part of the campaign to secure the release of two Scots Guardsmen who had been sentenced for the murder of Peter McBride (18), a Catholic civilian, in Belfast on 4 September 1992. [CAIN]

† Twenty-nine people were killed; the youngest, Maura Monaghan, was only eighteen months old. About 220 were injured. The bomb had been planted by the RIRA (Real Irish Republican Army) and exploded at 3.10pm. The RIRA were a breakaway Republican group who disagreed with the leadership of Sinn Féin.

TV straight away. There was a problem in that he had arrived ahead of his clothes and he was scruffily dressed. I asked which cops were with him, and he ended up using Bill Lloyd's suit and a shirt borrowed from one of the neighbours. We also had a conference call with John McFall, newly appointed NI minister, who was on duty. 'What a baptism,' said TB. It was clear John was nervous and I was worried he would hit the wrong note in extended interviews. For example, when I said what do you say if they ask if it harms the peace process, he said it's too early to say. I said we had to get over that the peace process is bigger than a group of fanatics who want to derail it. TB weighed in, saying we had to be making clear every peace process always faced disruption from people who wanted to destroy it. TB said this was the last resistance, and if we saw it off with public opinion there totally on our side, it could be another turning point. But how we react now will dictate that. It was pretty clear if the death toll was as bad as feared, he would have to break his holiday at some point, but I suggested for today JP went there. I spoke to JP, who said he would do whatever we thought was required, and we fixed it for the afternoon. I said the line we wanted to push was that we would not let a small bunch of psychopaths disrupt the will of the majority. We also had to get SF up on the right side of the argument. I called [Mike] McCurry, who was playing golf with his son, and said BC would be key in making the kind of noises SF would want to echo. PB called [Sandy] Berger and [Jim] Steinberg to brief them and try to get Clinton engaged early. We had to pull out all the stops to make sure SF said the right thing. Adams was on holiday in Italy but announced he was coming back. McGuinness put out a very strong statement. TB said that what we had to engineer was a situation where people felt the IRA were isolated from these people, that they were seen as a rump, that there was now an internal battle between the democratic process and renegades. TB did his clips, which PB watched, and said he was quite emotional. When I saw it on French TV later, it looked fine. It could have been anywhere and the tone was good. In a later conference call we had a longer discussion about whether he should go. It was pretty much inevitable he would have to, the only question was when.

Sunday, August 16

I barely slept and I guessed that TB wouldn't and phoned him early. I found it hard to understand how people can be so psychopathic, so dumb, to think this will work. Unless there was a strategy so deep and so sophisticated that it was beyond the comprehension of mere mortals, I couldn't see it. It was hard not to feel emotional about it after the real sense of progress there had been.

TB said there will be obstacles along the way but the forces of good have to prevail. He had got over the initial shock and was now working on next steps. He said he felt if he went he should go today but PB said there was a problem getting a plane. I said it was important he didn't just go in and come out but did something only he could do – like get DT and GA together to say the same thing, or get Adams to make clear in the tone of his denunciation that so far as he was concerned, the war was over. PB finally tracked down John Holmes who had been travelling and had been oblivious to what had happened. He too counselled caution, but TB sounded like he had made his mind up. He said if you go, you go today, you steady people, you give momentum to the process and you spell out a message of hope. It was obvious to me TB had decided to go so I said to PB and John we should just plan for it because it is going to happen.

After church TB got ready to go back and called from the car to go over the basic line – peace process can prevail, we can be stronger than these evil people, etc. Godric and PB had flown to Hull to meet up with JP. I spoke to John as they landed and said he could say that TB was cutting into his holiday to come over. JP wanted to go over all the difficult questions and we had a long briefing session – he was worried about getting the tone right on decommissioning. I said best to avoid difficult interviews until TB got there. This was about empathy and about making clear the extent of both our condemnation and our determination to prevail. TB's feeling was that the debate would move quickly to what kind of security measures were being put in place. As he flew I put together a long briefing note for a phone lobby. TB had asked me to keep control of the briefing which meant the only way to do it was do it myself in a series of conference calls, which was pretty irritating for Fiona and the kids so I tried to do one before they were up and out and another when they were just chilling out in the afternoon. He called me after his meeting with Ronnie Flanagan who was clear it was [Michael] McKevitt and the Real IRA [RIRA].

TB said I could announce Flanagan was going to meet the Garda and together they would make recommendations to the two governments. It had definitely been the right thing for him to go today and given how much time I spent on the phone it might have been easier to go with him.

TB asked me to speak to McGuinness to agree what they were going to be saying and keep them in the place we wanted them to be. It then emerged Mary McAleese [President of Ireland] was going to Omagh and TB was to meet Bertie at Stormont tomorrow. I said they should do a joint doorstep. TB went to the hospital and then met Trimble at Hillsborough. The scale of it was becoming clearer now and it had definitely been the right thing to go. Indeed I was worried Mo was going to take a hammering for still not being there, with the world waking up to the enormity of it. There was also the fear TB would look a bit cruel ducking out after a day or so. Prince Charles was due to go on Tuesday. At the moment the main focus was on the carnage.

Again, I didn't sleep too well. I was just dozing when TB called around 1am. He had been up till 12 with Trimble but the real reason for the call was he said he was deeply affected by the visit to the Belfast Royal [Royal Victoria Hospital]. He described some of the scenes he saw, the wounds and the scars and the mutilated bodies, and all the human suffering around them. But basically they were all giving him the same message – keep going, don't give up, work for peace harder than ever. He said it was really humbling. He felt it had been right to go but it was also OK to leave. He had seen victims and families,met the politicians, talked to the police.

TB felt what we really needed was something strong from [Ronnie] Flanagan on the security front out of his talks with [Garda Commissioner Patrick] Byrne. Flanagan told TB he was sure the IRA had nothing to do with this. I said it was important he make that clear today because we were still getting reports implicating the IRA. TB did another round of calls before heading back to France. I did another lobby briefing from the house in Flassan on to the squawk box in the lobby room. The questions were much the same as yesterday – worries about decommissioning, about prisoner release, interest in arrests and any planned new security moves.

TB said it was vital that we came up, whatever the legal hurdles, with a security package that gave people confidence we were on top of things. TB was worried that Mo would find herself surrounded by the usual NIO dynamics and we would lose grip. But Tom Kelly [NIO spokesman] was doing well on the media front and Bill Jeffrey [political director, NIO] seemed OK. Add to which a combination of Prince Charles' visit and then the funerals would be the main focus for the next bit. There was a lot being done that people did not know about. The problem with some of the new ideas was the requirement of primary legislation.

TB said he was not convinced these people had intended to do quite as much damage as they did, but I doubted that. * They had totally set the agenda on their terms and in different ways made life difficult for every part of the political debate with the possible exception of Paisley. On the flight back he wrote a very emotional reflection on what he had seen. It showed he felt it very deeply. What was

---

* The RUC, misled by confusing phone warnings, had directed people towards the bomb rather than away from it. The code word used was that of the RIRA.

amazing was that even before I had told Fiona or anyone about the new security measures, Rory said to me 'Why don't you just pick up the top man on phone-tap material, then the other top people, and find excuses to keep them inside until you find all their weapons, then break the organization?' Not bad.

In one of the briefings I did, I pushed out the boat for Adams and McGuinness. I said TB was totally convinced of their sincerity, which again was the right thing to say for now, but a potential hostage. At 5pm I listened in to a TB/Mo call. Mo read through the joint statement she planned with the Irish justice minister [John O'Donoghue]. It was wordy and woolly and with no specifics to drive things forward. There was no reference to the things we had instructed yesterday, e.g. changing the balance on evidence, ending the right to silence, proscription, use of phone-tap material. I said that if she read out the statement she had just gone through with TB, she would be panned.

TB said he wanted to see the police chiefs' ideas and then take half an hour to redraft and get back. I said to Mo the press can wait. Mo sounded like she always did when we were involved – pissed off and sullen, but the truth was it was a second-rate piece of work. As TB was redrafting, she called me back to say the police were pissed off hanging about and so were the press. I said neither were good reasons to do it half-cock. Every time I tried to push back she said she was surrounded by officials shaking their heads. I said look, there is no need for anyone to get antsy about this. It is not unreasonable for this to take a bit of time. It is not surprising that the PM would want to be involved, and consult Bertie. She didn't like that at all.

Then another extraordinary conference call with him and Mo. The police chiefs [Flanagan and Byrne] want to leave, the justice minister wants to leave and they cannot renegotiate because Bertie is in a meeting in Dublin. TB was pretty firm with her. He said 'I'm very sorry, Mo, but I am going to have to press you and you are going to have to press them because the statement is not adequate. It needs a strong intro and it needs three specific areas that have to be addressed. 1. Proscription and a specific criminal offence. 2. Measures to make it easier to secure convictions. We do not need to go into detail here but people will know this is phone-tap material. 3. Specific operational measures, where there has to be a sense of detail.' We then had the ludicrous situation of TB having to ask Mo for her fax number, and her shouting out 'Anyone out there who knows the fax number?' and then saying the officials had disappeared. It was the Mo manner that was fine when things didn't matter, but deeply irritating when they did. She sounded more and more exasperated. 'I'll say whatever you want, Tony,' she said, at which point TB exploded at her: 'It is not a case of saying what I want. It is a case of doing the right thing and then explaining it to the public, who may have cause to be concerned about recent events.' She then lost the plot completely. 'You cannot do this to me. I'm sick of the long-distance control. You are making it impossible for me. I can't do it any more.' Well, you're going to have to, he said. Just calm down, Mo, we have to do this properly. Ronnie Flanagan came on the line and was like a voice of reason and sanity. He did not sound like a man trying to charge out of the door. TB took him through some of the changes and he sounded fine. But Mo was getting near hysterical. TB said to her if you went out and read that statement as you read it to us earlier, you will be dead. I mean dead, totally out of the game. Nobody would take you seriously. She said 'I'd rather be dead than carrying on like this. I don't care any more.' TB said 'Yes you do, and that is why we do the extra bit to get it right.'

Tuesday, August 18

I listened by phone to Mo's doorstep, which was pretty grim stuff. She got the three areas for action mixed up and had to be rescued by O'Donoghue and she got muddled with the Irish on internment. She was clearly in a bit of a state. Then I learned she wanted to resume her holiday tomorrow, which would be a disaster area for her locally. TB called, having been told by Mo that her statement went fine. 'It was tough but I did it.' I told him what actually happened, that she had got things in the wrong order and did not even get out the line that PIRA [Provisional IRA] were not involved. He said 'You are going to have to take charge of this, and do a lot of one-on-one briefings.' I was genuinely worried about Mo, and what she might be saying. She said she wanted to go back to Greece because it was a waste of time constantly being second-guessed by remote control. The TB article [about his visit, in the *News Letter* and *Irish News*] went down a storm and was picked up by several of the nationals. It was the emotion that drew them in but it also included the main political points. In between dealing with NI, trying to spend time with Fiona and the kids, we also now had Don Macintyre up with us for a couple of days because I had promised I would help with his book [a Mandelson biography]. Peter was helping him, and Don was trying to be fair, but I sensed that his real interest was TB/GB or certainly GB/Peter M.

TB was less pissed off than I thought he would be about the *Sun* leader attacking him for going back to France. We were not making much progress on the Trimble/Adams meeting and we were not getting far on the security measures either, with NIO in a state of shambles from what I could glean from my various phone calls. Then news came through that the Irish president and Bertie were going to a service in Omagh on Sunday, which would put pressure on TB to go, so we had another round of circular conversations about that. TB said he desperately needed a rest but was getting none. It didn't help that he was worrying re Mo and the NIO the whole time. Prince Charles' visit and the Real IRA claiming responsibility was the big news. Re the church service TB felt it was OK for JP to represent the government and he would go to a memorial later.

Wednesday, August 19

The right-wing press was starting to be difficult, trying to link RIRA and IRA as pretty much the same thing. Their desire to fuck us over on this was pretty powerful. The Gerry Adams/David Trimble situation was going backwards, SF rejecting the language we had tried on them. It was making the UUs uneasy again. The RIRA called a ceasefire which we rejected in contemptuous tones, saying it was an insult to the dead and an attempt simply to stall the new security measures. The RIRA were intimating it had been intended as a big commercial hit, not heavy loss of life. That had been TB's view, that it caused more damage than intended. Mo was still intending to stay only until tomorrow, which was worrying me.

Thursday, August 20

TB called early, and we had a circular conversation re who should attend the service on Friday, what kind of memorial there should be, and what if any legislation we should be bringing in as a response. He felt we would probably end up recalling Parliament so it was probably as well to say so and set the terms ourselves. We were due to go with the Senes [a French family] down to the river so I wanted to get today sorted before we went. I organized for TB to do a pooled clip responding to Bertie's new measures, with an appropriately tough line. I told him of some of the right-wing articles being run and we agreed I should ask Geoff Martin [*News Letter*] to take an article warning these armchair generals risked provoking a Loyalist backlash. The basic points had to be rooted in what the peace process was for, and why people wanted to disrupt it.

We were effectively briefing that TB's holiday was over, though he was spotted up a mountain by photographers. Fiona and the kids were getting a bit fed up with me being on the phone, several hours a day, with today around nine calls with TB alone. We were doing OK re the message on legislation but going backwards re the war being over. I recalled the time I saw Bertie at Newcastle vs Man U last year and him saying he would come down like a ton of bricks on anyone who went back to violence and he had been as good as his word.

The last week of the holiday had been pretty much wiped out. Today was the last full day I had and most of it was spent working. We had to agree representation for the Omagh service tomorrow. In the end we opted for JP who did it perfectly well. I put together a briefing for the Sundays, TB to go there Tuesday and also decision to be made re recall of Parliament. I stressed that this could be the final such act in this particular chapter of Irish history. That was probably pushing it but there was a sense that people were longing for that to be so. I did the briefing by squawk box, and they were clearly desperate for a Diana [first] anniversary story. Mike Prescott [*Sunday Times*] said at one point 'Alastair, can I level with you – we are desperate for anything re Diana.' I said we would be doing nothing, apart from half-mast flags and TB at Crathie [church at Balmoral].

We were out at lunch when TB called after the doorstep, said it went fine and he had pushed again the line re new measures post Omagh. He kept asking if I had been able to have a rest because he needed me to be on form for the conference speech. In fact the first two weeks we had been able to rest and relax but the third week was a total write-off. Fiona had done a brilliant job keeping the show on the road while I was busy, and I think understood I felt there was no choice. People had said when I first started that NI would get to me, and it had.

We set off at 6. TB was on the phone at 8. We got home in around fifteen hours.

For the first time in three weeks I slept past 9. TB woke me at 9.30 to have a natter and go through where we were. He was really starting to focus on the conference speech and so we were into long circular-conversation mode as we started to develop and hone the main arguments. The Sundays were generally OK re our handling of Omagh. TB had been thinking about PR and had grown more persuaded against and regretted getting into the argument for reasons of Lib-Demery. TB feared Bill [Clinton] was getting really damaged by the Lewinsky affair now.* He said he should really try to engage in the Middle East, one because it was right and he could do it, but also because he needed something major to focus on to get away from the US obsession with his sex life.

---

* Following allegations of impropriety, in January 1998 Clinton had claimed: 'I did not have sexual relations with that woman' – i.e. former White House intern Lewinsky.

First full day back in the office, and it wasn't too bad. The main focus of the day was to decide whether to recall Parliament. There was a school of thought that we did not actually need to for the measures we wanted to get through. But equally I felt we needed to send the signal of the importance of it, and the added legitimacy it would give if we had a full vote of the HoC. TB had read the various different pieces of advice and his basic judgement was that it was probably the right thing to do. Lockerbie and NI were the main focus for the eleven o'clock. We were pushing the line that if we did recall Parliament we were also looking at measures to allow terrorist offences committed abroad to be tried here. I spent most of the day with Mark Bennett [AC's researcher] briefing myself back in. At 7pm we had a final conference call and TB gave the green light for a recall [of Parliament].

We headed for Belfast. TB drafted his own press statement, which was strong. He focused on the emotions aroused, the recall as agreed by the Speaker and the general thinking behind it. He was worried though that the political situation was fragile. Trimble and Mallon were barely speaking, DT was vile about the service he was getting from the Civil Service, Sinn Féin were attacking everything we did and saying Trimble's sole aim was to ensure the GFA [Good Friday Agreement] was not implemented. DT was a very difficult personality to deal with. When he was good, he was very good, but at times he could become very distant and disengaged and not focus.

Mo and Tom Kelly were both worried that [Seamus] Mallon would quit if things did not improve. We were flown by helicopter to Omagh, where the atmosphere was very subdued, as expected. TB did a meeting with local leaders and then groups of emergency services in little knots, all very friendly but some of them clearly shaken up. He talked to some of the locals in the street and though there were one or two difficult questions, he handled it all well. He was saying the measures we planned were tough but I thought he was wrong to say draconian. We had an unbelievably awful helicopter flight to Belfast, foul weather, low flying, dodging pylons, etc.

We arrived for the talks, first Trimble, who was clearly under pressure and not very friendly. Several of the UUs were making clear they would not sit on the executive with SF. They were also – in part fuelled by the Tories and the *Telegraph* – driving decommissioning up the agenda again. TB was seething afterwards, felt that whenever we took our eye off the ball, things slipped, and that DT was failing to offer leadership. We had an equally difficult meeting with McGuinness, Doherty and Bairbre de Brún [Sinn Féin's policing and justice spokesperson], who felt Trimble was stalling while they were constantly being asked for more. TB felt if we did not get progress going soon, the thing was in danger of collapse, and he was worried about the attitude shift on both sides.

Over dinner at Hillsborough, TB agreed he should do a statement on Omagh on the day Parliament came back, both to set the tone and give a broader context. DT came back for another meeting and TB decided to do it mainly tête-à-tête to try to get him to get a grip. It was a better meeting and TB had bought the line that Trimble was not trying to screw things for SF for the sake of it, but taking a tough public line to try to win more of his own people round behind him. They agreed to work towards a series of steps, e.g. 1. SF say something indicating the war is over, 2. DT calls a meeting of all parties, including SF, 3. McGuinness agrees to speak to the decommissioning body, 4. Trimble/Adams bilateral. Over a massive bowl of raspberries and strawberries, TB said he felt DT was a curious mix – he wants to lead but is needy about how to do it. It was as if he needed lessons – for example, he should bind in Donaldson and then every time Donaldson slips outside the net he diminishes himself not DT. He felt Donaldson was the one person who could really damage DT.

Wednesday, August 26

Over breakfast TB said he felt DT could get SF on to the executive but if he did it without decommissioning he was pretty much finished. He told Adams as much later. We left by helicopter then flew to Knock airport, which was a pretty extraordinary place, a huge runway in a small airport taking a few planes a day to get people to the shrine nearby. The Irish had laid on a helicopter to get us to Ashford Castle hotel, a fabulous building, part of it thirteenth century, set in beautiful grounds. We were met by Bertie and Paddy Teahon, Bertie being positive and constructive and helpful as ever. We agreed the same first four steps plus then, 5. real decommissioning, and then 6. SF on to the executive. Bertie believed it was doable. TB thought DT wanted to move but he thought it would be very hard to have an executive with SF on it by September 14. BA felt Adams was almost irrelevant to the decommissioning argument. McGuinness was the key.

We agreed it would be good to get one of the big steps taken while Bill C was here, to use his presence but also help him. The Clinton people advance team were giving us the usual headaches. They wanted a speech opportunity in Omagh which we thought might not be appropriate. They wanted a visit to the new university site in West Belfast. TB was opposed and John Holmes and I had a difficult discussion with Steinberg later.

Lunch was pretty relaxed, fabulous food and Bertie on cracking form. On the flight back, TB was more confident we could do something to push forward politically. He said it was like playing multi-dimensional chess. We got back for a long meeting with Mo, Jack S, RC et al. re the planned bill. Jack was excellent on the detail. We agreed not to go down the road of phone taps being used as evidence partly because most were not transcribed but also so that we were not pushed into detail of who and how.

We then had a meeting, including with TB, re the Clinton visit. TB was keen this was a good visit for Bill, who he felt was looking pretty close to being knackered. We had to stand by him and show we stood alongside people through bad times as well as good. There were a number of joint things planned but we decided it would not be a good thing for TB to be driven around in Bill's presidential limo. The palaver preceding the visit was appalling. They had too many people and a lack of clarity about who could actually make decisions on BC's behalf. Christ knows in how many countries his advance teams were currently causing chaos.

Saturday, August 29

TB was pushing us to keep the momentum going forward re NI. He believed after the talk with Bertie that we could get Adams close to saying the war is over and DT to agree to chair a meeting of party leaders including SF.

Sunday, August 30

Another fairly quiet day. The Sundays were trying to build a sense of rebellion over the new NI legislation and Mo had sent a letter to the *Observer* promising an annual review as a sop to the civil liberties people. TB spoke to more of the G7 leaders and he and Clinton did a bit of NI. We really needed some movement pretty quickly.

Monday, August 31

I was trying to have a lie-in but TB called early, worrying whether we were in the right place re Russia. He felt there had to be more done by the G7 and people were looking closely at how we handled this. John Holmes was urging caution, saying there was no point signalling momentum if ultimately it went nowhere and the reaction of the others was not yet clear. The other thing I was dealing with was the media making something out of the shortage of time the NI bill would get. I called Jack S who said it was being sent to Opposition leaders today and MPs tomorrow. In addition we agreed we should brief the new element of forfeiture, seizing the homes of people involved in the Real IRA, which was the one thing people were seizing on as being a bit draconian. We were also still hopeful of some movement on 'the war is over' scenario we had discussed with Trimble and Adams. We had a pretty relaxing weekend. I listened in to TB's Yeltsin call and briefed a line on that, though it was not clear yet what exactly we would be doing.

Tuesday, September 1

Over the weekend TB and John Holmes had been toing and froing between Adams and Trimble trying to agree some form of words that would allow DT to react positively and convene a meeting of party leaders. Today it seemed to be coming right. Apart from Clinton in Russia, NI was the only big story around and we put together a briefing for the 11 on the bill, which was being published in draft today.

After the eleven o'clock, it was pretty much all Northern Ireland. The feeling was growing Adams would do something significant today. I spoke to Joe Lennon [Ahern's press secretary], Richard Macauley [Sinn Féin spokesman] and David Kerr [UUP] and we agreed similar responses from different perspectives. We were still slightly operating in the dark because we didn't yet know exactly what Adams would say. TB had to speak to him again to try to pin him down. John said the problem was every time we suggested the slightest hardening of their position, Adams and McGuinness had to take it away and re-sell and it was not easy for them. But the key was to get Adams to say something Trimble could cautiously welcome, and then DT convene an all-party meeting. It took another round of calls before finally we pressed the button.*

It quickly replaced Bill [Clinton] and Boris [Yeltsin] as the main story of the day. Though Trimble's words were not strong, I got Kerr to put 'cautious welcome' in the headline. Kerr then came on and said DT didn't like the statement, felt it was full of coded threats, it didn't go as far as they wanted and there would be nothing more positive from DT tonight. I said that TB had an agreement from DT that if words about violence being over were in there, he would

---

* Adams announced in a statement that 'Sinn Féin believe the violence we have seen must be for all of us now a thing of the past, over, done with and gone.' Trimble then invited Adams to a round-table meeting.

respond as agreed. I said he could not possibly go back on that. He said DT had shut up shop for the day and they had real political problems. I got TB to call DT who actually sounded a lot better about it than [David] Kerr indicated. He said it was welcome but he didn't want to make too much of the convening of a meeting. TB didn't want to keep him on the line too long in case he went into textual analysis and instead asked me to call DT back straight away and persuade him that he should announce the all-party meeting rather than have it dribble out on someone else's terms. DT said he didn't want it all to look choreographed. I said he was in danger of letting GA take the initiative. He said only for the short term. He said he had always planned this meeting of leaders so it was no big deal. In which case why had we taken so long to get here? Because they refused to say the war was over. But Adams WAS saying he would bring forward the date announcing McGuinness was to liaise with [General John] de Chastelain. So it was all going well, if only Trimble could seize the moment.

News-wise it was running fine, everyone saying this was a significant moment but there was a residual concern DT would cock it up. TB, Jonathan and John Holmes had done bloody well to get things to where they were today, and the media operation had got it in the right place so there was a sense of progress. TB and Bertie did most of the heavy lifting but Clinton was also getting credit because it was done to coincide with his visit. Joe Lennon called and said there was no substance to Clinton's Dublin visit.

I got home to Calum having fallen off his bike and Rory and Fiona fighting about something he wanted to watch on the telly, and I felt myself getting depressed again at the lack of time I had spent with them.

Wednesday, September 2

TB called early on, saying he was worried re Trimble. It was so obvious what they had to do but they were terrified of Sinn Féin stealing the show. He spoke to him later and DT was at his disconcerting worst, humming while listening, humming when he should have been speaking, and making clear the only people whose views he considered were his Assembly members. TB also called GA to try to get a better fix on where decommissioning was going. We had to get a response re ITN and the moving of *News at Ten*.

I drafted a couple of strong sound bites for the NI statement, of TB speaking direct to the bombers, which made all the bulletins. Then came news re McGuinness being appointed [by Sinn Féin] to deal with de Chastelain [on decommissioning], another big hit, and they [the media] were starting to say it was all being choreographed to coincide with the Clinton visit. BC was clearly having a terrible time [over Lewinsky], as was clear from my various calls with [Mike] McCurry. Even he was a bit more tense than usual. It also took me ages to persuade [Jim] Steinberg we should have a pool camera in the meeting with the Assembly. Their worry was that Paisley would give him a big lecture on morals. I vowed they would not be there long enough and we would keep them off Paisley's lot when they met him. I spoke to Kerr several times to make sure DT was responding OK [to Sinn Féin]. He was, though you had to read between the lines to get there. Kerr asked me to 'leave it to me', but I was worried at the pace and so got several of the Westminster political editors to call and ask for confirmation this was leading to a Trimble/Adams meeting.

TB's statement in the House went fine. Kerr then briefed Irish journalists that there would be no decision [on a meeting] until a meeting of the UUP executive on Saturday. [Richard] Macauley and Joe Lennon both called, worried. I tried to assure them this was just DT's way and we would get there. But TB and John Holmes were both worried. I had Brunson and others saying this all basically meant a Trimble/Adams meeting on the cards, but the Belfast media were not really going for it. TB was very down on DT at the moment, said he found it hard to imagine him actually running the place.

Thursday, September 3

I was up just after 5 to get to Number 10 for the convoy to Northolt. It was pouring with rain. Some of the broadsheets were clear re a DT/GA meeting but there was still no confirmation it was going to happen. TB and John H were getting anxious Trimble may stall right through. On the way to the airport, TB and I were discussing how he should handle Bill [Clinton]. I said there was no mileage in any distance and he should be close. The speech should be a mix of where we are in the peace process, but also talk up BC's role. Trimble was waiting for us on the plane. TB was working on the speech for the Waterfront Hall [Belfast], while DT read the papers. I made sure he didn't see the *Independent*, which was the most firm re a meeting with Adams. We then had a discussion about what DT might say. Trimble said he didn't intend it to be a big deal, as both TB and Clinton were around and bound to take the headlines. We persuaded him there was an opportunity here and TB asked me to draft a few lines for him. I did, including a further clear hint that he would meet Adams. I never imagined he would deliver them, especially when he just folded the paper and put it in his pocket without comment, but later he did deliver them, as drafted. He told us he was having problems with Ken Maginnis and also with his executive but he believed it could be done. We got TB's speech finished, arrived and waited for Bill C to arrive.

There was the usual over-the-top security getting on everyone's nerves. I told the advance guy he should get hold of a copy of the *Independent* for Bill to see. They took it a step further, gave it to Sandy Berger as he landed and he had it under his arm as he walked across the tarmac. But they were clearly desperate for a success story with all the other stuff going on back home.

We left for Stormont, good pictures of TB, BC, Trimble and Mallon on arrival, then upstairs for a meeting. Bill asked a great question – 'What can I do to help?' TB said 1. show the three governments working together, 2. put pressure on SF re weapons decommissioning, 3. isolate pro-violence opinion in the US, and 4. economic help. DT was pretty churlish throughout and afterwards BC said to me 'Someone should tell him that part of the art of politics is smiling when you feel like you're swallowing a turd.' He also used that great line from Mario Cuomo [former governor of New York]: 'You campaign in poetry. You govern in prose.' It's about who clears the drains, he said. The Yanks were keen to be seen to be doing something for Adams.

Trimble said we were aiming for transfer of functions by February. Anji had a tight control on the cameras and we got our pictures of BC in the Assembly before he could be harangued by the UUs let alone the DUP. But now the US and SF wanted more – they wanted GA on the platform, claiming that is exactly what would happen with a constituency visit, and he should speak for a minute. John Holmes and Jonathan seemed surprisingly relaxed but TB and I were both worried that would wipe everything else out and send real bad waves through the Unionist community. But the Americans were really pushing, and Adams was pressurizing Mo. It was a classic last-minute SF bounce and I felt we had to resist as we had not thought through the consequences. Jim Steinberg came to our offices but after ten minutes of toing and froing we couldn't agree so I went to see Bill. I explained why we thought it was a bad move and said instead it would be better that TB said some warm words re GA and his role when he was making his remarks introducing Margaret Gibney.* Bill, who was a bit distracted as he was working on his speech, was fine with that.

He was very friendly with all of us, but Hillary was pretty icy, and the more he tried to bring her in, the more rigid and fixed the smile became. She was clearly finding the whole Monica thing hard to bear and he was clearly still being punished. The speeches went fine. TB got a good reception. His words on Bill got the balance right. DT said what we had suggested for him and though it was

---

* As a twelve-year-old in 1997, she wrote to Blair asking him to continue the search for peace, and imploring terrorists to give up violence. After Blair read out her letter on American TV, she caught the imagination of many in the United States, including Hillary Clinton. Subsequently she became a UNICEF Young Ambassador.

Fiona Millar and Alastair Campbell in his office overlooking Downing Street. (Author's private collection)

Tea at Chequers. Fiona Millar with Cherie Blair after Fiona had formally joined the team. (Author's private collection)

The room in which the Stormont peace talks get under way at Block 'B' Castle Buildings in 1996. Two years later the negotiators emerged having signed up to the Good Friday Agreement. (PhotopressBelfast)

G8 Denver 1997. To the mild consternation of Mike McCurry (standing far right)
*White House Press Secretary, President Clinton is being briefed on Northern Ireland
by Tony Blair* (seated) *and his team.* (Standing left to right) *Jonathan Powell,
John Holmes and Alastair Campbell.* (Author's private collection)

*President Clinton jokes about job-swapping Alastair Campbell for Mike McCurry
like the professional sports world, July 1997.* (Author's private collection)

John Hume and David Trimble, after the signing of the Good Friday Agreement, 10 April 1998. (PhotopressBelfast)

Tony Blair and Bertie Ahern celebrate the historic deal on Northern Ireland at Stormont, 10 April 1998. (PhotopressBelfast)

Waiting for the verdict of the referendum. David Trimble, Tony Blair and John Hume after breakfast at a hotel in County Antrim, May 1998. (PhotopressBelfast)

Martin McGuinness, Gerry Adams and Sinn Féin team after the signing of the Agreement, 10 April 1998. (PhotopressBelfast: Justin Kernoghan)

Mo Mowlam in upbeat mood at Stormont Talks press conference as talks edge closer to a deal, April 1998. (PhotopressBelfast: Justin Kernoghan)

On a flight back from Northern Ireland, Alastair Campbell dons Mo Mowlam's wig. She was given to removing her wig because it was itchy. (Author's private collection)

Moment of history for Northern Ireland as David Trimble and Seamus Mallon are elected First and Second Minister respectively while the speaker Lord Alderdice looks on, 1 July 1998. (PhotopressBelfast)

Waving to the media, George Mitchell arrives at Castle Buildings, Stormont for another day of talks with Sinn Féin and the Ulster Unionists, 23 October 1999. (PhotopressBelfast)

Tony Blair listening to the Ceann Comhairle, Mr Séamus Pattison, before addressing the joint houses of the Oireachtas, 26 November 1998: the first-ever speech to Dáil Éireann by a UK prime minister. (The Irish Times: Frank Miller)

Media squeeze into the press pen as DUP leader Ian Paisley gives a press conference at Castle Buildings, Stormont, 25 June 1999. (PhotopressBelfast: Justin Kernoghan)

A wall mural in the Ardoyne area of West Belfast illustrating Tony Blair's involvement in the Kosovo crisis and the Ulster Peace Agreement.
(Pacemaker: Stephen Wilson)

President Clinton arrives at Stormont with Tony Blair, Peter Mandelson and Senator George Mitchell, February 2000. (PhotopressBelfast: Justin Kernoghan)

never enough for SF, it was what was needed. He was an odd speaker. He waved his hands around at the wrong times, and he couldn't work out whether to hold the lectern or not, but it was OK. John [Holmes] and I had written a kind of tribute to GA from TB, which we showed to Steinberg. We set off for Springvale [new education campus], the crowds getting bigger as we went through West Belfast. A huge tent had been erected where the new university was going to be. TB, BC, Cherie and Hillary travelled together. Mo did a little speech, then a young boy, then TB, who went off the cuff and called Adams 'Gerry', I think for the first time in public, which John H hoped nobody would notice. Berger said to me I looked pained when he said it. I said we were always pained when we saw and heard things which we knew would see the other end of the see-saw tip over again. Adams looked pissed off though. He said that unless Trimble confirmed a meeting officially, this was all meaningless. I said it would be fine because Trimble had given his clear commitment to TB. He shrugged at that.

Bill had a little catnap in the holding room, and looked pretty shattered when he woke up. Hillary looked tired too and there was nothing between them when they were together. He did his best, and chatted to her and what have you, but she was having none of it. Icy does not do it justice. This was the deep freeze but he was bearing it well. TB was pressing Adams on decommissioning. He said whatever the GFA said, the reality was without decommissioning it was hard to see how they took seats on an executive. Adams said how difficult it was.

We were taken by helicopter to Omagh. We went straight to the local leisure centre to meet families of the victims. There was a little boy there, wearing a Leeds [United] shirt, who was the double of Calum. It was very quiet, a few sobs around the place, but as BC and TB toured the tables, the noise levels picked up a bit and people started to pour out their stories. But it was pretty harrowing. I chatted to a policewoman who was helping some of them through it and she said she had never known anything as bad as this. There was no media at all, just a sound feed for TB's and Bill's little speeches. Then they went round every single table and by the end people were mobbing Bill asking for photos and autographs. The atmosphere lifted as time wore on, but you knew it would fall back soon after they left. We were briefed by one of Clinton's people on the walkabout and he referred to how we were meeting 'some of the fathers' of Omagh. Hillary cut in, 'and mothers,' cutting the guy right down.

They set off to the scene of the bombing, laid flowers and then walked slowly down the street. The crowds were warm and friendly, and Bill was clearly getting a lift from the crowds and their reaction to him. TB said to me later he felt Bill was very down, but hiding it well, and also feeling very damaged. A role in the peace process meant a lot to him, for lots of different reasons. We flew to Armagh over some stunning scenery. There was a big crowd – up to 11,000 – waiting for them and the US team had told Bill he had been a bit down in his earlier speech and this was the one to get pumped up for. He did, and got the best reception yet. [Seamus] Mallon spoke really well. Trimble was flat and unyielding as ever. TB said later he had the worst personal skills of any top politician he had met. He just couldn't rise to these big occasions. DT looked gobsmacked for example when TB said he should try to develop a good relationship with Adams. He was still avoiding any official acknowledgement of a meeting. Both TB and BC felt today had gone well. We saw him off, then set off for home ourselves. It was getting massive and positive coverage here but a lot less so in the US, which is where he needed it. TB was anxious for him. He said if things were that bad with Hillary in public, heaven knows what it's like in private.

Just as the Ballymoney killings somehow turned the mood so, on an even greater scale, did Omagh. Whereas once such atrocities fed a feeling that it was hopeless ever to imagine that peace could come to Northern Ireland, the reaction to Omagh fuelled the determination of politicians and people alike that the peace process had to work. The reaction of Sinn Féin's leaders was crucial in this regard. Think back to the comments of Adams and McGuinness in reaction to bombings of the past, the weasel words and semi-justifications, all whilst claiming no link with the organization that carried them out; a stance which led to the Tory government banning broadcasters from using their actual voices: a boon to Northern Irish actors, and possibly to Sinn Féin recruitment and propaganda as well. This time, for all that their opponents were looking for weasel words, Sinn Féin leaders were clear that this was the way of the past, democracy and dialogue the way of the future. Again, the process was lucky to have a Clinton visit to Northern Ireland already in the diary. His visit to Omagh, with TB, Hillary Clinton and Cherie reminded me in terms of mood and emotion of the visit TB made with John Major to the Scottish town of Dunblane after the school massacre in 1996. There is a power in grief, especially when those grieving are urging those with power to work even harder for peace. That was the message TB and BC took from their visit.

Friday, September 4

For the first time in weeks, Bill C had a good press, and a sense that he had rediscovered his old magic touch. However, it didn't last long as by the time he got to Dublin, a Democrat senator [Joe Lieberman, Connecticut] was stealing the show with an attack on Clinton as immoral, and though he later said sorry, the damage was done. TB having agreed with Clinton that there should be a G7 deputies group to look at the Russian [economic] crisis, I put together a briefing note prior to a conference call with GB and Ed [Balls]. GB was opposed to trailing a summit because he worried it would overinflate expectations. I briefed up Mo's visit to the US. The Belfast *News Letter* was critical of Trimble's speech yesterday. I got a few calls, including from relatives saying they hated seeing TB call Adams by his first name.

Saturday, September 5

Joe Lieberman's attack on Clinton was going big and TB was more and more supportive. The bottom line is he is a good president but we have a 24-hour media fuelling constant denigration of anyone in public life who dares to make a difference. The whole thing was now totally out of perspective. He said we should be totally supportive. He had watched a bit about it on CNN last night and they were totally hysterical. I took the boys to Luton vs Burnley and at half-time got a message from David Kerr – 'We are winning' – which meant the UUP executive were about to give their backing to a DT meeting with Adams. Clinton drew massive crowds in Limerick but the good vibes from there were being drowned by the bad vibes in the States.

Sunday, September 6

The confirmation of the DT/Adams meeting was going fine but Trimble was briefing there would be no handshake because a handshake was a signal that you had no arms in your hands, which could not be said for SF/IRA.

Monday, September 7

TB and Bertie had a phone conversation, in which BA said the Real IRA were about to disband and would we still go for them?

Tuesday, September 8

The Real IRA ceasefire statement came through and we got TB out to do a doorstep. He also went to [Lord] Rothermere's funeral and the nurses' awards lunch. Clinton's position was looking ropy and people seemed to be deserting him.

GB had had his front teeth capped and the smiles were even scarier than usual. TB was getting more concerned re Clinton and wondering whether the New York visit was a good idea. Blunkett came round for dinner. He was worried TB was getting a bit remote from people who only ever see him getting on and off RAF planes, or hear about him being at Chequers or Balmoral. As ever he was going on endlessly about GB. He said he would stand, as would JP and JS, if TB fell under a bus. But GB would win.

Pressure on Clinton was now really intense, with a lot of new voices saying he should go. We had to deal with a problem on the way down, a US agency having put out a story that TB told congressmen we would demilitarize in exchange for decommissioning. We put out a line making clear there were no such trade-offs.

With the [Kenneth] Starr Report due for publication, pressure was really mounting on Clinton, and there was a lot of interest in how TB would handle it. I spoke to him at Chequers and he said though we should keep out of it as best we could in relation to the detail, basically we had to stand by him. There was no merit in distancing ourselves at all. Yet he then told John H he wanted to fix a call with Clinton later to discuss NI and Russia, with [Yevgeny] Primakov being confirmed as [Russian] PM today.

The Starr Report was published, and was grim for BC. It was wall-to-wall on the media all over the world. At 9.30, with the world just digesting the whole damn mess, TB's call with Clinton went ahead. Considering what was happening around him, he was amazing. It was as if nothing was going on. 'Tony, hi.' If he was acting nonchalant, he did a great job. TB said we were thinking of him. He said he was confident, people were rooting for him, Starr was just a politically motivated rumour-monger. Then they were on to Northern Ireland and Russia. The DT/GA meeting had gone better than anyone expected, forty-five minutes instead of ten, and with at least some engagement. TB stressed again how important decommissioning was going to be, but it was difficult for Adams. BC suggested token decommissioning plus – as it was assumed SF knew who was responsible – an Omagh arrest with briefing that SF were helping with the tip-offs. Then Russia. 'The good news is they have a new government, the bad news is they have put troglodytes in the economic portfolios,' said BC. He said Primakov was smart but knew jack all about the economy. TB was straight on after the call ended – what a guy, that was not someone who was going down. He believed the process would start to turn in his favour, that people had heard all the reasons why he should go and would now be looking for reasons why he should stay. I spoke to McCurry, who was literally counting down [to leaving his job] 'x briefings to go'. Mike said BC was more confident than he had been, felt Starr had overplayed his hand.

Sunday, September 13

TB said re Bill C, of course he can deal with these things but the question is whether this is what politics has now become. He said if you looked at any sexual relationship in the context of a report like that, it could be made to look terrible. Likewise, he said, if every conversation you and I ever had was published, we would be dead – the lewd comments, the impersonations, the rudeness about other leaders and Cabinet members. Every leader had to be able to let go a little.

Tuesday, September 15

TB came round to my office first thing and said it was right to stay close and there should be no distancing but he thought my line 'One report on the Internet won't change his view of the president' was a bit close to saying whatever the facts, we would support him. It was right to stay close but we should not go over the top. He felt Bill would survive, and be an even bigger star on the global stage, but he wasn't out of it yet and we did not want to be exposed. He was also worried about the format for the Third Way event in New York – 'Me and the prime ministers of Sweden and Bulgaria sitting around gassing on comfy chairs' – but Hillary was very keen. I had a sharp written exchange with Piers Morgan re the *Mirror's* ludicrous line on it – the idea you dump Clinton because of this was absurd.

Wednesday, September 16

CB was interesting re Hillary. She said she clearly found the whole Lewinsky thing 'yucky', but there was no question she was going to dump him. She had decided her marriage was a compromise some time ago and there was no going back on it now, despite the humiliation. She felt there were three possibilities: 1. she was religious and her marriage was a religious union, 2. she was besotted, could not believe she was married to Bill Clinton – I don't think so, she added, or 3. it was a power partnership. CB tended to the third of these, that Hillary knew what he was like but lived with it for the access to power, and the feeling of power, and occasionally the reality of power.

Thursday, September 17

TB was at Chequers all day, working on his boxes and trying to get going on the [conference speech] draft.

Friday, September 18

Clinton was the big running story. TB was at Chequers and called a few times, ostensibly to talk about the speech, but I could tell he was worrying about New York. I said it was going to be a bit of a nightmare but we just had to get through it. Wilson came to see me, worried about his profile, and how he was seen to be clearing everything we put forward. On GB, he agreed we had to get [Charlie] Whelan out. He said Peter M was a 'star – he will transform DTI [Department of Trade and Industry]'.

Sunday, September 20

TB called and said we needed to be far more positive re the NY visit. I pointed out I had been saying so for days, and he was the one sending out the negative vibes. He said we needed to show why we were going – to give leadership. He wanted to do a piece for *The Times* about why he was going. I talked him out of that, thinking it was far too defensive, but he called three or four times on the same theme. TB said this could be the last time we see Bill as president, but that does not mean we have to be totally paralyzed by it.

I kept pushing the positives in the briefings I did, saying we kept focused on the things that mattered. Jeremy [Heywood, TB's principal private secretary] was working on the NYSE [New York Stock Exchange] speech, which GB was trying to neuter because he didn't really want TB launching a big economic initiative. TB was never off the phone, constantly pressing for new storylines and ideas to carry us through the visit without the only story being him and Bill. Magi [Cleaver] called and said the NYSE did not expect a speech so we had to get that changed. TB said it was important the US felt we were doing right by them, and standing by friends, but we also needed people to see we had our own agenda being driven forward.

And so to what, in a note to TB yesterday, Jeremy Heywood called 'the day trip from hell'. In fact the briefing overnight had gone pretty much word-perfect, several broadsheet splashes, with all the main points we put out yesterday and a lot of interest in the IFI [international financial institution] reform. There was only a little bit of 'why is he still going?'and TB was strongly of the view now that strong support for BC would stand us in good stead for the long term, not just with Clinton but with the US more generally. Needless to say the *Today* programme was less focused on anything we were saying, instead resorting to the old 'will be overshadowed' [by Clinton's situation] cliché. By the time we got there, the organizers were still arguing about what kind of chairs to use! BC was said to be keen on a dialogue of the leaders followed by a Q&A.

Doug Senior [Clinton staff] told me they were totally confident he would get through OK, that the worst had been thrown and he was still standing and there was a backlash in his favour. The public totally got why he lied about it, and didn't think it meant he was a liar in his political life. The discussion over lunch [at the New York Stock Exchange] was mainly Northern Ireland, plus EU regulation. Nobody mentioned Bill.

Bill and Hillary arrived, and he was in pretty upbeat form. 'Hey buddy, we just had a good day,' he said to me. Sandy Berger said it would be very good if TB could at some point make a reference to the importance of BC's leadership, which I passed on to TB. Sidney Blumenthal [former journalist, adviser to Clinton] said it would be 'appropriate' for TB to talk up BC's leadership! Whilst they were all being briefed on the format, Bill was again trying to get some kind of contact going with HC, without success. She was icy cold, literally froze when he touched her, and avoided any eye contact at all. With everyone else she was perfectly nice and friendly. I dread to think what the mood is like when they're on their own.

We then had the TB/BC bilateral – NI, economy, G7–8, Kosovo – then to the reception. BC told him that Prodi [Italian prime minister] had done a big number for him yesterday and it would be good if TB did the same, which he did with the students. Jim Steinberg felt he was still in difficulty. On the way out, Clinton asked me how it all felt and I said I thought he was through the worst and he needed to keep doing what he was doing. In the airport, TB was beginning to unwind. The whole day had indeed been a bit surreal, he said, but it could have been a lot worse. TB was by now on his world-celeb high, felt the day had gone a lot better than it might have done.

I went to Chequers where TB was working out in the garden. He wanted me to do something on NI. He also needed something that said no U-turn without saying no U-turn. We settled on backbone not backdown. I stayed down for dinner with TB.

Although Chequers was not my cup of tea, I could see why he liked it on days like this. He spent most of the day just sitting out in the garden, surrounded by papers, taking an occasional phone call, the Wrens who work there serving him tea whenever he wanted it. The food was good and the atmosphere relaxed, and he did at least get a lot of work done on the speech today. He was a bit worried that he was not in his usual panic. Panicking about not panicking, I said, is hardly leadership. In any event, he has the Sunday Q&A to panic about instead. We watched Man U vs Liverpool, and he looked hurt when I told him Cathy [Ferguson] thought he was basically a Tory.

I had breakfast with TB, going over the speech pretty much line by line. We discussed Bill C again. He said he totally understood how it happens. He likes women. He needs release from the pressures of the job. He wants to be a normal person. He said he still found it hard to deal with the fact that everyone has a view about him, that people talk about him as though they know him.

I felt that today we broke the back of the speech. We still had two drafts but they were merging into one. I fought hard for my version on Ireland because I felt it captured more both the emotion and the importance of what had been achieved, and how it related to politics.

Rory seemed fine about both Fiona and I going to Blackpool, but Calum was really upset, so I was feeling down most of the day. Once we got there, I was pretty much stuck in the room where we were working, our bedroom, and TB's room, except for twenty minutes when I went down to join Fiona for dinner with Neil and Glenys [Kinnock].

TB was up around 6 and when I went in at half past, I was pleased to see he was reading through it calmly, rather than slashing out great swathes or scribbling madly. He made a few changes, and some good cuts, but by and large we were in shape. We ran the final fact and policy checks with the office and departments, then did the autocue rehearsal. TB was very happy with it now, said he felt, on going through it, it was the best exposition of the Third Way he had done. We made only tiny changes as we went through it. He was much calmer than at this stage in previous years. He looked very calm just before going on. Accidentally, though no doubt some would say it was planned, his tie almost exactly matched the set. He looked and sounded very prime ministerial, very in control. He delivered it brilliantly. There was an extraordinary standing ovation for Mo when he paid tribute to her in the middle of the speech, which added to the sense of occasion.

Later, I couldn't face going out so I just stayed in my room, cheered only by the fact the cop on the door was a Burnley fan and we nattered a bit about that. I watched the main bulletins and the speech coverage was fantastic.

At the Winter Gardens, TB had a very difficult forty-minute meeting with Gerry Adams. He had been pretty provocative at the *Tribune* rally, talking about the need to take the united Ireland campaign forward, and a veiled threat when he said if you kicked the dog too hard, it would bite, which was seen as hinting about going back to violence. TB felt both sides wanted to make progress. But GA was clear how near impossible it was to get the IRA to decommission, and DT was saying he could not get the executive up and running without it. Worryingly, GA was saying that it may reach the point where people felt they would rather have a different leader. GA agreed to be reasonably upbeat afterwards at his press conference, while I just stuck to the line that we were determined and would get there in the end.

Cherie and Fiona were already at the dreaded *Mirror* lunch when we arrived. Monty put a shot right across his own people's bows saying he wanted a debate about the papers and how they covered the country. He said he felt this was a government with a real project for the country but he didn't feel that came over in the [Mirror Group] papers. He felt they were looking tired and cynical. Piers [Morgan] had a smirk on his face, but not one that hid his hurt. It was a pretty brutal assault on Piers and the other editors and at the end of it, Piers said 'Bloody hell, Alastair could have written that.' TB said he felt there was a time-warp mentality going through the media. They still saw politics through the prism of Thatcher, so everything had to be set by comparison with her, not a new and different agenda. He said he felt the *Mirror* ought to be a place for lively debate and intelligent criticism, not knee-jerk criticism set in an outdated agenda.

Then on Clinton, TB said he felt they were totally out of touch. People had a gut instinct on these things, and they felt if the Republicans wanted Clinton out, they should do it at an election, not by this kind of stuff. It all became pretty aggressive and Piers was handling it badly. He had a lot of front and he could talk, but he only had one tune and when you had the prime minister and your boss there having this kind of discussion, it wasn't the right tune to play.

[David] Montgomery said why couldn't the papers take the same approach as they did to Northern Ireland – be critical if necessary but basically supportive and wanting things to succeed? To pile on the pressure, I asked Monty if he wanted a lift to the conference to hear the NI debate, so he travelled with TB and said that had been a warning to the editors that if they kept on with the totally cynical approach, they would be out. By mid afternoon, there was a lot of talk about it. I got Anji to call Piers and tell him we had not been involved in orchestrating that, but he was clearly suspicious. The question was whether Monty had the power to deliver. TB met Trimble and Mallon. 'Well how do we get out of this, because I'm buggered if I know,' said TB. I went briefly to the Women in Journalism event, where Piers was making a big drama out of the lunch, and Rebekah [Wade, *Sun* deputy editor] was having to calm him down.

Thursday October 1

The papers were quiet apart from Kosovo and Ireland. I was getting focused on the briefing for China. [TB was about to make a bilateral visit to China.]

Wednesday October 7

Talks with [Chinese President] Jiang Zemin, which were a lot more formal, and a lot more small-talky than with Zhu. He told TB he was jealous of his youth. He also treated us to a lecture on Tibet. He was pretty scathing about the Dalai Lama, suggested he was influenced by young people in his entourage and said things he wasn't sure of. TB was a lot less nervy about raising things than he had been at that awful meeting in Hong Kong. TB said he understood because of Northern Ireland how they felt about irritating outside interference.

Friday, October 9

Godric called at 7am, midnight UK time, to tell me Clare Short had said on *Question Time* that Clinton was not fit to be president because he lied. My instinct, as so often with Short, was that TB should sack her. His argument was always that she would become a martyr and cause more trouble outside. But I wasn't convinced she actually had a following. She had got herself into a position where the press lauded her publicly, because she gave us a headache, but in truth did not see her as a very credible figure. Of course Clinton had done things that were hard to defend, which is why it was best to be in the position of defending in general while avoiding the specific. When I told him about it, he just said what a silly woman she is – does she have any redeeming features? Then he added 'I'm probably asking the wrong person.'

Friday, October 16

TB was in for the Nobel Peace Prize [for Northern Ireland] and we put out words and then did a pooled interview at Chequers. Nobel Prize was a massive story all day. I left for home early, and headed north to see Mum and Dad.

Monday, October 19

The main story for us today was Northern Ireland with McGuinness in in the morning, and Trimble in the afternoon. We placed expectations very low and by the end of the day it was clear that we were right to. McG told TB they would decommission but not right now. TB said that wasn't good enough. DT was trying to get SF on to the executive and he needed better cover than that. McG had someone called Jim with him who asked TB to sign a good-luck card for someone called John. As TB signed, I said it's not for someone who has a contract out on Paisley is it? Jim said it's for a good Republican friend. McG did his door-step outside and was very aggressive – it's all about Trimble (he had a wonderful way of pronouncing his name to make it sound like a really unpleasant illness). It also made it easier for DT when he came in, not harder. He didn't have much new to offer. Both he and Taylor were pretty clear they could not move without actual decommissioning. I said to TB afterwards 'Your one great triumph and it's going up in smoke.'

'Going up in smoke' was an overstatement, but decommissioning was further establishing itself as perhaps the trickiest issue of all. For very different reasons, it was a

huge stumbling block for both sides, and a permanent headache for TB, not least with a steady stream of convicted terrorists being released from prison. The next few days, which saw Margaret Thatcher wade into a row about the upcoming visit of Argentine President Carlos Menem, were almost light relief by comparison.

Saturday, October 24

I couldn't think of many worse ways to spend a weekend than at a summit hosted by Viktor Klima, but here we were in Austria [Pörtschach]. Very annoying. We had a bilateral with Bertie [Ahern] back at the hotel, up on the third floor. I think Bertie and I rivalled each other for who found all the palaver and protocol of these summits the most irritating. Bertie said his people thought the Real IRA were planning something, and it might be a hit on McGuinness. McGuinness meanwhile had told Bertie, with a view to him telling TB, that Trimble was at risk and needed to up his security. He seemed pretty serious. He wanted to push on and get the implementation bodies agreed by October 31. TB said he couldn't understand why they could not do some symbolic decommissioning.

Sunday, October 25

TB went off to church and had been expecting a quiet time but the Austrians had turned out the whole village council in traditional uniforms bearing gifts etc. Klima said it was fantastic because none of the other leaders would be seen by the public, but Paddy Teahon was pissed off because he had been trying to get to the same church and the Austrians wouldn't let him through.

Monday, November 9

TB had a one-on-one with Gerry Adams and called me in at the end. The mood wasn't great and it was clear they had made no progress. 'So what do we say to our friends outside?' asked Gerry. I said we should say you had confessed to being gay and therefore TB was putting you straight into the Cabinet as Northern Ireland Secretary.*

---

* Nick Brown (Chief Whip 1997–98, Minister of Agriculture 1998 onwards) had just been outed as gay by the press. Ron Davies (Welsh Secretary) had also resigned after a 'moment of madness' prompted a bizarre encounter with a West Indian man on Clapham Common.

Martin McGuinness gave us a problem on the *Today* programme when he said that the reason they couldn't get the IRA to decommission was because the IRA 'won't do it'. I replied as best I could on it but then PA ran my quotes as indicating we were no longer saying SF/IRA were part of the same thing. Trimble complained and I had to square him and then clarify at the four o'clock, they were two sides of the same coin etc. What I didn't want to do was lay into McG at this stage. But we had to put the pressure on. With 200 prisoners now out, it was very hard that there was no decommissioning. The morning briefing was better humoured than last week.

Bertie [Ahern] caused a bit of a flurry, which I had to damp down at the 11, when he said there would be a united Ireland 'in my lifetime'.

On the plane to Belfast we were working on the Thursday speech for the Dáil, which TB wanted to go big, and be about more than the usual stock of Anglo-Irish issues. He even threw out the idea of speculating that one day Ireland could join the Commonwealth, before John H and I persuaded him it was a barmy idea. Over dinner, he said he wanted to frame a context for the debate on decommissioning, that we had to break the ideological grip they had against the physical handing over of weapons. John H and Mo were worried about getting into that territory too. Seamus Mallon came up for a drink and did a doorstep saying the process was in danger unless we made progress before Christmas.

Hillsborough. TB was worried that the process was in danger of moving backwards and felt we had to make progress soon on the North-South implementation bodies. He was also concerned at the feeling in the security services that the Real IRA would be going for a big assassination soon. We headed for Stormont and there was a lot of tension between Trimble and Mallon at the first meeting. They could barely bring themselves to look at each other, and Seamus looked both hurt and angry whenever DT spoke. TB felt he was close to the end of his tether and after seeing them together he had a session with them individually, told DT he had to be more understanding of what SM was trying to do; told Seamus to keep going, not let the lack of progress get to him, keep working away. SM said DT saw the implementation bodies as a Fenian plot between us and the Irish. Then Adams, and TB trying again to push on decommissioning but getting nowhere, with GA constantly moving back to DT being obstructive. I ducked out of some of the meetings to work on the speech for the Dáil, marrying John H's draft with TB's comments overnight.* It was a strong speech which I started to brief. I particularly enjoyed briefing the 'new positive relations with the Republic' line with Ian Paisley sitting on the edge of my desk looking at a newspaper. He looked around at me, shook his head. I winked and he laughed.

TB did the smaller [NI] parties pm, then left a group of UU, SDLP and Irish officials to work up new ideas on how we take forward the North-South implementation bodies. He did his third doorstep of the day, said he remained optimistic but there was a lot to do blah. We carried on with the speech for Dublin where the Tony and Bertie show was going well. I really like the Irish political class. They seem far less hidebound and of course they love talking about UK politics. They [the media] wanted a response to Bob Marshall-Andrews [Labour MP] saying I was Pontius Pilate's spin doctor. Ignored.

Thursday, November 26

Dublin. It was only as I filled TB in on the Irish media that it dawned on him how big and how historic this speech was being viewed in Ireland. We had a meeting with Ruairí Quinn [Irish Labour Party leader] who briefed him on the planned Labour/democratic left. We set off in a very long convoy for very few people and at the Dáil there was a real excitement in the air as he walked through, that buzz that you normally associate with weddings or big sporting events. The mood was really good. Fiona and I sat up in the gallery behind CB and Celia Larkin [Ahern's partner]. It was a good speech and he delivered it really well. The UK press picked up on the very positive mood music re the euro. But generally it was the history and the sense of occasion that dominated.

We left for a visit to Bertie's old school, St Aidan's, really bright kids, and did a computer link-up with other schools, then a walkabout, where the mood again was terrific. Over lunch they were crunching hard again on implementation bodies and also re Vienna – no to tax harmonization, yes to dealing with unfair

---

* In the first ever speech to Dáil Éireann by a UK prime minister, Blair appealed for nationalists and Unionists to work together.

competition. TB said he was worried 'the crazies' would do something soon. Martin Mansergh [Fianna Fáil politician] said he was worried if the IRA moved to decommission, the Real IRA would strike. Mo called me out halfway through to say TB really must speak to Trimble to seal the deal on implementation bodies. TB and Bertie were really working together well but both agreed the whole thing was in danger of stalling unless they managed to get a shove forward soon. They did a short doorstep before we left for the plane.

Friday, November 27

We got pretty good coverage for Ireland and now we were heading straight for Wales. TB spoke to Trimble again, who was cutting up rough re implementation bodies and TB felt he may need to go again soon.

Monday, November 30

I did a foreign press briefing in the afternoon, and there was an on-off drama re whether we were going to NI again. TB was keen, but DT was so difficult at the moment, and also so under pressure from [John] Taylor and others, that it might prove fruitless. Eventually the decision was made for us when we were told Trimble had flu, though there were mixed views as to whether it was the diplomatic variety. TB said there is a real risk we lose this whole thing because these people are so impossible.

Thursday, December 3

TB got back from Ireland at 3am after the talks on the North-South bodies. They had been close to a deal and he thought it was to be sealed but again, as he left the thing slipped away. By the time we got to France [for the Anglo-French summit] it was all falling apart and there was a growing sense of crisis.

Northern Ireland was a big problem again, and TB was blaming Trimble and Taylor. 'I sometimes wonder if they are just thick,' he said. 'They do not get it.'

Friday, December 4

TB was really pissed off re NI. Mo called to get me to get TB to call Trimble but he didn't want to in case he lost his rag. It's a joke he's off for the Nobel Peace

Prize [won jointly with John Hume] next week. This thing could tip over. He felt generally that sometimes the NI politicians were more interested in being feted than getting the job done. In the car on the way home TB spoke to Jonathan re NI and was absolutely livid they had let it slip back. We got in for a meeting with Mo who was convinced now we were going to miss the February deadline. She blamed the UUs straight out for moving the goalposts again.

Saturday, December 5

I was due to take Fiona and the kids for one of Mo's Hillsborough Castle weekends so I was hoping for a quiet time work-wise. We got to Hillsborough and went straight out to a pub lunch nearby – Mo and Jon [Norton, Mowlam's husband] and his daughters, Will Hutton and family, DB plus his three boys and a girl-friend, Chris Smith [Culture Secretary] and Dorian [Jabri, Smith's partner], Tessa Blackstone [Baroness Blackstone, education minister], Ross Kemp [actor] and Rebekah Wade [engaged to Kemp]. Mo was a good host and everyone seemed to enjoy the whole weekend. Even the charades game, which was normally the kind of thing I hated, was good fun. I was called out of the dinner God knows how many times when the papers dropped, and there was a lot of interest in my dealings with Cranborne. [AC had been involved in a series of secret negotiations with Cranborne, behind the back of his leader William Hague, to secure a deal on Lords reform, and the expulsion of most hereditary peers.]

Sunday, December 6

My meeting with Cranborne was running second on the news. Ridiculous. I had breakfast with Mo, Will Hutton and Tessa B. They were all doing in Geoffrey Robinson, on whom there was more stuff in the Sundays.* We touched on whether Mo should go for London mayor. She got a call from a UUP contact saying [Michael] Mates and [Brian] Mawhinney [Conservative MPs, former Northern Ireland ministers] were making calls in advance of Wednesday's debate on prisoners to stir things up and raise pressure on the UUs to be difficult. Mo was worried the Tories were preparing to end bipartisanship. They were even sug-gesting Hague might lead the debate for them. She was clearly worried at where things were. Trimble wasn't leading and the vacuum was being filled by trouble-makers. It made it harder to put Adams under pressure.

---

* Geoffrey Robinson, the Paymaster General, was revealed to have an off-shore trust.

I spoke to TB who was minded to speak to Major and line him up to step in if need be. They basically want us to end the Agreement, he said. We won't do that. It is despicable if they talk bipartisanship while trying to undermine the Agreement at every turn. I had a long chat with DB who seemed fairly relaxed for once. His boys were terrific with him, very solicitous but also taking no nonsense. The kids really enjoyed the weekend and even though I had spent several hours of both days on the phone, I was really glad we went and felt refreshed by the time we got home.

Monday, December 7

TB spoke to Bertie and Adams and was getting more and more fed up with it.

Friday, December 11

TB's day started with a gloomy bilateral with Bertie. BA was really down, felt Trimble – either because he wanted to, or because of the pressure from within the UUs – was holding up on North-South bodies, and this was stalling any progress on the debate inside the IRA. He agreed with TB that it was crazy they were going around collecting peace prizes when there was no peace. 'These people drive me crazy,' said TB. 'Sure, they're not easy,' said Bertie. Our intelligence on the IRA meeting at Cavan at the weekend was that basically they had decided not to decide yet, but it was going to be tricky to handle if word came out.

TB felt we were in a strong enough position to do a round of interviews, and the sense was growing we were on a bit of a roll. We had a secure line brought in for TB to speak to Bill C about Iraq. They agreed we would go in if there was more obfuscation over the weekend. RC was still totally opposed. The IRA's briefing led the news. Robin Oakley had tipped me off in advance and I put a note through to the office and the NIO that we must not overreact, and demand people keep it in perspective.

Monday, December 14

TB was called by Bill C early, his second call in thirty-six hours, and it was pretty clear he was gearing up for action on Iraq. [Head of UNSCOM inspection team Richard] Butler was due to report for UNSCOM tomorrow. If he said he was being obstructed, BC was clearly on for a strike. The problem was Ramadan was due – Saturday – so the strike would have to be soon. TB was supportive but worried that the public would simply think the whole thing was a diversion from impeachment; or that Butler would not be crystal clear, and we would be going to war on an ambiguity.

Tuesday, December 15

Northern Ireland was getting more and more difficult and TB was several times on the phone to BA, DT etc. Bertie wanted him to go out there and try to drive it on.

Wednesday, December 16

TB was clearly having a bit of a wobble about Iraq. He said he had been reading the Bible last night, as he often did when the really big decisions were on, and he had read something about John the Baptist and Herod, which had caused him to rethink, albeit not change his mind.*

TB spoke to Bill C again and it was now very much when not if, and we were into working out the media management detail. He was less worried about the impeachment situation now than the possible loss of innocent civilian life. He said he worried about our forces losing their lives, and he worried about the people on the receiving end too. 'I think if ever you lose that, you risk making the wrong decision, and you cease to do your job properly.' It was at moments like these you got a proper sense of the enormity of his job. Dealing with this, on the same day as the Irish were pressing him to get more involved in their problems, and with a stack of difficult domestic issues too, it was pretty impressive the way he kept these different issues under some kind of control, and was able to move from one to the other and box them off where he needed to.

Thursday, December 17

Peter M, out of nowhere, asked me if Geoffrey Robinson was being sacked. At lunchtime, it became clear why he was asking. Ben [Wegg-Prosser] called me and said Routledge's book on Peter was going to reveal that Robinson had given him a £300k loan to help buy his place in Notting Hill. Peter felt they should get it out through e.g. Bevins as part of a story about dirt being dug on Peter. I said

---

* After John the Baptist denounced the marriage of Herod Antipas, Herod ordered him to be imprisoned and later beheaded.

hold fire. There was no way the story would be anything other than the existence of a loan that most people would find very odd. 'Do you think it is a problem?' asked Ben, knowing the answer. I do, I said. A big problem? Well, it sounds like it. I went round to see TB, who was in the loo. I took Jonathan into TB's room and waited for him to come back. He was in upbeat mood, which I was about to deflate. I told him the facts as I knew them, and he was horrified. First, what on earth was Peter doing taking out that kind of loan from Geoffrey, who was not an uncontroversial figure? Second, we were immediately on to the angle that Peter was ultimately in charge of the DTI investigation into Geoffrey. Third, it was bound to be – or certainly seen to be – part of the ongoing GB/Peter M nonsense. We assumed Geoffrey had told GB's lot, and someone had fed it to Routledge as a way of doing in Peter if Geoffrey was going to go down anyway. And all in the middle of a bloody difficult international situation which required us to keep our eye on a very different kind of ball. TB was not best pleased, but quickly calmed down and went into his usual 'we need the facts' mode. I found it astonishing Peter wanted to brief preemptively, which would never work on this. He [TB] wavered between anger and exasperation. 'I hate this. I cannot believe this. The Tories will murder us for it.' Yet when I spoke to Peter, he couldn't see it, or at least pretended not to. It was a loan between old friends who go back a long way. What about the DTI angle? I would not be making the decisions. Charlie [Lord Falconer] came to see me, and asked me what was wrong with Geoffrey lending him money? Possibly nothing, but the politics are fairly obvious and you can't just ignore them.

Friday, December 18

Again, our press was going better for us than the US press was for BC. There was good news overnight in that there was finally agreement on North-South bodies, and we put out TB words of welcome.

TB told me he had spoken to Peter and warned him his instinct was that the Geoffrey Robinson loan story was potentially very dangerous. We had asked Charlie F to do a report on the facts, and when I spoke to him later, he seemed to think it was pretty serious. Peter was still of a mind to brief on his terms, and later Ben W-P told me Tom Baldwin knew about it. Then [Richard] Wilson came to see me, said Michael Scholar [DTI permanent secretary] had only been informed of the loan once Peter knew the book was going to divulge it. So there would definitely be questions about non-declaration as well. I felt it was a no-hope situation for him. It could easily be seen as bad as anything the Tories did, and it showed poor judgement, first to get involved, and then not to be up front when there was the possibility of a conflict of interest re the DTI investigating Geoffrey.

Saturday, December 19

I had a long chat with Peter M, who claimed not to see what the problem was re the loan. He said what is wrong with a friend lending money to someone? I said it had the potential to be a big bad story and surely he could see that. He said I was overreacting, I had always been a bit of a Calvinist, and it was all a bit 'Alastair and Fiona-ish'. He was adamant it would not be much of a story. I said it had the potential to be the worst thing to hit us yet. 'Would it be the same if it was Sainsbury?' he said.1 Probably not, I said, but politics is not science. So it is a Geoffrey problem, he said. I said it is a Geoffrey problem, but it is also a Peter Grand Panjandrum problem, and it is a GB/Peter M self-destruct at the heart of government problem. He was adamant I was overreacting.

Tuesday, December 22

The Iraq fallout was bad enough but the Peter M situation was a wall-to-wall disaster area. Every paper led on it in later editions, and it was grim.

Wednesday, December 23

The papers were absolutely ghastly for Peter, massive coverage and relentlessly negative. Could I go to a meeting at 10.30? I spoke to TB who, as I thought he would, had pretty much made his mind up. 'I'm worried what this is all doing to the public, never mind the press,' he said. He said in the end it was the concealment that was the main problem. Everything else was secondary but they would pick away. I said if Peter went, Geoffrey would have to go too. I know, he said. We had a conference call with GB, who was still asking if Geoffrey could stay. Re Peter, somewhat disingenuously I felt, he was saying maybe an apology and a reprimand would be enough. TB said that didn't do enough. He felt Peter could only rebuild from a fresh start. He had spoken to Peter late last night, and he sensed Peter was coming to the same view. Peter had spoken to GB this morning too, and one of the odder aspects of this was that as it got worse, he turned to GB for advice and support, despite being pretty sure he had been involved in setting the whole thing up.

I got a lift in with Fiona, feeling pretty stressed and depressed. I met up with

Jonathan and Lance [Price] and we went to the DTI. Jonathan was scruffily dressed as he was due to go to the Lake District. Lance was due to be heading to Chile for a break. We were driven into the underground car park, met by a very pretty girl who took us upstairs to an outer office that was deathlike in its atmosphere and then in to see Peter, who was at his desk, reading the papers. He had done the office very much to his taste, modern and brightly coloured furniture, a minimalist desk, nice pictures. A Christmas card from Prince Charles had pride of place on his desk. I asked everyone else to wait outside and told him TB wanted to talk to him. I didn't listen in so only heard Peter's side of the call, that he knew he had made a mistake, wished he had handled it differently, but was it really a hanging offence? I could tell from the vibe coming back that TB was in steely mode, and saying that it was. His argument was that an apology would just be seen as a piece of spin. There had been a deception, or at least a concealment that could be construed as such. Added to which neither party nor public could really grasp the scale of it. I was pacing up and down by the window and after a while Peter's tone changed, became one of resignation. He said 'You have clearly made up your mind and I have to accept your judgement, which of course I do. I'm obviously very sorry.' The call ended, he looked at me, shrugged and then went out to see Ben.

I spoke to TB and began drafting resignation letters. I told Lance to put out a line that the PM was looking at the detail. I called Jack C[unningham], who was still manfully doing bids on it, and warned him it may end with his resignation, so change the tone. I spoke again to TB who said we now just had to put sentiment to one side, and deal with it. He wanted it made clear that we were not the Tories, and never would slide to standards as low as theirs. He, Jonathan and I worked out the reshuffle and agreed the sooner it was done the better. I felt desperately sad for Peter, who came back in looking wretched. I said this is not going to be easy, but we are just going to have to do it, and be professional about it. I know, he said, I know. He had clearly been crying. He collected himself and then amazed me by saying he felt he ought to call Gordon. Again, I only heard his side, but it sounded as though sympathetic noises were coming from the other end. Peter said he had been foolish, he was desperately sorry it was ending like this, and he hoped they would maintain some kind of relationship. It was extraordinary considering all that had gone on. GB was clearly saying he could trust him because Peter said on more than one occasion 'Yes, I know I can trust you, I know that.'

I wanted the letters done and dusted and out by the lunchtimes, and started to read the draft of Peter's letter to TB. The first line was 'I can scarcely believe I am writing this.' We were both quite emotional by now. I went over to him, said this is all absolutely dreadful but we just have to get through it. He kept saying why, why, why, but I was unsure whether he meant why did he do what he did, or why was he being forced to go. He felt if it was anyone else, we could have fought on. He made a few small changes, I got Lance to type it up outside, and then spoke to TB re his reply. Again, Peter startled me re GB. 'It's important Gordon sees them before they go out,' he said. He saw my surprise. I sat alongside him as he read through the letters, tears cascading down his face, and I gripped his shoulder and told him he had to be strong, and just get through the next ghastly few hours. I watched the news with Peter, who was calmer now, more focused, but still regularly bursting into tears. 'Please do your best,' he said. 'Don't let them portray me as some kind of felon.'

Michael Scholar popped in to say he was sorry, and seemed genuinely moved. Peter was fine when someone else came in like that but when it was the two of us, he kept breaking down. 'You don't deserve this Peter, you really don't.' Yes, I do. 'Well,' I said, 'even if you do, you don't really, if you see what I mean.' How many times had I warned him that what I called his 'lifestyle ambitions' would do for him? His desire to be famous and mingle with the rich and the great and the good. What the fuck was Charles' card doing there like it was the biggest thing in the mailbag? I really felt for him though, and felt wretched that I was having to act like some kind of undertaker to his ministerial career, doing the letters, shaping the media, telling them it was all over and soon he would be gone. We had had so many moments, good and bad, but when push came to shove, he was still one of the best and it was a dreadful fucking waste. I'd done Ron Davies' [Welsh Secretary] letters, and others, and it was just a job really, just helping sort things tidily, but I really felt this, and felt dreadful for Peter, for whom politics was wrapped up in everything he had.

As we left, I took him to one side and hugged him, and he me, and my mobile phone went off inside my jacket. We laughed. Be strong, I said. Do not let those bastards take any joy in seeing you broken. Stand tall and give every sense that one day you'll be back. I left feeling absolutely drained. TB called to go over the lines we should be pushing. It's grim, I said. Yes, he said, but we just have to get on with it now. I was back in the office and did a full briefing at 2, gave out the letters, took all their predictable questions. I felt OK, apart from when pressed on whether it was a breach of the ministerial code, and also why he hadn't moved on it earlier.

[1999]

I left for what was going to be a difficult meeting, to discuss Peter, with him, Anji, Philip, Ben [Wegg-Prosser], at [Labour peer and media entrepreneur] Waheed Alli's office. There was the usual jokey small talk at the start, Peter talking himself down as a disaster area a bit, then I kicked it off properly, said we all started from the premise – and this includes TB – of wanting Peter back in the front line at some point. This meeting was about how we suggested he conducted himself in the meantime. My own judgement was that he should have a reasonable period of radio silence, at the end of which he emerged as a reformed character who had learnt from the experience, was more humble, less media-focused, more substantial. Peter said he agreed, then seemed to contradict that immediately by saying that he thought he should use the time to write a book about his personal journey in the party, his upbringing, his sexuality, his politics, his strengths and weaknesses, and that he should also make a film about the Third Way.

I knew about the book idea already because JP had mentioned it to me. He was pushing for Peter maybe to get involved with the ANC [in South Africa] in their elections – a [Richard] Caborn [regional development minister] idea. Re the book he said he thought 'later rather than sooner'. Peter said JP supported the idea. Ben said he didn't think Peter would be happy until he was out of politics. Peter said on the contrary he was only happy when he was in politics. 'I am not, contrary to what some of you think, interested in wealth. I was put on this earth to do what I've been doing.' When it was suggested he spend more time in Hartlepool, he said his constituents didn't want to see him in Hartlepool as much as they wanted to see him in the Cabinet. 'Indeed they do not think I should have left.' This was not making progress. When Anji suggested he did back-bench committee work, and Philip said other MPs found it interesting and satisfying, he said the vast bulk were bored out of their skulls. He then said, not really meaning it and exaggerating to make a point, 'If I can't come back and make a difference, then I may as well take my own life.' 'The Third Way,' I said, and he laughed, but we were getting nowhere. He then turned on Anji in particular, said she did not have his interests at heart and we were all just trying to find ways of keeping him out. 'Anji, if you want me to be a vegetable, to just vegetate, well I won't.'

He said he was fed up with being talked about, now he intended to do the talking, to let people see him as he is. We went on for an hour, by the end of which all we had concluded was that we all wanted him to make a comeback – apart from Ben – but there was little or no agreement about how to lay the ground for that. He had lost weight, as had Ben, and at times he looked close to the edge. Later he called Fiona and said he would like to come round and see us on Saturday. TB's worry was that he was incapable of living without the limelight. He couldn't do without it. He said he was getting fed up with the lot of them. There was too much to do without having to worry about all this the whole time. We had left the meeting, particularly Anji, in a state of some agitation. I had tried to be conciliatory re the book, though I was unconvinced it was a good idea, and TB was sure it was a bad idea. There was a bit of a feeling around, articulated by Peter Hyman [strategist and speechwriter], that if he was not careful, Peter was finished.

Monday, January 18

TB was seeing the Garvaghy Road residents' association, which had a big media crowd outside. I left early to go to Edgware with Philip who thought I should see for myself the way the mood had changed in the focus groups.

Wednesday, January 20

For PMQs, we thought Hague would do health, Kosovo or maybe Jack C's expenses, which hadn't really taken off. In the end he did Northern Ireland in a way that was very tricky for us re prisoner release. PMQs was OK, and TB on good form, but Hague got very close to busting bipartisanship on N Ireland. TB said afterwards he felt he was getting more into his stride. TB was also sure Hague was in trouble, and that the skids were possibly under him.

Wednesday, January 27

Northern Ireland was the main story and Hague was diddling again, really trying to crank it up, and we decided to up the ante a little by saying he was being dragged into this by [Andrew] Mackay. PMQs was dominated by Northern Ireland and the Tories got perilously close to ending bipartisanship. TB saw Hague afterwards and Jonathan said he looked pretty low. His confidence was not good. Paul McCartney popped his head round the door of the Cabinet Room. He was in seeing CB and Fiona about a charity event. He was funny and charming and the guy from the *Liverpool Daily Post* thought he had died and gone to heaven.

Thursday, January 28

Cabinet went over pay, Kosovo, NI and Iraq. Kosovo was getting heavier by the day. On NI, TB said the Tory shift was really unhelpful. Prisoner release was difficult and unpopular and it made it harder for the Unionists to move. The more the Tories made it an issue the harder it was. If the Tories move to the right of the UUs, it will be very hard for Trimble, who has a tough enough time as it is.

Back in Opposition, TB had refused even to consider breaking with a bipartisan approach to policy on Northern Ireland. Part of his thinking was that if we did get into government, there would come times when we needed Tory help in keeping the process going forward. But Hague did not enjoy the strength of position as leader that TB had enjoyed. Also, there was almost universal support on the Labour benches for what John Major had tried to do. By contrast, there was a significant strand of Tory opinion that was against the process, both because of the perceived bias against Unionists, but also because of a desire to cause TB trouble. Hague was responding to these different pressures, in a way that had the potential to damage Trimble, and so damage the process. The politics of the Province were complicated enough. This was a further complicating factor that we could have done without.

We got back to Number 10 to wait for Al Gore. He arrived late from JP, so TB and CB worked the crowds in the street. Gore arrived, did a bit of glad-handing and we went into TB's room to prepare for the business meeting. He was wearing the most extraordinary boots. He was still a bit wooden, but more relaxed than before, and showed the odd flash of humour, e.g. when I warned him pre-press that there was a situation to be aware of re the Falklands and he said 'Falklands, that's what I have to call the Malvinas, right?' I looked horrified, he started laughing. 'Got you.' Asked by TB what he could say that was helpful, he said Jefferson, Kennedy, Clinton, Gore. He was good on Europe, really pro the argument that Britain strong in Europe was good for the US/UK relationship. The media were in for the business meeting and I thought he did well. We then had a meeting with kids from the New Deal, and once the media were out, he was really relaxed, good with them.

Like Clinton, he was excellent on policy detail and more focused on the ends of policy than the means. We had agreed to do two joint interviews, Sky and CNN, and as with Bill C, Gore was good at taking a brief, wanted to know the goal of the interview and then would go out and deliver. We went over some of the areas that might be tricky – death penalty, Ireland, Falklands – and he was pretty much up to speed. The [Adam] Boulton interview [on Sky] was good, a mix of the political and personal and I thought both came out well. CNN was almost all Kosovo, with RC out there today. Gore and TB set off for dinner at Chequers. JP, who had been unbelievably status-conscious in the planning of the visit, was going too.

TB said the dinner went really well, that once JP relaxed a bit, they had a great time, the right mix of politics and just letting their hair down. He found Gore more impressive this time, and Gore felt we had pushed the boat out. TB was keen we stay out of the elections when they come, but he felt we had done enough for Al to be a friend for life if he got in.

[In Jordan, for the funeral of King Hussein.] We were out and about at 8. There was a fair bit of hanging around, and when you saw the list of leaders attending, you realized the enormity of the logistical and security effort. Clinton had suggested a bilateral so we went up to the American room, where he was having a nap but his people felt he wouldn't mind being woken up. He was the one most into the whole atmospherics, 'What a day, what an amazing event, how many bilaterals you done, Tony?' kind of thing. We did Kosovo then Ireland, with BC clear the IRA had to decommission real weapons before Trimble should be expected to have Sinn Féin on the executive. We were called out because we now had a session with the new king, Abdullah, so we walked up the winding hill, and in for a fairly brief session.

Tuesday, February 9

We had the farewell dinner for John Holmes, which Sandy Berger flew over for. John was unassuming as ever, but I think even he was moved by TB's speech, which really laid out how important he had been. He said TB, JH, Jonathan and AC would always have the bonding of the Good Friday Agreement days to remember. He spoke with real warmth about John's commitment and expertise. Richard Wilson said to John that he had heard a number of insincere farewell speeches, but that one was as genuine as it got.

Friday, February 12

Clinton winning his impeachment battle was the big news.

Tuesday, February 16

I went north to see Mum and Dad, who was not looking too great. They had the telly on in the afternoon and on one of the quiz programmes, there was a question: 'What does Alastair Campbell do?' Good question.

Friday, February 26

TB had a bilateral with [Jacques] Santer [president of the European Commission], who strikes me as hopeless. It is as though he is surprised to be there. Then Ahern, and decommissioning, which was at a difficult moment. There was a wonderful moment which cracked everyone up when TB, exasperated, said 'If it is in the Agreement, I cannot see why it should not be in the treaty, and if it is in the Agreement it NEEDS to be in the treaty,' to which Paddy Teahon replied 'You are applying logic, Prime Minister, and that has no place in this process.'

At the 11.30, I got a lot of Northern Ireland and said we were likely to miss March 10 – there was a bad poll today – and a Good Friday Agreement Mark 2 was now more likely. Mo had told the Cabinet March 10 wasn't going to happen.

NI was coming back up the tracks and at the office meeting, Jonathan said it was needing TB's attention. Gerry Adams claimed we were in crisis. On the press, we agreed there was no point going to war, but we did need a proactive strategy for putting over arguments about them and about the nature of political debate.

I had another fight with the *Record* over their dishonest stitch-up. They had done an interview with Mo, she had talked about the importance of integrated education and they had presented her comments as though about Scotland, not NI. I spoke to Mo who wrote a letter to [Martin] Clarke and suggested there was now malice in their coverage of us. Word then came back they were going to splash on the letter, and attack her. The guy [Clarke] should be a down-table sub on the *Mail*, not editing what was once a decent newspaper. I suggested to Mo we pre-empt with a statement put out generally. DD was worrying the row with them was escalating out of control. I said this was the result of not standing up to them when it started.

The *Guardian* had a story saying TB wanted Mo to be London mayor. She called in a huff about it and I said she should ignore all reshuffle stories.

We got a call about the car bombing of nationalist lawyer Rosemary Nelson.* Grim. I put together a TB statement, which we released on return.

---

* Leading human-rights solicitor Rosemary Nelson was killed by a car bomb in Lurgan, County Armagh. The murder was claimed by a shadow loyalist group, the Red Hand Defenders.

Thursday, March 18

Cabinet was mainly EU crisis then Kosovo. TB was worried the public were not remotely prepared for what might be coming, namely a pretty difficult military operation. Ireland was bubbling up and we finished the joint statement, which was still weak on decommissioning. The four o'clock was mainly about Ireland, George Jones [*Telegraph*] in particular giving me a really hard time re the lack of toughness of decommissioning.

Friday, March 19

On Kosovo, TB said there is a chance we will be launching bombing raids next week, at the same time we are trying to sort Ireland and negotiate a good deal for Britain in the Agenda 2000 talks.

Tuesday, March 23

TB did a clutch of Kosovo interviews, then we set off [for Berlin]. On the flight we sat with RC, David Bostock [head of European Secretariat, FCO] and Stephen Wall [UK Ambassador to the EU] and went through the real nitty-gritty. We arrived, got to the hotel then had a long session with Bertie Ahern and team, which was pretty gloomy. Bertie said he was not sure it was worth holding talks in Belfast because we could be up seven nights and still not get them to say they would decommission. TB said if we didn't go, and it subsequently all collapsed, we wouldn't be forgiven. He felt we had to inject a real shock into the system. TB was sitting in the only comfortable armchair in the room, the rest of us on hard-backed upright chairs, and he was clearly the man calling the shots. Bertie ended up agreeing they should go next week, but he was down about things. TB said if the two of them, plus Bill C, all made the same points powerfully, it would have a big impact on public opinion. Joe Lennon said the IRA never gave two hoots about public opinion. TB said yes, but we have to separate the moderates from the extremists.

Saturday, March 27

I slept solid for twelve hours then took the football club at school. I was also working on a joint TB/Bertie Ahern article, the Irish as ever trying to get a bit weasely on the decommissioning issue.

The US fixed a TB/Bill C call for 7pm so I had to leave the kids' school disco to get home and listen in. They did a bit of NI, BC saying he would do whatever it takes and we briefed that too. Good call, and he sounded a lot more sharp and clear than last time they did Kosovo.

Another day from hell really. The refugee situation was getting worse, and there wasn't much sign the military campaign was getting better. Some of the papers, especially the *Mail*, were positioning for failure. Another ghastly Scotland call. [Alex] Salmond was to do a broadcast on Kosovo and I said we had to be ready to pounce if there was the slightest equivocation. Back came the line he might get support. Added to which NI was upon us again, at another crisis point. I asked Julian [Braithwaite, press officer] to do a proper report on how the Serb media worked, so that we could start to inform our own media as much as anything else.

Plane to Belfast. TB asked me to work with George Robertson on plans to neutralize or turn the negative effects [Slobodan] Milosevic's media machine was having on our media. We helicoptered to Hillsborough, where TB did a fairly downbeat doorstep, less 'hand of history' than 'we have come too far to stop now'. TB saw Bertie, then Trimble, then Mallon, then he and Bertie met Adams and McGuinness together. Everyone seemed to think we were in the shit. I had a chat with McGuinness re Kosovo. He said he [Milosevic] would be a hard nut to crack and 'bombing into submission' isn't always a sensible policy. Pots and kettles. The only breakthrough of sorts came when Adams said to us 'Look, we know the score, there has got to be decommissioning.' It was the first time he, rather than we, had been that blunt. It had also been announced where nine of the 'disappeared' were. The downside of that was it reminded people the IRA were killers. As TB said, are we really expected to be hugely grateful that years after they did it they told us where they killed and disposed of a few people?

Kosovo was not looking good. The humanitarian crisis was becoming a disaster. TB saw the Orange Order before we left for Stormont for talks mainly with the smaller parties. He and Bertie saw [General John] de Chastelain, who must live a very weird life, backwards and forwards to NI, with large periods of literally nothing happening to bring him into the picture. But TB stressed de Chastelain's credibility was vital to the process. He felt we might get something, possibly an act of decommissioning, videotaped by SF, verified by them. Paisley was out and about rowing with the Irish, but the one TB really couldn't stand was Brendan McKenna. He said he was making things worse and people would die as a result.

We flew back to Hillsborough and over lunch TB and BA agreed they would really try to work on Sinn Féin. They went into a two-hour meeting with Adams and McGuinness, while I put together another vacuous space-filling briefing about it all being 'difficult but doable'. We were literally having to just dream up lines to keep the news guys busy whilst TB and Bertie tried to put the pressure on. The BBC ran a story, based on God knows what, that the UUs were now saying an act of decommissioning was not required. John Taylor went straight out and said it was nonsense. GA and McG were basically saying they would decommission – not least because they knew they had to – but they could not be sure how the IRA would react to that idea. We set up a SF/UUP meeting for 8pm, beforehand TB/BA seeing GA/McG again to suggest the UUs were not as insistent on prior decommissioning as a precondition. He tried to get them to have a drink, but they refused. Even Taylor had said he could see it was a problem for SF if they were seen to be responding to pressure on this. Taylor wanted to delay but we were saying we had to move on it now. I felt TB was being too open with them and that they would brief the SF position and then move SF back. John Sawers [foreign affairs adviser and successor to John Holmes] came in with tonight's [Kosovo] targets, mainly defence ministry buildings. There was a North Atlantic Council meeting going on and Italy was getting more and more nervous. The truth was we were not in control of events. TB was keen to get more and more involved 'but I'm here having to deal with this nonsense.' He said if it was left to him and Bertie, they could sort a deal that most people would support in five minutes. But the NI politicians were a nightmare. They delight in being prisoners of their own history. There were meetings going on all over the place but the one that mattered was SF/UUs. Adams and McGuinness were always on their own, Trimble always with a huge entourage to keep an eye on him. The aim was to try to get some kind of sequencing agreed. GA/McG agreed there would have to be decommissioning within two years, which was an advance. TB felt Trimble was keen to get off the precondition hook but he needed at least the sense of a time-table and we were not able to get it.

About 9, they came through into the big lounge where we were just chatting and Adams said 'I'm afraid that rather than wasting everyone's time we thought it best to tell you we have a real problem.' Trimble said 'We are not in the same ball-park.' Very calmly, GA went through the main difficulties – the UUs need some kind of act, and we cannot deliver it in that way, while we cannot have decommissioning as a precondition for joining the executive, and political realities make that impossible for David. There was a long silence, TB a mix of frustration and anger, and he just sat there stony-faced for a while.

We talked round the problems for a while, but it was impossible. We met the SDLP delegation who had been hanging around getting more and more impatient. Seamus Mallon said he had to 'fight his way in to see the prime minister'. TB explained that he was not the problem, and charmed him round. Seamus said it was not sensible to keep the other parties feeling uninvolved. He felt de Chastelain's remit should be widened to give him control over a timetable. Officials were put to work on drafting overnight a proposal to kick things off in the morning. Earlier, we had been genuinely optimistic. TB said we should stay another night to give it a go, but there was a sense of deep gloom. TB was pretty much fed up with the lot of them. We were saying progress had been made but in reality all that referred to was SF acknowledging they had to decommission sometime in the future, but without a commitment it took us nowhere with the UUs. Even they accepted it wasn't enough for DT.

TB's only hope was GA and McG were off seeing the IRA guys to say 'Do we really want to be the people who bring this crashing down?' There had been something pathetic about the way they came through to TB and BA to say they couldn't sort it. It made you worry they could never work in government together, which was meant to be the aim. TB called Clinton to brief him. A group of loudmouth Loyalists appeared at the gates to abuse just about anyone who came near the place.

Wednesday, March 31

I had a bad call with Fiona first thing because she said it was impossible for her to plan anything when she never knew if I was going to be there. It put me in a foul mood for the day. Kosovo had had another night of bad weather so military frustration. TB was worrying about that, and about NI, where he said at the first meeting he just felt we were too far apart. We're wasting our time here, he said. I had a brief chat with McGuinness in the corridor and said I thought TB was getting to the end of his tether on this, so they needed to work out their lines for failure. He said it was all down to Trimble (or Trumble as he says it). TB saw the UUs. BA saw SF and gave them a hard time, said TB had a 'war to fight' and they were keeping him here, buggering him around and getting nowhere. 'I told them in Dublin Central language to "stop fucking about".' Obviously nobody wanted to be seen to bring the whole thing crashing down, and they had to feel more pressure. That did require us to stay a little longer, whatever the frustrations. I agreed with Bertie that when we left we would say if left to the two PMs it would be sorted in minutes, and people had to face up to their responsibilities, to give the sense there was a solution but the two sides would not embrace it. TB was a bit worried leaving Mo in charge of the talks, as her relations with the UUs were so poor. Yesterday she asked him what job he was going to give her post-devolution. She was making clear she felt she deserved one of the big ones. TB felt Cabinet Office was probably the best he could offer her. He had not been impressed by the way she had let the UUs stray more and more offside.

Bertie and Liz O'Donnell [Irish foreign minister] came in after a meeting with Adams and McG who had said the IRA were issuing a 'helpful' statement. We eventually got it and what was helpful was that it did not say there would be no decommissioning. It put in all the usual stuff but did say they wanted peace and that the IRA guns are silent. We had the usual analysis chat re what it meant and agreed it was broadly positive. We had another session with the UUs and I could see DT reading the draft declaration upside down on Bertie's foot-stool. I motioned Joe [Lennon] to go and drop something on top of it without it looking too obvious. DT did not go bonkers, but did say he would have real difficulties with the parts about SF being on the Shadow executive. While we were in the meeting, Mark Bennett paged me to say Sky were quoting a Trimble spokesman [David Kerr] as saying the talks would adjourn for two weeks, and TB was not able to focus properly because of Kosovo. I was pretty pissed off at that, told DT it was a low blow, and went out to deal with it. Bertie was getting more and more impatient.

We had to leave for PMQs. Re the *Mail* and the Tories, TB said their patriotism is as deep as the next opportunity to attack a Labour government. We got to Northolt, were driven straight to the House, where we were expecting Kosovo and NI to dominate. He got very little on either. On Kosovo, we worked up a line re the damage being done to Milosevic. The word from Belfast was not good. McG had basically said piss off to the paper. Bertie was threatening to go home. TB's view was the IRA were just unable to move. We also had intelligence reports on their worries the Real IRA would move if the IRA decommissioned.

We left for Northolt again. We met Bertie at [RAF] Aldergrove, got a heli-copter to Hillsborough, then took stock. Clinton wanted to speak to Adams but he was away 'consulting' IRA members, which meant we couldn't get hold of him, as he went without a mobile, presumably because he knew he could be tracked on it. DT was at Stormont, telling everyone he intended to go to the opera. You sometimes wondered if they were serious. We started the next round around 8, first BA/TB, then the UUs and then a possible breakthrough meeting, just TB, Bertie, Adams and McGuinness. TB called us in after a while, saying 'I think we are in go mode.' He said they had definitely moved on decommissioning, however dressed up. By now most of the top IRA guys were in the building, including [Thomas] 'Slab' Murphy. 'Don't give him your home number,' Bertie said. Alongside the supposed shift, they had put down a list of demands on so-called 'normalization'. It went too far, as did the stuff agreed earlier while we were away between the Irish and the NIO, all about the dismantling of the police and security apparatus which, when you set it against a vague and unspecified act of decommissioning, did not look that great. Mo was getting really steamed up that we were trying to water down what she had agreed, but it would tip the UUs off the other side. John Sawers was arguing against some of the specifics she had agreed, and she virtually stormed out. But he was right. They had gone too far. TB felt the SF meeting went well though, and GA went off on another round of whispered conversations and walks in the garden.

The news from Kosovo was dire, with the refugee crisis getting worse. TB saw Trimble and Taylor. DT was down because Adams was being quoted as saying there would be an agreement in the morning, and they would take their seats, which was not where DT was. But he was misrepresenting what SF were saying. They had been talking about 'no precondition', not 'no to decommissioning'. I was briefing the BBC that DT was hanging tough for deeds not words, to try to help him with his own people on the later bulletins. We were obviously set for the talks going into the night. McG was due to come back with specific comments on the paper and all the various objections to it but came back around 1.30 to say there was a problem, they had political difficulties and needed more time. I did a fairly positive briefing because I think they sensed things were moving, though SF were trying to move without saying they had. DT and Taylor said their Assembly people were getting very fractious and maybe TB should speak to them.

Ken Maginnis gave me a real bearding about how awful Mo was, how she didn't understand where they were coming from at all. He said there was no way they would accept all these normalization measures 'and remember I am relatively speaking one of the liberals'. They all later surrounded TB and mon-stered him with the same kind of message. John Taylor said Mo was a liar. TB said afterwards, I think now I understand better why Trimble is like he is. While SF were away again, I had a very nice quiet chat with Bertie and Mo. Bertie said even though it is all so frustrating, it is worth remembering that not long ago, people inside this building were trying to kill each other. He was right. Earlier, I had briefed the PUP on what was going on, and they had gone to seek out some of the SF people to get clarification on one or two points. TB was less sanguine than Bertie. 'We are in a fucking madhouse,' he said as the next round wore on. Yet somehow I thought we would get there.

We rolled into the early hours. Taylor said his troops were getting more and more fractious and wanted to go home. TB talked them into staying. I said to Taylor why don't you go up for a nap? I suggested he take TB's bed to which he said 'I could not possibly use a bed reserved in the main for the Queen and the PM.' So he took my room instead, and Maginnis, clearly no possessor of false modesty, took TB's. When I wandered up later he was snoring loudly at the ceiling. We had another mad moment shortly afterwards when McG was talking us through a SF statement as though he had literally nothing to do with the IRA, 'the other people who are being chased about the other thing'. BA, TB and I had a very jokey conversation re having conversations between various parts of your body but pretending they were not part of the same thing. By 5 or 6, there were people kipping in chairs and lying out on sofas. The staff were providing an endless supply of food and coffee, and somehow we kept going. Bertie was convinced there was a real and substantial discussion of the [seven-member] IRA Army Council, inside the building, and that GA and McG were genuinely trying to win them round. At 5.55 we had a meeting with the Irish and it was gloomy as hell. Bertie felt they were at the bottom line. TB felt we were going nowhere but was striving to find another way of moving it forward. TB was looking a bit grey by now though, and the briefings on Kosovo weren't helping his mood or morale. TB had another session with Adams and McGuinness. I went in, and later got DT in, and said we had to publish something today, or else people would feel we were totally hopeless and this was all going nowhere. Mo and I were both getting really pissed off at the way the SF people were handling it all. Mo said they have got two PMs totally tied up in this, and a US president, yet they are giving nothing at the moment. It reached a low point when we got Clinton up at 5am US time to speak to Adams, who was busy delivering a history lesson to TB and too busy to take the fucking call. [Sandy] Berger was raging about it. We were moving to the idea of publishing the document and simply saying the parties would have to consult on it, and we would give them ten days to do so. Then, cheek of all cheeks, McGuinness said 'You realize we will be bound to oppose the delay.' Bertie, by now getting fractious, said 'That's a good one – you'll oppose it when you've been calling for it.'

Joe Lennon and I were now both imploring TB to go for them, put some real heat on. He said he was, but it was all still a bit matey. The PUP said we were kidding ourselves if we thought they would do something in ten days that they couldn't do now. Around 12, TB, Bertie, Paddy [Teahon] and I went for a walk in the garden at the back. TB said we had to get DT signed up to the text, then work on the smaller parties, then publish. TB spoke to Clinton at 12.30, who was also preoccupied with the three US soldiers being paraded on Yugoslav TV. TB said we were going to put down the declaration – D'Hondt*, act of reconciliation, full devolution – and we wanted him to say to GA he should go for it. Bill spoke to him, then to TB again and we could see the SF people getting very tetchy and feeling the pressure. The BBC did a story that SF were asking for an adjournment, which pissed them off, but Joe and I both felt they should stew a bit. TB asked me to draft a positive press statement, which I did, and there was enough to build up into something. Mo liked it. TB thought it went too far and needed toning down a bit. Adams was saying to TB that they would get there, but not today.

The important thing was to give at least some sense of progress and movement. We did a joint TB/BA press statement, probably too positive, with a bit of TB emotional uplift at the end. I got Tom Kelly and Sheree Dodd [NIO] to get the press in place at the back of the castle, and told Mo and Liz O'Donnell this should just be TB and BA. They were very pissed off but what I was trying to do was create a sense of occasion, because the fact was the agreement itself would need to be carried by more than the words. What I didn't want is for it to look just like any other NI doorstep mess. From the look Liz gave me, I think I made an enemy for life, and Mo was steaming too. The last meeting was with de Chastelain to go over what he would do. We went through the difficult questions in the pre-briefing. People were reasonably upbeat apart from SF. I got them to agree an order in which they went out, so that everyone could hear everyone else. Everyone was very tired and the mood at farewell and handshake times was not great, though the TV were just about buying the line. We got a helicopter to Aldergrove and then flew home, TB and I impersonating the main players for much of the flight. What a crazy place to work. TB was still worried that if we pushed SF too hard, they would be unable to shift at all. I got home, and crashed out.

Friday, April 2

I was very tired still, and starting to get that achy feeling that exhaustion brings. We were losing the propaganda battle with the Serbs. The press for NI was OK without being great.

---

* A method of proportional representation voting named after Belgian mathematician Victor D'Hondt. The D'Hondt system, electing candidates in constituencies as well as party lists, had been used in the Scottish Parliament and Welsh Assembly elections.

The need to grip the Kosovo media operation was now a running theme, though our press had settled down a bit. Today was manifesto launch day in Scotland and DD sounded up for it. The talk in the press was now of the SNP in crisis, with senior figures not talking to each other. At the office meeting, TB seemed a bit more relaxed re Scotland. Ireland and Kosovo were the big worries. He wanted new structures on the Kosovo operation, and wanted to get more directly involved himself.

I had a meeting with the Home Office Security Unit re my own security. They said the current Security Service assessment was that I was moderate risk but that it would rise to significant if things went backwards in NI. He said it meant I needed protection mainly focused on home and cars. He said, in a very matter-of-fact way, that in some ways Jonathan and I were at greater risk than the PM because the terrorists know he is so heavily protected whereas they know we are one layer out and not subject to the same level of protection. Very cheery. I was a bit worried about Fiona's reaction. She was OK about it, though it was going to mean work on the house, blinds on all the windows and cops wandering up and down the street every few hours.

In Brussels, TB saw a very depressed Bertie [Ahern], really down about things. He was coming under a lot of attack but more than that, he said he couldn't see where the next bit of progress was coming from.

TB called again. He was worrying about Ireland too, and anxious that with us so focused on Kosovo [AC had been seconded to Brussels to revamp NATO communications], Ireland and international stuff we'd drift on the domestic front. I said to him that two years ago, tomorrow was election day '97. Christ, he said, nobody could say we haven't done a fair bit. 'Is it really two years?'

I said to Fiona – two years to the day since the election. It feels a lot longer, she said. Things were certainly feeling different to how they were two years ago.

I woke up exhausted and with Rory ill, I decided to have a day at home. We had the security people in putting in the new security stuff on the house. TB was doing a stack of Northern Ireland meetings, and felt we were making progress, that he was beginning to think we could get decommissioning.

I went in for a TB meeting on office structures. He still wasn't happy. He was also arguing that Jonathan and John Sawers should be in proper offices, with proper support, not stuck outside in the crowded private office. Truth is they prefer it there, whatever the inconvenience. Siobhan Kenny [press officer], who was doing a great job for me, was leaving because we couldn't match the money she was being offered by the private sector. I tried to talk her out of it but I couldn't really blame her. It made my blood boil that we lost good people while people thought not to be up to the mark got promoted.

Michael Howard did his second attack in two days on Kosovo. They were doing what they did re NI, saying they were bipartisan but acting very differently. I had a go at Howard, said when things get tough is not the time to show lack of resolve and determination.

I had been ignoring toothache for ages, and today it was really bad. TB was holding another round of NI talks and by the time I got in with my tooth sorted, he was having lunch with Bertie [Ahern]. They had obviously been talking about me because at one point, when I asked Bertie what Mary Robinson [former Irish President, now UN high commissioner for human rights] was up to in her criticisms of NATO, TB laughed and said 'Told you, he is obsessed with Kosovo.' I said that was because he told me to be.

NI seemed to be going a bit better. The current plan was to reaffirm commitment to the GFA [Good Friday Agreement of 1998], set a deadline for June 30 for full devolution, run D'Hondt [voting system] and let de Chastelain decide if decommissioning was taking place. The meetings went well, much better mood than of late, and then ran late into the evening, with some decent food being served, to sort it out. By the end we were close to a line that said we had a process all of them would support, which would be seen as a breakthrough of sorts.

Saturday, May 15

I picked TB's brains on NI before doing a Sunday lobby briefing by phone to try to get the NI statement when it came in the right place. They were straight on to the right questions though – namely if we were running D'Hondt and appointing ministers designate, it was clear what Sinn Féin were getting, but what about the Ulster Unionists? During the day, the UUs started to move to reserve their position, so it was looking tricky again. I took Grace and her friends to the cinema, but was in and out dealing with the NATO people.

Monday, May 17

TB and Bill had not spoken for more than a week, which was bad. This was going to have to get cleared up. I was asked about when they last spoke and just dodged it, said they kept in touch the whole time. We got a message that the UUP [Ulster Unionist Party] had rejected the Friday proposal, so TB dictated a letter to DT [David Trimble] urging him to think again.

Tuesday, May 18

Just before midnight, John Sawers woke me up to fill me in on a 'very difficult' BC/TB phone call. They had spoken for over an hour, and the first five to ten minutes were taken up with Bill in a total rage. He had seen the UK reports [on Kosovo] and the stuff in the US and he 'knew what was going on, it was deliberate and it had to stop'. He said it may play well with the UK media and public but 'there is a price to pay and you will pay it'. John said he was clearly suggesting I had been briefing deliberately to build up TB at his expense. TB protested as best he could, said he was appalled they would think we would undermine him when he was leading the whole thing, to which BC said in which case it is happening without you knowing – the implied notion being that was even worse. John said he didn't name names but it was obvious who he meant. He had never heard him so angry and TB was taken aback. On the substance, however, BC appeared to be moving. He shared TB's view that the D'Alema option* could be a way of getting

---

* The Italian prime minister had proposed a 48-hour ceasefire on condition Russia and China support a UN Security Council resolution imposing the G8 terms on Milosevic to withdraw.

the ground force option out there. TB put it in terms – we have a 48-hour pause while we agree a new UNSCR, then if Milosevic does not comply, based on the five NATO demands, we bomb again and plan for ground forces. Bill leapt at it.

PMQs preparation was mainly Kosovo, disability and NI. We had another round of talks today, as if Kosovo wasn't enough to be dealing with. At one point, TB's kids were trying to show Adams and McGuinness how to use a skateboard.

Cabinet was NI, Kosovo, plus GB on the economy. TB and Mo both said they had never known a situation where there was such a desire for progress, yet they couldn't take the last vital steps. The UUs won't form an executive without IRA decommissioning. SF say they will work for it but it cannot be a precondition.

The *Guardian* led on a rewrite of the *New York Times* account of the TB/BC call, which was clearly going to run big through the day. 'There's the revenge,' said TB. 'It's silly because the people rubbing their hands at this are the Europeans and in the end the people the US will need to stand by them are us.' He asked me to call Joe [Lockhart, White House press secretary], which I did. I said once more that it would be stupid to get into a briefing war, and if we did we knew we could not win it. He said he had discussed it with the president yesterday and everyone had moved on. TB, on his way to the North-East, said he sensed BC knew he was in the wrong position and took it out on his friends. Maybe, maybe not. The RC/Madeleine [Albright] double act was going fine, and we did need to work to get back on the same songsheet.

It was FA Cup Final day, and I took Rory and Calum into Number 10, and went upstairs to see TB. He was wearing a Real Madrid tracksuit and doing lots of different impersonations, much to the boys' amusement. We got an escort up to Wembley and on the way he had a couple of difficult calls with Trimble and Adams. I had fixed an interview with Jim Rosenthal [sports commentator] on the live coverage with both Bertie [Ahern] (Man U) and TB (Newcastle). He got a pretty good reception from the Newcastle fans, apart from one in a wheelchair who yelled out 'Tony is a Tory.'

TB and Bertie did a bit of NI in the margins, but they were pretty much on show here at events like this and expected to mingle etc. We were taken up to the wives' section beforehand and TB chatted to Posh Spice [Victoria Beckham] and her dad, while I chatted to Bertie and Celia [Larkin, Ahern's then partner]. It was an OK match, without being storming, and I was chuffed for Alex [Ferguson, Manchester United manager] that he won. He was loving it at the end and when I spoke to him later, he said he had a feeling about the treble. TB called on his way home and said Newcastle just weren't at the races.

'In the margins' – given the extent to which Kosovo was dominating TB's agenda, and the difficulties with President Clinton over the threat to use grounds troops, these chance meetings with BA were useful opportunities to take stock, but having survived the recent NI crisis, TB worried he did not have sufficient time for the issue. He often said the process either moved forwards or backwards, but it never stood still. This was one of those rare periods when it felt like it was standing still.

Thursday, May 27

I got in to see TB, who was doing another note to Clinton about how we would explain the ground force option. TB spoke to Clinton again. He said Bill basically felt we had shafted him and we now had to help him get back to the position he wanted to be in. The problem was that within NATO, the truth was we really were more like the Americans and we were not like the Europeans in the final analysis. 'That is exactly what Thatcher said when I saw her on Tuesday,' said TB. Her view was the Germans try to be disciplined and so become inflexible. The French can't be trusted. The Italians are too weak and the Spanish don't count. The only people like us are the Dutch and they are too small. TB said he didn't necessarily agree with it all but there was something in it.

Wednesday, June 16

I did the eleven o'clock down the line after talking to TB. He said Ireland had gone well [TB flew to Ireland on June 14, AC to Kosovo on June 15] though at the Orange Order meeting some guy was literally foaming at the mouth. He said I had to get back on the domestic agenda, which was right, but I was glad I had gone to Kosovo. I felt it was without doubt one of the most worthwhile things we had done since the election and I was proud of the job I had done. I had brought together a disparate group of people from different parts of the world and from Clinton and [General Wesley] Clark [Supreme Allied Commander Europe] down, I think they acknowledged that we had used communications strategically to make a difference on the military side too.

Saturday, June 19

Had breakfast with TB and a pretty circular conversation about the domestic agenda. He was worried about the health department. I said he had to reconnect with the domestic agenda with the same zeal he showed for the war and Northern Ireland. He did a pre-record for Adam Boulton [*Sky News* political editor] mainly focused on Europe. Adam somewhat tendentiously compared me to Goebbels.

We went back for a meeting with Bono and [Bob] Geldof [musicians campaigning to cut Third World debt]. First we had to get them there, because Bono for some reason told Boulton he wasn't going. I called Geldof and got him to persuade him that it would be seen as total grandstanding not to turn up when the media were already there waiting. In the event, we had a very good meeting. I liked them both. They were really funny but also incredibly committed, and they knew what they were on about. They had facts at their fingertips. There was no way this was just a spray-on cause to help their rock-star image. TB said at one point that we were pushing as hard as we could but there was a lot of politics, different countries with different agendas, and it was like climbing Everest. Bono said 'When you see Everest, Tony, you don't look at it, you fucking climb it.' We got the cameras in and they went a little bit rock star-ish but it was impossible not to like them.

Tuesday, June 22

Northern Ireland suddenly flared up. Trimble had an article in the *Times* and later he called on Mo to quit, which put TB in a total rage. Jonathan and I had tried to calm TB down but he was really pissed off. Jonathan felt it probably wasn't worth going there on Thursday as there was no give or take on either side but we had to push on.

Suddenly there was a sense across the media that NI had become very gloomy. TB was tired, and really pissed off at the Trimble situation, and generally downcast. He hated it when he couldn't see a way forward. Normally, no matter how bad everyone else was saying it was, he would always find some ray of hope somewhere, but today he was as down as any of us.

TB was good at PMQs, didn't let his mood show, and was a lot more political than of late. He did say he would 'listen to the debate' on PR [proportional representation], which was a bit weak, was defensive on NI but he was definitely back on form on Europe and the domestic agenda. Mo came in to tell me she believed GB was really stirring at the moment. Anji, who was not normally paranoid about GB, also thought he was up to no good just now.

Trimble came in to see TB, TB still in a bit of a rage with him. He wanted to do a piece for *The Times* which took up a bit of the morning. Mo was quite chirpy re Trimble, said it was the tenth time her resignation had been called for this year – slightly down on a year ago. TB worked on the NI draft [article] and really put a lot into it. It was going to land with a big hit, a small nuclear device into NI politics, basically spelling out the reality and the reasonableness of the deal which they had all conspired to fuck up.

The [*Times*] NI article, though rushed, had the immediate effect of putting the story up in lights and at least with the sense of a plan, even if all it did was state the blindingly obvious in a very direct way. I called Joe Lennon [Ahern's press secretary] to make sure the Irish didn't go offside on it. TB now wanted to push hard on a statement of general principles – 1. an inclusive executive; 2. decommissioning by May 2000; 3. de Chastelain judging. It was ridiculous, given that it was all pretty much agreed at the time of the GFA, that we were having to portray this as progress. Jonathan and I saw TB to go through PG's latest, unbelievably gloomy note. TB thought he was overstating it, that the problem was really lack of progress in public services. He looked tired and drawn though and I think felt that having done as much as he had to win a war people had said they supported, it was odd not to get at least some credit for it. Equally, they did not seem to want to give us credit on the economy.

Bertie came in around 9 to take stock. They were both wearing black ties for the [Cardinal Basil] Hume funeral at Westminster Cathedral. The Irish seemed OK with TB's article, though the UUs were already out attacking it on the grounds that it conceded to SF on the question of prior decommissioning, and SF were attacking us because it made it look like they, not the IRA, were responsible for arms. TB said 'If you ask me, I think we are pretty fucked on this. I can normally see a way forward but at the moment I can't.' He said the UUs were fighting like ferrets in a sack. Also we sometimes underestimated just how important the Drumcree march was to them. He felt if we could get a breakthrough on the march, the door would open on the bigger picture. He even wondered if Clinton shouldn't call Brendan McKenna [Garvaghy Road residents' spokesman], which on one level was absurd but if it shifted it, it would be worth it. I could just see McKenna pocketing a call from the most powerful man in the world and then carrying on buggering us about. There was actually a simple enough formula, easily put-downable on a postcard, and all his article did was make the obvious explicit – there would have to be an inclusive executive and there would have to be decommissioning – but getting there would be hard.

We headed to Northolt, on the plane with Bertie. We arrived at [RAF] Aldergrove, jumped on a helicopter and headed straight for a quick round of talks, TB and BA together, with first SDLP, then UUs, then SF. TB felt there was room for some progress, and suggested I brief the same message as the morning, but more upbeat. Things were made more difficult though with [Jeffrey] Donaldson [Ulster Unionist MP] in the Trimble team, as he was constantly second-guessing, and throwing in unhelpful observations. He was clearly having none of the TB stuff in the *Times* on prior decommissioning. Donaldson looked to me to be taking Trimble close to the edge. TB could barely bring himself to be civil. Joe Lennon and I worked up a press statement around the three principles and then briefed that the last-minute changes were because DT would not agree on the timings or sequencing.

TB said on the flight home he had started out in government determined to like the Unionists, and always to try to understand their point of view, but they made it bloody hard. 'The other side may kill people but at least you can have rational conversations. When the UUs are like this, they are so ridiculously unreasonable. They are too stupid to realize they have won and SF are too clever to admit they've lost.' It had been a beautiful day but we were potentially a day away from political disaster.

Saturday, June 26

TB called just the once. He was back totally focused on Northern Ireland. He was feeling a bit more hopeful but thought there would have been a more positive response re them seeming to sign up to decommissioning. On Kosovo, we needed a major plan of repatriation.

Sunday, June 27

Trimble was putting out a less grudging line re SF/decommissioning, but when TB called, he said he was really worried about him, felt the others were getting to him big time. He was also worried Jonathan was getting too emotional about it, which I felt was a good thing. But TB was alarmed last week, e.g. when the Orangemen were attacking TB and Jonathan really went for them, saying you cannot talk to a prime minister like that. I don't know why but I felt we should be more confident. The engine was in place, the carriages were waiting, and it was just a question of getting the carriages in the right order.

Monday, June 28

With NI, Britain in Europe, welfare to work, we were at least back dominating the agenda, even if not all on our terms. I left with TB for Northolt just after 8. He said he had slept really badly, didn't get to sleep till 3 and then was waking up on and off after that. NI was occupying his mind, along with delivery, and someone was definitely getting at him re GB. It was true there was stuff in the papers today we didn't know was coming, but it wasn't really stuff we could object to. TB was also wondering whether he could send Peter M to NIO. On the plane he mapped out the various approaches to take with the different parties. He was pretty fed up having to go through it all again. Jonathan had spent the whole weekend out there, poor sod, talking to the Garvaghy Road residents' association and the Orange Order.* On arrival we worked through a plan for the day with Bertie. We wanted SF to agree that they would say they would persuade the IRA to decommission, whilst the UUs would accept a statement that the war was over. But a lot of his time was taken up with the residents and the Orange Order re Drumcree, which was dire. Whenever we got on to these marches, even TB's patience wore thin after a while. Both sides just lectured from their different takes

* The Parades Commission that day ordered the Orange Order's annual Drumcree march to be re-routed away from the Garvaghy Road. In the end, despite an Orange Order protest meeting, the march passed off relatively peaceably.

on it. He told them this was never going to change until at least they tried to see the other point of view, but he might as well have asked them to dive into a vat of burning oil. They were not listening let alone changing their minds. As Paul Murphy said, fighting for this was all some of these people felt they had, and they were not prepared to lose it.

After doing various meetings at Stormont we left for Hillsborough [Castle] by chopper to meet Bertie and have lunch with de Chastelain. He too seemed pretty downbeat, was not confident of getting anything out of SF. Bertie was fairly quiet but when he did speak was constantly trying to come up with practical suggestions. Joe Lockhart called as Clinton was about to do a BBC interview and I sent through a note on the lines we had been pushing over the past twenty-four hours. BC did fine, as ever, and gave it a bit of impetus media-wise. We flew back to Castle Buildings [Stormont] for a long session with GA/McG and then Trimble. We were waiting for the Parades Commission announcement on Drumcree and DT was really on edge. TB suggested all I could do was put the best face on this, and keep talking up DT and at least give the sense of progress. But Drumcree was taking the meat out of the negotiations. Bertie came in at one point and told me he felt Adams and McG were ready to say they would act as persuaders for decommissioning. But even that was probably not going to be enough for Trimble.

TB and I went for a walk round the gardens after dinner. He said he felt if we had nothing else to deal with, he could sort this. But it needed even more time than we were giving it. At times, he said he felt like we were dealing with madmen. He was also fretting still re lack of strength in depth in ministerial ranks. 'I am a bit of a fluke. So is Gordon. We are both a cut above your average politician. But we are exceptions.' That was why we needed Peter back. He gives us problems, but he gives us extra intelligence.

Tuesday, June 29

We needed to keep up at least some sense of momentum so after a long meeting on the way forward, I went out to brief a mix of atmospherics and an outline plan about how to move on. Gerry Adams was already there, planning to brief, and said he intended to be positive, which he was, saying some progress had been made. Trimble said the opposite not long after. The problem on the talks was that we were getting vague agreements but whenever we looked like getting closer to pinning them down, something would get in the way. DT was saying we had to have decommissioning in two weeks, SF that we might be able to see something by December.

We kept going, and TB and BA just went from one round of meetings to another. I did three full briefings through the day and by the third, there seemed to be an acceptance of progress, created largely by the fact we were still persevering, and people thinking there must be a reason for that. TB and Bertie did a five-sider, with SF, UUP, SDLP, then we left for Hillsborough. TB gave instructions that overnight we had to get words from all three signalling the direction of travel on decommissioning. De Chastelain called, and I briefed him on what we had been saying publicly, and also the mood inside the talks.

Wednesday, June 30

Over breakfast with Bertie, TB said he feared real problems with the UUs today. They were imagining that by the end of the day, there would be a commitment to acts of decommissioning but of course even if we got decent words, there would have to be an IRA convention to get it agreed. SF were going to make a historic statement of intent of their commitment to decommission, without any guarantee of how it could be delivered. Overnight we had worked on a single text – 'Essential elements for an understanding' – based on the various drafts and statements. TB was going to use it as a speaking note first before seeing whether we could bind the parties to it. First he went over it in detail with Bertie at Castle Buildings. The Irish were getting pretty impatient.

TB said we had to lower the bar for SF and we had to lower it for Trimble. We got DT in and he was pretty nervy. We tried to persuade him that the media was actually worse for SF than for him, and the pressure was still on them more than him. If they were to make a commitment as historic as the one we were working on, he had to seize that as major progress won by his side. We knew it didn't mean for sure all the weapons would go but it signalled a direction of travel that was surely worth seizing on. He didn't look so sure. We were now into a round of long, long meetings, and with little to brief of any substance, there was a bit of a vacuum developing. I was trying to put out the mood that we were in for a long haul, but we wouldn't be doing it if we didn't think we had a chance of real progress. SF presented to us their own version of what they could do – the overall commitment was there but it was clear there would be no product before October at the earliest.

A while back that would have been seen as real progress, but in the current mood it would be difficult. On the one hand it was remarkable that they were prepared to say 'total disarmament' but on the other, if that was the case, it would merely confirm and strengthen suspicion on the other side if they could not go further and talk about how, when, etc. It would be hard to take the UUs forward on the basis of what they were saying. DT saw TB alone at 2pm, and left looking really downcast. I went in to see TB, who was now just sitting there looking out of the window. He looked up, shook his head, and he said he could scarcely believe it – the UUs were about to turn the victory of the IRA handing in weapons into a defeat because psychologically they were incapable of getting out of defeat mode. If they see a Republican with a smile on his face, they assume they have lost something. They were incapable of seeing a bigger picture.

At 2.20 Trimble came in, and alongside him John Taylor, Reg Empey, Donaldson and Ken Maginnis. TB was very curt with them, less of the small talk and the bonhomie he usually doles out. He said he was trying to get a statement from SF, and from the IRA, effectively that de Chastelain was the means of decommissioning, the process, and the failsafe. But it was clear from their faces, barely reacting as he spoke, that they would not be able to go with anything other than a 'jump together' – the executive set up at the same time as arms were handed over. Trimble said that with Drumcree rerouted, and with the [Chris] Patten review on policing due, and bound to be terrible for them, they could not hold their own people with this. If we push too far, we risk the UUP falling to the extremists. Whether Donaldson, smirking a bit throughout, was the target of that one I wasn't sure.

Maginnis said the release of prisoners 'cost us 45,000 votes and we have bugger all to show for it'. 'With all due respect,' TB said – which he tended like me to say when he meant to indicate a lack of respect on a particular point – 'I think you have a tendency to snatch defeat from the jaws of victory and you are in danger of doing that now. In the GFA, you got a good deal – especially the principle of consent re constitutional change. Now you have the IRA making a commitment to decommission and you are saying it is not significant.' Empey said it may be, but they were being asked to accept a post-dated cheque. 'We give them a whole load of cash now, but we have to wait to get anything in return.' Also they hated the failsafe idea because it suggested SF/IRA had a veto on the whole thing. Trimble said the people who were trying to make it work would be the ones who end up punished. TB said if we fail to reach agreement he could not defend spending days and days of his time trying again. 'People will not understand if we pull the plug at this point. There is a Rubicon to be crossed and you have to lead the way.' If we could get an agreement around this, and sort Drumcree, we are back on track. If we don't, we will never get it done. Empey said nobody doubted his commitment or seriousness of intent but it had to be a good deal.

So off we went again, trying to recalibrate the atmospherics to benefit the UUs. I put together a briefing note based on some of the intelligence re key IRA figures moving, which we put on hold pending another round of TB/Bertie meetings, the most important of which was with Adams and McGuinness at 4 to 5.10. TB was saying we could transform the whole picture if we could get a deal here, and they responded with a magnanimous gesture re Drumcree. They said it was impossible. TB said it wasn't. It was essential. If we didn't get progress on Drumcree, Trimble's position was very difficult. Adams gave a picture of how horrible life was for the people they wanted to march through. They could not countenance a march this year. Joe Lennon came in, very flustered because Donaldson and Taylor had been out briefing that actual guns and explosives had to be handed over before they could sit on the executive. Joe said if SF went out and reacted badly to that, we were dead in the water. I went out with Tom Kelly and did a massive briefing – massive re the numbers present rather than the content – to the effect that we had the makings of a deal, that the two sides were testing the quality of the other's commitment before going snap. They pointed out I said the same at Hillsborough and at Downing St. I pointed out I said the same not long before we secured the GFA and we were hopeful again. So based on nothing, we somehow managed to inject a sense of forward momentum, enough for us to keep going into the next few hours. I got back in to find TB with the Orange Order, the usual barrel of laughs – not – with him trying to calm them down re Drumcree. Then into another round of talks and the gap was getting closer.

We were in a TB/Bertie stocktaking session when Jonathan came over to me and said two of my best friends were at the door wanting to see me. I went over and it was Adams and McGuinness, with some of their other key guys behind them. 'Here's the guilty man,' said Jonathan in that wonderfully flip way he has. They claimed I had briefed they were going to get an IRA statement. I had done nothing of the sort and I explained they were confusing two things. I had briefed that there were SF/IRA meetings going on (which they later denied). I wasn't convinced they believed me, and there was something pretty heavy about seeing them lined up demanding explanations. They were jovial, but there was a real hint of menace. 'Look Alastair,' said Adams. 'We live here. We know what is going on.' I said I wished to fuck I did, because so far as I could see, we were going nowhere. Back inside, TB was looking downcast again, but we decided to keep going through 9, then 10, then 11, when Adams did a pretty positive briefing, followed by Trimble being very negative, prompting me to go out and say de Chastelain was putting forward his report shortly, and that both GA and TB were keen to see the UU Assembly members. It was time to put the pressure on Trimble. I briefed [BBC journalist] Mark Mardell and [ITN political editor] Mike Brunson that there was real movement from Adams and the pressure was all on Trimble now. TB had talked to both the Queen and the president by now. We regrouped with the Irish after 11, TB having done another sweep of the smaller parties to stop them getting too fed up. It was all getting a bit high-wire again, but we had rediscovered a third wind and we were determined to sort something.

The problem was that the UUs were feeling a real blow – Drumcree – and it kept them in a very negative mindset. I played the bagpipes out on the terrace at one point – the acoustics were terrific and it seemed to cheer people up a bit, but we were drifting a bit. We got a helicopter to Castle Buildings. TB saw Trimble while Bertie saw Adams. TB called me in to say David felt all the public pressure was on him, and we needed to balance up by getting some pressure on SF. I said we should say there was still the chance of progress and that on the question of decommissioning, TB and Bertie were 'one hundred per cent' behind DT's demand for a clear and unequivocal commitment. DT was pretty calm by the usual standards. I briefed as agreed, both in person in Belfast and down the line to London. Bertie felt we could get 'the war is over' from SF, and a commitment to try to persuade the IRA re decommissioning but we were still a long way off. Then we discovered de Chastelain was about to publish a gloomy report making clear there had been no real progress on the decommissioning front. There was no way we could let him publish as things stood. We got TB to speak to him and they agreed to meet at 1. The only defensible line was to say that we had asked him to postpone because we believed we were making progress on decommissioning. De Chastelain was happy to delay publication for a day. We now had to pin them down.

McGuinness had called de Chastelain to say they would be making a statement making clear their commitment to decommission, though not speaking for the IRA. He accepted it at least as a step in the right direction. They then went into a more detailed discussion on the modalities, and a plan for a timetable. I was intending to go out and brief a sense of progress but both Joe Lennon and Paddy Teahon nobbled me to say we could not mention the commitment to decommission as it would send SF off the deep end. We retreated to Tom Kelly's office, where we agreed a toned-down briefing. At 3.15 TB/BA met Adams and McGuinness for one and a quarter hours, after which TB said we were moving in the right direction. They didn't like the idea of a named person dealing with de Chastelain. They wanted to be more flexible about things. We were still a huge way apart on the timetable for the establishment of the executive. TB thought it significant they had themselves put forward new ideas, e.g. a South African to verify decommissioning.

We were now working on a paper with a variety of options. We told them what we needed by way of amendments. We needed an IRA statement. They had to accept the executive will only come into being once the process starts. The process must start, then the timetable will want weapons a few months later. TB said they will want to see if it beds down. Bertie said they still feared if they did this, nothing would change. Trimble would still not speak to them. McGuinness came to see TB. Their problem was going out and saying decommissioning will happen. In some ways it would be easier to do if they didn't have to say they were doing it. De Chastelain is the key to determining any progress. The Irish were seeing Donaldson who was seemingly being more reasonable.

As midnight approached, TB called me in and said what do we do by way of fallback? What do we say if we make no real progress? He was really tired and tetchy. 'I can't understand them. I am really scared about it this time because I don't have a clue what I would say to the country and I don't have a clue what the consequences will be if we have to walk away without real progress.' DT was seeing GA at midnight but was unable to get real detail on what they planned. TB set out for DT what we saw as a best-case scenario for him but even that wasn't good enough. He said to him he (DT) was the leader who was getting the IRA to commit to decommission, and he was walking away from it as though it were a defeat. All we could really do was let them sweat – put out details of the kind of deal on offer and let them consult. I worked on a draft failure statement, with the key line 'I believe the parties are sincere, but the parties do not believe each other.' Trimble took TB's best-case list to his people and reported back that not one of them supported it.

He came back with Seamus Mallon at 1.05am for an unbearably gloomy meeting. Even Jonathan and I had given up on the black humour for now. Trimble said he had no support for what was being proposed. They did not believe we would kick SF off the executive once they were on, and they did not believe decommissioning would happen. TB was tired and saying little for once. Mallon quizzed Trimble, said there was never a good time but real opinion out there supported him more than he thought. Trimble said that didn't matter, because the Unionist Council would not support it. TB was getting close to the view that deep down they just didn't want to share power with Catholics. Mallon felt DT lived in permanent fear of political crucifixion by [Ian] Paisley [DUP] and [Bob] McCartney [UK Unionist Party].

Bertie was patient as ever, trying to coax out DT into a more positive position. TB said 'If I get them to agree to decommission within a month, would that do?' He said 'I wouldn't be there. They only need two weeks to get me out.' He was clear his Assembly people just wouldn't wear it. Mallon said 'David, think the worst the whole time, and we all go down, but Adams goes out smelling of roses, while you are there with your party intact but you'll be wrecked.' 'I'm wrecked whatever,' he said. Mallon: 'Who dares wins.' Trimble: 'I'm always wary when others are urging me on to what I know will be my own destruction.' TB: 'At least give me a counter-proposal.' Silence. TB turned to me and said what do we say? I said all we can do is say we have failed and you give an honest assessment of where we got to, what was on offer, and let people make their own judgement. TB said if we go out there and offer no hope at all, we have a bloodbath on our hands. But he also said he wasn't prepared to keep coming again and again to put in day after day on negotiations going nowhere.

Then at 1.55am, Adams came in and made clear there was no way he was going to sign up to a deal that had decommissioning prior to the executive, or to a shadow executive going nowhere. I had now drafted a three-page statement setting the context for failure but TB was for now determined to keep going. We cannot go out of here having failed, he said. Adams and Trimble had another meeting but as ever came out with totally different interpretations of what had been said. The problem was DT kept going back to his own people and instead of offering leadership around a position secured by him, he took all their criticisms like a sponge. We had another round, then TB spoke to Clinton around 3.45, gave him his assessment and got him to speak to both GA and DT to urge them on.

DT was in our office when the call came through from the US and he was almost embarrassed, looking away from us, whispering and mumbling, humming like he did when he was nervous, then turned to us, wiped his mobile on his sleeve and said 'It's President Clinton.' BC took the line that the world would not understand if we failed to take this step forward now. As we left TB was pretty apocalyptic, could see it going nowhere fast, and then with dreadful consequences on the street as the blame games and the retreats started. In the car, he said he felt the Irish were not putting enough pressure on SF, whose position was a mirror of the UUs, and they were both as unreasonable as each other but because SF were cleverer negotiators and media operators, they got away with more. I reckoned he had about eighty meetings long and short behind him, and he was looking really tired. 'I have to find some verve and energy from somewhere. Otherwise this is going down.'

Thursday, July 1

The press was full of the knife-edge stuff re NI. At breakfast, TB said it was time to put real pressure on them. He intended to say it was now or never, that the civilized world would not understand if we did not do this now, and that we agree the coordination of two historic steps. The IRA will disarm. The UUs will share power with Catholics. No sane person outside of this place would remotely understand how you can turn your backs on that. He intended to do a round-table talk and say all that on arrival. We had the full-cholesterol Hillsborough breakfast, which was one of the delights of NI, and then flew off by helicopter. He was fired up by the time we landed. We linked up with Bertie and they did the last bit of the journey by car together, TB spelling out his plan of action. We got inside, then they went out again to do a brief doorstep, during which Adams came down, very wired for him, close to hyperventilating, saying TB had to meet them because Republicans did not understand why the deadline passed, why they had made this huge shift on a commitment to decommission and they were still waiting for a proper response.

TB spoke to Clinton, who had had another go at Adams, but felt he had pushed him as far as he would go. TB was just as angry with Trimble because the reason he had been negotiating on the basis of no prior decommissioning was because at one point DT had signaled he could live with that. The media were just about buying the line that we could make it, but there was not a lot of optimism. At 4.40 we got Bertie and co back in, TB briefed them on Trimble's position. Bertie was really down now, said he thought we were pissing about, that the UUs were not serious about sharing power, but he would give it a go. When Paddy and Dermot [Gallagher, Irish diplomat] came back and said they had to be clear that if they went for this, that was it so far as further demands were concerned, we were a bit more hopeful again. But then TB was downcast again, struck by the logic of what we were saying, set against the seeming near impossibility of making it happen. But Trimble and Taylor were still hanging out for the IRA statement, which made us think it was still worth persevering. Taylor definitely seemed to have shifted gear. He said at one point 'I agree with the prime minister that if the IRA stuck to their word, we could ride out a storm, but it would depend how quickly.'

TB to DT: 'I need to know you can back me on this.' DT: 'Sorry, I can't.' It seemed we had Taylor in a better position than Trimble. TB explained, as if they didn't know, that it took the IRA six to eight weeks to get round all their people. To which Trimble replied – OK, let's wait a few weeks then. But he also knew that they needed to be able to take with them the power sharing. TB said that if they signed up to the 'possible sequencing' paper, that was an enormous step for them, and he couldn't ignore that. We went round and round in circles, having hit the absolute nub of the problem – they wanted decommissioning prior to the executive being established. SF wanted it the other way round. And neither trusted the other to deliver if they were meant to go second.

Trimble went off to see Bertie while we worked on Sinn Féin, just to see if changing the mix might produce something. One-hour-plus TB meeting with Adams and McGuinness who was in full flow about how he and Gerry were being ripped apart for their 'peace strategy', their people feeling they were giving all and getting nothing. Decommissioning in days was not a runner, he said, it just was not possible. It was hard enough to get an IRA statement on the general commitment. They felt I had been pushing too far in briefings on the seeming progress they were making with the IRA. They lived in fear, he said. I said I know sometimes they thought I pushed too far, but they needed to understand I did nothing without TB wanting it done, so if he wanted the pressure shifted one way or the other, that's what we did. 'Alastair, that stuff (IRA statements re decommissioning is what I think he meant) is sacrosanct. Youse cannot get involved like that, and sometimes you scare the life out of me.' He said he would decommission 'the day before yesterday' if he could, but we had to deal with the realities we had before us. We pressed on and they finally agreed to put a proposal to the UUs. BA gloomy again. Trimble in again. TB said he was going to speak to Clinton and together the three leaders would put the deal to Gerry.

Trimble was talking about not making a specific comment on the specific proposal. Unbelievable. Adams had talked of this being the beginning of the end of the IRA, but Trimble would not seize it. We were now going round in circles and getting very ragged again. Sinn Féin were more nervous than usual, e.g. at one point before a bilateral with Trimble coming to ask TB for advice. We briefed on TB's meeting with the UUs and agreed after tortuous meetings with the Irish that Joe [Lennon] and I would go out with a package of 1. SF/UUP bilateral led to 2. round-table talks, led to 3. de Chastelain report in the morning, led to 4. the joint paper. We gave out the text, absolutely mobbed. There were dozens of journalists, God knows what kind of life they are leading in this crazy media village. But at least we had a process story to keep going.

Friday, July 2

Breakfast was pretty gloomy. Jonathan reported that de Chastelain was getting restless and feeling messed around. TB was worried it was all going down the pan again. Bertie was equally gloomy. The date of an IRA statement and lack of certainty about decommissioning were holding us back. Trimble seemed on for it early on but Donaldson could see his moment and was trying to undo the whole thing. The good news was that Taylor and Maginnis seemed better than before. But TB was exasperated that they could not grasp the fact they were about to deliver the death of the IRA, if only they would seize it. SF were being difficult. McGuinness and Gerry Kelly [Sinn Féin] came in while I was talking to TB and Jonathan. 'We're here about him,' said McGuinness, pointing to me. He said I was currently spinning the line that we were about to announce there would be legislation to exclude them if there was no decommissioning. I said it would be far better if he focused more on the talks inside and less what was said out there by the press. Kelly, sharp-eyed and sharp-suited as ever, flashed one of his looks. People still said McGuinness and [Martin] Ferris [Sinn Féin] were the real hard-nuts, but Kelly could be pretty disconcerting.

De Chastelain came over with his report and had half an hour with TB while we waited for Bertie to come back from Sinn Féin. He was effectively talking to the Provisional Army Council, pushing for a statement. De Chastelain, and perhaps more importantly Ambassador Don Johnson,* clearly did believe the IRA would decommission and that SF had moved. At 4.10 Trimble came in on his own and said he could not go for it. Then exactly half an hour later he came back and said he would go for it. He may not survive but he was willing to give it a go. TB said it was the right thing to do. It was better than the Hillsborough deal and there would be the legislative failsafe. By 5 I was telling the broadcasters we were on for a deal, that Trimble was hanging tough. Trimble came back in again and I gave him the line which he seemed OK with, 'Are we really not prepared to test for thirty days a process that could end thirty years of violence?'

At 5.20 Paddy Teahon came in saying SF were having big trouble with anything that suggested days and weeks. Joe Lennon was pissed off I was briefing on the deal at all. But TB, who was now seeing the smaller parties, was keen to press the button. We gave the thing the title 'The Way Forward' and some new lines to inject forward process.

Then at 7, Trimble came back in with Taylor and Reg Empey, said sorry but he couldn't do it. His party could not support it, they would split and he would be gone. TB said let me go and speak to them. They didn't want that. He said it was an own goal of potentially historic proportions. They could be the people to end the IRA and see off violence for good but for the sake of a few days' uncertainty they weren't prepared to take a risk. He looked pretty close to despair. They all went over to shake TB by the hand, Trimble said nothing, Taylor said thank you for everything you have tried to do. TB said 'I fear you will deliver public opinion to the nationalists at a time they don't deserve it. It is a real error and you will take time to recover from it.' TB had to go through another session with the Garvaghy Road residents' association. Then finally we were off, and on the car radio on *The World Tonight* [BBC radio] the reporter said he had a sinking feeling. So did we. On the plane Jonathan and I tried to keep up TB's spirits but he was as fed up as I've seen him, veering from silently looking out of the window to looking back and muttering about the UUs' zero strategy. In the car he called

---

* Career diplomat, US ambassador Donald C. Johnson, one of three members, with General John de Chastelain and Brigadier Tauno Nieminen of Finland, of the Independent International Commission on Decommissioning.

Clinton, who was also amazed they rejected the deal. TB said only the Unionists could throw that chance away.

This really was one of the low points. As at the time of the Good Friday Agreement, TB felt we should stay for as long as it took. In some ways the gaps were narrower than at the time of the GFA, but what became clear was that for Trimble, actual decommissioning had to happen, and his people were not prepared to trust a promise. TB felt Sinn Féin and the IRA really had crossed a Rubicon, and that had the UUs taken this deal, it signalled the death of the IRA, but they couldn't make the leap. Throughout the process, the pressure Trimble was under was clear for all to see. Even if he did not exactly wear his heart on his sleeve, his mood and the reasons for it tended to be pretty transparent. Adams was usually harder to read, but during this marathon session, the pressure he was under not to go too far was all too clear. The combination meant that the progress we had hoped for was not going to come, and we made the best of a bad job and left. The contrast between the flight to London now and the Good Friday flight could barely have been starker. It is to TB's eternal credit that no sooner were we back in London than he was sitting down trying to work out how to keep the hopes of progress alive. Not for the first time though, we quickly found that in trying to meet Unionist concerns, we risked losing Sinn Féin. In addition, the normally patient and resilient SDLP leadership were also reaching the end of their tether. Rarely had so much activity produced so little progress as during this period.

Saturday, July 3

TB was desperate to breathe some life into the NI process. We wrote a piece for the *Sunday Times* and for Monday's *Belfast Telegraph*. He called several times to ask how it was going and all I could say was it wasn't dead yet but it felt fairly close to it. He was now being accused of having misled them by giving the impression that only Sinn Féin could be excluded. So as well as failure, he was getting blame. The *Sunday Times* piece was designed to meet Unionist concerns, but TB felt let down by Trimble, first because he had agreed to the plan and second because some of the changes had been his ideas. We have given up a week and got nowhere, he said.

The press were pretty much writing the deal off. TB said there was real malice in the way some of the papers wanted us to fail on this. It made him more determined, but there was a danger of him being continually distracted from domestic policy. If we were able to put the same kind of energy into health and education, we might make more progress. Trimble was doing *On the Record* [BBC television] and, speaking to TB, said he was worried he wouldn't get a word in edgeways with [presenter John] Humphrys. I spoke to Humphrys to say Trimble wanted to get himself to a position where he could at least not totally reject it and he said he would help, but they would need to explain the thinking behind the failsafe and the need for the IRA statement. Trimble was pretty negative, saying it was a con job and Adams duped him.

I was feeling Northern Ireland was pretty much all over but TB wanted to press on. There was another bad story in the *Telegraph,* Sinn Féin people telling their members there would be no decommissioning. But Drumcree went OK and TB was not too downhearted when I went in to brief him for the *Today* programme and *Good Morning Ulster.* He did well on both. The problem now was that in trying to please the Unionists we risk pushing Sinn Féin off the deep end. We went over to the House for the statement on Ireland. TB had seen Hague and Andrew MacKay at 9, but at 3, Trimble was pretty clear with TB that he was being wound up by the Tories to press for more. The statement was fine but at the four o'clock I was pressed on prisoners, was unsure of my ground, and ended up with them filing stories about us reviewing prisoner legislation if they didn't decommission. This was a real problem area for Sinn Féin. Throwing a prison review into the mix had the potential for disaster. What I had said was factually right but politically difficult.

I slept badly. Even though I had been factually right on the prisoners, it was a fuck-up to get drawn, and provoke Sinn Féin. They were livid. Joe Lennon said Bertie also felt we were doing too much for the UUs now. TB could tell I was worried and he said it was fine but I hated messing up.

We decided to cancel Poland and Kosovo visits because of Northern Ireland.

I was speaking at an Irish press ball in Dublin and [UK ambassador Sir] Ivor Roberts, our man in Dublin, had invited the whole family out for the weekend. The dinner itself was a pretty drunken affair. It reminded me of Fleet Street in the eighties. We auctioned me playing the pipes and raised £3,500 out of a total of £75,000 for Kosovo charities.

The Sunday papers were really quiet, though full on inventive reshuffle rubbish. After breakfast we went off to the beach and after a while I realized I had left my phone behind. Once I got used to not having it, I rather enjoyed it. But by the time we got back, there were stacks of messages to deal with, most of them Northern Ireland related.

Northern Ireland was the main story all day. The bill on the Northern Ireland Executive suspension [allowing devolved government to be suspended in certain circumstances] was being published. John Sawers had been in late last night for final bit of drafting. It was due to be published at 3.30 but it quickly became clear we would have to wait. The Irish weren't happy because it was obvious we were talking about Sinn Féin exclusion. But the UUs weren't happy either. I went through it with John to work up an idiot's guide for the eleven o'clock. The four o'clock briefing must have been the longest ever, taking them through the details of the bill whilst saying I was not able to give it to them yet. This stuff was never easy. But it was very difficult to sell it properly when we weren't in a position to publish it. They got a sense of how difficult when Mo called halfway through and said the Irish had effectively rejected the bit about Assembly meetings. I did OK I think, but God was it long.

TB wondered if we shouldn't get out that the Irish weren't happy. I called Mo, who was very opposed on the grounds it would provoke a big-split story, and she was right, though they would probably brief it themselves anyway.

I didn't think there was much intellectual coherence to their position but they were genuinely pissed off at the moment. Trimble and Maginnis for once did a fairly helpful doorstep and didn't get drawn into questions and it wasn't running too badly on the news. Also the marches were going off fairly peacefully so perhaps we were going somewhere.

Tuesday, July 13

Ireland was the main story again with the bill due in the House today. Jonathan, John S and I were called up to the flat first thing. There was a sense of political crisis out of yesterday but the marches going well is a bonus. TB was worried that we were stumbling towards the end of the road and we had no real strategy. The eleven o'clock was again totally dominated by Ireland. We were pressing for a statement from the IRA but we didn't even have one at the moment from the SDLP.

TB felt we were going to have to give even more to the UUs. Mo came over at 12. [John] Hume [SDLP leader], Mallon and [Eddie] McGrady [SDLP] came in and they were very unkeen on saying they would sit on the executive without Sinn Féin. Both they and TB were pretty vitriolic about the Tories, who were deliberately making things more difficult for the Unionists. Went over to the House. The Tories abstained, Trimble voted against but without going over the top. Mo was pretty poor. Hume was dreadful, Trimble not as bad as he might have been. TB had a private meeting with Trimble and said afterwards he felt DT really wanted to help, and TB was the only person he trusted to deal with, but it was difficult for him. He felt we might need to park the whole thing for the summer, which would be a big disappointment.

Wednesday, July 14

Northern Ireland was still dominant. John Sawers had put together a number of amendments to the bill. There was a lot of excitement at the amendments plan though I was careful to say we didn't know if it would be enough and by now Adams and McGuinness were spitting fury. The briefing went on for an eternity. Now we were just waiting for the outcome of Trimble's meeting. Elinor Goodman [*Channel 4 News* political editor] called to say they had rejected the deal. It also meant there was no longer a need to rush through emergency legislation. TB agreed with Bertie there was no point doing the legislation now. But Sinn Féin and SDLP were livid. Mallon sounded close to quitting. TB spoke to an as ever graceless DT who sometimes spoke as though he wasn't actually involved in the process at all, as if his party was some kind of distant entity. The rollercoaster was rolling in the wrong direction again. Denis Murray said to me even you cannot persuade me this is anything but bad news.

It was descending into farce and chaos. Trimble didn't go to the Assembly meeting. Mallon resigned despite TB personally calling him on his mobile and urging him not to. Recriminations were beginning, with some of the blame going towards TB, but Trimble taking the bulk of it. Cabinet was pretty downbeat. TB said neither side was really ready for this. He said we would put those limited issues into a review process and the Assembly would effectively be in recess. But he believed there was something to come back to. He asked me to speak to Trimble and urge him to be more positive, at least give the sense there was some hope there. TB's view was that provided we could limit the recriminations, and give the sense there was something to come back to, it would not be so bad.

I took a day off. TB called a couple of times re Ireland.

Work-wise it was fairly quiet all weekend and I was starting to think about what we needed to do to start planning the next election. The party machine did not feel to be in very good shape. There was loads in the papers about Peter M going to Northern Ireland.

The Sundays were totally crap. There was loads of reshuffle stuff. Peter M called, said he was worried he was being set up for a job he wouldn't get and that he would get mauled if he didn't get it. We had a problem with Bertie who was quoted as saying decommissioning may go beyond the May 2000 deadline.

Another Northern Ireland day with both Bertie [Ahern] and [Senator George] Mitchell coming in at 4.

Mo had made some comments about wanting to stay at the NIO. I was asked about it at the 11 and stressed only TB decided and we never talked about reshuffles. Mo called to apologize, and yet she was saying that in the US she would say the same thing. Later, she was behaving a bit oddly, e.g. walking out with TB to meet Bertie, interrupting and contradicting TB during the meeting and overdoing the touchy-feely stuff with some of the officials, who looked a bit taken aback. And after Bertie's doorstep with Mitchell, I had a meeting of [Civil Service] heads of information, which was as depressing as ever. No matter what I did, they seemed either cowed and intimidated, or they just didn't get it.

Jonathan called to say the IRA were putting out a statement. For one great moment, I thought it was going to be the statement we had been working for but in fact it was deeply gloomy, critical of the government and with a clear veiled threat to return to violence. Denis Murray did a pretty breathless two-way. TB, who was seeing the Sultan of Oman, was pretty fed up.

The IRA statement was leading the news. TB was due to see Trimble and Adams, and TB, John Sawers and I felt there was a case for cancelling the meeting but Jonathan was strongly against. TB saw George Robertson re the NATO job. He was clearly keen but worried Sandra [his wife] was totally against. As well as it being a good thing to get a Brit there, TB was limited in his room for manoeuvre on the reshuffle. He later asked me whether he could send Peter M straight to the DTI. John Sawers was pretty desperate. He said the NIO were for a move there but if Mo was the only move that was a problem. Mo was worried that the Cabinet Office job was all spin not substance. Cabinet was a very political discussion on dividing lines.

Meeting with Adams, McGuinness and Ferris. John Sawers thought Adams and McGuinness had asked Ferris to be there to show they weren't patsies and could be really tough with TB. TB was pretty tough back and there was a fair amount of mutual fed up-ness. TB said, re the IRA statement, 'Well I get the message, and it's a pretty heavy message too.' McGuinness said 'Nothing to do with me. Not guilty.' In a different context, it would have raised a smile but on both sides, there wasn't much humour. Adams said, rather patronizingly, we think you are trying your best but the Unionists have no interest in sharing power. The Mitchell review is a waste of time. We have been sitting on the Agreement for fifteen months and getting nowhere. He said that TB was the best guarantor of not going back to violence, but as an organization they were not as disciplined as sometimes we thought. 'I know you may have doubts about us but we are the best you've got. We have our own reasons to do this and the main one is a better future for our young people, and the only person that can make it work is you. They have to know change is coming.'

TB said both sides operated according to norms that they couldn't imagine changing. He believed the Unionists did want to make it work, but they had people capable of talking themselves into despondency greater than any people he has ever met. 'That doesn't mean they don't want to share power. You have a real understanding. I can put pressure on them as the Irish put pressure on you. I also know that if you go back to violence then I see none of you again. I'm a pragmatist but I feel things deeply. I felt Kosovo. I feel this peace process and if I get an IRA statement like that on the day Gerry Adams and Martin McGuinness are coming in, I don't like that. I don't like the threat. I don't operate like that. And just understand if you go back to violence, I see none of you again.'

McGuinness said their only strategy was to stop power sharing. TB was having none of it. 'The problem with you is that both sides have absolute clarity about the wrongness of the position of the other side. They say to me the IRA will never do it and I say, you're wrong. Just as I'm telling you you're wrong about Trimble.' They seemed a bit taken aback by how heavy he was with them and Adams tried to soften it, said he accepted part of Trimble wanted it to happen. TB said so what the hell do you want me to do? Adams: Implement the Agreement. TB: What the hell do you think I am trying to do? I am implementing the damn Agreement. McGuinness: The only person that can sort this is you, by making them do it. TB: You still can't see it from both sides, as I have to. He said the relationship between Britain and Ireland would change when we joined EMU, 'which we will'. At last there was a bit of laughter, and TB said that's about the only story that can knock the IRA off the front pages. I said I'd be grateful if they didn't brief that historic commitment. Adams said they couldn't believe it when TB had talked about there being decommissioning within days and weeks. All that pressure piled on them, all the compromise going the UUs way, didn't we read the barometer of opinion on Seamus Mallon's resignation? If we had behaved the same as they [the UUs] did, would you have been so benign? TB: Yes I would. McGuinness: But would Alastair? He was obsessed with this idea that I somehow had a different agenda to TB when in fact if anything instinctively I was much more on their side than TB. Adams had a go as well. He said this is going to be bad long after me and Alastair have gone. It's a life-and-death situation. Jonathan made a joke about that being a direct threat to me, which again lightened the mood, and I said to McGuinness 'You're obsessed with this media stuff.'

TB joked he would tell me to be nice and gentle with them, but then went back to being serious bordering on heavy. 'If there is a return to violence, just be clear I will have absolutely nothing to do with any of you. I will pursue the justice and equality agenda because I said I would and because it's right. But do not lose your patience so quickly. I will keep mine and get it done. I regard Unionist supremacy as an intolerable historical relic. But it won't go just because you will it to go. And it certainly won't go through more intimidation. My doubt about you is not that you don't want to do it but that if you do not get what you want, you can revert to a situation where you become an enemy when you don't really want to be. I don't want to sound like some kind of Relate counsellor but you should work harder at finding out what the other side is thinking and why. Retreat into your boxes and you will squander it all.' McGuinness said TB and Trimble have to come to terms with the fact that they have more influence on the IRA than him or Gerry. They hung around for a fair bit, obviously trying to work out how best to deal with it.

An extraordinary meeting; extraordinary because of TB's absolute frankness. As the person essentially holding the ring on these negotiations, there was usually a sense of diplomacy to his utterances. Often things that were broadly understood nonetheless went unsaid. He was also capable, as are all top politicians, of finessing a message to suit a different audience; indeed one of his key roles was the ability to speak directly to all sides, so that sometimes he acted as a spokesman for Sinn Féin when seeking to persuade the Unionists, and vice versa. But in this meeting, weeks and weeks of frustration seemed to build up, and he just decided to say it as it was. Adams in particular, he who was something of a master at conveying hidden meaning in seemingly insignificant-sounding words, was taken aback. TB rarely lost his temper, and this was the closest Sinn Féin got to seeing him do so. His reference to Relate marriage guidance was a direct reflection of how he felt a lot of the time – as the person both sides came to to complain about the other.

The difference with a failed marriage is that SF and the UUs did not see TB as a mediator, so much as the man with the power to sort the other side out. And it was always the other side which was at fault. SF/IRA made a tactical error in the timing of the statement, and although there was a bit of humour towards the end, they left very clearly understanding that if there was a return to violence, TB would never see them again, and he would be clear about where the blame lay.

A footnote on this meeting: to this day, despite having seen McGuinness in particular over recent years, I never understood why they assumed, as they seemed to, that I had a different agenda to TB, and used the press to put out harsher messages about them than he was delivering to them. We were the ones often accused of being obsessed with what appeared in the papers. But we had nothing in that regard on some of the main players from Northern Ireland.

Over at the House, I bumped into [Nicholas] Soames by the cash dispenser. He was raging at me about hunting. 'How would you feel if we got back into power and passed a law banning Burnley fucking Football Club?' He said he had told 'that fucking halfwit [Bruce] Grocott' [MP, Blair's parliamentary private secretary] it was war. To add to the lively scene, Trimble and his wife wandered by, Trimble saying he wished he had his camera, then Andrew Lansley [Conservative MP] who gave us a quizzical look, provoking Soames to yell at him 'Well you can fuck off for starters!' He said he was desperate for ten minutes with TB to talk him out of 'the worst decision he's ever made' re hunting. I stayed up late for the [Eddisbury] by-election which came through at 2am. 1,606 [Conservative] majority.

Friday, July 23

I briefed the Sundays, largely on the [government] Annual Report as well as batting off endless different reshuffle stories. The best today was the *Telegraph* saying Ashdown was in line to be Northern Ireland Secretary.

Sunday, July 25

Out for dinner with Peter M and Reinaldo [da Silva, Mandelson's partner], Philip [Gould] and Gail [Rebuck]. Philip felt we were in quite poor shape at the moment. TB called, not knowing till I told him that I was with Peter. He said he had spoken to Mo and was wondering if he could put Peter in as Mo's Number 2. I said it was sellable but was it the right thing to do? I spoke to Mo who was about to go on holiday to Turkey and we needed to agree a line in case he went ahead and did it. She sounded pretty mad about the whole thing, saying it was all about Tony and why did he need Peter back at all blah blah blah? I raised it with Peter at the end of the evening and he went into ultra-haughty mode, said it was a total non-starter, he could not possibly work with her. I said I wondered if that was the wrong approach and whether he shouldn't give it a little bit more thought.

Tuesday, July 27

We went back and into a round of reshuffle meetings, the first time we had really gone into it in any detail. TB said at one point 'We are not exactly greatly blessed with talent.' TB was wondering whether twelve to fifteen ministers going was enough. He still wasn't sure about what to do with Peter M. Truth be told, he didn't like the personnel side of stuff and was not looking forward to it.

Wednesday, July 28

TB hated doing this [reshuffles] and it brought out the worst in him. We were getting a bad press mainly because the feeling was out there that he had wanted to make more changes but his colleagues had hemmed him in. But we couldn't afford an offside Mo plus an offside Frank [Dobson] let alone JP. They knew he was in charge but there was no point picking too many fights at once. JP was grateful TB was consulting him the whole way through but he was definitely feeling bruised. It was impossible not to have something of the feeling of an undertaker hanging around waiting for people to come out and then discuss how we handled their demise. It was definitely better doing this in the Commons but it was going on far too long. Bits of the jigsaw kept changing. At one point we had both [Peter] Kilfoyle and [George] Howarth [Merseyside Labour MPs] going to NIO, which would have been like a scouse outing, so [Adam] Ingram stayed despite wanting to go to MoD.

Thursday, July 29

I was in at the crack of dawn again. We were being savaged by the press for alleged weakness because he hadn't moved the Cabinet. I spoke to Jack C before his *Today* programme interview to get over that TB ran the government for the country not for the media. Margaret Beckett [Leader of the Commons] did the same thing brilliantly on *The World at One*. TB called and said we have a problem. He had also had a difficult call with Peter M to tell him he wasn't coming back in but he would be putting him in a party role later. He was very down on Peter at the moment, felt he had been diddling through the media to try to put himself in line for a recall. GB was being very onside, as was often the case when Peter was down. There was a real sense of payback in the vehemence of the media attacks over this. In the end we just had to take a hit and get it sorted. TB loathed the whole thing. He hated doing the sackings, didn't like pressures being put on by ministers looking after their friends, or the desperate pleas from individuals.

We got out a few more names for the lunchtimes and finally got it together for 4.30. I had a copy of a CD someone had sent me by a group called Garbage and I gave out prizes for the biggest and most garbagic reshuffle stories. George Jones [*Telegraph*] won for his Ashdown to Northern Ireland story.

Saturday August 28

Back to earth with a bit of a bang. The *Mail on Sunday* had a really nasty piece about Mo, with a 'source' claiming she would be 'left to twist in the wind'. I assured her it was nothing to do with us. I genuinely believed the bulk of anonymous quotes particularly in the Sundays were routinely made up. But Mo was very gloomy. The IRA had threatened four kids with death over local crimes and the 'ceasefire intact' line was looking a bit shaky. I put together a line defending Mo to the hilt.

Monday, August 30

There was a terrific leader in the *Sun,* which said I was brilliant and should be left alone. Both the Tories and the SNP [Scottish National Party] had piled in but it was all inside page and reasonably light-hearted. The main story on our watch was Ken Maginnis calling for Mo to go and I put out a very strong line in her defence, saying TB is fully behind her. In truth, he felt she should have moved on when the going was good. I took Calum to Bristol Rovers vs Burnley and on the train down, a young black family sat opposite and told first me, and then the whole carriage, that this was the best government we had ever had.

Tuesday, August 31

Trimble was demanding a meeting and TB, Jonathan and I all felt we needed to push them back a bit. TB felt the UUs were using what was happening as an excuse not to go into further discussion with Sinn Féin. Peter Hyman had done a very good note on the need to focus on the domestic agenda. It didn't bode well when TB said he wanted to go to Chequers when everyone else felt he should be in Number 10. I had a good meeting with Philip. He felt that spin was not yet a real problem, as it was confined to being a chattering-class obsession. I had thought a lot about this on holiday, and felt we had to make the nature of the modern media part of the debate about modern politics, because they were setting themselves up as a kind of alternative Opposition and becoming a barrier to any communication of political progress at all.

Saturday, September 4

There was a lot of interest re George Mitchell [commencing a review of the Northern Ireland peace process] on Monday and Chris Patten [delivering his report on policing in Northern Ireland] and Mitchell would ensure it was a big Northern Ireland week but we really had to try to stay focused on the domestic policy issues. Joe Lennon and I agreed we should try to stay out of it and see whether we couldn't keep the meeting with Bertie on Monday a secret.

Monday, September 6

TB saw Patten about his report on policing with Mo who was looking pretty stressed out. He had done a really serious piece of work but as he was also giving it to the Irish and to Trimble today the chances are it would get into the press. There wasn't much we could do about that. But I felt uncomfortable, as I think did he, not really being in charge of how this thing landed.

Thursday, September 23

TB asked me to go down to Chequers in the evening. Over dinner, we discussed GB and whether he would make a good prime minister. TB said he believed he was one of the top five politicians this century, that he was a Lloyd George figure, had massive qualities but was flawed and he worried whether the flaws would harm his judgement. His biggest worry was whether his general take on the world – that you were either for him or against him – would lead him to promote bad people at the expense of good. Charlie Whelan [Brown's former spokesman] had done an interview saying TB had apologized to GB re psychological flaws. TB said to me he had never done that because although he believed somebody did say something that made them feel justified in running that story, he was not prepared to say as much to GB.

TB was now sure Cherie was pregnant. They worked out it happened at Balmoral. A royal baby. He said he felt a mix of pleasure and horror. Thank God I'm a Christian, he said. It allows me to assume there must be a reason. We discussed it on the train. At the moment, TB, CB, Fiona and I were the only people who knew, and I was winding them up as to how much money we could make by tipping off the press. There was a part of it that was just funny, but it was also clearly worrying him. Once we got to the hotel, any time the two of us were together, he would just want to talk about it, what impact it was going to have.

Monday, October 4

I had a really bad asthma attack overnight and [Tom] Bostock [AC's GP] came round at lunchtime. He said it was not possible to operate under the pressures I did without suffering illness. He said given my history there were three possible routes for that pressure – head, chest and stomach. There was a chance, if I was not careful, of me just dropping down dead and he didn't want to be responsible for the 'second most powerful man in the country' dropping down dead. He said he was only half joking. He put me on antibiotics and said I had to rest.

Friday, October 8

We had a reshuffle meeting. TB was thinking of Peter M for NI, [Geoff] Hoon for defence, [Alan] Milburn for health. He didn't want to put out Jack C but he was looking to free up room and there was a lot of MoD lobbying of me, John Sawers and Jonathan for Jack C not to be sent to the MoD. I was pretty horrified at the idea of Mo coming to the centre [as minister for the Cabinet Office]. Jonathan was very funny describing what she would be like chairing meetings of the SCU and sorting out the Grid [news calendar designed to coordinate government announcements]. I had very bad vibes about it. Charlie [Falconer] was probably the best person for that job but with Peter coming back in, it would risk making the whole reshuffle about TB and his mates.

Monday, October 11

I got in early to see TB and Jonathan. I was moaning about Mo, but his constant refrain was give me alternatives. I said Jack C, but that deed was done. We went over various possibilities for [minister for] Europe. RC rejected Kim Howells [education minister]. TB then overruled Ann Taylor [Commons Chief

OCTOBER '99: TB REACTION TO CB PREGNANCY

Whip] and RC to go for Keith Vaz [a PPS]. At the office meeting, TB had still not decided re Ken [Livingstone], but we were all growing increasingly alarmed about Frank's lack of any campaign. TB was getting more and more frustrated about delivery.

Jack C was in first and came through with a handwritten note that he intended to put out as his resignation letter suggesting he offered to resign some time ago. I told him that the press team would really miss him because he had been reliable and a team player and I hoped we could still call on him. Then Mo came round after seeing TB, all lovey-dovey, burbling away about how she saw herself as a coordinator rather than an enforcer and she wanted to go to Belfast with Peter tomorrow. I had to persuade TB not to move Charlie F, who would be essential to making sure that Mo didn't run amok. Then [Alan] Milburn, then [Chris] Smith, and then Peter to Northern Ireland. I was glad he was back. He looked genuinely shocked and wasn't himself at all. He went to the loo and when after a few minutes he hadn't come back, I went looking for him and found him, still in there, saying he had never felt so anxious. I took him back through to my office and then got Mo round again and suggested they went out together and travelled off in the car together. He said he was due to see Gordon and then said, as if an aside to Mo, 'In this government I am appointed by two people not one.' TB claimed that when he saw him one-on-one he had been very hard on him, told him that if he didn't really behave, not diddle, just do the job properly, he would be finished. That may explain why he was so shell-shocked. I also wondered whether he might be worrying about needing round-the-clock protection.

At the briefing, most of the questions were about Peter and also whether Mo was pushed. I got Mo to do the media for tonight and Peter tomorrow. I had been pushing for promotion for Brian Wilson [Labour MP] but TB had been unsure. Like all reshuffles, there had been difficulties but this one had probably been easier than most. Mo's interviews were pretty hopeless. The 'hiya babe' approach had a certain appeal I suppose, but she was incredibly loose with language. I spoke to Peter later, who was settling in. He was seeing his new protection team and said 'I've just introduced them to the concept of Reinaldo.' The general media comment was that TB had the modernizing Cabinet he wanted, in his image. But Peter M would dominate the coverage and there would be a reaction at some point from GB at not having got what he wanted. We organized a series of baton-handover type pictures, Peter and Mo, Dobson and Milburn, Robertson and Hoon.

We got a pretty good press for the reshuffle, and only a few really hostile remarks re Peter M. He did the *Today* programme fine and his visit with Mo was the main story until the coup in Pakistan.*

Mo had, as was often pointed out, brought a breath of fresh air to politics in Northern Ireland. But though her personality and vivacity went down well with large sections of the public, her relations with the Unionists in particular had become dysfunctional. Perhaps some of them were not ready for a woman, and certainly not a woman like Mo, fond as she was of dirty jokes, belching, and slapping her wig down on the table at the start of meetings. Also, they became adept at exploiting the fact that Northern Ireland was so clearly a priority for TB, and Trimble in particular would often bypass Mo and go straight to the top, which annoyed and frustrated her. The aftermath of the Omagh atrocity was perhaps the high point of her antipathy to Number 10, but it was a recurrent theme, even though personal relations tended to be kept in reasonable order. One of the great frustrations for Jonathan Powell and me was her – or certainly some of her staff's – belief that we briefed against her. We never did. On the contrary, when she was under attack from the Unionists in particular, we were out there defending her to the hilt.

It also became a given among the commentariat that TB resented the standing ovation for Mo during his party conference speech. In fact, it was the Blairites – not least Peter M seated alongside her – who led it. She was an unusual politician, but that was a strength, and her role in bringing peace to Northern Ireland has rightly been recognized. I think she knew she had run her course in Northern Ireland, but it quickly became apparent she was not going to enjoy the Cabinet Office. Peter M is also an unusual politician, not least because of the passions he is able to inspire among others, and he was always going to bring a different approach. Instinctively closer to the Unionists, much more cerebral, but he too would develop a resistance to TB being involved in micromanaging affairs in Northern Ireland. TB had long believed Peter had very special political skills. No sooner had he resigned from the DTI than TB was thinking about when and how he could bring him back. Peter and Mo could not have been more different, but both helped to deliver important steps as the process inched forward.

---

* The Pakistan Army, led by General Pervez Musharraf, overthrew the government headed by Prime Minister Nawaz Sharif.

Thursday, October 14

I drove back with TB and we had a wonderful moment crossing Westminster Bridge when the phone in TB's car went, he answered, and it was a phone company asking whose phone it was, saying that they had a bill and didn't know where to send it. He said try the Cabinet Office in Whitehall. We got back for Cabinet. Afterwards TB saw Gerry Adams and Peter M privately. At Tampere [special European Council summit on justice and home affairs] we met with Bertie [Ahern] just to take stock.

Tuesday, October 26

I had another problem with Mo. She'd told Richard Wilson that she wanted to make public she'd taken cannabis 'and inhaled'. Nigel Warner [Mowlam's special adviser] called to say the *Mail* had asked her and she was inclined to answer. Pure self-indulgence, which would put pressure on other ministers re all manner of personal life questions. Mo could get away with it, and she knew it, which was why she was keen to do it, but it was a bad idea. The problem was she had too much time on her hands, loved the image stuff and this kind of thing just appealed to her for all the wrong reasons. I raised it with TB after he got back from the Palace and he said he did not want anything done until he had spoken to her. He said we had to find ways of harnessing her popularity.

Friday, October 29

I slipped off to the dentist. Bad news. She reckoned I needed twelve to fourteen hours' work on my teeth. I had a meeting with Mo who was desperate to get out the line that she once took cannabis 'And unlike Clinton, I inhaled and didn't like it.' She felt there was no way of not answering it sometime and she wanted to tell the truth. I saw it as being no problem for her but a problem for others who would then be pinned down on the basis she had been upfront. She said it would connect with people and in particular young people. I wasn't sure about that either. Bizarrely, she said it would help her do her job properly.

Wednesday, November 3

George Mitchell came in to see TB [re Northern Ireland] and felt things were moving in the right direction. He said Peter M was a real help because he was not Mo and that helped on the Unionist side.

I don't know what triggered it but last night I plunged into depression which stayed pretty much through the weekend. Partly I think it was tiredness, but also the feeling that whilst Fiona gave me all the practical support I needed, emotional support was lacking because by and large she was against the fact I had to put so much into the job. I was definitely feeling under more pressure. Her basic take was that I just wanted everything on my terms and had to understand that it could be tough living with someone as driven as I was.

Mo was still pressing me to do a statement on cannabis. She also had this mad idea that she sign up to do a book from which she, Nigel [Warner] and Jon [Norton, her husband] all take a third but Jon would get his third now. She said it wasn't an autobiography as such but it was all about 'how famous Mo coped with it all'. I said I couldn't see how a serving minister could do it and benefit financially from such a book. Added to which I thought the cannabis thing was just self-indulgence. She left by saying if she didn't hear from me tomorrow she would go ahead.

I went back to Number 10 for a meeting with TB, Mo, Richard W and Jeremy H and we had to go through all the crap about drugs again. We got her to agree to say she was never into drugs and she wasn't going to go over her whole life. On the book idea, both TB and Richard felt there was a problem with it because she was earning money from it while in office. She then said 'Well, I hear what you say and I'll have to decide whether to go ahead and make a decision.' TB: What do you mean? Mo: Well you'd have to decide if you wanted me to stay in government. TB: There's no need to think like that, but it would not be sensible for you not to be in government but you would get badly hit if you went ahead with this, so I just say don't do anything without coming back to me. I said to her later if they had problems with money why doesn't Jon write a book himself, but even that had its own problems. Later she agreed she would not take any money.

Wednesday, November 10

Peter M called TB to say the Unionists had come in with yet another list of demands, and it was dreadful. 'Boy, have we been here before?' TB said. He just had to keep going.

Thursday, November 11

Cabinet was Northern Ireland and beef. Peter M called, pretty exasperated, said Northern Ireland was looking really difficult and could even go belly-up today. There was a story in the *Mirror* that Mo hated her new job. She was going to become a real problem.

Friday, November 12

Crisis time in Northern Ireland. Tom Kelly [NIO] called saying it would be helpful if TB did a calming clip on Northern Ireland. TB [in Durban, South Africa, for the Commonwealth summit] was reluctant but did it. TB spoke to Gerry Adams, said he really understood why they were so fed up with the UUs but just give us the weekend. Mugabe [who had attacked TB for running a government of 'gay gangsters'] was running big, then Northern Ireland, then beef.

Saturday November 13

TB was pretty much focused on Ireland, though there were some tricky issues at the [Commonwealth] summit. Mugabe took up most of the press coverage.

Monday, November 15

The eleven o'clock was Ireland and beef. I was asked about a story about Peter waiting till he got the Ulster job before getting his flat refurbished, and I suggested he should sue over it. Both Mitchell and de Chastelain made good statements suggesting progress and we got a broadly positive response from the parties.

Thursday, November 18

Cabinet was Ireland, beef and the Queen's Speech. Peter M said part of the IRA statement was written by the UUs, which was a measure of how far we had come.

Mitchell was due to make a statement at midday, that he believed it was possible for devolution and decommissioning to proceed. He said it was fragile but there had definitely been progress.

The [Florence seminar] dinner was in a fabulous setting but organizationally a total shambles. Clinton's speech showed once more how brilliant he was at connecting, not just through what he said, but how he said it, through the pictures he painted in words, and through body language, but above all through making the most of what he knew and what people told him. You always had the feeling with Clinton that he was just hoovering up other people's stories and experiences, because they interested him, but also because he could use them. I discussed TB image problem with him. He said Hillary was being hit with exactly the same thing, that it's an obvious thing for the right-wing media to do, because it helps put up a barrier between the left in power and the people who elected them. All you could do was be aware of it and always strive to be in touch. Clinton was also asking TB to get more directly involved, given the success of his approach in Northern Ireland, in Cyprus and Kashmir. I was horrified at the prospect. I said I thought you were trying to help us get him back in touch, not find more reasons never to be at home.

We were in Norfolk for [special adviser] Tim Allan's wedding. The Ulster Unionist vote [backing the peace process plan and paving the way to devolution] went through. I did a conference call with Jonathan and John Sawers to agree a TB statement, but then we had to deal with the surprise move by David Trimble saying that he and his colleagues would issue pre-dated resignation letters by February if there was no decommissioning by then. We got our line agreed, playing it down, emphasizing we were still moving forward together. Peter M was at the wedding so he and I were able to sort it. I played the pipes outside the church and they sounded fine considering how little I had played recently. As weddings go, it was quite a nice do and the speeches were pretty high quality.

Tuesday, November 30

The news was still dominated by Northern Ireland with the devolution order to be laid soon and inevitably a lot of interest in Martin McGuinness as education minister.

Wednesday, December 1

The Northern Ireland order was laid after Peter M went to the Palace so we get devolution at midnight tonight.

Thursday, December 2

Power was devolved [in Northern Ireland] at midnight last night. Cabinet was fairly brief, Northern Ireland the main thing. GB was in a foul mood, came in, head down, spoke to nobody, scribbling the whole time, or just raising his eyes to the ceiling. There had been a definite change in him, probably a combination of the baby [announcement]* and Peter M doing well in Northern Ireland.

Ireland was massive but I wrote the hand of history-type sound bite which Jonathan was against, but which made all of the headlines.† Gerry Adams called me and said he wanted to say thanks to TB and to all of us. He said it was a really emotional day which many thought they would never see. It was wall to wall on TB all day and Peter M was doing stacks of media well. There was one less pleasant fallout we had to deal with which was that with power devolved, John McFall and Alf Dubs were now surplus to requirement as ministers. They were both very grown-up about it and just pleased the thing was happening.

A genuinely historic moment, and one which, after all the crises and the times we thought this could never happen, almost crept up on us. The diaries for this period are full of other issues, notably tricky negotiations in the EU, the attempt (failed) to stop Ken Livingstone becoming London mayor, and TB becoming a father again. The key moment was the vote at the UU conference. Once that was through, the rest followed almost effortlessly for the next few days, until the order was laid, and power was devolved.

---

* Cherie Blair's pregnancy had just been announced.
† Recalling Blair's words following the Good Friday Agreement that he felt 'the hand of history' on his shoulder, Campbell wrote for Blair of 'the hope that the hand of history is at last lifting the burden of terror and violence.'

'Inevitably a lot of interest in McGuinness as education minister.' The fact of those words in back and white, let alone in such a low-key, understated manner, underlined how far we had come, and how much all the ups and downs and the crisis summits had been worth it. So another big step forward, but plenty more ups and downs and crisis summits to come.

Monday, December 6

TB did a [Manchester] city centre visit with Mo, then out to see the Commonwealth Games site, then to east Manchester to see the New Deal for Communities at work. We were also getting enormous coverage in all the regions, not all positive, but with the main messages out there. Mo was looking a bit fed up. Earlier in the car, she had intimated to TB that she would stand for mayor [of London] if we could get Frank to quit.

Tuesday, December 7

TB was talking to Charlie [Falconer] and others about whether we could get Mo into the mayoral contest. Charlie felt legally there was no problem.

Wednesday, December 8

We heard from Gerry Adams that he was going to make public that they had found a bugging device in his car. It was going to be a huge story. I stuck to the usual line about not commenting on such issues and I strongly defended the security services. PMQs was a bit flat. The four o'clock was all about Adams. Mike White seemed genuinely concerned that it was history repeating itself, security services fucking things up for a Labour government. I said I didn't share his concerns.

Thursday, December 9

We were still getting a bit of flak about the Adams business but TB seemed totally relaxed about it. On the flight [to Helsinki European Council], we went over with Robin the various tricky issues we had to deal with. TB spoke to Adams about the bug, a call we had agreed to simply to let GA say that he had raised it and protested. But he seemed fairly relaxed. 'Sorry to bug you with this,' he said. Both of them laughed.

While TB was at the dinner John Sawers and I went over to the Irish hotel and had a good chat with Bertie [Ahern], half work, half play. He was regaling me with stories about [Cork-born Manchester United footballer] Roy Keane's dad who was called Moss and now they call him Sterling Moss because Roy sends so much money home. When TB arrived, he was raging about the French [continuing their ban on British beef] and Bertie said 'You wouldn't have to read too many history books to know they were a bunch of untrustworthy bastards, Tony.'

PG and PH called having been to a couple of focus groups which they said were the best for ages. There was real goodwill towards the government. TB got respect out of Northern Ireland, they felt warmer about him because of the baby, and they felt the report on the North–South divide took them seriously and didn't treat them like idiots.

Tuesday. December 14

I got back for a meeting with TB etc. on the mayor situation. Frank was going absolutely nowhere. TB was also worried about Mo. Margaret McD[onagh, General Secretary] said she had had dinner with Mo and Jon last night and he was saying that it was unbelievable that Mo wasn't at least Foreign Secretary by now. But TB was clearly moving to the view that Frank shouldn't stand.

Wednesday, December 15

TB saw Mo and told her to stop giving out so many vibes that she was fed up with the job. She claimed she had said nothing to anyone, which of course was nonsense. She had put it around variously that she should be Foreign Secretary, Defence Secretary, NATO Secretary General. She certainly had qualities, but she overestimated them and had over-inhaled the positive publicity she got for being a different sort of politician.

GB had another strategy meeting I couldn't go to. I was sorting out Friday's arrangements for the Northern Ireland meetings. I went out with TB visiting some of the down-and-outs near the Savoy, which was really grim, and then to [the homeless peoples' centre at] St Martin-in-the-Fields [Trafalgar Square] where he did a couple of interviews and then the press conference with Louise Casey and Hilary Armstrong [local government minister].

The BIC/BIIGC [British-Irish Council and British-Irish Inter-governmental Conference] was running fine, though the arrangements were all a bit shambolic. Peter M was very funny quizzing me about what happened at the Good Friday Agreement that led to the Isle of Man being part of these discussions.

We went over to Lancaster House to greet all the different delegations like Guernsey, Jersey, Isle of Man. Bairbre de Brún [Sinn Féin Assembly Member and minister] was late and so came in on her own. TB realized straight away that if he greeted her, it would be the first ever public handshake with Sinn Féin, which was straight away the main story. TB and Bertie's opening statements were carried live. Then TB and Bertie left for Number 10 for the BIIGC. Trimble and Mallon were a bit late. The Irish were keen that Bertie did the press with TB, as a head of government, Trimble and Mallon to do it later.

The other amazing thing today was that GB popped up on the nine o'clock news saying he was going to write off all Third World debt to the UK. Nobody, not even TB, was aware that he was going to do it today. TB tried to get hold of him but he wasn't returning calls. GB had gone right offside. The debt story led the news and some of the papers, especially of course the *Guardian,* relegating the Irish stuff, which was being seen as a success for TB and Peter M.

The eleven o'clock was about Shaun [Woodward, Tory MP who had defected to Labour] and Northern Ireland, where we were changing the law in relation to taking the oath. Piers and [David] Yelland [editor, *Sun*] called to say someone was flogging a picture of Euan [Blair] with a girl at the Ministry of Sound [London nightclub] last night and Yelland offered to buy them out of the market, which was quite nice of him. Then we heard the *Star* was running the picture. I called them and they agreed not to. TB was seeing Adams and when I told him about the Euan snogging picture he said the one thing that would put him over the edge was that his kids were not allowed a normal life because of our wretched press. In fact the press were being pretty good about it.

TB called. He said he had spoken to GB re [Third World] debt. Asked why he did it in the way that he did, GB said 'Because you asked me to.' 'When?' 'Six months ago.' We were able to laugh about it, because he had in the end done what we wanted him to but it was a very odd way to do it.

The Blair-Brown relationship did not play such a big role in relation to Northern Ireland, so this is perhaps not the book in which to add excessively to the many millions of words already devoted to the subject. However ... the truth is no book about one can really be anything like a full account without some assessment of the other.

As I think about the two of them with specific regard to Ireland, two immediate thoughts come to mind. The first is that when GB was called upon to act to help the peace process in his capacity as Chancellor, or as a campaigning mind, he always did so. The other thought, less charitable perhaps, is that one of the reasons TB performed so well in relation to Northern Ireland, was that unlike in most domestic policy and strategy issues, he was relatively free from the day-to-day relationships and pressures that sometimes ground him down. I found it striking, going through the diaries, how often we would return from an NI visit, or an overseas trip, and reflect that things went well, but almost immediately we would be dragged down into another difficult spat, often though not always with GB.

The tragedy is that the relationship never fully recovered from the immediate aftermath of John Smith's death in 1994. The day before he died, if asked the theoretical question 'Who will follow Smith as leader?' most people, including certainly GB, possibly TB, and the bulk of opinion formers, would have said Gordon. But the moment John died, and the question became real and immediate, not speculative or theoretical, a different answer emerged. As soon as I heard John had died, I knew Tony both should and would be the next leader. So did many others. That truth hurt GB then and I think it probably still hurts now.

As I recounted in the first volume of the diaries, Prelude to Power, *TB went to considerable lengths to ensure GB had a 'soft landing' from the hard-fought decision that he, not Gordon, should be the modernizers' standard-bearer in the leadership election against John Prescott and Margaret Beckett. But GB never fully reconciled himself to the fact that he, for so long the senior partner in a hugely creative and productive political partnership as they rose through the Party, had suddenly, under an intense spotlight, become the junior.*

When they worked together well, and when Peter Mandelson and I worked together well, and when John Prescott and the other 'big beasts' were on board, it felt like we were unstoppable. I can remember saying at times, when we were setting a clear agenda and the Tories were on the run, both in Opposition and in government, that it felt like playing for Barcelona against Hartlepool. And a lot of the best things the Labour government did came from TB and GB working together well. But too often, the team did not hang together. Too often, to take the football analogy a step further, it was as though we had a collection of people who would only pass the ball to selected other individuals within the team. Imagine how ineffective Barcelona would become if Piqué never passed to Puyol, Xavi would only pass to Iniesta, and Fabregas would not give the ball to the next man if it happened to be Lionel Messi.

I am obsessed with football, as fellow fans Bertie Ahern and Martin McGuinness know from the many conversations we had about Burnley and Manchester United at various lulls in talks. Also TB and GB both follow the game closely. Too often I felt like I was the guy on the pitch running around saying to the players it was not just ok to pass to each other, it was essential. That was a frustrating place to be, and with regard to Gordon, those frustrations finally erupted in the 'psychological flaws' episode, in January 1998. I always prided myself, still do, on being a team player, and I regret that I let my frustrations get the better of me, to the detriment of the team. But at the time, it felt like GB and Co were not simply refusing to pass the ball, they were running around the pitch hacking down their own star player. We had had a tricky but successful trip to the Far East, with Northern Ireland high up the agenda and any spare moment on the visit to Japan going on making calls to keep the process moving forward. But TB had reached a judgement that GB was 'deliberately destabilizing the government', and we came back to a real struggle to find out what was being planned in the upcoming Budget. It was a nonsense, which was making teamwork impossible, and I lost it. What I actually said to Andrew Rawnsley of the Observer *was that those who thought GB would have beaten TB in a leadership election needed their heads examined, and that the whole TB-GB problem was fuelled by resentment; a misguided belief that somehow TB robbed GB of what should have rightfully been his. It happened to be true, just as it was true that GB's team spent far too much time telling themselves and others that whatever TB was doing at the time, GB would have done it better. All true. But I should not have said it.*

I think there was always a wary but mutual respect between Gordon and me, and he fought hard to get me to go back and help him when finally he became Prime Minister. But at times the relationship between him and Tony could only be described as awful. For large periods it was possible to argue that there was a creativity to the tensions that helped sharpen the government machine, get people working harder, thinking better. But over time that eroded and it was hard to find any productivity or positivity in the negativity between them. I do believe GB and his team must take the lion's share of responsibility for that, for their failure to accept fully the basic fact that TB was the leader because he was the one the Party wanted, and the one likelier to deliver the kind of election victory we went on to secure. I also believe that if we had all hung together in the way we did when we were at our best, we would have kept the Tories out far longer than we did. And I believe that Northern Ireland is a good example of teamwork in politics at its best. Not just TB and his own team, which did indeed work well, but how that team worked with other teams – Ahern's and Clinton's on the easy end of the spectrum, SF's and the Unionists' on the not-so-easy end.

One of my favourite political quotations comes from US President Harry Truman. 'It is amazing what you can accomplish if you do not care who gets the credit.' To me, it sums up the centrality of teamwork to political progress, and indeed to any other meaningful project in life. I think the peace process was an example of that principle at work. From time to time, the spirit of that principle imbued our politics outside of NI policy too. But all too often, it did not. Again, sad, but true.

[2000]

I agreed with Mo that she would do a speech about the Tories on Friday and their 'lurch to the right'. She was very pissed off at Steve Richards' [*New Statesman*] article ['Mo Mowlam's fall from grace'] saying Number 10 was exasperated with her. I assured her we did not brief against her, and that she was the one who emanated unease the whole time. She was pretty antsy but agreed to do the speech. At one point, it was clear we were talking at cross purposes because she thought I meant us at first when I talked about lurch to the right.

Cabinet went over pay review bodies, flu, Northern Ireland. Peter M was very gloomy on decommissioning, said it was absolutely bleak. He said we were talking about very dark clouds. The decommissioning body would be unable to make a positive statement and that was very serious because decommissioning was to have started by the end of the month so that Trimble could report to his council in February. It meant the UUs would leave the executive.

We had a truly dreadful meeting of the TB/GB etc. strategy group. It was meant to be just the six of us (TB, GB, Peter M, PG, Douglas Alexander and I) but GB turned up with Ed [Balls], walked through the door saying 'This is an economics meeting, isn't it?' Ed marched in behind him. Embarrassment all round. At one point when TB asked what he thought was going to happen with long-term interest rates, GB said 'Ed's here, he can answer that.' At another point, discussing Europe, TB said the pro-Europeans were attacking him and making life difficult, Peter said we had to be more positive and Gordon literally turned away to look at the wall. He only opened up in any shape or form when TB and Peter left the room for a call with Gerry Adams. God knows what Douglas thought of all this.

Sunday, January 16

Mo did [Adam] Boulton [*Sky News*] and admitted she had taken drugs so she got her way in the end.

Thursday, January 20

Piers splashed the *Mirror* on Mo for mayor. Dobbo [Frank Dobson] was whacked in the phone poll. Piers was probably successfully winding Mo up. I told Dobbo about the dreadful *Mirror* poll but he showed no sign of wanting to pull out. I spoke to Mo, who came up with, even for her, an unbelievably up-herself statement, namely that TB was now so unpopular that 'even I might not be able to pull it off'.

Friday, January 21

The *Mirror* was massive again on Dobbo. [Front-page headline] 'Dead as a Dobbo'. The *Sun* asked Mo to do a piece backing Dobbo as a way of stuffing the *Mirror*. I had to get Mo to pull it on the grounds she didn't want to be used in newspaper politics. Mo was clearly keen to run, but very unkeen to say so.

Tuesday, January 25

TB was in a real state about Livingstone. Frank had refused to come out. He was not remotely bothered, it seemed, about going back to Cabinet or a peerage, or anything else. His pride was at stake and that was that. Also Mo was not willing to push him too hard. TB said it was the worst of all worlds – we had a candidate in the ring who can't win and a candidate outside the ring who would probably walk it.

I was pretty short with them at the 11 and really wanted to go for the *Sun* on [repeal of] Section 28 after they had said that children of five were to be taught about gay sex. We were due to leave for PMQs but an all-night and all-day filibuster meant we lost the day's business, which was ridiculous.*

Another meeting on London. Margaret McD said there was no way Frank would win and that Mo would, even though there would be a backlash. We all felt pretty desperate at the idea of Ken being a candidate. I said we had to do everything we could to get Mo in there. Margaret and Sally [Morgan] went to see her and eventually she said she would do it provided Frank wanted it, and we didn't pull him out. I went home briefly before going back in to join TB to see Frank and Janet Dobson [his wife], to try to persuade him to pull out. TB was pretty blunt, said he felt that the very best prospect was that he would only just nick it and then lose the election itself, possibly with Ken as an independent. Frank said he was convinced it was moving his way, but I said there wasn't much evidence of that. Frank also said, and he admitted there were personal feelings here, he didn't believe Mo would do much better. If he really felt she would, he would have no problems pulling out. Janet said she thought party members in particular would be gobsmacked and appalled if we did this, that it was the worst kind of fixing. TB said what he cared about was the impact on the party and the government if Ken won. It would be a big disaster and he didn't want that. All the evidence suggested Frank wouldn't win, and Mo might. That says to us that we should get her in. Frank was adamant he could do it and that she would do no better.

He must have been hurting to hear what we were saying, and maybe it just made him more determined. I said Mo would totally change the dynamic because she had an anti-politics persona and it was clear that several of the papers, including the *Mirror*, which a lot of members read, would just shift behind her. It may be unfair but the press had not let Frank put over a persona. Between us, TB and I must have tried eight or ten times, but he wouldn't move from the basic point, that he didn't think she was the answer. TB asked him, if he carried on and things didn't pick up, whether he would pull out later in the contest and he said no.

---

* Conservative MPs filibustered for twenty-nine hours to oppose the Disqualifications Bill, which sought to remove the disqualification for membership of the House of Commons and the Northern Ireland Assembly of politicians who were members of the Irish parliament, while still disqualifying Irish ministers from holding ministerial office in Northern Ireland. The move meant that parliamentary business was cancelled on Blair's thousandth day, though it deprived William Hague of an opportunity to confront Blair at Prime Minister's Questions.

So that was that, we were stuck with it, we were going to have to try to get him a proper message and a proper campaign and try to get him to win but it was going to be very, very difficult. I gave Frank and Janet a lift home and we really just talked small talk. I felt sorry for him. He was almost certainly going to lose, and surely he must know that, and he'd be left with nothing. I had one last go, saying he could come out with dignity, but he didn't buy it. There was real pride involved there and nothing we could do. The truth was we were heading for Ken as mayor. TB called just after 11 and said 'I suppose you think I wasn't tough enough.' I said no, I thought you got it about right. And given Frank wasn't budging, it was important not to destroy his morale totally.

Saturday, January 29

The papers had lots of stuff about Mo being 'whispered against' and losing her bodyguards, of which she was probably the cause.

Monday, January 31

Mo came to see me just before the 11, in a real strop. She really did have the look of a wounded child. She wanted to know what I would say about the story that her protection was being scaled down, and about the so-called whispering campaign against her. I said there was no whispering campaign from here or anywhere else that I knew of and on protection, it was purely a matter for the security people and I would discourage people from writing about it.

Tuesday, February 1

Peter M called, said that the Irish were in a real state and living in denial about what was going on. They didn't want to publish de Chastelain's report [on decommissioning], and they were just hoping something would turn up. But nothing was emerging. Peter said he wasn't at all sure how we take it forward. The feeling was we would keep going through a day or two, make a statement on Thursday about legislation to suspend, unless we got more progress now, which was doubtful. We had to steer the line between realism, accepting this was bad, but not tipping it into disaster areas. It had to be clear we were fighting to save it and we had to do what we could to prevent violent reaction. If it was usually two steps forward, one step back, this time it was a very big step back.

Both the *Mail* and now [*Sun* columnist Richard] Littlejohn had run dreadful pieces about whispering campaigns against Mo. I complained to Yelland, said they had no evidence of it.

Peter M, Tom Kelly and I were all working on the Irish to try to get them to see we had to publish the report, but they were adamant we couldn't. Hague did a reshuffle and I agreed lines with the party about judgement and moving to the right.

Wednesday, February 2

We were trying to get the Irish over for tonight but it was difficult. Bertie [Ahern] was seeing Adams and McGuinness. We had one of those classic little logistics fuck-ups that becomes a story. When I was speaking to Joe Lennon about the idea of meeting tomorrow, and we fixed Northolt as a precaution, the office was talking to the BBC and somehow the conversation got mangled into them thinking we were about to meet at Northolt for a crisis summit.

Thursday, February 3

Cabinet was all about Ireland. TB and Peter M both spoke at length and didn't hide how bad things were. Peter was due to do a statement and we were looking like we would have to suspend the institutions which, as the Irish said, was going to lead to no decommissioning at all. Jonathan, John Sawers and I were in constant touch with the Irish re meeting up later after TB's West Country visit [for the rural report].

TB spoke to Bertie, who was saying there was progress. Peter warned us to be very sceptical. We agreed the tone and tenor of the statement with him, deciding to go for legislating to take the power to suspend, rather than just to suspend. TB wasn't convinced the IRA were really moving. It wouldn't be enough for Trimble just to get more words. I did a briefing for the UK and Irish press and I think got the balance about right, as did Peter on the broadcasts.

Bertie was flying into RAF St Mawgan [Cornwall] and we met at a nice hotel at Carlyon Bay. He arrived about 9.15 and we got straight down to it in a room set up with a mix of hard chairs and overly comfortable sofas. Paddy [Teahon] showed me the second de Chastelain report, which was further down the road and they believed showed they were ready to do the business. The problem was it was all just words. Only under pressure did Bertie admit that what we were talking about was that the IRA would disband in May, send in their weapons and say that war was over. I said would he be able to be that blunt with Trimble and he was honest enough to admit both that he probably wouldn't, and that it didn't go far enough. TB was sceptical. If Adams was asked 'Did it mean the IRA was definitely beginning to decommission?' he would just say it was a matter for de Chastelain. TB said without clear answers, Trimble was dead. We had to give Trimble some succour. We all understood though that suspension was incredibly difficult for Sinn Féin.

Paddy Teahon warned that if de Chastelain said he was content, there could be no suspension of the executive. Bertie said we had to get it. Brian Cowen [new Irish foreign minister], who always strikes me as a pretty tough cookie beneath the laid-back manner, said to TB we cannot proceed on the basis of irrationality. TB said why not, virtually every argument I hear from Trimble and Sinn Féin has large elements of irrationality. They did brief statements which were fairly strong, saying there had to be decommissioning and there had been progress, and then I did a longer briefing. John Sawers felt we had gone from 0 per cent to 15 per cent.

Friday, February 4

We did a round of interviews. Peter M was very cautious about so-called progress. Gerry Adams had a real go at Peter today.

It was remarkable how quickly we had gone from devolution to decommissioning once again rearing its head as the main stumbling block. Or perhaps it was more accurate to say it was remarkable we had managed to get to devolution with all the ambiguity surrounding the various statements and approaches on decommissioning. Interesting too, to note that Peter seemed to be becoming quickly to SF what Mo had been for the UUs.

Sunday, February 6

TB called on his way from Chequers, and we agreed he would do something on Ireland at the top, then the big One Nation message as I had drafted it on the train yesterday. He was very keen on the argument he developed up to last Friday. His car and the cops collected Calum and me and we went off to wait at Blackpool airport. We went through the speech [to Labour's local government conference in Blackpool] and he liked it. Ireland was tricky. We took out the line that he believed that the IRA had not broken their word. It was an attempt to recalibrate because the sense was Peter M was really hitting Sinn Féin and putting all the pressure on them. It was a good, rounded, measured statement but maybe there was too much in it because the press could only take one simple message. So when PA headlined it 'Blair issues decommissioning challenge' I was a bit pissed off. TB chucked away most of the prepared text and did a big-picture explanation of all that we were trying to do, and did it well. He took them through the whole argument in all the big policy areas and they liked it.

Monday, February 7

At the morning meeting, TB went through some of the problems we had – Dome, NHS, delivery, Ireland, Scotland and Wales, Europe, transport, welfare. He felt we were in the right place on the big arguments, particularly the politics of unity.

Tuesday, February 8

TB was in worried and reflective mode in the flat first thing. He said we had a lot of problems. Cherie told me he was not sleeping well for the first time in ages. He was definitely worrying about GB, the latest thing being said was that GB was saying to MPs that TB was trying to block a rise in the minimum wage. TB asked me if I honestly thought GB could be prime minister. I said possibly but I would be worried how he would be in a real crisis or up against some of the big cheeses when they were on the rampage. TB was really fed up at the moment. A lot of it was about Ireland, but a lot of it was also about GB and the sense that there were a lot of problems mounting up.

I got back for the Sinn Féin meeting but it was clear we weren't moving anywhere. Even though we were on a new time frame [for decommissioning] of December 2000, it wouldn't be enough to move Trimble. I had the usual line to take discussion with Adams and McGuinness and Gerry gave me his notes, including his warning about the slippery road back to conflict.

Wednesday, February 9

After I had gone to bed, I got an extraordinary call from Mo. She had seen Tony. She wanted to be Foreign Secretary but she realized it wasn't going to happen. She was not very happy where she was and she was going to be looking for something new. She *did* want to be mayor, and she suggested to TB that maybe she could be an independent. Two businessmen had offered her forty thousand quid. She said people were coming up to her the whole time urging her to go for it. She was looking for a way in. TB had grimaced at the idea of her being an independent. Amazingly, it was the idea I had put forward weeks ago and I still felt surely it was possible. Mo said whatever she did she was going to be a problem area for him and she needed to be out of it. She said the Tony crony thing was a real problem.

Thursday, February 10

We got no news back from Mo re her independent bid. TB said it was crazy that she felt so badly she now wanted to do it but we just couldn't find a way. TB spoke to Bertie, put together a very downbeat line for the four o'clock where I virtually said we were going to suspend and it was important not to lose Trimble.

Friday, February 11

The *Telegraph* were gleeful about 'Labour hit in the polls' though when you looked at it we weren't that far down. It was more the raggedness that was worrying us. TB was on the phone re Ireland all day trying to get a situation where de Chastelain could produce a report showing progress. Peter M was being very hardline, for example not buying the line about new words from the IRA being enough. He had signed the order suspending the institutions so Adams, aware of what Peter was doing, put out a statement that there had been a major IRA development, so putting us in the position of looking like we were at fault. Peter was not at all happy with the game-playing. De Chastelain was due to produce a report that would show progress which we wanted out there to welcome but which the Irish wanted us to say was the basis of reinstatement of the institutions. We couldn't do that because in the end the progress was just words.

TB spoke to Bertie and after the Adams statement to Bill Clinton and told him they were 'dicking us around'. But Bill was taking Sinn Féin's side, saying Trimble had to get out and sell this. Our view was it was best just to get Trimble through tomorrow and leave it at that. Adams took the high ground for a bit. Peter was slow getting out that he'd suspended. Trimble struck an OK note. I got Denis Murray to say there could be a second de Chastelain report and tried to persuade the Irish we would put it out by nine o'clock. Joe Lennon was up for it but Paddy Teahon was insisting it was accompanied by a statement from the governments that we could use it to reinstate the institutions. TB and Bertie discussed it right up to 9pm, when I cut off from the call and gave Denis the go-ahead to brief on the de Chastelain report and say there would be a statement from the governments welcoming this as a development of real significance.

As ever we were walking a tightrope between the two sides and trying to get the media not to be too downbeat so that we could avoid overreaction, not least on the streets. And as ever, I was grateful for the honest discussions you could have with Denis Murray. TB was pretty fed up with it. Bertie was realistic and pretty clear we had to suspend but desperate for us to indicate we wanted the institutions back up again. Paddy got more and more emotional. I came on at 8.45 to say it was important to get the dynamics changed and get this reported in a more positive light. Literally, seconds before nine o'clock, with the titles running and Denis Murray holding on for me, I said right, decision time. TB said go and get Denis to do it, as agreed. Paddy started up all over again about the need to say that Peter would now be going to Parliament to rescind. Denis did an absolutely brilliant job, got the balance right, and put it in the place we needed it.

Saturday, February 12

TB thought last night's conversation with the Irish had veered from hilarious to surreal. Paddy had been unbelievable. Most of the time, it had been Paddy not Bertie doing the talking, and so emotional. The papers weren't bad, many following the same line as Denis. We got Joe Lockhart [White House press secretary] to be reasonably positive. Calum was grounded so we couldn't go to Bournemouth vs Burnley and I got Rory on at me to go to Newcastle vs Man U. Bertie was going to be there too. TB gave me a brief for when I got there. It was pretty rollercoaster stuff and even though we were nowhere near where we needed to be, it did feel a bit better. Bertie was in great form. I said our biggest problem was that we never seemed to get clarity from Adams. The IRA had to be clear or we would lose Trimble off the other end. He [Ahern] was a lovely bloke. Alex [Ferguson] popped up for a drink before the match. He looked really tired. Man U played badly and got hammered. On the train back, Mo called, emphasized she wanted to do it [run as mayor as an independent], said she was destined for it. The journey was spoiled by a dreadful hoity-toity public school women's hockey team making a racket in the carriage.

Monday, February 14

Northern Ireland was tricky, with the Irish briefing they were on a different tack to us, and that was the main focus of the 11. Mo came to see me after calling me at the weekend about going for the mayor's job. She was up for it, knew it would be a disaster for the party and that she would have to leave but she said it would be better than the life she had at the moment. TB had told me it must not happen but she had the bit between the teeth. I got her in to see him. She said she was very keen and it was him who had put the idea in her head, at which point he grimaced. She was eating a huge pear very loudly, with juice all over her top by the time she had finished. TB's view was that it was impossible for her to stand as an independent. We ran round in circles and eventually agreed she should place a story that she wished she had gone for it, then build a clamour about it, particularly through the *Mirror*.

It was an odd meeting. It ended with her thinking she was going to go for it but she later came back to me and said she would wait for Frank [Dobson] to win and then get TB to do the dirty work. She definitely bought the argument that Frank's and Alun Michael's problem was that they were seen as TB's people against colourful independent-minded people, whereas the problem was that they didn't have clear personalities and message. I had a dreadful cold and got very bad-tempered later in the day.

Tuesday, February 15

We had a big meeting on drugs planned for tomorrow and I was trying to get stories up on that, but both Mo and [Keith] Hellawell [former senior police officer now Labour-appointed 'Drug Czar'] were a bit of a nightmare to deal with. Then at 4.45 Jon Smith [of PA] called to say that P. O'Neill [IRA spokesman pseudonym] was putting out a statement about the IRA pulling out of cooperation with de Chastelain and what was our response? We discussed calling off tomorrow's meetings on Northern Ireland but TB said no. I had a meeting with Hellawell, who constantly needed reassurance that we rated him and wanted him out there on the media, but he was finding the system very difficult. He was basically fed up because he felt he lacked any real clout or power, felt that [former Minister for the Cabinet Office Jack] Cunningham had a problem with him because of his ego whereas Mo was useless and unfocused.

Wednesday, February 16

The Ireland meetings were leading the news all day. I was pretty clear we would get nothing out of today beyond SF and UUP grand-standing. The drugs coverage went pretty well all day, despite Mo charging around saying it was all a waste of time.

The meetings were OK, first Bertie, then SF, UUs and SDLP. Peter M was getting very Mo-ish, claiming to be isolated, Number 10 taking up too much of the reins, etc. Joe Lennon and I worked on joint statements, but we really were in verbiage territory. Adams and McGuinness were pretty surly, lecturing TB. People were just going through the motions and going to their default positions. There was a natural cut-off point because TB had to leave for a banquet at Windsor for [Margrethe II] the Queen of Denmark, which was a white-tie job, prompting me to feel even more sorry for him.

Thursday, February 17

Cabinet was mainly Ireland, Peter M just taking them through where we were, good news and bad. He felt Adams and McGuinness had indeed stuck their necks out, perhaps too complacently. He said Trimble was saved but in a difficult situation. TB said later that Mo going through the Grid had been 'unbelievably excruciating'.

I had another discussion with TB re GB, but he didn't buy my basic argument that GB was currently doing him in. He said they would get there and I would have to leave it to him. In some things, his judgement had to be paramount, and he was in no doubt that if he and GB fell out publicly it would destroy the government. Peter M felt GB had made his operation more subtle but he was still steadily building up support and subtly undermining TB, and the aim was to build a sense that TB was shallow, without values, that New Labour was just a brilliant piece of spin, that GB was the real driver on substance so why not let him take over and be the real PM? Peter M said he felt a bit out of it in Northern Ireland but his sense was GB was motoring, that the whole 'psychological flaws' episode slowed him for about a year, but he was back in gear.

Saturday, February 19

We were in the final build-up to Sunday's mayoral announcement. Mo was on again, desperate to do it.

Sunday, February 20

TB was very agitato, must have called about ten times. The first was to say that Frank had won [Labour's mayoral candidate nomination] and that I needed to speak to him and talk him through the day. The focus was all really on whether or not Ken would go as an independent. I was pretty sure he would. TB asked me why I sounded depressed. I said I wasn't aware that I did, but he was back urging me to rest whilst at the same time calling me every few minutes either for the same conversation as before or with a new set of instructions. TB said that the mayoral situation was bloody but a lot better than if we had been landed with Ken. Norris said that if there was a God, clearly he was a Conservative, and I managed to crank up a bit of a storm.

Tuesday, February 22

Livingstone was still the dominant political story and now we had the *Guardian* saying TB had a secret plan to dump Dobbo and put in Mo. The story could only have come from Mo or, TB and others feared, possibly Peter M, which I didn't buy. Mo insisted she was not responsible but it was odd that it was out there just as Frank was looking better. We were also having to deal with a story being whipped up about the idea of the army handing over guns in an act of NI reconciliation. Godric did the 11 and it all got a bit tricky because he couldn't rule it out. I didn't really get focused on it but later Trevor Kavanagh [*Sun* political editor] called and I sensed it was going to be big. I spoke to Tom Kelly in the States [Washington DC, on a trip with Mandelson] and we agreed a pretty robust line to get the thing in perspective. But we had too many of these ragged situations.

Stephen Lander [director general of the Security Service] had asked me to go for lunch at MI5. We went over a brief history of the service, in particular what they did during the war. He said there were three main parts to what they did – first, following people, at which they were reckoned to be the best in the world. Second, interception of communications and third, counter-terrorism and increasingly, working on organized crime and drugs.

As with MI6, they had in my view an overly negative view of their own profile and image. Most of our discussion was about Ireland, drugs and the media. They had someone who responded to media enquiries but they were resisting the idea of having an official press office and I said I would continue to resist it if I were them, but they did need to have lines out that allowed them to explain properly when they needed to, or when they needed political support. I said they should always feel free to use us. Lander was clearly more strategic than hands-on. He said the organization had changed beyond recognition since he joined it twenty-five years ago when women were only allowed to be secretaries. Northern Ireland was clearly his focus and he said it was important that even decades after the event, sources should be protected. I understood better after talking to them why they needed a bit of distance from government but felt there was a good story they should be telling about an old organization responding to new challenges. He said the CIA's press operation cost more than their entire budget. It was gone 3 by the time I left.

Monday, February 28

Peter M called, said that he had had a very thuggish meeting with Adams and McGuinness. He also said his security advisers had admitted that decommissioning would make little practical difference to security and that it was a non-issue so far as the real security situation was concerned. The problem was the Tories had got on that hook and we were on it too.

Tuesday, March 7

Livingstone choosing to stand as an independent was wall to wall and he got a very good press without necessarily being endorsed. There was a sense running through it that we had really fucked it up. He was running rings round us.

Wednesday, March 22

Peter M called, angry that Bertie had said there would be a new initiative from the two governments when there was no such thing. On the flight to Lisbon [for the European Council meeting], TB said it was becoming a problem that I was seen as such a figure in my own right, because it made the straightforward job of briefing harder.

Thursday, March 23

TB did bilaterals first with Bertie and then [Lionel] Jospin, which we had to break up for the family photo [of leaders]. It was comic to watch because TB was placed next to [Austrian Chancellor Wolfgang] Schüssel and it really looked like he was trying to avoid him. Schüssel was desperately trying to talk to him and TB just carried on talking to Bertie. TB insisted afterwards he wasn't being rude and hadn't deliberately ignored him but the press were convinced it was a deliberate snub.

I had to deal with an Alex Ferguson problem. He had agreed to do an RUC dinner in Belfast tomorrow and the press there were whipping it up and the club was getting lots of calls. He was in Portugal for a match. I called him and he said his instincts were to get out of it, so I did a statement for him to the effect that he was not prepared to be used as a political football.

At his NHS [pre-summit] meeting,* Alan Langlands [NHS chief executive] slipped me a note saying I must press TB not to micromanage from Whitehall because it was a disaster waiting to happen. Peter M clearly thought the whole thing was a nonsense and arrived totally unprepared and talked about the Northern Ireland Health Service much as he might talk about life on Mars.

We were back on to Northern Ireland. Jonathan's meeting with the UUs was leaked, so it was out TB was going tomorrow, which gave us another set of problems. I agreed a line with Tom Kelly and Joe Lennon to keep expectations right down.

We set off for the airport and out to NI, with Michael Cockerell [BBC political documentary maker] and film crew in tow.† We got helicoptered over to Hillsborough where TB did a brief doorstep before beginning his meetings, first with the chief constable and the General Officer Commanding, then Trimble, then the other parties. TB was trying to get a new IRA statement out of Adams and McGuinness, who Tom Kelly and I met going round the gardens at one point, Gerry pointing at the plants and telling us which ones he had in his own garden, being very much the nice middle-aged woolly-jumpered gardener. Tom and I did a fairly full briefing, but made clear to them all there was very little going on, and

---

* Blair had called a summit with ministers from the devolved governments – the first of its kind – to discuss NHS investment and reform.
† A documentary about the government's media operations, which ended up attracting more attention to AC than he wished.

that they might as well leave for all the hanging around they were going to have to do for not very much to report.

TB remained optimistic though and when we went back in said he felt we might end up making progress. Paisley absolutely tore into him, and he more or less just let him. We then left for Dublin by helicopter. He and Bertie did another brief doorstep. They had a private session one-on-one and came out to say they had decided to meet on Thursday. Over dinner I was getting calls from Burnley where we lost 3–0 to Gillingham to pretty much fuck our promotion chances. Bertie was on good form, and interested in how the asylum argument was playing out. I think he felt NI was in danger of going backwards again but he was determined to keep going.

On the flight home, while TB talked to Jonathan re NI, Peter M and I talked about what to do re Millbank. He felt there were several big downsides to me going there – Fiona's opposition to a bigger workload, Number 10's capability, and whether I could manage Margaret. I was worried more generally about my management skills. I was fine at the inspirational leadership stuff but less confident at all the more classically managerial stuff. Peter was curiously disengaged from it all, as if he were talking about something that was not really anything to do with him, giving advice from afar. He said it was impossible for him to do anything because in NI he was pretty much running the show and it was full on the whole time. TB was still very antsy re Cockerell, wouldn't let them film on the plane for example. Peter said it was a great big ego trip for me, and I would regret it.

Thursday, April 20

There wasn't much appetite for an eleven o'clock so I delayed and we waited for Bertie's arrival. Grace was in when he came in and he made a real fuss of her sitting in the chair in the corner of the hall. The meeting went well and there were clearly the makings of a plan on the table. We needed a joint statement by the two governments, an IRA statement, confidence-building measures to help both sides. Bertie as ever was more optimistic about the IRA going further than we thought they would. Peter wasn't there and pissed off not to be, but it would have meant Brian Cowen being there too and sometimes these worked better just with the leaders. They were at it for ninety minutes or so, then did the joint webcast.

I persuaded Joe Lennon not to go overboard about progress today, as this was not the time to overclaim. We were discussing third parties, who could verify arms dumps. When someone suggested an American, I ventured Oliver North,

APRIL '00: AHERN MORE OPTIMISTIC THAN TB RE IRA

just to lower the tone.* I did a briefing, also told them about TB being called up for jury service [as an MP and barrister Blair was disqualified], then home to collect the boys and head north to see Mum and Dad.

Tuesday, May 2

My routine was now see or speak to TB first thing, GB meeting, my own government meeting, see TB again, then do what was needed to get everything ready for the 11. I did both briefings today, mainly focused on Ireland, Rover and the [London] riots, all quite difficult. We had to organize TB a postal vote for Dobson, having decided on the next trip to Ireland. Peter M was working out of my office most of the day because he was not at the Northern Ireland meetings and very pissed off not to be so. He felt Number 10 and Jonathan in particular were not setting meetings up well, and also that TB was too prone to buying the line from Adams. There was a rather nasty little scene at the end of the day when, in front of officials, he rather mocked TB when he referred to 'demilitarization'. Peter M said 'We call it normalization. Don't use your Sinn Féin methods just because you've been absorbing them all day.' Peter was clearly feeling a bit isolated and undermined. He was also getting more and more grand in the scale and nature of his anecdotes.

Today was a good example of how hard it was to separate day-to-day and strategic. The politics of Northern Ireland was such that TB wanted me briefing on it, to get the sensitivities right, which Godric would be able to do in time, but you only got them if you were immersed alongside TB. I was trying to work up a new strategy paper but was constantly interrupted. I announced at the four o'clock we would be going to NI on Thursday, but Sinn Féin threw a wobbly, said it was all pointless and then Bertie threw his own spanner in the works. Jonathan and Bill Jeffrey [political director, NIO] went to see Adams and McGuinness at the Irish Embassy. It was all very touch and go and only TB seemed at all hopeful. I bumped into JP and we agreed that at the count for the mayor, he should shake Ken by the hand and be reasonably friendly. He sounded very fed up. Everyone seemed a bit fed up at the moment. I got home and worked till 1 after the kids had gone to bed.

---

* US Marine Lieutenant Colonel Oliver North, involved in the clandestine sale in the 1980s of arms to Iran, the proceeds of which were used to fund Contra rebels in Nicaragua.

I woke up to the feeling that we had a bad day ahead, on the mayor and electoral front and also re Northern Ireland. TB, having worried for so long about Ken, seemed alarmingly indifferent, said Ken was going to be a problem but there we are. TB, for reasons best known to himself, was having lunch with [right-wing journalist and historian] Paul Johnson. We collected him from there and headed off to the airport to head for Belfast. Bertie arrived. Adams and McGuinness came privately for a couple of meetings before going off to get the IRA to agree a statement. Things felt a little bit more hopeful. Over dinner, which was pretty relaxed, Bertie said there were three options. They come back with a good statement and we go snap. A bad one, and we go home, or one somewhere in between that means a long negotiation. I felt a little bit unworthy that my principal selfish thought in all of this was how to make sure I managed to get home to collect Calum and get to Scunthorpe on Saturday for what was, after our recent run, Burnley's biggest game in years. The big bad diversionary story – there always seemed to be one – was a leak of an Ivor Roberts [UK ambassador in Dublin] telegram saying Brian Cowen was basically a Sinn Féin supporter. TB spoke to Clinton and said at one point the big difficulty was losing the word Royal in the new Northern Ireland police service. Bill said why can't you call it 'former Royal' or 'Royal pain in the ass'?

I woke up to pretty nightmarish headlines.* I went to see TB in the Queen's bedroom [at Hillsborough Castle]. He was pretty unfazed. Said he wasn't complacent and he didn't think this was so significant, though he didn't like us being neck and neck in the GLA [Greater London Assembly, Labour nine, Conservatives nine]. He was furious at a *Times* piece by Linda McDougall [documentary maker] on her programme with Mo, which was all about us doing her in. TB said he was fed up with this stuff and wanted to speak to her. He did, during a lull in the talks, and though he wasn't terribly stern, she probably got the message. He said we had never briefed against her and it didn't do her or us any good to have this take hold as some kind of truth. He said he was fed up with reading we had done her in because it simply wasn't true.

---

* Livingstone had won the mayoral election with 57.9 per cent of the vote. Dobson came third. Labour had won only nine of the twenty-five Assembly seats. Elsewhere in the country, Labour lost seventeen councils and 574 councillors, while the Conservatives gained seventeen councils and 594 councillors.

TB and Bertie did a series of meetings and the parties were all coming and going, but it wasn't clear where we were heading. Adams and McGuinness came through with their IRA statement, which was fine though slightly watered down, Brian Keenan [IRA representative] having insisted on putting in a line about 'the causes of conflict' next to the line about decommissioning. But it was pretty good. However, it was becoming clear through the day that Trimble, whilst reasonably happy on the decommissioning front, was desperate for something new on [the recommendations on policing in Northern Ireland by Chris] Patten to avoid problems being generated by David Burnside [Ulster Unionist candidate in the forthcoming South Antrim by-election]. We had a whole series of arguments about the title of the new police service, with Trimble desperate to get some kind of reference to RUC in the title. John Taylor suggested we say it incorporated the RUC but Trimble rejected that. It was all a bit rollercoaster-ish. We all had our own reasons to want to get away. TB for his birthday, Bertie was intending to go to Old Trafford tomorrow, I was desperate to get to Scunthorpe.

We seemed to be on for progress again after a Sinn Féin/UUP meeting upstairs went better than we thought it would. Ronnie Flanagan was around and was keen to get on with it. Stephen Lander let us know he didn't much like the IRA statement but even Peter was satisfied it was progress. We had to go out and do the media both on this and London. I did a script for TB after he spoke to Frank. The backdrop was good, out at the stables, he got the tone right. There was an embarrassing moment, me having lined up Mark Simpson [BBC] to do something on Ireland and TB slapped him down, saying he was really focusing on London. His best answer was when he said he wasn't going to pretend he had changed his views about Livingstone but he was going to do his best to make it work.

I did a phone briefing with the political editors, who had realized Romsey was significant. It was pretty vile watching Ken on the news. The Northern Ireland stuff was really up and down and TB was getting a bit frantic. He spoke to [former President of Finland Martti] Ahtisaari to get him lined up on arms dump verification. We were also going for [South African lawyer and politician Cyril] Ramaphosa. So there was lots to move on but it was hard. I asked TB if I could leave early and he said yes. I had a long walk with Peter who felt that the Irish were being unreasonable, that if everything could be left to Bertie, it was fine, but his people kept getting to him. He visibly cheered up when I told him that Ken had said of GB that a Chancellor who wanted to be prime minister would have to look after London as well as he currently looked after Scotland. Earlier, TB and GB had had a bit of an argument on the phone about the nature of reform and the extent to which we made that our key argument.

I did the Sunday lobby down the phone with Cockerell filming in Number 10 and Alison Kahn with me. Godric said Cockerell then interviewed Jon Craig [*Sunday Express*] and Mike Prescott [*Sunday Times*] who were quite hostile. TB was really getting down at the idea that this thing could come crashing down over what we called the police force. As the thing dragged on, eventually I left in an armoured police car that whisked me through to get the 9.40 flight. I felt personal pleasure at leaving and knowing that I would make the match tomorrow, but professional guilt because I could sense both TB and Jonathan felt I should stay.

On the flight, I watched a couple of women reading the [Linda] McDougall piece in *The Times* [re Mo Mowlam], which they read from beginning to end, and I could see them thinking it was true. By the time we landed, I called through and it was all moving. They had pretty much got the deal. There would be a joint statement, a brief doorstep with TB and Bertie, the expectation of an IRA statement within twenty-four hours, Trimble not too bad about it. Jonathan and Tom Kelly both sounded genuinely excited about it. TB sounded tired but the atmosphere had been transformed. The key was the SF/UUP meeting. It also allowed us to say that Peter M had done a real job in talks, getting the UUs to move. There were all manner of questions but it was pretty good. I followed it late watching Sky News. We could be pretty pleased with the last few days' work.

Saturday, May 6

The NI breakthrough came too late to prevent the papers from being a real Livingstone orgy. Peter M did some excellent interviews as we waited for the IRA statement. TB was in better mood re Ireland but still felt we should try to persuade the Irish to move on the question of the RUC.

I got on the train with Calum and Charlie [Enstone-Watts, friend of Calum] and set off for Scunthorpe. I did the Sundays in a conference call from the train. I was setting out the difficult questions on the NI process, making clear that we were almost there. As I was speaking, Adams called Jonathan to say that the IRA statement, exactly as agreed, would be out in half an hour at 1. So at Doncaster Station, I did a conference call with Tom [Kelly] and Julian [Braithwaite] to agree what we should do and how we should announce it. There was a fantastic feeling among the Burnley fans but Scunthorpe scored, and we went through a pretty dreadful phase and it looked grim. But we equalized, setting us up for half-time. We scored again and somehow we hung on. Everyone piled on to the pitch to wait for the other results, then it came through that we were promoted [from Second to First Division]. Fantastic celebrations. Somehow Calum and Charlie managed to get on the team bus and got their shirts signed before they got kicked off. On the train back, Peter M called to say the Channel 4 documentary on Mo was an outrage, and totally libelous of me.

Happy days. To get Burnley promoted on the same day as we finally seemed to get back on track re decommissioning made this a close runner-up to Good Friday Agreement Day in terms of the sense of progress. Yet again, it had required longer-than-expected negotiations, sleep deprivation, a shift from unexpected quarters at unexpected times and (see below) setbacks following on quickly enough. Peter's harder approach to Sinn Féin also appeared to be a positive factor at this time, much as Adams and McGuinness would deny it. But there was a spikiness to the relationship – Peter was good at spiky relationships – which did seem to have injected a new energy on that side of the equation.

Sunday, May 7

Ireland was dominating, with the IRA the lead in most papers, Clinton up on it and Peter M on *Frost*. I was working on the *Times* interview, saying to TB that we had to get back into a sense of conviction, that he was doing what he was doing out of belief. Alex called re our promotion, said that Darren (his son) had been man of the match for Wrexham beating Gillingham, and that there had been hundreds of Burnley fans there cheering them on. His take on the local elections was that it was a bit of a wake-up call. TB was pretty close to the end of his tether re Mo, who was clearly pushing all this stuff about being done in by us. Julia Langdon had a big piece in the *Mail on Sunday* saying Jonathan was 'the Downing Street poisoner'. TB felt Mo had made up her mind to get out and had decided to go as a victim rather than have anyone think she'd been a failure. He felt that she was trying to damage others as a way of protecting herself.

The [*Times*] interview was in the flat with Phil Webster and Peter Riddell and we went for it as a kind of New Labour relaunch. TB was good on Ireland, excellent on the big picture, London, the baby, and volunteered a few lines on the Mo stuff being a tissue of lies. He said afterwards he was tempted to write a piece himself setting out the truth – that he did ask her to go for mayor but she didn't want to, the opposite of what she was saying now. Both he and JP, who was mega-supportive at the moment, agreed that she was behind all this stuff. TB reckoned JP's current support was because we had stood by him so strongly when he was being kicked about.

Monday, May 8

Jonathan was in Dublin and although Ireland was in a better place, there were still problems to sort. TB was supposed to see Pat [McFadden] to get him to go to Millbank but he did it so badly that Pat just felt he was being shunted aside and he thought fuck it.

Wednesday, May 10

I was hoping to get Cockerell out of our hair by giving him some TB access today but at the first meeting, TB was so obviously not himself, and by lunchtime he just wasn't in the mood for it, and we called it off. By then the Northern Ireland situation was going backwards again. Sinn Féin was saying the CBM [confidence-building measure, e.g. verifiable evidence of IRA decommissioning] was off if we changed Patten, which was a real problem because we had already done a deal on changing Patten with the UUs. TB had a stack of calls on it through the day. He wasn't in a great mood all day, probably because of Ireland.

Thursday, May 11

There was meant to be a TB/GB pre-Cabinet strategy meeting but Northern Ireland was going wrong. It was another of those issues that you couldn't believe might scupper the whole thing, namely flags. [John] Taylor said there could be no question of any Union flags being removed from public buildings. Sinn Féin was saying that any retreat on Patten would lead to the IRA statement being withdrawn.

I went with TB for lunch at the *Observer.* He was on much better form, terrific on Ireland, relaxed about Ken and good on Europe. He was on the phone re Ireland all day, and at 11pm Trimble was virtually in tears, saying it was over, he was finished, and TB trying to assure him he would stand by him but eventually saying 'I can't believe we are going to lose this because of the bloody flags issue.'

Friday, May 12

TB was really struggling to get Northern Ireland back on track with flags and the RUC still the main problem. Peter M was losing patience with the Irish. GB came in for part of a strategy meeting, but wasn't really contributing because Peter M was there.

Northern Ireland and Sierra Leone were the main issues for the day.*

The *Guardian* poll showed TB's ratings now very low, comparatively. Mo's were very high. She came to see me at 11.30 and we agreed she should go on *The World at One*. But she was all over the shop. Wanted to say we had changed course, kept scribbling things I was saying then playing them back at me, usually with a totally different meaning. I thought she should be on social exclusion, she just wanted to 'do drugs'. She said she ought to explain how many Cabinet committees there were, as if that added up to a row of beans. She said she wanted to say TB had 'gone through his strong leadership phase'. We also agreed she would say we didn't comment on polls, but she ended up thanking people for their support for her. Mike White [*Guardian*] called me after the interview and asked, genuinely, if she was ill. I think her basic problem, and she said as much to me, was that she hated the job and was desperate for a real role.

GB came for a meeting with TB and had a copy of Peter M's speech in Belfast, which he felt was a real problem because he was pushing the boat out on the euro, suggesting we could not get stability for our businesses until we were in it. GB was in a total rage, said it was an outrage and why didn't he just stick to Northern Ireland? He felt it was crazy to get the euro up in lights at a time we didn't need to. I spoke to Peter in Belfast and he did his usual feigning ignorance as to why there should be a problem.

Fiona had gone off with Cherie to the hospital and they were pretty sure the baby was going to be born fairly soon. TB stayed in the office till about 8 and Anji said later he had been really nervous, nervous about the politics of where we were, nervous about the baby and what it would do for him, Cherie and the way we work. TB called as he was going to the hospital. I called Anji to get Cockerell

---

* David Trimble was asking for three points to be clarified before deciding whether the UUP would return to government.
   1. What exactly did the IRA mean by putting its arms 'beyond use'?
   2. How did the two international arms inspectors intend to carry out their inspections?
   3. Other issues of concern for DT were the retention of the RUC name and the flying of flags from public buildings.

down there to film the media outside. Fiona kept me in touch through the night. It finally came at 12.25 and we decided not to put anything out until they got home. I was in bed when Fiona texted that it was a boy. I called through, spoke to TB who sounded very happy about it. I heard the baby and TB said 'Here you are Leo, talk to your spin doctor.'

Friday May 26

I had to deal with [Labour MP, former arts minister] Mark Fisher's nasty letter to his constituency members about me and the 'nauseating' campaign against Mo, so I put together a reply on that.*

Saturday, May 27

There was a narrow but successful UUP vote on the IRA statement, leading to restoration of the institutions.

Monday, June 26

IRA decommissioning was massive on the news.

Tuesday, June 27

I woke up to Zimbabwe and more intimidation of the Opposition, followed by a story that Mo was calling for the Queen to move out of Buckingham Palace. Lucie [McNeil, press officer] called to ask if I thought Mo should go on. I said no. She went on anyway but with TB as the ardent monarchist, anything we said would take us to 'slap down' territory and so it duly proved. The full transcript was even worse. It was now becoming a given that we saw her standing ovation at conference as a problem, and also a given that there was a Number 10 briefing operation against her. Both were nonsense. We had pretty much organized the reaction during the speech, with Peter M deliberately sitting with her, and I was now pretty convinced the so-called briefing operation consisted of her and her friends just going around saying it. It just wasn't serious.

---

* Fisher's letter had found its way into the *Daily Mail* and elsewhere, saying, 'The nauseating spin campaign against Mo Mowlam suggests that Downing Street is still in the grip of the southern, modernizing spin doctors.'

Mo apologized for the Royal gaffe, ensuring it ran for another day.

Through the evening, I got a stack of calls about a vicious attack from Ken Follett [author and husband of Barbara Follett, Labour MP] in the *Observer*. Really lurid over-the-top stuff and very personal. I got the *Observer* to change two lines, first to deal with the bollocks that TB tried to blacken Mo's name, and second that I poured poison into their ears. I gave PA a statement that it was sad that there were always people on the left willing to peddle the propaganda of the right.

Mo called, bright as a bee, and said 'Hi Ali, just to say if you want me to go up and say whoever's doing all this to me, it's not Tony, I will,' and I really lost it. I said the best thing she should do is what she should have done months ago and tell the truth, namely that it's total balls that anyone was doing her in from Number 10. She could say that she was too busy dealing with serious issues like drugs and social exclusion to worry about gossip, but no, we had to deal with this fucking rubbish every weekend because people were too self-indulgent and because wankers like Ken Follett wanted a few more minutes of fame. She was clearly taken aback and for a while there was total silence. She said was I aware of her discussions with TB about leaving government to try to get an international job and we needed to talk about how to make it a good story for Tony. I said I wasn't in the mood.

I spoke to TB, who also said to her she had to make it clear that the stuff about her being briefed against was rubbish. He was pretty forceful and she sounded close to tears. She later called Anji and said I had blamed her for the whole thing, which indeed I did. I knew TB hadn't said anything untoward about her, I knew I hadn't. Most of the journalists Jonathan spoke to complained he never said anything to them. I was convinced she and her pals were the ones putting it about.

The press was full of spin stuff, several pieces vile about me. The GB meeting was more angst than anger. I was working on Thursday's speech on race and exploring whether we could take the fixed penalty idea further, e.g. for parents of unruly kids. TB called me in and asked if I was all right. He said there was so much anger in me at the moment and it's not sensible. He said there weren't many people he was dependent on but I was one of them and angry advice was not always the right advice. He relied on me for the right advice. He said he relied on me more now than ever because GB was always in a rage and always calculating, which meant he gave warped advice, whereas Peter M was incapable of not being devious. But they were both brilliant and we still needed them.

He said my problem was that most Cabinet ministers, certainly the important ones, trusted and respected my judgement, so I was unique. It wasn't like [Bernard] Ingham because in the end I was on a par with the senior Cabinet guys. He had thought about whether I should go upfront as a government spokesman but felt that would just lead to more noise about propriety, but he just wanted me to get in a better frame of mind so that I wasn't always fighting. He said it wasn't sensible to be at war with the press the whole time. It's what they want. He said in the end he had to take most of the strain because he was the top man. But when it came to taking the strain and the pressure, I was second in line and he knew that I was talking more than most people were capable of. But somehow I had to get more time off and I had to delegate more, and I had to try to rebuild some of the relationships with the media.

We had an office meeting on the reshuffle and the restructuring of government and every proposal seemed to bring its own problems. I felt the most pressing question was whether to put Peter M in Millbank. Stephen Byers [Trade and Industry Secretary] to Northern Ireland might be seen as a bit of a slap down. We rejected the idea of [John] Reid, [Alistair] Darling or [John] Denham for Millbank because we knew Peter would still be diddling.

Thursday, July 13

The press went in droves to a screening of the Cockerell film, which I watched in the office. It seemed fine, worthy, neither great nor disastrous. The only moment I cringed was when I seemed to be taking the piss out of TB. There was a real sense of access but some, e.g. Peter H, felt it made TB look weak and me look strong. Jamie Rubin did me proud on *Westminster Live*. It certainly wasn't a hatchet job, though the press were bound to go for the bits they wanted.

Northern Ireland was the big story because of prisoners leaving the Maze [prison].*

August holiday, France

We had a house in Puyméras, a little village on the other side of Ventoux. We had an OK time, though there were too many party people around in one go – Neil and Glenys [Kinnock] at the bottom of the road, the Goulds in the village, Jonathan and family about a mile away, and the Kennedys [Ian and Andrea, with their sons]. Some days, I was chronically depressed. Philip's view was that I had moved from characteristic glumness to anger. We were all pretty much agreed by the end of the holiday that I felt I had to give my all and was asked to do too much and pick up too much of the slack left by TB and his colleagues. Neil could tell I wasn't terribly happy and after ten days or so we sat down at the bar in the village and talked it over. He asked what was wrong and I said I felt I had to work round the clock to hold the show together. I asked if he thought there were any circumstances in which I could quit. He said no, because he worried it would fall apart. I said that was the pressure I felt. Northern Ireland took up a bit of time. Peter M called when he put Johnny Adair [notorious Loyalist paramilitary leader] back inside.

Monday, September 4

I went back to see TB to try to resolve the Mo situation. Yesterday the *News of the World* said she was thinking of going at the election and today's *Express* had a quote from her agent saying she wanted to go. TB said we should deny it but that wasn't possible. He spoke to her by phone and though he believed she said she was staying, that was not the impression either Jonathan or John Sawers got listening in. She came to see him. She decided she was not standing at the next election and wanted to make sure she didn't damage the party or the government. She wanted a different job and didn't want to be a running sore between now and conference and beyond. She wanted to announce it today. TB wanted to stop her but I felt the sooner we got it out of the way the better. She had drafted a statement, full of sentimentality, which included the line she was resigning today. I said 'I thought you were announcing you were standing down at the election,

---

* Seventy-six paramilitary prisoners were released from the Maze Prison. This brought the number released under the Good Friday Agreement to 428.

not that you are resigning today.' She said simply 'Is that a bad idea?' And I said 'I think it probably is.'

TB then got a little bit heavy with her, said that if he was to have any chance of getting her a big international job she needed to understand it was hopeless if this line kept running that he was trying to get rid of her. He wasn't and never had been, and yet all this victim stuff meant that people would think twice. He said she was the only one who could kill the idea that we had done her in or forced her out. After she left, he said we underestimated the extent to which good media could turn people's heads. I said she had inhaled the propaganda in full. What had been extraordinary about the conversation was that basically she had just talked about herself. She had said she was worried that she might dominate conference so maybe she should 'get ill' during her visit to Colombia. Maybe she should 'disappear' for three weeks. TB had been pretty frank with her, but was trying to be helpful. He said she would be wiser to make sure something was lined up before she went because 'politics is a very rough trade and people can be quickly forgotten'.

She and I met in my office and agreed a plan. We would announce it at the 11, she would put out a statement then do interviews today and tomorrow. Mo was fine but of course the press had their line – she had been forced out and we couldn't cope with characters and there was very little we could do to stem that tide. What was awful was that they knew we hadn't briefed against her, but they couldn't resist running with it. TB didn't like how big and bad it was running but I felt we just had to be confident and relaxed. If we briefed the truth, e.g. that TB had offered her Health and later asked her to be mayor, it would just be seen as more briefing against her, so we were as well just to stay schtum. TB called after the Jospin dinner and said re Mo that he didn't believe she had thought this through at all. He felt her husband had bought into this whole notion that she was briefed against after the standing ovation at conference.

Thursday, September 21

There was a mortar-bomb attack on the new MI6 building, which would dominate the news for a while.*

---

* A missile believed to have been fired from a rocket launcher, from a range of between 200 and 500 metres, shattered an eighth-floor window. Dissident Irish Republicans were believed to be responsible.

Saturday, October 7

Trimble did well in his no-confidence conference.* TB said that every time he has forced a fight he does well, but he always takes too long to get fighting and he is too slow to see the problems emerging.

Tuesday, October 10

The Middle East was bad and getting worse. Ditto Northern Ireland, and TB was having to get more involved again.

Monday, October 16

Middle East was the main story but Geoffrey Robinson book, *The Unconventional Minister* in the *Mail*, and the allegation that Peter M lied [about the £373,000 loan from Robinson], was going big. Peter called, anxious, and I said he should just put out a short but non-inflammatory statement. GB was really firing and there was a bit of contrast when we went over for TB's office meeting. TB wanted to be dismissive of Geoffrey's book but knew it was bad and may well be TB/GB-related, with [Charlie] Whelan almost certainly operating for GR. He spoke to GB and we suggested he make clear he hadn't wanted the book written and that he thought Peter M was doing a good job.

Wednesday, October 25

I left after the four o'clock to go to Notts Forest with the boys. I had a stack of calls on the way, mainly from JP and DB. We got there a bit late, were 1–0 down when we arrived, then 3–0, finally 5–0. For the first time, I had a bit of aggro from some of the Burnley fans who were involved in the petrol protests, and they warned it was going to get even nastier. On the way back, I was dealing with the response to the IRA statement [on arms inspections, accusing the British government of 'bad faith']. I also dictated a speaking note for TB at Cabinet tomorrow.

---

* Trimble had survived a vote of no confidence in his leadership orchestrated by disaffected Ulster Unionist Party members who felt he had been too conciliatory towards Sinn Féin.

TB had been in Northern Ireland and we had got another statement from the IRA.*

Fiona and I had dinner with TB and CB in the flat. TB knew I had not been very happy of late, and also that Fiona was pressing for a decision on how long I went on. I said I would probably want to go after the election, and he needed to understand others would want to do the same and so he should be looking around for new people. He said there was no way I would go because I would not be able to resist the challenge of a euro campaign, and if we went for it, he would want me around. I said I was not that bothered about the euro. It didn't move me like a Labour vs Tory battle did. He said it would be tailor-made for me because we would have to win the argument with huge swathes of the media against us, and it would be the time to make them part of the argument. I said we needed a get-out date, and he said he couldn't give one at this stage. He said if he could get new people, that would be great, but he didn't know where they were. He said New Labour was largely built by him, GB, Peter M and me. We were all better than anyone else at what we did. He accepted that GB and Peter could not really work together but even with that, they were still brilliant.

He said he would love to rely on more people, but he came back to his basic point – GB was special, Peter M was special, I was special, there were plenty of very good people but very few who could just take you to a different level, and I had to understand he would not let go easily. In between the heavy stuff, we had a lot of laughs and Cherie was back to her old self. Between us we gave TB a bit of a hard time, said he *was* becoming a bit out of touch, that he was no longer seen as having North-East connections, that he spent too much time at Chequers, that he didn't get the empathy stuff. But as he said himself, he was about as normal as any politician could be given the weird circumstances of his existence. 'There aren't many prime ministers who could sit and listen to their missus, their spin doctor and their spin doctor's missus all telling him how useless and out of touch he is, and still keep smiling.' He then pretended to call through for executioners to come and take us out and hang us on Horse Guards [Parade] for rank insubordination. The upshot was he was determined I should stay but accepted we might have to do things differently.

---

* The IRA stated that they would permit a further inspection of some of its arms dumps and that they would hold further talks with General de Chastelain.

Mo was pushing to get herself in charge of a committee looking at some of the longer-term problems we were likely to face around the election, but neither TB nor JP wanted her doing it.

Bush was declared US president but Gore was fighting on.

I went up to see TB who was exercised about getting the right message on health and working up to the Queen's Speech debate. He was also trying to think through the Clinton visit, and how we put together the right relationship with Bush. Jonathan and John Sawers were feeding him the usual diplo stuff, but this was going to require some pretty acute political skills.

I was called out to deal with another Peter M problem. He had hosted a party yesterday that was interpreted as him saying that Bush would be pro Sinn Féin. Pretty idiotic. Sometimes he just couldn't keep his mouth shut.

The last bits of haggling [at the Nice EU summit] were done in the margins and largely by officials. Finally around 5am it was all done. Bertie [Ahern] and I were chatting about the need to change the way the whole thing works. It's ludicrous that these negotiations were sorted in this atmosphere of frenzy, with everyone exhausted and losing their tempers. Bertie was really grateful to TB for sticking out as hard as he did on tax and was full of praise at his own press conference. We got back to the hotel for a couple of hours' sleep.

We flew on to Belfast [from Nice] where the plan was that we try to get something done on the observation towers as a signal of commitment to the normalization agenda being pushed by SF, and get them to do some kind of engagement in decommissioning, but it was going to be tricky. We met up with Peter M at the Hilton. He said we wouldn't be able to do the normalization measures because all the towers were essential for the security operation vis-à-vis the Real IRA. The plan was that we try to get Clinton to put the deal forward. Bill and Hillary arrived and after the small talk, and a bit on Ireland, Clinton wanted a rundown on Nice. He had an extraordinary grasp of detail on the varying economic performances round Europe. Like TB, he found it hard not to like Chirac and his roguish qualities. TB put to Bill the specific plan on Ireland. He felt sure Clinton would be able to give it a real push.

Wednesday, December 13

I went for a run in the pitch black round the grounds of Hillsborough, falling over once or twice and landing really badly on my shoulder. After breakfast, TB had a session with Ronnie Flanagan and the new head of the army in NI [General Officer Commanding (GOC), General Sir Alistair Irwin]. They were reasonably helpful in trying to get some moves on demilitarization but the big symbolic things Sinn Féin wanted were not going to be possible. Peter was a bit odd at these meetings. He was obviously so used to being the main man here and lording it and found it hard to adapt when TB came in and was clearly the focus. He was very good in describing other people's positions, usually in exaggerated and sometimes disparaging terms. TB was getting more and more exasperated by his manner. We left for Stormont and were left hanging around for ages waiting for Bill, who was seeing Adams and Hume at the hotel. He finally arrived forty-five minutes late and did the rounds of Assembly members and we then met some of the leaders. We did a photo call, TB, BC, Trimble and Mallon, before a meeting of the four of them. Trimble was worried about Patten and the effect it would have on the Unionist community.* Seamus was clearly worried that Sinn Féin would outflank the SDLP. TB was worried later re Seamus, felt he was a lot more difficult than before, that he was being driven by the SDLP not being clear about their purpose in all this. The politics were clearly in flux and all of them seemed a bit unsure how to deal with it. It must have been odd for Clinton to be trying to help us deal with all this, in what was ultimately a fairly small part of the world, albeit one that had a resonance elsewhere, and back home there were

---

* The Patten report included recommendations that the Royal Ulster Constabulary be abolished and that recruitment to a replacement force establish parity between Catholic and Protestant officers.

pretty seismic events going on. I spoke to several of the Clinton people about the Gore situation. They obviously felt the campaign could have gone better if Bill had been more involved. The Supreme Court judgment had basically been that a recount was unconstitutional so that was basically that. Gore was planning to concede 2am our time, then Bush would speak an hour later. Clinton was reasonably discreet but he clearly felt his legacy was at risk, that they lost by allowing the Republicans to neutralize the issue of the economy, by allowing their basic message to move leftwards, and by not using him properly. He was right on all three counts. He also clearly felt some of the strategists had not done the business.

TB saw the UUP, SF and SDLP, and the meetings were more convivial than usual, which sometimes meant progress was not being made. Trimble was pushing hard on decommissioning. Ken Maginnis was pressing for proper recognition of the RUC and said we were playing a very dangerous game if we were going for an amnesty for the 'OTRs' [on the run terrorists]. Then Sinn Féin. Martin McGuinness said he liked doing education and he felt most people felt he was doing his job. But we kept coming back to all the old impediments to progress and it pissed him off. He said he would welcome it if more of 'our people' joined the police but they are not convinced that a new police force genuinely represents a new beginning. He said he was the guy going out to Republicans saying Blair is a good guy, different to every other prime minister, but they laugh at me if I say that policing is a good deal for us. Patten did not go far enough for them. He said we don't come from where they come from and we have to understand the psychology. People hate the RUC even more than the British Army, but there is an appreciation that there must be a policing service. People are up for that but are badly disappointed. TB said what's your beef? We've done everything the SDLP asked for in the implementation plan. Bairbre de Brún [Sinn Féin public safety minister] said their people just weren't going to join as things stood. It was interesting that McGuinness did more of the talking this time than Adams. Gerry Kelly and [Martin] Ferris did the strong silent bit as usual. Policing, demilitarization and decommissioning were coming together as real problems. TB wrote a passage for Bill that put pressure on all sides to move.

We set off for the Odyssey [Arena, Belfast]. Tom Kelly [NIO] and I did a briefing which went fine. It was an OK venue. TB didn't really get going. The audience wasn't as fired up as when BC was in [Courthouse Square in] Dundalk yesterday. He had some good lines but he must have been depressed by the Gore/Bush situation. We were getting something out of the tripartite attack – UK, US, Irish – on terrorism though Hague was about to wade in on a different front with a hit on the liberal elite re the impact of the MacPherson Report on police morale. The *Sun* was driving some of this and was hitting us pretty hard, as well as welcoming Bush like a best friend. Clinton seemed more tired than usual, at one point nodding off on a long black sofa in the holding room. Hillary was also clearly having to really fight within herself to put on a brave face about what was happening back home, and she was if anything even more discreet re Gore. But they were very anxious about the future.

Thursday, December 14

I went in with Philip and chaired a meeting on next steps but the only thing that mattered today really was Bush. It must have been so weird for Clinton, who was down at Chequers and giving TB a tip or two on how to make sure he got in with Bush. TB and I spoke a couple of times before he came out at 11.30 and did a big number on the US–UK relationship and how we would work with Bush. He also lacerated Hague for his MacPherson speech. He was up for really going for him for bandwagoning.

We got flown up by helicopter to Warwick University, where TB did a little walkabout and then he, Jonathan and I were taken up to the vice chancellor's office where a phone had been put in for his call to Bush. There was something almost weird about us sitting there waiting for the call while outside, everyone was getting very excited about Clinton. Bush came on, and made a point of saying it was the first call he was making. Neither of them mentioned the recent turmoil. Bill arrived and we were put into a very poky little holding room before they went down to do the speeches. He was going out of his way to help. I had been trying to get their speeches to work together to show the Third Way as being something more than just an electoral device. As he came off the stage he said 'I hope that did something for you.' I said I wasn't the biggest Third Way fan in the world, but we may as well try to get something out of it. He said he always preferred the first way.

There was definitely an end-of-era feel to things. He said he wanted to thank us for all the help we had given him. I said he was the best political communicator I had ever seen or heard and he said thanks for everything. I reckoned he would find it quite hard to adapt out of power. Hillary looked sad as well. She said say hi to Fiona and keep in touch. Then they walked out, smiled and waved at the small crowd over the road, into the car, and off they went. There was something about a presidential motorcade that looks both impressive and sad at the same time. Impressive in that it sweeps all before it, but sad that they need that kind of support and protection, and for an outgoing president what was once a symbol of power becomes a symbol purely of status of what he once was. You could feel that the power was no longer there, but had moved.

TB called me as I was on the way back and said he had been unsettled by the idea of me and maybe Anji leaving after the election. He said he had a very clear idea of what he wanted to do in the second term and he really needed me to be there. He said if I could find someone else he would be happier letting me go, but currently he couldn't see it. GB would be hovering, the press would be after us more than ever and he would need his key people around him. He was also worried that Peter M was having judgement problems. His Christmas card with himself and his dogs [Bobby and Jack] at Hillsborough Castle was the latest little thing to suggest detachment from political reality.

[2001]

Even though we had trailed it, there was inevitably cynicism at TB heading off for NI on the day of the hunting vote, though we made clear he would have maintained the same position as before – voting for a ban – had he been there. PG had the latest poll in, which was pretty good. GB felt we were lacking message about a forward agenda. TB was worried we had peaked, and also that we were about to take an onslaught on public services. Once we briefed we were going to NI, we decided it was also time to kill the TV debate idea. I was working on a letter to the broadcasters ruling it out. When I briefed on it, they were all pretty sceptical about the arguments, but I was sure it was right just to get it over and done with. I genuinely worried that if we went for it, process not policy would become even more dominant in the election coverage, but they basically felt we were ducking it because it was a risk it wasn't worth the favourite taking. In Belfast we had dinner with the SDLP, who were not at all happy, and clearly felt the UUP were driving our agenda, but it was definitely the UUs' precarious political position that was worrying TB.

We then had a meeting with Sinn Féin, who were doing their usual of maintaining they were being reasonable given the difficulties whilst maintaining everyone else was not. TB spoke to Clinton by phone. He said he was happy to do anything we wanted, now and in the future, so long as it didn't cut across anything the Bush people wanted to do, 'Not that I guess they will want to do that much.'

TB said he was really worried, that he had not quite realized how much ordinary Unionist opinion had moved away from us. He had been alarmed by the meeting with the DUP. Even without Paisley there, they had been very chipper, cocky even, and he sensed that they sensed things were moving their way. They told him straight out that Trimble was going down the pan and he'd better get used to dealing with them. I didn't like the tone or feel of it one bit. TB now felt that unless there was decommissioning – and that meant product not words – then he feared Trimble was dead, and without him there was no peace process as things stood. He felt that was confirmed by the Alliance [Party] and the women's group, who though not big players were very good barometers. He really was worried, more worried than I had heard or seen him for ages. TB told the Irish it was not good enough for us to be expected to do something on normalization in Armagh now, whilst all we got from SF–IRA was the vague promise of something down the track. He said we had to get a deal that would help DT. He said without Trimble there was no peace process and no Good Friday Agreement worth saving. He was getting irritated by the way the Irish officials overstated where we were with SF. They were saying what they wanted to be true, rather than what they knew to be true. He said he feared we were going round in circles.

He spent hours with SF, then said to us he wasn't actually sure what they were saying any more. They were pushing for more demilitarization measures and up to twenty changes to the Patten proposals. The SDLP were nervous about SF getting the political credit for any change. They constantly felt squeezed, and maybe felt they were punished for being reasonable, whereas the UUs and SF got somewhere by shouting louder. TB was trying to persuade the Irish and SF that electoral disaster for Trimble would not be good for any of us. He called me through to a meeting with Adams, McGuinness and Gerry Kelly, who all seemed very relaxed and jolly given the circumstances. TB asked whether we could get away with a meeting at Chequers without the media knowing, and I said of course. We ended up talking about TB's neighbours, and chatted re Jackie Stewart [former Formula 1 world champion] and somehow we ended up discussing whether we liked Des O'Connor [TV entertainer], and Adams said maybe in the absence of anything else concrete to report, I could go out and brief that there was agreement that we all liked Des O'Connor. I said you just like his surname.

I had to fish TB out to meet Ronnie Flanagan and the new GOC [General Sir Alistair Irwin] who had been flown in by chopper to avoid being seen either by the media or SF. TB was very upfront with them about wanting to concede something on the demilitarization front, provided we got something back, but he also wanted to assure them if they had genuine security concerns, he would not press. I sensed Flanagan was more up for doing something, but this was very tricky stuff. On the flight home, we chatted re Europe. TB was going off Jospin. I stopped by at Philip's on the way home to see the agency efforts on £16bn cuts posters. I spoke to Peter M in Paris and took the piss out of him being there for the Anglo-French colloque rather than doing his real job(s). He said it was important someone flew the flag for a positive European policy. Maybe, but it was also important we got our act together for an election campaign.

The combination of Clinton's departure from office, and the seeming shift away from the UUP to the DUP, made this a troubling period for TB. Clearly he would need to develop a relationship with George Bush. Indeed, on some issues, like Iraq, both would come to be defined for some by the issue and their relationship in relation to it. But though Bush would signal support on Northern Ireland, and at times actively help, it did not mean as much to him as it did to Clinton who followed, and often influenced, every twist and turn, and who was always ready to help whenever TB felt his involvement could move things forward. As for the shift in Unionist opinion, that was less easy to explain, but it was real, and meant that Ian Paisley was set to become an even more significant voice.

Friday, January 19

TB was down at Chequers seeing SF and the Irish, and we were putting together contingency lines. The SF lot were staying at a local pub and they were bound to be seen by someone. It wouldn't be the end of the world, but we were likely to get more done if we could keep it quiet.

Saturday, January 20

TB was very buoyed up by the talks yesterday which, amazingly, hadn't leaked, even though Gerry etc. were seen in Amersham. He felt they made real progress and felt that if we could pull them off some of their demands on policing, and above all get actual decommissioning, it would be the biggest thing since the

GFA itself. Bush's inauguration provided a news sponge for the day, so work-wise things were quiet, though we were planning another possible NI trip on Monday to keep the thing moving. TB was saying if we went we may need to stay to Tuesday too, if we felt progress was being made. He clearly thought yesterday had turned things. Yet again, the lack of the 'crisis talks' spotlight had helped. There were one or two pieces in the press re a new play, *Feelgood*, which was meant to be based on me. TB called after his Chequers dinner, which must have been a collectors' item – Bono and Bob Geldof, Jackie Stewart, Polly Toynbee and her dreary bloke [David Walker, also a journalist], John Denham [social security minister], Kate Garvey [TB's assistant]. He said it was totally surreal, but the real star was Dickie Bird [former cricket umpire], who was singing my praises all night, saying I was a good lad because I stuck with Burnley, and how he was so honoured to be there he would happily have walked all the way from Barnsley. TB said he arrived two hours early and was mesmerized by the place. Dickie asked Bono whether he had had many hits. TB said Bono and Geldof were a good double act, and deadly serious on the policy front.

Sunday, January 21

I went for a run and then was playing tennis at Market Road when I finally got hold of Peter to get a line on the story in the *Observer* that he tried to help the Hindujas get a British passport.* He denied it but I could tell he was in a real state. There was something bizarre about the sound of tennis balls getting whacked all around me as I tried to concentrate on what he was saying.

He said it was unacceptable to have a group of people determined to destroy him and all I could do was say that it was six of one and half a dozen of the other. He said he did not know when, but he intended to remove himself from the situation before too long. He was basically signalling he had had enough. I tried to pin him down a bit more re the Hindujas but he just said the story was wrong.

Monday, January 22

Hinduja/Peter M was low-level but had a bad feel to it. I didn't do well at the 11, because I think they sensed my worry about Peter M, and I was not sufficiently on top of the detail. Peter had been very dismissive yesterday and I did not follow

---

* It was claimed that Mandelson had helped Srichand Hinduja's application for a British passport. A subsequent inquiry found he had not made representations but by then he had lost his job.

my own instincts sufficiently to get to the bottom of it. It went on for ages and had a bad feel to it and they clearly sensed something here. Then it emerged that we having said it was all handled by a private secretary, Peter M seemingly did speak to Mike O'Brien about it. So we were heading for a process/handling drama that would have them obsessing. Peter M had been adamant yesterday re non-involvement. The Home Office finally told us of there had been a call with O'Brien at 3.45 and we went into a stack of conference calls, the most important of which was me, Tom Kelly, Godric, Peter M and Mike O'Brien, where I said we had to get all the facts. The position was defensible but not if we were saying different things or the story was changing and we had to get the facts quickly. It was another wretched weekend situation, where departments had not bothered to grip until the next day when things were often too late. I should have done so myself yesterday. TB was adamant we must not let the press create a false firestorm if Peter had done nothing wrong at all. Even if he had pressed for citizenship, there would be nothing wrong with that provided the normal rules and procedures were followed. The problem was the changing line, Peter having first said it was all handled by a private secretary, us sticking to that, but then the Home Office saying there was this phone call. It was not good. I called Peter M to say I was really worried about the Hinduja story and we had to get it sorted.

Tuesday, January 23

Peter came over for the Northern Ireland talks and was nervous. The eleven o'clock was not as bad as it might have been, but we were still far from out of it. I did my best to appear calm and controlled but it was going to be grim, as was clear with the BBC now leading on it and by the four o'clock, they were in full cry and the facts were getting lost. Peter was in and out of my office. TB now felt the situation was bad but we had to get the facts out. Peter and I agreed he should do the rounds at Millbank and defend himself, but he opened new loose ends, for example saying he had not forgotten anything, alongside unravelling the Home Office version too. He was strangely detached through the day, almost as if he was talking about someone else, not himself. TB was by now irritated we were having to spend so much time on this, which he said had nothing to do with real people and real lives and yet would get millions of words devoted to it. He accepted it showed a loss of judgement by Peter, who had damaged his chances of a top job post-election. I meanwhile was fed up having to pick up the pieces and draw so much of the blame. This was going to do us real damage. The press could sense how bad it felt. I was up till past 12 briefing people for the morning programmes.

I was also sensing that if Peter was moved on, I would be the next target, and I was going to take a hit on this stuff anyway.

I said to TB that the worst-case scenario was that he was asked direct in the House whether he had been aware of any evidence that Peter did know about the call. TB would have to say yes. TB spoke to Jack [Straw] himself and I could tell from his tone of voice was satisfying himself that there were grounds for Peter going. He was asking whether he could stay for the duration of the next part of the process but we all agreed that wasn't possible. Also, whether he should say he was satisfied there was no wrongdoing in relation to the application but in any event we should have an inquiry. That's what we did in the end, and RW got hold of Anthony Hammond [QC, asked by the government to carry out the inquiry]. I was clear we had to get this sorted before PMQs, preferably by the 11. Derry was clear we either had to get rid of him or have an inquiry, or both. The mood was ghastly and it was pretty much curtains. TB said I cannot believe we are going through this again. The guy is finished. Is there nothing we can do for him at all? If not, it's his life over. He also said to me later that GB would feel more emboldened. Peter came to see TB at 10.45. I went in at 10.55 and said I needed a line for the eleven o'clock. Peter said things weren't resolved. He was resisting the idea of going. I said we had to be clear that if any new information came out, for example Jack's call last week, it was curtains, and I feared that was where it would end. TB said can't you just busk your way through it? I said no, I had to have something to say. He and I popped out and agreed I should say Peter was here because TB wanted to establish for himself the facts before being questioned in Parliament.

I did the 11, was as calm as I could be, maybe too calm, because they read from the body language a mix of feeling down and accepting inevitability re Peter going. I hadn't deliberately signalled it, but they sensed something was going on. After a while I said I was no use to them down here, I was better off upstairs, establishing what was happening. I went back up and TB looked absolutely wretched. Peter looked becalmed. TB said he had made clear to Peter he had to go and that though he wasn't sure, over time he would see why it had been necessary. TB seemed much more emotional about the whole thing than Peter. TB was writing what Peter might say. Peter went up to Anji's office to do the same. Up till now, I had pretty much dealt with it like any other difficult handling issue, but seeing him sitting there, looking pale, almost poleaxed, but trying to keep a very brave face on it, I was suddenly hit by how awful the whole thing was. Also there was a line emerging, e.g. via Andy Marr, that what this was all about was a blazing row between me and Peter, that I had said to TB it was him or me. It hadn't been like that, but here I was again, just me and Peter, drafting resignation letters, statements to the press, etc.

Peter was far less emotional than the first time, much more matter-of-fact. I said he was a good thing, and he didn't deserve this happening to him again. He said maybe I did. He was strangely quiet and unmoved, maybe even relieved. We agreed he should be allowed to do Northern Ireland Questions and we went round to my office with Tom Kelly to prepare for that. In between I was backwards and forwards to TB to agree lines and letters and help him prepare for PMQs. Peter finally went out to the street to face the media. It was windy and his hair was flapping about but he was pretty dignified and his fears that he would fall apart were unfounded. Fiona and Cherie came into my office to see him, and again he seemed strangely unmoved. In the House, Hague was too shrill and misjudged it. Because it had been Northern Ireland Questions, Peter was on the front bench alongside TB and only now I think started to realize this was probably the last time he would be there.

We now had to work on the reshuffle, John Reid to NI, Helen Liddell to Scotland. Brian Wilson was really unhappy about it. In the end, TB got [Peter] Hain to move to DTI and Brian into Hain's job. In all of the calls, TB said it was a tragedy for Peter M, that he had paid a terrible price for a small sin. Peter called me from the airport and was perfectly nice. There was a delayed reaction to come, I was appalled at Robert Harris going on TV effectively saying I had pushed him out. GB was advising TB to use the cover of the reshuffle to get me to go to Millbank, which was positive on one level, but TB was still worried it would make it impossible for me to go back after the election. There was a real sense of vengeance in the media, Peter getting his comeuppance. TB said Hague would regret being as lowlife as he had been today. TB said he was heartbroken for Peter but now we just had to pick up and move on. Peter H said I must get Tony to look a little less like his child had been run over by a bus. PG, as ever looking for the bright side, said maybe now GB would start working properly with us. I had my doubts. The only good thing out of today was people saying we had acted decisively, but by the time I got home, I felt drained and low, and Rory and Calum were both sad for Peter.

To this day, I am not entirely sure what I think about Peter's second resignation. I certainly think he allowed a muddle to be created, which led to us misleading people. I also think he was strangely detached, and lacking in his customary determination to grip a situation. But I also think had it been anyone but him, with a sense of the baggage left over from the first resignation, that we might have made a more deter-mined effort to fight it out. The whole operation, for various reasons, felt weakened at this time, and he was a victim of that, as he was of the fact that his enemies in the government and in the press were not exactly rushing to support him. I think also that I did allow my own mood – this was not a happy period, what with workload and domestic pressures combining to make neither work nor home particularly pleasant at the time – to affect me in a way that was not conducive to helping Peter. He may have been distracted by the GB story in another paper, but I can hardly claim to have been fully focused on getting to the bottom of the situation from a tennis court. And though I felt let down by his failure to grip the situation, and get us the facts straight away, he was entitled to feel we should not be allowing a media briefing to dictate the pace of events. I have managed to straight bat far trickier situations and yet my body language definitely created a sense of momentum towards his demise. I think all of us – Peter, me, TB – contributed to making a bad situation worse. When the Hammond report concluded, it found Peter not guilty of the main offence of which he stood accused. But Peter knows as well as anyone that sometimes in politics facts will take second place to events and perceptions, and this was one of those situations, with horrible consequences for him, and despite both of us trying to make amends from time to time, for our relationship.

Thursday, January 25

Papers totally crucified Peter as expected. There were loads of predictable inaccurate pieces about me being the assassin. TB said all we could get out of this now was a sense of government as normal straight away. Peter, having slept on it, was now feeling a sense of injustice and was penning a self-defence that was wrong. At Cabinet, TB opened by saying there would a political Cabinet on Tuesday, and there then followed a totally political Cabinet anyway. He dealt with the Peter business fairly quickly, said it was a tragedy for Peter, serious for the government, but provided we moved on quickly, and got back on to the fundamentals, we would not sustain lasting damage. I was always struck at how quickly Cabinet business returned to normal, got over the shock of something like yesterday.

Friday, January 26

I chaired a handling meeting and made the mistake of mentioning the JS/Peter call, and became worried it would come out not on our terms. Peter then called on the mobile and said his ex-assistant private secretary, Emma Scott, had called him and said she was absolutely sure that it was she who spoke to O'Brien's private office, she did not recollect Peter speaking to O'Brien and therefore she vindicated his account. He had recovered himself, and was now convinced he was the victim of an injustice, not the perpetrator of a resignation-worthy mistake. He said there had been funny business at the Home Office and he intended to speak to Richard Wilson. He had been treated unfairly, his career and his life had been destroyed and he had to get his side of the story out. He said it was possible that everyone was telling what they thought to be the truth. There were funny things going on at the Home Office, but I couldn't ignore what Emma Scott was saying. He said I had a responsibility to sort it out. I said I had thousands of things to do. He said this is my life, my reputation, my future and you have to grip it because nobody else can. I said this was why I hated my life, because everyone told me only I could grip these things, but how was I to make sense of the conflicting stories, the Home Office clear there had been these calls, him denying it, not recollecting fairly recent events. I said I will try, but he had to understand why it was difficult. I had taken the call at Alison's desk, and it was becoming embarrassing because there were people walking in and out, and he started to sob down the phone, please, please, please help. This is my whole life being destroyed and I don't know why. I have not been wicked. He said he got something wrong but was it really such a bad mistake? He said he was in there seeing Tony and he hadn't even marshalled all the facts, then you come in saying you have to have a line for the wretched eleven o'clock, a bunch of total bastards, and we didn't have all the facts, hadn't examined all the facts, and on that basis I am destroyed. You have to believe me, please believe me, I've been telling the truth. I said OK, I'll try but please understand the pressures I am under. He said he was desperate. We had pushed him out and he was a dead man. Jack Straw's version was wrong.

He then called Derry and RW, both of whom called me to say they were worried enough to want to shut Jack up. We had various calls on it ending at 8pm with TB, Jonathan, Jack and I agreeing we should just say the Home Office handled it properly and we would now leave things to the inquiry. We got Richard to ask Hammond to make clear he did not want potential witnesses to give interviews whilst he was conducting the inquiry. Peter agreed to that and also said he was thinking about his future. TB had said to me Peter might not stand again but when I put that to Peter, he said it was nonsense. I said he definitely needed a break from it all, but he was talking about fightback. TB felt I was being too brutal with him and that as a result Peter had refused to take our advice. He had to feel we were on his side. The Sunday lobby was the usual crap, going over and ver the same questions. Again though, I didn't handle it well and inadvertently gave them the idea that Peter had been a bit mad. Peter called late in the evening and was very different to earlier, calm, friendly, asking about the kids.

Sunday, January 28

The broadcast media were still talking about little else and there was endless stuff about my relationship with Peter. I felt I had to do something to correct the dreadful coverage of my Sunday lobby briefing, 'Number 10 knifes Mandelson' kind of thing. I put together a statement after an early morning run making clear I had been misrepresented. The truth was I should not have got involved in their amateur psychology games. I called Peter and he too felt they were worse in the cold light of day than when we had first seen the papers last night. He said he was determined to rebuild his reputation. He repeated that there had been funny stuff going on at the Home Office. TB, Jonathan and I had a conference call. TB felt it was all going to move to questions about me and Peter, and they would also be piling in on Vaz. He said Peter was in a dangerous mood and would be assuming we were advising him for our purposes not his. TB said he intended to have very sharp words with Richard Wilson on the quality of factual material that came back from departments. TB was clearly beginning to doubt whether he should have gone. He said it may have been he genuinely forgot, and it may be it was O'Brien who placed the call, and a private secretary who made the enquiry.

Friday, February 2

TB was quizzing me about going, said that Anji was determined to go some time after the election but there was no way I could leave. I said he may not have finished his job but I felt I had done the bulk of mine. He said I was like an alter ego, that we had done it together and he couldn't believe I didn't want to see it through. I said I had to get a life back outside.

Sunday, February 4

I dreamt that I had my left leg blown off in a bombing, and at the hospital where I was being treated, they didn't allow family visits. They said they only made exceptions for people who could sing like Barry White! Philip had spoken to Peter who was by all accounts still very much on edge and determined to prove he had been wronged.

I got woken at 3.30am by someone saying they were the IRA and there was a bomb in the house. I ignored it, but then couldn't get back to sleep.

TB was fretting we did the wrong thing re Peter. Peter M called me and was asking me to go over old conversations we had had. He was clearly putting together a case.

On Hammond, TB was hoping that we would end up in a position where it was clear Peter didn't lie, but he had been responsible for creating a muddle. According to Charlie [Falconer], Richard [Wilson]'s basic view was that we panicked. Meanwhile, Peter M was putting his version of events all over the place.

TB was very keen for Peter M to have some way of rebuilding his reputation and the best possible outcome was for it to be clear he did not lie but he did cause an avoidable muddle. He was worried my account would basically be of a changing story. However, I felt that tonally I could do it in a way that did not need to 'kill' him. And as Richard W said when I discussed it with him, 'Better you kill Peter M than kill the PM.'

I went up to the flat on my own, and once we had settled down in the sitting room I told TB I was feeling tired and demotivated. I felt I had given him my best for several years and I no longer felt on top form, and I wasn't convinced I would recover it. He said he went through phases like that too, and felt election years always produced this kind of mood, particularly at the start of the year. He said the problem was a quality-of-life issue, and we all felt our quality of life was poorer than it should be. He said I was key to the election and after that we had to make sure I had less pressure, less to do with the media, became more strategic. He was sure we could make that happen.

I said that was all fine for him but I did not believe my job would change. He said it would if I let it. CB came in and he picked up his guitar and started strumming it, which clearly irritated her. Fiona arrived, while Cherie was telling him he had to listen to people more, and listen to their concerns. Fiona pitched straight in, said our education policy was crap and the party was moving too far to the right, and she had a pop at Jonathan and Anji for good measure, saying that if they were given more responsibility, I would end up doing a load of their jobs for them. TB seemed taken aback. I tried to calm it down, said that he had to understand we had given an awful lot and Fiona's worry was that the changes he planned would just load more on to me, and that had a knock-on effect at home. I repeated my view that I didn't feel I was as effective as I used to be, and it meant he should be thinking of how to find someone who could do better. He wouldn't have it. He said I had a special talent and he needed it, and at the very least I should give it a go for a few months after the election. This went on for an hour and a half, fairly heavy at times and I did feel I would be letting him down badly if I left when he wanted me to stay as much as he did. I said I was unconvinced things would change.

CB and FM said a lot of people feared he was taking the party further and further to the right. He said that is a different argument, and it is wrong. We have moved to the centre and we are staying there so long as I am leader, and none of us should forget the mistakes we made in the past that kept us out of power for so long. He was perfectly nice but by now getting irritated and feeling he was being overly attacked. Fiona and I had a row in the car home, because she said it was clear I was going to stay. TB called as I arrived home and said 'Be nice to her.' He was taken aback at how angry she was. He said she probably felt totally boxed in and subservient, and I had become such a big thing in politics that it was difficult for her, and I had to be more sympathetic to that. But the scene was bad all round.

Wednesday, February 21

The argument with Fiona continued once we got to bed and the cloud had not lifted by the time we got up, so our farewells were very muted, and I felt really low. She asked what I was going to say to TB, and I said I would tell him I wanted to leave still. 'Good.' She said she had found him patronizing and insulting, that he thought he was always right and he basically thought she was an imbecile. When I saw him later, he said 'God, do I have a problem with your missus – I had no idea it was so bad.' He said he was willing to work at improving things but he could not have Fiona telling him whether he could or could not keep Anji or give Jonathan more responsibility. He had to be able to make judgements himself. I said the problem was Fiona was not happy with our existence at the moment, felt I was so immersed in the job I had no time for her, and he was copping it as well as me.

Friday, February 2

Washington: I was up before 6 to prepare TB for three US interviews, which helped us straighten the lines on NMD, European defence and Iraq. Bush let [Colin] Powell do a fairly long spiel on the Middle East. TB thought Arafat was a problem and did quite an interesting read-across to the Irish situation, said the Israelis were the Unionists, the PLO were the Republicans, for the Irish read Egypt, for the Americans read Britain. Bush wasn't as up to speed on the NI detail as Clinton, but he asked the right questions and said if we needed help, pick up a phone. He was a curious mix of cocky and self deprecating, relaxed and hyper. He liked to see everything in very simple terms, let others set out complicated arguments and then he would try to distil them in shorter phrases. He was very clear about his own positions on the big foreign policy questions. After lunch they went out to do some pictures and there was a dreadful moment when Bush clicked his fingers for his dog to follow him and the media were trying to make it look like Tony turned and walked towards him.

Saturday, February 24

TB said that on one of their little walks they talked about God and about their kids and Bush, clearly having read the potted biographies, asked TB why so many of his senior staff weren't married, and TB said he was constantly trying to persuade us.

We talked about Bush over dinner. Cherie and I had both felt a bit uneasy at times, but you couldn't deny he had a lot more charm and nous than the caricature. TB said he liked him, thought he was straight.

As ever, there was disproportionate interest in TB's terrible sense of style, e.g. the awful pullover he wore on his walk with Bush and the dreadful creation he wore on the plane. He was hopeless at casual clothes. He had put on what was to all intents and purposes a vest and I said you can't wear that, and he said why not? I said because it's a fucking vest and you're the prime minister. Eventually he agreed to put a sweater on, which was some ghastly Nicole Farhi creation, on top of the vest, and it looked ridiculous. I said please, please take them off and year something else when we see the press. Eventually, by persuading him that he would have to answer questions about foot-and-mouth [the disease had broken out during the recent trip to Canada, and was becoming a full blown crisis], which was getting more serious, I persuaded him to wear a shirt and tie.

Thursday, March 1

The Hammond report came in. Jonathan basically said a call took place but Peter M wasn't happy with it. It was actually not that bad and probably got the balance about right. Peter had not been dishonest but had created a bit of a muddle and a call probably took place.

Monday, March 5

TB was growing more and more concerned about Northern Ireland again. I told the lobby we wanted to go there later in the week, but tried to play down expectations, so it didn't become a great media circus.

Tuesday, March 6

Fiona told Cherie she was definitely leaving. She said she was not going to allow me ever to blame her for me leaving so I had to make my own judgement. It ended in another row, and her in tears again.

Wednesday, March 7

I had another bad scene with Fiona, her saying she was no longer prepared to take second place to TB and saying if I stayed it meant the job meant more to me than she did. I said the family meant more to me than anything but it was very hard to give this up when there remain so many challenges. Surely we could find a way of doing it differently. I worked on TB's Inverness speech before we set off for Belfast.

Thursday, March 8

Despite all the worries, the Budget got a very good response. TB was focusing straight away on the Northern Ireland talks. The IRA statement took everyone by surprise, and by the end of the day the feeling was of progress, if not perfectly so. John Reid seemed to have settled in pretty well [as the new Secretary of State for Northern Ireland], though my God does he smoke. In between the various meetings I was working on the Inverness speech and preparing for Hammond. Peter M called first thing as I was looking out over the gardens at Hillsborough and he asked 'How exactly is my castle from which you evicted me so forcibly?' It was a joke, I think, but he was pretty focused when we got on to what we intended to say about Hammond's report tomorrow. I said we had to give a plausible reason for his resignation and that was that people came to be misled and he had taken responsibility for that.

Later in the day TB spoke to Peter from the sitting room upstairs at Hillsborough and when he said he intended to say it cleared Peter but that he had inadvertently caused the public to be misled, Peter became quite menacing and rude. 'I see where you're coming from. It's all about saving your face. You say what you have to say. I'll say what I have to say.' He said the whole thing was a squalid exercise, that he had been pushed out for the sake of expedience, that I had hardened up the line and created the problem. TB listened for a while, then lost his rag, said 'Just listen to me for one second. I have bent over backwards to get this thing to help you and I have to tell you I don't think you come out of it as well as you seem to think. There are real difficulties there for you and we are still trying to help.' Peter said there was confusion, that's all, and he should never have been made to leave the Cabinet. TB said whether he liked it or not, people had been misled but Peter would not accept that.

TB eventually hung up but, showing Peter's intimidating manner can work, TB did take out some of the more critical parts of the draft statement. They spoke again later. Peter said the top line had to be that he had been cleared. He said you have given me no adequate explanation as to why I left the Cabinet. 'Liable to misrepresentation' is hardly a hanging offence. He said resigning was the biggest mistake of his life, that we should have waited for the inquiry but that we had pressed him. If a bit of confusion was the problem, why am I alone in being blamed? He said I [AC] contributed to the confusion and so did the Home Office. TB asked if he intended to shut it down tomorrow. He said it depended on our reaction, and if we were unfair, he would react. He said the whole thing had been squalid. TB: 'I resent that.' Peter read out his draft statement and TB shook his head at me as we listened and mouthed 'impossible to reason with'. TB was dreading tomorrow now. Philip called, said the groups had been really bad.

Before I left for the office, I said to Fiona, maybe the only way we can get a life back is for us both to get out of Number 10 but I would be very worried about leaving TB right now. The problem was she had grown pretty much to despise him, and therefore didn't share my sense of commitment and support. Jeremy told me his and Jonathan's meeting with Fiona and Cherie was the most difficult he had ever had to handle. Meanwhile Anji told me she was definitely going, because she felt she had CB, FM, SM and DM [Miliband] all ganging up on her and if that continued, she wouldn't last. Fiona was in tears again later, said this was about whether I had proper respect for her or whether I would just always do whatever I wanted.

asked the boys what they thought about me packing in the job. Calum seemed to think it was a good idea. Rory was appalled, said it was the best job I'd ever get and added 'You have to understand that it's good for my image at school.' Fiona was really piling on the pressure though and said she just couldn't understand why I would not give it up when she was asking me to do so. Also, as I had ended up pretty much hating the press, being driven crazy by the politicians, she didn't understand why I didn't want to leave anyway, and she was totally unconvinced his planned changes would make any difference at all.

The foot-and-mouth epidemic became one of the biggest crises of TB's time in government. Northern Ireland barely figures in the diaries for the next few months as TB seeks to get the disease under control, but is finally forced to postpone plans for a May election. With the military brought in, eventually FMD is managed, albeit at great cost to agriculture and tourism, and the election announced for June 7. The campaign launch was enlivened by TB being harangued by a woman outside a hospital, and John Prescott thumping a male member of the public. Despite these twin setbacks, plus race riots in various northern towns, and continuing difficulties managing GB and Peter M, TB led Labour to a second landslide victory. I meanwhile was coming under mounting pressure from Fiona to leave the job.

I didn't sleep well, woke up feeling really tired and thinking how crazy it was that we helter-skelter round the country for weeks, work round the clock, then have one day – the election – to start getting your mind in shape for what follows if and when we win. The papers weren't bad, though the *Sun* was still slightly playing it both ways, and the *Mirror* was hopeless. I went for a run, found a nice hilly area, and loved the feeling of being out on my own, with the wind gusting every now and then, and feeling I had done all I could and though it had not been perfect, we were definitely going to win.

Friday, June 8

There were hundreds of media in the street shouting at me as I walked in. The Number 10 staff seemed genuinely pleased to see us back. I had a quick walk round the press office to say hello to everyone, then up to the flat to see TB and work out what we needed to do for the day. The start of the election felt a long time ago, it was also odd how quickly it was back to an almost 'business as usual' feel. We had one final go on the reshuffle.*

Friday, June 15

I felt like I had some kind of post-natal depression. We'd won the election, which ought to have been great, but virtually every day since it had felt like swimming through shit. The only good thing to be said for it was that the only way was up.

Monday, June 18

The Northern Ireland talks were going badly.†

---

* In the Cabinet reshuffle, Robin Cook became Lord President of the Council and Leader of the House of Commons; Jack Straw, Foreign Secretary; David Blunkett, Home Secretary; Margaret Beckett, Secretary of State for Environment, Food and Rural Affairs; Alistair Darling, Secretary of State for Work and Pensions; Patricia Hewitt, Secretary of State for Trade and Industry and Minister for Women and Equality; Tessa Jowell, Secretary of State for Culture, Media and Sport; Estelle Morris, Secretary of State for Education and Skills; Charles Clarke, Minister without Portfolio and party chairman. Nick Brown was appointed Minister of State for Work.
† TB and Bertie Ahern held talks with the three main pro-Agreement parties: the Ulster Unionist Party (UUP), the Social Democratic and Labour Party (SDLP) and Sinn Féin (SF)

Before TB left for Northern Ireland, I went to see him and told him I thought he had looked weak and nervous and they had left with bad vibes out of that. He said Anji had already told him the same. He called again after he got back from Belfast and sounded a bit more chipper. He said the best thing to be said for the meetings in Northern Ireland was that they were short. And he had a lot of work to do. Milosevic was taken to The Hague [International Criminal Tribunal]. It was a huge story but, as Fiona pointed out, TB seemed to be getting none of the credit that he deserved for the fact it was happening at all.

Trimble resignation [as Northern Ireland's First Minister] due soon.

Trimble quit at midnight.* TB called to go over his weekend note, back on the same themes. I ran for an hour or so and felt a lot better.

TB had been having breakfast with Clinton before heading on to Weston Park [Staffordshire stately home, location for Northern Ireland peace talks].

---

* David Trimble resigned as First Minister of the power-sharing executive in protest against the IRA's failure to redeem its pledge to decommission all weapons. Trimble called on Tony Blair to suspend the Northern Ireland Assembly and the other institutions established under the Good Friday Agreement. The procedures of the NIA allowed for a six-week period during which a new First Minister and Deputy First Minister would have to be elected; otherwise new elections to the Assembly would have to be called. Another option would be for the British government to suspend the Assembly and the institutions and reintroduce Direct Rule. The final option was for a temporary suspension, which would extend the period in which to find agreement. The Assembly was suspended for twenty-four hours beginning on Friday 10 August 2001. [CAIN]

The NI talks at Weston Park were going nowhere, and there was a feeling it wa going belly up.

TB being tied up with NI, Robin [Cook] was doing PMQs and he came over for a meeting with TB's usual team. He was comic in his pomposity. He would regularly get up and stroll around the table, rehearsing lines and arguments. He came in carrying a clean suit and shirt in a suit carrier. I suggested he sit in TB's chair at the Cabinet table, and his chest puffed out and he did a little chirrup of delight. He really was beyond parody today. I had sent him over a note about the Tories/ *Big Brother* [TV programme] and he was up for using some of the lines. As we worked out a few different options and lines of attack, he was off wandering up and down the room again, loving it. I suggested we get someone in to take notes of what he was saying. A secretary came up from the Garden Room and tried to make sense of what he was reciting as he marched around with his head up, his chest out and his belly breathing in and out. He was fine on all the policy stuff but spent ages worrying about how to handle the Tory leadership.

He asked me what sort of state JP got into at this stage. 'Oh far worse,' I said. 'What about Tony?' 'Cool as a cucumber.' Humph. I went over to the House with Robin and he was on much better form. I had David Hanson [Blair's parliamentary private secretary] trying hard not to laugh when I slipped him a note saying a Rory Bremner [TV satirist] researcher would have an immediate multiple orgasm if he walked in and saw Robin right now. He was so puffed up I thought he might explode. But he did well. He had a real presence in the House and he got into his stride quickly. I had TB in hysterics later describing the scene. It was interesting how even though he and JP had been in the House for years, they found the step up to PMQs such a big thing. TB said it took him ages before he was basically confident about it.

We were entering a phase of the commentariat being very down on us. We were getting a bad press re NI and there was a feeling around that we were not really motoring. At Cabinet, Northern Ireland was the only other big issue being discussed, and things were a bit bleak at the moment. GB was doodling madly with a big thick pencil, covering page after page with odd scribbles. He left his pad at the end and I went to have a look. Really thick black lines, up and down, a drawing of what looked like a dustbin, with the lid on the ground, and then the single word HARD written with real force on the page so that the impression went through several pages of the pad. There was a lot of anger and frustration there, even in his doodles.

Friday, July 13

TB and Jonathan etc. set off for Weston Park* again around 3. He called me up again before he set off, said he was sure things would be fine after a holiday. He said he would rather have me for two hours a day than most people for twelve, though he would prefer me to be motoring full-time. There were riots in Belfast† so the backdrop to the talks was worse than ever.

Saturday, July 14

The Tory leadership contest was still the main political story. TB called from Weston Park, clearly a bit agitato. There was no doubt we had been drifting a bit. He said Bertie had a different take, that the Tories seemed to be in self-destruct mode and people would instinctively understand that was because of the changes we had made to get into the centre ground. He seemed to think I needed to be out there with the media more, that the one big downside of the changed role [AC had cut back on day-to-day briefing to focus more on strategy] was that my voice was not out there clearly heard speaking for the government. Remember Clinton's edict, he said – never stop communicating. He was a bit worried we had.

Wednesday, July 18

Ian Austin [adviser] called but I was tied up and then five minutes later it broke on PA that Sarah [Brown] was pregnant. We had to go along with the pretence that TB had known about it for some time. It didn't exactly engender a lot of

---

* The talks had been suspended for the 'Twelfth'.
† These riots were the worst for years. The RUC shepherded an Orange Order parade along a route close to the Catholic Ardoyne, blocking roads to try and prevent conflict, without much success. Ten RUC officers were injured. Nationalists claimed that plastic bullets had injured twelve people. Senior police officers later blamed the IRA for inciting the violence, a claim denied by Sinn Féin. There was also violence in the Short Strand after an Orange parade.

warmth around the place. Bush arrived [in the UK]. Magi [Cleaver] said she was absolutely at the end of her tether with the Yanks [White House visits team].

Thursday, July 19

Early afternoon, we travelled down to Chequers to wait for Bush and go through the difficult stuff, Kyoto and NMD in particular. TB seemed pretty nervous, and was repeating the same arguments again and again. There had been a total fuck-up earlier re the reception we had planned for the White House press corps because someone at the White House had cancelled the visit to Number 10 and Buckingham Palace. Tanya Joseph [press officer] just about rescued it. Magi said Bush's advance people were even worse than Clinton's. Total nightmare. Bush arrived by helicopter, and we were surprised to see him not wearing a tie, his advance people having said that he would be. He and TB had a very long chat one-on-one, mainly going over the tricky stuff before they came through for a session with the rest of us in the room upstairs with the Cabinet table. Bush seemed a bit more on top of detail, though had to ask at one point whether Trimble had resigned.

Wednesday, July 25

TB called later to say he wanted me to go with him to Hull tomorrow and for the meeting with Bertie on Friday, but I had fixed all my August planning meetings for the next forty-eight hours. He said there was a fair chance he would be fighting for his political life quite soon, and GB was limbering up. He felt our discussions had shown where the divides would come but he felt this was the time to go more New Labour, not less.

August holiday

It was incredibly hot part of the time and we had the World Athletics Championships [in Edmonton, Canada] on TV to keep me and the boys occupied during the day and we were out pretty much every night. I was out running most days but just couldn't get my head straight as to what I wanted to do. Fiona was convinced that I was clinically depressed again. The kids were brilliant but I was definitely worried about the old demons coming back, and about my falling off the wagon.

I'd never drunk enough to be 'drunk' but I had been testing myself with it a it. Interesting that this is the first time I've actually put anything in here about it. Maybe denial, don't know. Fiona seemed to think it was no real problem, provided she knew, and provided I drank no more than she did, which was never more than a glass or two at dinner. I had a chat with Neil about it. He felt it was OK too but I had to watch out. I can't remember the first time I actually had a drink. I can remember having a couple on the boat coming back from the Dome on Millennium night. But that wasn't the first time, I know that. As I went so long without – thirteen, fourteen years – you'd think I would remember. I can't. I remember having a drink on one of the EU trips, Germany I think, I remember being worried about it, so stopped again. But this holiday I was drinking more, not every day, far from it, and never a lot. But I must be worried, or else I would have recorded it before, I think.

It must be part related to the mood too, so I knew I needed to watch it. Funnily enough, on one of the calls, when I was at the bar, TB was asking how I was feeling, and I said OK but he could tell not, and he said 'Thank God there's no danger of you hitting the bottle – now that really would freak me out.' I said to Fiona partly it was a desire to feel 'normal' but I really did not want to get into the habit. I said she would have to keep an eye on it, as would I. Only she and the kids, and now Neil and Glenys, Philip and Gail, knew that I'd had these mild falls off the wagon. It wasn't a great sign, and yet it was interesting that I had no sense I was going to go off on a great bender.

Tuesday, September 11

These are the Irish diaries, and it is hard to maintain there was a specific Irish angle to the September 11 attacks, though six Irish citizens and countless Irish-Americans were killed. But I include the account of this epoch-making day because it consumed so much of TB's time and attention both in the immediate aftermath, and also in the wars in Afghanistan and Iraq, which to some extent flowed from September 11, as the US waged the 'war on terror'. It perhaps explains the low-key attention I give in the diaries to the fairly seismic move announced by Gerry Adams on decommissioning on October 22, and the IRA actions the following day, good news delivered as I landed with Jack Straw and David Manning in Washington. It is also perhaps the case that the sheer scale of 9/11 confirmed IRA thinking that their brand of terrorism had had its day. They had had hunger strikers, but not suicide bombers killing thousands.

For long periods of this latter part of my time in Number 10, sometimes lasting months, Northern Ireland barely gets a mention. Partly this was about the sheer weight of foreign policy dominance of TB's in-tray. But it was also a sign – once SF–IRA had delivered – the UUs were back on board, and devolved institutions back up and running, that the political process was operating as it should. TB often said in speeches and interviews that his dream for Northern Ireland was one where the politicians were dealing not with stories about bombs and bullets and peace talks, but all the boring things that hardly ever got on the news – schools, buses, drains, refuse collection. For now, for a good few months at any rate, that is what seemed to be happening. Northern Ireland was always a priority area for TB, and when it required his attention, he gave it, and he knew there would be many times it would be needed. But from September 11 onwards, there is no doubt the foreign-policy side of the job – always large – grew even more.

TB's agenda literally changed, and for some time, we seemed to be spending more time in aeroplanes than offices as he lifted a large part of the diplomatic load, with Bush confined to the US by his anxious security advisers. And on the broader point about how history will see TB, pre 9/11, plenty of people would have said his legacy was defined by Northern Ireland, Kosovo, the minimum wage, Bank of England independence, devolution, great historic achievements, not to mention two landslide election victories, with a third good win to come even after the Iraq war. Post 9/11, the agenda changed, and so did the prism through which many now see the Blair legacy. I can, and I do, argue that the critics are wrong, but I cannot dispute that many exist because of TB's sharing of the Bush agenda in the aftermath of the attacks on the twin towers.

I woke up to the usual blah on the radio about TB and the TUC speech, all the old BBC clichés about us and the unions, the only new thing GMB ads asking if you trust TB not to privatize the NHS. Peter H and I went up to the flat. TB had done a good section on public-private, an effective hit back at the John Edmonds line. With the economy, public services, Europe/euro and a bit on asylum which was really worrying, we had a proper speech. We sharpened it and honed it a bit. He was furious at the GMB ads, said he intended to give Edmonds a real hammering. We finished it on the train, were met and driven to the hotel. We were there, up at the top of the hotel putting the finishing touches to the speech, when the attacks on the New York Twin Towers began.

Godric was watching in the little room where the Garden Room girl had set up, came up to the top of the little staircase leading to the bit where TB and I were working, and signalled for me to go down. It was all a bit chaotic, with the TV people going into their usual breathless breaking-news mode, but it was clearly something way out of the ordinary. I went upstairs, turned on the TV and said to TB he ought to watch it. It was now even clearer than just a few moments ago just how massive an event this was. It was also one that was going to have pretty immediate implications for us too. We didn't watch the TV that long, but long enough for TB to reach the judgement about just how massive an event this was in its impact and implications. It's possible we were talking about thousands dead. We would also have to make immediate judgements about buildings and institutions to protect here. TB was straight on to the diplomatic side as well, said that we had to help the US, that they could not go it all on their own, that they felt beleaguered and that this would be tantamount to a military attack in their minds. We had to decide whether we should cancel the speech.

There was always a moment in these terrorist outrages where governments said we must not let the terrorists change what we do, but it was meaningless. Of course they changed what we did. At first, we felt it best to go ahead with the speech but by the time we were leaving for the venue, the Towers were actually collapsing. The scale of the horror and the damage was increasing all the time and it was perfectly obvious he couldn't do the speech. We went over to the conference centre, where TB broke the news to [John] Monks [TUC general secretary] and Brendan Barber [Monks' deputy] that he intended to go on, say a few words, but then we would have to head back to London. We would issue the text but he would not deliver the speech. John Monks said to me that it's on days like this that you realize just how big his job is. TB's mind was whirring with it. His brief statement to the TUC went down well, far better than his speech would have done.* We walked back to the hotel, both of us conscious there seemed to be a lot more security around. We arranged a series of conference calls through Jonathan with Jack S, Geoff Hoon, David B. We asked Richard Wilson to fix a Cobra meeting as soon as we got back.

We set off for Brighton station. He said the consequences of this were enormous. On the train he was subdued, though we did raise a smile when someone said it was the first and last time he would get a standing ovation from the TUC. Robert Hill [Policy adviser] was listening to the radio on his earpiece and filling us in every now and then. TB asked for a pad and started to write down some of the issues we would have to address when we got back. He said the big fear was terrorists capable of this getting in league with rogue states that would help them. He'd been going on about [Osama] Bin Laden for a while because there had been so much intelligence about him and al-Qaeda. He wanted to commission proper reports on OBL and all the other terror groups. He made a note of the need to reach out to the British Muslim community who would fear a backlash if this was Bin Laden. Everyone seemed convinced it couldn't be anyone else.

We got back and before Cobra he was briefed by Stephen Lander [director

---

* Blair told trade union delegates: 'This mass terrorism is the new evil in our world today. It is perpetrated by fanatics who are utterly indifferent to the sanctity of human life and we, the democracies of this world, are going to have to come together to fight it together and eradicate this evil completely from our world.'

general of MI5], John Scarlett [chair of the Joint Intelligence Committee], RW, DTLR [Department of Transport, Local Government and the Regions] had closed airspace over London. There had been special security put around the Stock Exchange and Canary Wharf. The general security alert had been raised to Amber. Three hundred companies were being contacted to be given advice. Scarlett said OBL and his people were the only ones with the capability to do this. Neither he nor Lander believed other governments were involved. TB said we needed a command paper of who they are, why they are, what they do, how they do it. He said at the diplomatic level he felt the US would feel beleaguered and angry because there was so much anti-Americanism around. Lander felt the pressure on the Americans to respond quickly, even immediately, would be enormous. Afghanistan was the obvious place. Iraq, Libya, Iran, the Americans will be trying to find out if they helped in this. He said there were a lot of people sympathetic to Bin Laden, more than we realized. TB said they will move straight away to the international community and their response. If I were Bush, I would demand the Taliban deliver him up.

Scarlett and Lander were both pretty impressive, didn't mess about, thought about what they said, and said what they thought. Scarlett said this was less about technology than it was about skill and nerve. Lander said this was a logical step up from the car bomb. Turning a plane into a bomb and destroying one of the great symbols of America takes some doing but they have done it and they have been able to do it because they have any number of terrorists prepared to kill themselves. TB's immediate concern, apart from the obvious logistical steps we had to take, was that Bush would be put under enormous pressure to do something irresponsible. If America heard the general world view develop that this happened because Bush was more isolationist, there would be a reaction. He felt we had to take a lead in mobilizing diplomatic solidarity in the rest of the G8 and the EU. We had to start shaping an international agenda to fill the vacuum. He spoke to Schroeder, who wanted a G8 meeting, Chirac and Jospin, who were not so sure, and then Putin, who had a real 'I told you so' tone, said he had been warning us about Islamic fundamentalism.

TB and I both pressed Scarlett and Lander on why they were so sure there were no rogue governments involved in this. They said because Bin Laden was able to do it himself and that suited his purposes better. We all trooped over to the Cobra meeting, which was a bit ragged, but that was to be expected given what people were having to deal with. There were contingency measures that had gone into effect. Private flights had been stopped. There were no commercial flights to go over the centre of London. All small-plane flights were being grounded unless they had specific clearance. Security was being stepped up around financial centres and major computer sites. The Met [police] were raising numbers on visible patrols, particularly at Canary Wharf, Heathrow and in the North London Jewish areas. We had upped protection on our premises in the Middle East. There was talk of moving some of the planes based at RAF Leuchars to London in the event of a hijack. Jack S said the EU GAC [European General Affairs and External Relations Council] was planning to meet. Geoff Hoon gave a briefing on what troops were where in the Middle East.

TB did a very good summing-up, first going through all the different measures that I should brief, then on the specific reports he wanted to commission, then on the importance of a diplomatic strategy to support the US. He said they would feel beleaguered and all the tensions that had been apparent before would now become more open, whatever the warm words around the world. He asked Jack and Geoff to come through to Number 10, said it was vital that we worked up an international agenda that went beyond the US just hitting Afghanistan. He felt NMD would quickly rise up the agenda.

He intended to say to Bush that he should deliver an ultimatum to the Taliban to hand over Bin Laden and his people and then hit them if it didn't happen. He had been reading the Koran over the summer. [The Prophet] Mohammed had lost battles but there was a belief that if you died in the cause that you believed in then you went straight to heaven. That was a very, very powerful thing to work against. TB's public words were very much in total support of the US. He said this was going to be a nightmare, as big and as bad as any we had endured. It was interesting that he had not asked GB to come back for the smaller meeting. I asked him why and he said because in their recent discussions he had been monosyllabic. The Israelis were making massive attacks on the terror groups. TB said we were going to have to work exceptionally hard on the international response. Bush was getting it in the neck for not being in Washington.

Everyone was in bed when I finally got home, and Fiona had fallen asleep watching it all on the TV. I did a call with Jonathan to go over how much we would need to kick out of the diary in the coming days. Pretty much all of it, at least for a while. Jonathan said the Americans would be unlikely to let Bush travel – it was a bit much that he couldn't even go to his own capital – but the fallout from this was going to need an awful lot of diplomatic activity. I think we're going to be seeing a lot of the insides of planes, he said.

I turned off the TV in the bedroom and went downstairs to channel-hop while writing it all up. The TUC felt a bloody age ago. Some of the footage of the aftermath, clouds of dust and debris literally rolling down streets, was extraordinary. So were the eyewitness accounts. Gut-wrenching. What was amazing about this was that people like Bush, TB, Chirac and the rest were having to react and respond in exactly the same time frame, and with pretty much only the same knowledge of the incident as people watching on TV. The difference was they were going to have to take some huge decisions about it too.

Monday, September 24

TB and I had a long chat re GB. TB had asked him what he thought of what was happening [after 9/11] and got the monosyllabic treatment. Eventually he said 'How am I supposed to know what to think? I don't know what is going on.' TB said there was not a word of support, or a hint of understanding of how tough this was. He even got back to the point of demanding a date for TB's departure, at which point TB snapped, said he was fed up of the way he spoke to him, the way he treated him. 'You say I have a choice about when to go. It's you that has a choice, about whether you work with me or against me, and get it into your head that if you work against me, you'll get no help from me.' He said GB was also urging him to cut loose the IRA from the peace process, which was ridiculous. I sometimes wondered whether he wouldn't actually be a total disaster as prime minister and whether in fact we weren't duty-bound to ensure it didn't happen.

Tuesday, October 9

TB was seeing Adams and McGuinness at 8 and we had to choreograph the arrivals to avoid any crossover with the War Cabinet – not what we needed right now. At the morning meeting, there were two immediate problems to address – the first was that the BBC were reporting TB was going to Oman. They just would not listen to our concerns on this. And the second was the leak of a Jo Moore [special adviser to Stephen Byers] email from September 11 saying that it was a good time to 'bury bad news'. I didn't allow much discussion of it at the morning meeting. It was perfectly clear someone inside had leaked it and it was a classic Civil Service move on a special adviser. It was a stupid thing to say, and knowing Jo she would be mortified, but I didn't like the idea of her being hanged, drawn and quartered for it.

Monday, October 22

I got home fairly early as it was Rory's birthday tomorrow, but was dead tired again. The news was all [Gerry] Adams after he had called on the IRA to disarm, which was a big moment.*

Tuesday, October 23

We landed [in Washington] to be met by Tony Brenton [deputy head of mission [UK Embassy] and two pieces of news – the IRA had delivered,[†] and Burnley had beaten Crystal Palace [1–0].

Wednesday, October 24

We had got the cuttings and Northern Ireland decommissioning was getting big play, but positive.[‡]

Friday, November 16

From left field, Mo [Mowlam] had done a [Michael] Cockerell film [*Cabinet Confidential*] and said TB was presidential, had killed Cabinet government and

---

* In his speech Adams said: 'Martin McGuinness and I have also held discussions with the IRA and we have put to the IRA the view that if it could make a groundbreaking move on the arms issue that this could save the peace process from collapse and transform the situation.'

† At around 4 pm the IRA issued a statement that announced that the organization had begun to decommission its weapons. The statement included the following: 'Therefore, in order to save the peace process we have implemented the scheme agreed with the IICD in August (2001).' Later in the day the IICD issued a statement part of which read: 'We have now witnessed an event – which we regard as significant – in which the IRA has put a quantity of arms completely beyond use. The material in question includes arms, ammunition and explosives.' [CAIN]

‡ There were a number of statements in the House of Commons. Tony Blair welcomed the decommissioning by the IRA. David Trimble said that he had reappointed the three UUP ministers to the Northern Ireland Executive 'without prejudice' to the decision to be taken by the UUP executive on 27 October 2001. However, Trimble asked Blair: 'What sanctions will the government apply to them [those who had not decommissioned by February 2002] so as to avoid others having to apply sanctions?' Trimble was thus explicitly setting a new deadline in the peace process.[CAIN]

the TB/GB relationship was unhappy. JP was asked about it in front of cameras and used the line 'She's daft.' He called me afterwards. I felt he wasn't far wrong.

Thursday, December 13

I watched [Sir] Ronnie Flanagan [Northern Ireland chief constable] on *Newsnight* when he was given a really hard time [Flanagan had been accused of 'flawed judgement' over the Omagh bomb inquiry], a really unpleasant interview. I felt so strongly about it that I wrote to him, said I thought he had handled it incredibly well and that the public would have ended up respecting him far more than the interviewer.*

Friday, December 14

Ronnie Flanagan called me while we were having dinner and said that my letter to him 'meant more to me than you'll ever know. That someone like you could be bothered to say that with all the other things you have to deal with.' He sounded very emotional, and was clearly feeling a lot of the pressure, but I thought he was basically a very decent bloke.

---

* Nuala O'Loan, then Police Ombudsman for Northern Ireland, met the relatives of the victims of the Omagh bombing and presented them with the findings and recommendations of her report into the bombing and the handling of the subsequent police investigation. The report also accused Ronnie Flanagan, then Chief Constable of the PSNI, of flawed judgement and of damaging the chances of arresting those suspected of being responsible for the bomb. The report also recommended that, 'an independent senior investigative officer from outside Northern Ireland be appointed to conduct the investigation and that that investigation be properly resourced and it be given access to all material.' (O'Loan had decided to publish the findings of the report when Flanagan failed to respond to the draft report by the set deadline.) Immediately after the release of the findings Ronnie Flanagan gave a press conference in Belfast at which he threatened to begin legal action on a 'personal and organizational basis' to have the report withdrawn. He claimed the report was full of 'wide and sweeping conclusions' and was unfair. He also said that if the conclusions were true he would publicly commit suicide. (Flanagan later withdrew the remarks about suicide. O'Loan later responded and said that the findings of the report were based on facts and were carefully established.) [CAIN]

was due to have lunch with Peter M, which had been my suggestion after he emailed me re an article he was doing. I asked Hilary C to find somewhere discreet and she had booked La Trouvaille in Newburgh Street. I arrived first, Peter a few minutes later and we were put in the window. Who should walk by, just seconds after we sat down, but Andrew Marr [BBC political editor], but he was so busy window shopping on the other side of the passageway that he didn't see us. Peter did most of the talking early on, re what he had now taken to calling his 'defenestration'. He was very calm and friendly, said he wasn't blaming me directly but described the whole episode leading to his resignation as a 'road accident' in which everyone accidentally conspired. I said if it had been anyone else, we would probably have survived but he had baggage that weighed us down. On the whole Geoffrey [Robinson, former Paymaster General] loan episode, he felt it was a case of the circumstances of one period being different to those of another. When he took out the loan, Geoffrey was not *persona non grata,* was not a media bogeyman, was a friend who had always taken an interest in helping Peter. Peter said he had always wanted a nice home and to find someone to live with. He hated [his former flat in] Wilmington Square [Bloomsbury] because it didn't feel like a home. The themes of his loneliness, and his sexuality making him more lonely, or certainly more secretive, came through. He hated being away from Reinaldo [da Silva, his partner]. His private life was happy, but why because he was a politician should there have to be comment about it at all, why? It was he who was the politician. Nobody ever disputed he was a good minister and he felt he had to get back to top-level politics. I said it was true, he rarely got criticized on ability grounds. He accepted a return to the Cabinet was difficult, so the options were probably Europe or the UN and he was intending to develop his international profile.

Despite it all, we were still able to talk openly and I still considered him to be a friend whose judgement I value. We went out, and stood there, in the middle of Carnaby Street, with a couple of bodyguards, passers-by shooting the occasional odd look and Peter said 'Happy Christmas. I had better do some shopping.' And off he went.

[2002]

To the Goulds' for dinner. Gail [Rebuck, publisher and wife of Philip Gould] asked whether Philip and I had ever had a discussion that did not cover TB, GB, Peter M and their varying relationships. The answer is probably not, at least none that lasted more than a minute or two.

I was in early, and up to see TB in the flat. It was dark up there and he seemed a bit down. He asked me if I was depressed. I said yes. Clinically I mean, he said. I said I think so. He said my problem was I was agonizing – stay or go. He felt I would hate it if I went, no matter how much I sometimes hated it now. I needed to see the press as the inevitable downside of a job that had a huge upside, namely doing an important job and being part of a huge process of change for the country. He came back to the theme over at the House pre PMQs, said I should remember what Leon Brittan [former Conservative Cabinet minister] said about leaving power, leaving powerful jobs – for a year you feel better, eased of pressure, able to do normal things, but then you realize what you miss, the ability to make change. He said 'If I die tomorrow, they would say he was the guy who modernized the Labour Party, made it electable, won two landslides, sorted the economy, improved public services, Bank of England, Kosovo, Northern Ireland. They would barely mention the frenzies we have survived, so always remember the big things, the big reasons why we're doing it.'

Friday, March 1

The Peter M report,* Hammond Mark 2, was the main political story and we went over backwards to be nice about Peter, to the extent that the story effectively became TB apologizing for him being sacked. I felt sorry for him. The reality was if it had been another minister, he or she probably wouldn't have paid with their job. Also, though we could present it in the way we did, it wasn't the case that the report fully exonerated him.

Saturday, May 25

Birthday. Forty-five today. The herald for a weekend of gloom. Feeling really down again. Best thing was that Rory was running in the South of England qualifiers, so he and I went out to Watford. Fiona had bought me a pedometer and I ran for over an hour to get it working. The Roy Keane/Mick McCarthy drama was for some reason really draining me too, even though I knew neither of them well.[†] I felt a real sense of empathy with Keane, felt he was driven but also haunted by demons, depression, violence, an inability to share all the same emotions as everyone seemed to have around the big moments. TB, coincidentally, said he had had friends over for dinner, one of whom asked what I was like. TB said he is the Roy Keane in the operation, driven, doesn't suffer fools, expects everyone to match his own standards, flawed but brilliant.

---

* Anthony Hammond had reopened his investigation into the Hinduja passports affair after Peter Mandelson submitted correspondence between himself and his private secretary, Mark Langdale. Hammond conceded that though the correspondence offered 'some support' for Mandelson's account of his conduct, 'it is still not possible to reach any firm conclusions about the contacts which took place between Mr Mandelson and Mr O'Brien.' Hammond's main findings, and Mandelson's situation, were unchanged.
† A public row between Republic of Ireland football captain Keane and manager Mick McCarthy during preparations for the World Cup in Japan resulted in Keane leaving the squad. The Irish team was defeated by Spain in the second round.

TB got back from the BIC [British-Irish Council] in Jersey. He said Northern Ireland was a mess and we may lose Trimble.

TB called me through and we went out for a chat on the terrace. Philip had briefed him on how his trust ratings had really dipped. He said 'In truth I've never really wanted to do more than two full terms. I could fight a third election *in extremis,* but it would have to be *in extremis,* namely that my worries about GB were such that I feel it would be wrong.' It was pretty clear to me that he had just about settled his view, that he would sometime announce it, say that he was going to stay for the full term, but not go into the election as leader. He had mentioned the idea to Peter M, thinking he would be totally hostile, but he wasn't, because he could see the logic. It seemed to me he was definitely moving towards it. We walked in from the terrace to the Cabinet Room, and I asked him whether he really thought this was the right thing to do, or whether in fact he was being intimidated into doing it, and thinking it was the right thing, by a mix of GB and the press. He said, I don't think so. 'You have to know when to go. I also think the history of leaders trying to choose their successors is a very bad one.' So far as I was aware, only Jonathan, Sally, Cherie and I, and now Peter, were aware he was even thinking about this. As we walked back to his office, I said 'Christ how much could I get from the press for this one?' He smiled, then stopped again and said 'Is it the right thing or the wrong thing? I want your best brain on it.'

TB got a good press at the Liaison Committee but of course the apology from the IRA yesterday was a massive story and took over.*

TB at the PLP, PMQs and the Northern Ireland statement at which we were raising the bar on a ceasefire judgement [amid renewed violence in Belfast]. He did well at the PLP and at PMQs and we were ending pretty well.

---

* The IRA issued an unprecedented apology to the families of those 'non-combatants' it killed during the thirty-year campaign of violence in Northern Ireland.

Today the second of TB's new monthly press conferences. He called me up to go over tricky areas, mainly Iraq, Ireland, unions. We had got Michael Barber [head of TB's Number 10 delivery unit] lined up to do the press conference with TB to try to get some focus on public service delivery. On Iraq, he said he didn't really want a big fight on this unless he has to have it. TB ran up the stairs for the press conference so started out of breath. Michael Barber did well and it was interesting enough. Questions mainly Iraq and Ireland.

Friday, August 30

TB also said, though we had heard it after holidays before, that he wanted to change the way we worked, so that we became more formal, with a proper approach modelled on a company board. On Ireland, he was more not less worried than when he went away.*

Tuesday, October 1

Of all the visitors we had had to the Labour Party conference in Blackpool, Clinton was the one with the most star quality, up there with Mandela. As we were heading back to his suite, BC said he fancied going for a walk. It was windy, a bit cold and it was starting to rain, but he was like a big kid enjoying the lights. 'I love this place. I love Blackpool.' The security guys were clearly used to these kinds of eccentric excursions. We passed a big bingo hall, which advertised itself as the biggest amusement arcade in the world. 'Hey, I wanna go in there. Let's go play the machines.' We got to the door and it looked a lot less inviting close up, so we walked on. We were trying to find somewhere to eat. He said he wanted some fast food, nothing fancy, but we walked past two or three places that were closed. By now the rain was getting a bit heavier. Kevin Spacey [actor and friend of Clinton] was with us, having been on a trip with BC. We must have walked on for a couple of miles. Eventually we found a McDonald's that was open. Bill was now on the phone to Hillary, a mix of heavy politics and small talk, going on with her too about how great this Blackpool seafront was. He made quite an interesting point when he came off the phone. All the delegates and the conference people are inside the security bubble, but more of them should get out here with the real people. The tighter the bubble, the more you should try and get out of it.

---

* There were worrying outbreaks of violence around the Short Strand area of east Belfast. A large security presence was criticized by Sinn Féin.

The staff were gobsmacked when we trooped in. There was a young kid behind the counter who was shocked enough to clock Kevin Spacey, but then saw Clinton and went a funny shade of pink, before getting everybody out of the kitchens to come and see. Doug Band [Clinton aide] ordered massive amount of burgers, chicken nuggets and fries while Bill went round saying hello to the small number of customers in there. There was a fringe event going on at a pub or hotel over the road and word went round there. [Former Labour minister] Margaret Jay's daughter Tamsin came back with a few journalists including Matthew d'Ancona [deputy editor, *Sunday Telegraph*] but they just sort of gawked, pretended they had just been going out for a night at McDonald's. I got them over to say hello a bit later on. Meanwhile a crowd was building outside, some of them classic Blackpool landladies out of the postcards, looking and pointing and then when he occasionally turned round and waved at them, they were waving back in a state of high excitement.

So there we were, sitting in a Blackpool McDonald's, drinking Diet Coke and eating chicken nuggets as he poured forth on the theme of interdependence, the role of the Third Way in progressive politics. He was also quizzing me about GB, and could sense that GB didn't really want to acknowledge TB's peculiar skills and talents, just as Gore hadn't used him properly in the campaign. He spent a while talking to the crowd on the way out, then we got driven back in a little van. He was like a man replenished, not because of the food but because he had been out with real people, and got something out of it. It was probably the single biggest difference between him and TB. They both loved political ideas, wrestling with policy problems and the rest of it, but of the two, Bill was the one who most saw politics in terms of its outcome in people's lives.

Friday, October 4

Iraq still really tricky. TB just wished the Americans would do more to put over a proper message to the world and worry less about their own right wing. First, a meeting in the garden, TB, AC, Jonathan, Andrew Adonis [head of Policy Unit], later joined by David Manning [foreign policy adviser]. First we had to work out how to respond to the breaking news that Sinn Féin members were being arrested for arms offences and the obvious worry the ceasefire was breaking. Just had to play it along. I called Doug Band in Germany, and Bill came on the line and said 'Hey man, what is going on in Northern Ireland?' I explained how some of the SF people were stuck in the arms game. He said if there was anything he could do, he wanted to do it, and he would go there at the drop of a hat.

Sunday, October 6

Philip called, said it was obvious that Jonathan did a lot for TB, particularly foreign and Northern Ireland, but that I basically held it together and I could not possibly leave. Also, he said, what else would I do? He felt TB was moving to a different phase, developing in an interesting way and I should be part of that history.

Monday, October 7

Quite a big news day with Northern Ireland still very difficult.*

Tuesday, October 8

TB did a brief doorstep on Ireland after his meeting with the Bulgarian president but wasn't happy with it. Then Trimble came in for a shouting match.† TB was going to have to go over there soon. We had a long-term diary meeting, desperately fighting to get more domestic stuff back in the diary but it wasn't easy with all the foreign commitments in there already.

Wednesday, October 9

I ran in, a bit sluggish. Meanwhile Northern Ireland was going bad. TB saw Mark Durkan [Social Democratic and Labour Party] and later Bertie Ahern and it was pretty clear that we were going to have to suspend the Executive.

Thursday, October 10

TB saw [Gerry] Adams, [Martin] McGuinness and Bairbre [de Brún, Sinn Féin]. I went in at the end of the meeting and GA was giving TB the usual rather patronizing history lesson. TB did though believe that Adams and McGuinness were genuinely trying to move towards non-violence and there was little chance

---

* Sinn Féin's chief Stormont administrator, Denis Donaldson, and Fiona Farrelly were accused with having confidential details of members of the police and British soldiers, following the PSNI raids at Sinn Féin's Stormont offices. [*Irish Times* 7.10.02] Donaldson was later revealed to be a British spy and was shot dead in Donegal in 2006. The Real IRA claimed responsibility in 2009. [*Irish Times* 13.4.09]
† David Trimble gave Tony Blair a seven-day deadline to propose Sinn Féin's expulsion or face an Ulster Unionist withdrawal from the Executive. [*Irish Times* 9.10.02]

of the IRA going back, but they had real issues in dealing with their own people. McGuinness and I had a long chat about football while TB and Adams had a little session in the corner of the room. Adams did a big number in the street.

Monday, October 14

The morning meeting was largely [the] Bali [bombs], A levels and Northern Ireland, with JR about to suspend the devolved institutions,* so it was a pretty big news day.

Tuesday, October 15

Ran in, thirty-two minutes. Home in 31.37.82, a homeward personal best. During the day I formally signed up for the [London] marathon. Back to meet Jeremy and Sally and go for a meeting on the honours list with [Andrew] Turnbull [Cabinet Secretary], Hayden Phillips [permanent secretary, Lord Chancellor's Department] and people from the [Cabinet Office] Ceremonial Branch. It was a really dull list and we were creeping back towards more Establishment dominance. We wanted more head teachers in there. We fought for George Best.†

Thursday, October 17

I made contact with Leukaemia Research [charity] re the marathon and they sounded very up for it. I spoke to [Andrew] Turnbull and Jeremy about generating sponsorship and they were fine providing I wasn't using government facilities. TB was off to Northern Ireland and his speech went really big, and we were pleased that Sinn Féin were not too dismissive.‡

---

* Dr John Reid signed the order to suspend devolved government in Northern Ireland, saying local administration had 'proved impossible in the short term'. He insisted that the nominated date of 1 May for the next Assembly elections stood and committed himself to finding a basis on which all the institutions of the agreement could be brought back into operation as soon as possible. [*Irish Times* 15.10.02]
† Belfast-born Best, a world-renowned winger who succumbed to alcoholism, would die in 2005 without receiving an honour. He has been honoured by a saying in Northern Ireland: 'Maradona good; Pelé better; George Best.'
‡ In the Belfast speech, Blair asked Northern Ireland politicians 'Do we have the courage as politicians to do what the people want us to do? Do we trust each other enough to make the acts of completion happen? I can only tell you as British prime minister that I have that trust in all the parties I have worked with. We must implement the [Good

Friday, October 18

TB, now in Sedgefield, got very good coverage out of Belfast.

Monday, October 21

My day was rather overshadowed by illness. After a few days of low-level colitis, it was back with a vengeance. By the evening, I was back on the steroids. [Professor] Michael Farthing [gastroenterologist] thought it was a mix of stress, lifestyle, plus maybe a bug. He was sceptical about me doing the marathon though he conceded I looked fitter and better than before.

Wednesday, October 23

TB was on great form at PMQs and was also strong on Northern Ireland. He didn't like having to defend the line about the army not crossing picket lines.

Thursday, October 24

Paul Murphy was replacing John Reid as Northern Ireland Secretary. [Reid was moved to Party chairman in a reshuffle following Estelle Morris' resignation as Education Secretary.]

Friday, November 15

To lunch at MI5. There was clearly a lot going on, much greater threat closer to home, and they said it was sometimes difficult for Western minds to come to terms with the added dimension of terrorists who in many ways didn't mind if they were disrupted because they didn't fear dying, but welcomed it. I said we had better relations at the centre of SIS than with them and we needed to keep more closely in touch because I was sure that as they spent so much of their time thinking strategically and thematically, there was a lot of their work that could dovetail with public communications. They were clearly worried that they were having to move resources from organized crime because of the growing need to keep tabs on Islamic fundamentalism, added to which for all the progress, Northern Ireland still took up a lot of resources, they clearly felt under pressure.

Friday] Agreement in full, because it is the choice of the people; the people here, the people in the South and the people of the United Kingdom as a whole.'

[2003]

TB called me in, was very friendly, and said he just wanted to know how I was. I said fine, up to a point. 'But only up to a point?' he asked. Yes. I couldn't deny that I felt pretty ground down by things.

I asked what he was going to do about his 'friend next door'. 'I'm going to sack him. I've come to a settled view that he has to go. There was a time when I could make the case that the tension was creative. But it has reached the point where it is destructive and it can't go on. I'm not prepared to be in a position where I have got the job, but I am not allowed to do it properly. It could be that it ends up with me being toppled but I would rather that than this situation. I remain of the view that the party will not get rid of a leader if they think the leader is doing basically what the country wants and needs.' He seemed fairly set on it, but doing it would be harder than saying it. He was also keen for Ken Clarke to become Tory leader, feeling it would waken up our lot and also help the country on Europe. The general feeling was that IDS was fucked.

The *Observer* sent me the magazine piece on me doing the marathon and Fiona went absolutely mental because of the ironing board being in the picture. God knows what that's all about.

TB lunch with Bertie Ahern, cooked by Jamie Oliver [TV chef]. I was just trying to plough through paperwork as they talked over where we were with the IRA. They were still thinking it was possible for a big-bang solution to end the IRA.

Tuesday, March 4

TB in Northern Ireland. The Iraq meeting was fine though I felt we needed to do more to get up the bigger argument about democracies versus dictatorships. We were in a very odd period where there was a strong sense of momentum towards war come what may, but with the dynamics feeling as though they were totally against us. He was doing OK in Belfast, though Trimble walked out at 7 and Sinn Féin kept chiselling away. They kept at it till gone midnight and TB didn't get back till 3am.*

Monday, March 17

TB started Cabinet, introduced [Peter] Goldsmith [Attorney General], then Clare came in and asked Sally where Robin Cook was. 'He's gone,' said Sal. 'Oh my God.' TB's only reference to Robin was to say that he had resigned.† He said French intransigence had made it impossible to get a resolution. We were at an end of the diplomatic process.

Wednesday, March 19

Fiona came to see me, said she couldn't stay in the job any longer and started crying. She said it wasn't the war in Iraq per se, but it had been the last straw. She felt it was a waste of time her being here, that she wasn't happy doing what he did. I said she should go if she wanted to, and if she didn't support what we were doing, to try not to do it in a way that makes us an issue. She said but you're a big issue, which meant that there was never a right time to go, but she really didn't want to stay. She went to see Sally, got very upset. Sally said she felt it was

---

While talks at Hillsborough Castle broke up shortly after midnight without the pro-agreement parties reaching a final blueprint to restore the institutions, Ahern and Blair agreed to push back the elections until May 29th to give the parties more time. [*Irish Times* 5.5.03]

Robin Cook resigned over the Iraq conflict, saying he could not support a war opposed by the UN and a majority of the British people.

as much about Cherie/Carole as being about me. It was about not being valued I didn't quite know how to deal with it. It's true there was never a right time but this was about as unright as it could be, in terms of us being made an issue It didn't exactly help that the message from the security people was that patrols around the house would be stepped up while the conflict was going on.

I told TB about Fiona. He reacted, as I knew he would, by saying he couldn't understand why people got so emotional about this. I said well, it's going to happen so I have to work out how to handle it. I said it's true she wasn't happy with the war, but there were other issues too, chief among them that she now had a bad relationship with CB, despite having successfully helped build a very positive image for her. She felt we had next to no life outside work, and that I gave too much for too little in return. He went into 'this is ridiculous' mode. I said Tony, you are talking about Fiona and I won't have it. He said for God's sake I was always saying things about his wife, but this stuff was very difficult, when big political issues were swirling around and they got mixed up with relation ships. But if she went and said it was about Iraq, that would look very odd for me because people would think that was my position too.

I asked what his plans were. 'I really don't know. I've never really wanted to fight a third election, but I don't know, I might.' I asked if he had done a deal with GB. Not at all, he said, but he didn't rule it out. He said it was interesting that GB had been more co-operative recently and said JP had been the key to that. JP had basically told him that if TB didn't want him to get the job, and JP was agin it, it would not happen. In the end, he said, I think it's wrong for me to think I can pick the next leader, or control what he does. But I do worry about him. I worry about the party and do want it to be well led. Things were definitely in flux again, and it was odd how often it was the really big moment that brought out these situations.

Wednesday, April .

Definitely a sense that the military campaign was going better, plus we had a strong humanitarian message running alongside. Sir Charles Guthrie [Chief o the (UK) Defence Staff] made a revealing comment when he said in Basra we were using lessons from Northern Ireland. Troops were getting to know people finding out who the ringleaders were, then seeking them out. 'Did you do that in Northern Ireland?' I asked. Laughter.

I had a separate chat with Dan Bartlett [Communications adviser to George W Bush] re the Northern Ireland visit. We were thinking about a joint interview and also getting over their guy from Homeland Security.

We discussed Bush visiting Northern Ireland at Cabinet. I asked what the US media would make of GW pitching up there. They said their approach was to say it was to show those involved in the MEPP that peace processes can work. Good idea.

Dan B called as I was leaving to say AP [Associated Press] were on to the Belfast visit. I knocked up a quick briefing note with Ben Wilson [press officer] to use it to get out basic message on Iraq, MEPP and NI.

Fiona picked a fight this morning as soon as I went downstairs with some jibe about 'the thought police'. I said it was time she got a grip of herself. She ended up calling me a bastard and throwing a cup at me, which smashed on the floor at my feet. She was more angry than I had ever known her and taking it all out on me. Part of me understood. Part of me resented it. But I had a terrible sense of foreboding about it. I left for the office feeling like shit.

On the flight to Belfast TB worked on a note for Bush setting out why it was so important to get the UN properly involved – to show our commitment to rebuilding after the divisions in the international community, for the Arab world, for Europe. It was a two-page note, very clear and rational. We landed, got a helicopter to Hillsborough. As I was making a few calls in my room, TB called me through to his room. He asked how my situation was at home. I said that unless I had an exit date, I had no 'marriage'. He said he was really saddened and disappointed, but he understood. He would not put me under pressure to stay. He felt it was a bad move for me, that I would forever regret not seeing the whole thing through to the end. 'But you need to know you have done more for me than anyone, more than I could have asked for, I could not have done it without you, and I will not feel let down, so let me relieve you of any pressure you may feel on that front.' But I did feel it, because I knew he valued the close team around him and I knew I made a difference. I felt it very strongly here at Hillsborough because there had been so many good and bad moments here, but I knew I had helped with both.

We stood at the window and I reminded him of the time we came here in Opposition and he looked out over the grounds at Hillsborough and said the Tories were not going to give it all up without a real fight. We had won that

fight and I knew a lot of that was down to me and the work I'd done for him
and it was not easy to walk away from it. He asked me when I wanted to go.
said summer at the latest, maybe conference, maybe before. He just nodded. W
went round in circles for a while and then he said I would have to help him fin
a successor. I felt David Hill [former Labour Party chief spokesman] was possibl
the only option. We went downstairs to wait for Bush and Co to arrive. The
flew in, then drove up, GWB, Powell, Condi [Condoleezza Rice] and Andy Car
in Bush's car. TB and Bush having a fair bit of time together. At one point the
came back from a walk and Bush was talking about his favourite presidents
Washington, Lincoln, Roosevelt, Reagan. He said Reagan made the country fee
good again and he saved the Republican Party. I tried to go out for a run but wa
stopped at every second tree by bloody American security men jumping out from
trees. Gave up after a couple of miles.

Tuesday, April

TB said 'this neocon stuff' was crazy. I had asked Dan last night what 'neocon
meant and he said it was the belief that government had a moral purpose. I said
does that mean moral purpose can only be right wing? TB felt today's meeting
with Bush was going to be tough. It was clear Condi was pushing a fairly hard
line re the UN. We had a fight on our hands to keep in a 'vital role' [in the pres.
conference script]. She wanted 'important', which sounded too grudging. 'It'
meant to be,' she said. My other worry was that it might be briefed they had
downgraded it. TB was determined we had to get something out of this and in
the end, largely thanks to Bush, we did.

Bush was excellent on Northern Ireland, and on MEPP, linked the two
well by saying he would spend as much time and energy on MEPP as TB did on
NI, then excellent too on the UN role. He was good on the war message too.
The general feeling afterwards was that it was the best media performance he'd
done. It was interesting to watch him in the main meeting today, where he was
letting TB do a lot of the talking, then taking in Powell's and Condi's views in
particular, then more or less saying what we expected him to in the first place.
He seemed restless too, a bit fidgety. He and TB were in the big armchairs by the
fireplace, the rest dotted around the room, Jack and Powell on the sofa together.
Powell was talking at one point when Bush got up, got himself a coffee, asked
me if I wanted one and came over to talk to me about the marathon. When is it?
What time will I do? How much money will I raise? Dan pointed out that I had
a piece in *The Times* on it and Bush picked it up and read it, getting to the end

ug for Leukaemia Research. 'You doing it for leukaemia? Did you know my
ster died from leukaemia? Would you like me to give you a cheque?' I certainly
ould, I said.

He went to the door giving on to the lounge, opened it and shouted out
Blake [Gottesman, aide], get my chequebook.' Later the cops said he created an
solute stir because nobody had a clue that he had a chequebook with him, let
one where it was, though they did find it eventually, and he wrote out a cheque
ere and then. He said his sister was called Robin and died aged seven when he
as four. 'I will do this because you are my friend,' he said, 'but I am also doing
for her.' I asked if the charity could publicize it. Sure, he said. TB came over
d asked what I was up to. I said the president had just given me a cheque so
here's yours?

Bush seemed to buy into TB's line that he had to develop a bigger interna-
onal message that was not just terrorism but MEPP, world poverty, environ-
ent, etc. He was pretty vile re Chirac, said he felt betrayed, that Chirac had
one against him not on the merits but as part of a general anti-US strategy
nd he would never forgive that. 'The only thing that would swing me round
France is regime change.' Bush said he would maybe rebuild with Schroeder
rst but he wanted TB to make sure he knew he felt personally affronted and
e would only think about putting things back together with them on the clear
nderstanding German foreign policy was not run by the French.

TB seemed to have worked a fair bit of influence on him because the general
eaction from the press conference was that Bush went well beyond what was
xpected. He also tore a bit of a strip off Condi at the pre-meeting when she was
till picking away at him, and he suddenly said 'There is too much tension in
ere.' He asked everyone to leave apart from me, Blake and Magi Cleaver. TB and
ush also had a fairly long stroll, just the two of them while Jack continued to
ork on Condi, Powell and Dan Fried [National Security Council], saying that
he warmer the words re the UN, the greater the influence within it. Jack and I
oth fought very hard to keep 'vital' in the text, and eventually they agreed to it.
ater Dan said, only half in jest I think, 'Can we win any of these arguments at
ll?' He obviously had the counter-worry, that if Bush was too warm re the UN,
e would get hit at home. TB said to Bush 'that was a very rash promise' – to
pend as much time on MEPP as he had on NI.

Bush knew he had done pretty well. I was trying to get them up to do the
raqi TV pieces to camera straight away while they were still in the mood. We
orted the filming logistics, then down to meet Bertie [Ahern] who was arriving
or lunch, and then the other parties. The press conference was running pretty
uch word perfect for us.

We gathered the parties, including Trimble, Adams, McGuinness, Ervin etc., in a rough circle inside the main dining room. Bush did the rounds and w pretty good at it, and did a little general number, saying he was there in the hop he could put some wind in their sails, and that when NI finally moved to lastir peace, it would be seen as a symbol of hope around the world. The meeting wer fine, and they all seemed to think it had been worth him coming. TB and Bus then walked down the hill to the helicopters. I was following on behind wit Condi. We joked about the next venue, maybe Cyprus. I said I thought it ha gone pretty well, but said she seemed a lot more wound up than before. They fle off and TB went back in for meetings with Bertie and the parties.

TB was full of himself on the flight home, really felt it had been good an positive, pretty much on all fronts. GWB was definitely moving a bit on the inte national agenda, and buying into the need for a new approach, but the tension internally had been very clear.

TB was seeing Fiona and seemingly told her he was sad things had reached th point, that she had done a good job, and he knew these were very high-pressur positions. She felt he was fine about us leaving but not yet. She told him sh thought the political side of our operation was weak, that too much fell on me She said it was fine on one level, but the reality was she didn't much like hir or respect him any more, and she was convinced we had to get out. I felt tha considering everything else he had to deal with at the moment, it was a bit muc to expect him to be on top of all the internal personnel issues too, even thos involving us.

David Blunkett came round for dinner and Fiona was now pretty open abou how she felt about things. He said to me when she was out of the room 'You mus not let her push you out. TB has to have you there, and so do the rest of us.' H was making clear he thought TB had to grip GB. He realized he couldn't sac him but he could swap him with Jack. GB might see it as a downward step bu you cannot be Chancellor forever and Foreign Secretary is the other big job h could do.

Jonathan had stayed out in Northern Ireland trying to get the final pieces i place for a deal but it didn't work out, so we aborted the plan for TB to fly ou nathan called early to say that they couldn't do it. TB worked on it for a while, ried out various forms of words, but in the end the IRA were not going to deliver.

was determined to be in the best possible shape for the marathon tomorrow so ested up a lot of the day, didn't go in for the morning meetings, watched Man Jtd vs Newcastle on the TV and took Grace to see *Maid in Manhattan,* which ad a seriously silly plot, though the relationship between the politician and his pin doctor was moderately amusing. TB left me pretty much alone, though he id call to ask why I hadn't been to the meetings. I said I really wanted to get my ead in gear for tomorrow, and in any event Jonathan had filled me in.*

t was a nice day, fresh but looked like it was going to be sunny, and the mood p at the start was terrific. The start felt great, and I reckoned I was in OK hape for sub four hours, which is what I really wanted. I did the first mile vell below eight minutes without even really trying, which was probably the drenaline getting me to start too fast, the second mile bang on eight, and then nto a fairly steady rhythm for a while. After three miles Charles Lindsey [one of 'B's protection officers] said I ought to run on ahead on my own. The hardest oints were nine miles, fifteen and twenty-one, but the bands and the crowds vere great. 'Rockin' All Over the World' [hit record by Status Quo] got me hrough one tricky part. A Jennifer Lopez song playing made me think of Grace t another and got me through. The crowd were fantastic all the way. I didn't et a single adverse comment, which surprised me considering how much war livisiveness there had been, and loads of encouragement. Philip and Georgia Gould] popped up a couple of times on the route. Andrew Turnbull, Alun :vans [Cabinet Office], others from the office though I missed Alison [Black-haw] and her crowd at Canary Wharf. I had been warned Canary Wharf would e quiet but it was about as noisy as anywhere on the route and I got a great lift here. There were no quiet and lonely miles at all. Also, on a couple of occasions

---

President Bush's special envoy on Ireland, Richard Haass, left Northern Ireland on Tuesday: however, after the British and Irish governments were forced to postpone ublishing their blueprint for restoring devolution, he flew back to offer US assistance nd support. He urged the IRA to make a 'historic transformation', which would allow olitics in Northern Ireland to move forward. [*Irish Times* 14.3.03]

when I was struggling one of the other runners would come alongside and help push me on, including a woman from Dulwich who suggested I 'lock on to her and follow step by step which, as she had a near-perfect bum, took me through another tricky mile before I recovered my strength and eventually left her.

The last few miles from the Tower were hard and exhilarating in equal measure. I hit twenty-two miles with fifty minutes left to break four hours so knew I was going to do it and could relax a bit. The crowds by now were just a wall of sound and encouragement. I was worried I was going to cry on crossing the line, so forced myself to do it as I ran towards Big Ben, lost myself in a crowd of runners, and just let the emotion come out, imagined friends on one shoulder, enemies on the other, friends pushing me on, enemies failing to hold me back, thought about John, thought about how long left my dad had, thought about the kids, really piled it on and cried for a bit as I ran, and then felt fine on the last mile.

I had trained hard in really difficult circumstances work-wise and I felt a real sense of achievement. I wondered around twenty miles if I could beat Bush's time, but as I tried to pick up the pace, the pain in the hamstrings really intensified and I just went back to my steady plod, and settled for sub four. I didn't realize the cameras were on me for the last couple of minutes, by which time I was swearing at myself the whole time, push yourself, faster, fuck it, keep going, push, etc. The last few hundred metres were a mix of agony and joy. The pain was pretty intense but by now virtually every second someone was shouting out encouragement, from 'Do it for New Labour' to 'I forgive you everything Tony Blair has done' to endless 'Go on, you can do it, not far to go.'

I was siphoned off at the turn into the Mall and could now hear the commentary. I spotted Fiona and the kids right at the end in the stand and ran towards them. They were screaming at me to head straight to the finish but I was seven minutes inside my target and just so pleased to see them. My legs buckled a bit as I stopped and my voice was unbelievably weak, but it felt fantastic to have done it. I posed for a few pictures for the snappers, did an interview with Sue Barker [former tennis player turned sports commentator], dictated my column to *The Times*, and also did a briefing at the ICA [Institute of Contemporary Arts] by which time my legs had pretty much seized up. We got home, by which time had a massive dehydration headache, and was drinking gallons of water. We went out for dinner with the Goulds. Philip had reminded me of the Woody Allen character Zelig today, popping up in incongruous places along the route. But felt really happy at having done it. Grace said she had felt so proud of me, and did I know what a fantastic thing I did for John? I was really touched, especially as she had never known him.

Tuesday, April 15

'B wanted me to go on the trip to Germany, but agreed I could come back after hat. He wanted to discuss the media and political plans for the next phase, and ve often managed to get some decent work done on these plane journeys. By the nd of the day I had put together an OK plan for the next few weeks.

As we drove to Northolt he must have said three, maybe four times, that e was just at a loss to know what to do about GB. He felt that he was now of a nindset that he needed to wage war on pretty much every front. To create the ircumstances to depose him, he felt he had to create and win power struggles. I elt if that was the case, it was totally the wrong approach. If I were him, I would ove TB to death, support him so closely that TB felt a certain pleasure in handing ver power. As things stood, he was making it harder and harder for him to do it. Ie seemed to want not only to get rid of him, but also destroy any sense that TB ad a legacy worth the name.

Saturday, April 26

Grimsville at home. I was feeling really down. I couldn't let things get so bad ve split up. I went out for a run, and came across a scene in Golders Green that underlined how much I didn't want it to happen. A young boy was screaming as is mother tried to hand him over to his dad, because it was 'his weekend'.

Wednesday, April 30

TB was heavily focused on Northern Ireland, where we were in a bad place again, leading towards cancellation of the elections, which we would do tomorrow. TB aid he was determined to treat Sinn Féin politicians like any other. His big worry vas that SF would not deliver on the final steps. The other big story was the *Times* xclusive on Special Branch transcripts of calls between McGuinness, Jonathan und Mo Mowlam, clearly genuine.*

Sinn Féin accused MI5 of tapping the phones and compiling the transcripts, which eature in a biography of McGuinness, *Martin McGuinness: From Guns to Government* by .iam Clarke and Kathryn Johnston.

I watched a bit of [political journalist] John Sergeant's BBC programme to coin
cide with TB's birthday. It was very funny in parts, though Mo and [Peter] Kil
foyle were exceptionally bitter. Overall TB came over fine.

We were already beginning to talk about elections and it just didn't hold out th
excitement it once did. Also Rory had an interesting take. He said he reckone
I wasn't as good as I used to be, that if I left soon, I would be a legend, the firs
person really to take communications to a level that made an actual difference t
politics, whereas if I stayed, it was downhill all the way. 'You're not enjoying it a
much as you did, you're not doing it as well as you did, and never forget that th
reason [former Manchester United footballer] Eric Cantona's a legend is becaus
he left at the right time.'

TB saw Adams and McGuinness and told them he thought it might be time fo
him to meet the IRA guys that they kept going back to see. Adams seemed keene
than McGuinness. TB felt they had to give something.

To the Ritz where I was having lunch with Clinton, with Peter M and Philip
Mary McCartney [photographer] was taking some pictures. BC had had just two
hours' sleep after getting in from Greece. He was dressed in golf-type clothes. H
was a lot thinner than the last time I had seen him. Doug Band [Clinton aide
had organized lunch, which seemed to be a succession of different meals, anc
Clinton was eating a lot of them. First a plate of eggs, then bacon, then ham-
burgers. First we talked about Bush. We talked a bit about the US scene. I askec
why he never stayed in embassies when he travelled. He said Bush had some
mean people round him. 'I could, but I'm not sure about the welcome.' He saic
he was not much for having things named after him but there had been a Clinto
Fellowship for Israeli and Palestinian students and at first the Bush administration changed the name and then they took away the money. 'These are ruthles
people you are dealing with.' On Marc Rich [indicted in 1983 for illegal oil deal

ith Iran and tax evasion] and the controversial pardon [by Clinton on his last
ay in office], he said that Cheney's chief of staff [Lewis 'Scooter' Libby] had testi-
ed for the guy. 'You have to understand that what they care about is power. They
ontrol the press, they control the agenda and they hoard power ruthlessly.' They
vere changing the law to allow the White House to be more secretive. He said
he view in DC was Bush had put all his [Texas] governor papers into his father's
residential library because that meant they couldn't be got at.

He said Bush liked TB because he stayed with him but if somebody came
long they thought would help them more, they would go for them. He was
peaking very slowly, calmly, matter-of-factly, probably conscious that we were
n the lookout for signs of bitterness, but there was precious little of that and it
vas pretty compelling. He felt Bush had lost an election and having 'won' it he
vas now behaving as if he had walked it. But they were clever, and so was Bush.
He was good at dealing with opponents. I asked him what Bush would do with
he BBC. 'If he could kill the governors, he would. But he can't, so he would do
deal.'

On Iraq, he said the Bush lot had never been keen on Blix. He said Powell
vas the one who really wanted to let the inspectors work, and now it was looking
ad for them, but because they still had control of the media, Bush was not yet
ınder pressure. September 11 had changed the American people's psychology.
3ush understood that and the Democrats had not worked out how to respond,
ıow to fight it. He was angry about Bush, philosophical about the campaign [Al]
Gore fought, hopeful for Hillary.

Peter M had to leave to do an interview. Philip, BC and I went over to the
ofas and out poured something of a masterclass in political strategy. He followed
our politics closely, and I asked him what his remedy would be for our problems.
He said he was touched that we trusted him so much that we could openly lay
out the problems we had. He said first, you have a weak Opposition. Keep them
veak by coming up with the forward policy positions and push them where you
vant them. Second, TB is about as good as they get. Keep reminding everyone
of that. Third, on the press, he said you need a strategy to get back credibility. He
aid he'd followed my troubles and was sympathetic. He said that I'd always been
he number two target after TB and that I'd taken a lot. I'd been right to fight for
nyself and I did a great job, but now move on. Don't keep digging the hole. Let
others do it. Go back to the media and say I didn't lie, but maybe I missed some-
hing. I always strove to tell the truth but I've thought deeply about it all. I've got
ı job to do and so have you, and it's best if we can do it without regarding each
other as subhuman. He said the problem was they felt it was a pattern of behav-
our – manipulation and bullying – and that I had to show them I was real again.

He said they don't like me in part because I was one of them and now I'm not.

Next, a strategy for the PLP. Understand their lives and reach out to them. They have shitty lives. You guys go to DC. You have real power. They get a weekend in their constituency. Give them some romance. They think you guys have gone Hollywood and they want more local. It's about their psychology. It's the same with the press. Some you will never win but others you will if you are nice to them, involve them. Your MPs know TB is better than them but that doesn't mean they are nothing. Fifth, you have to reconnect. People are falling out of love with Tony because they think he has fallen out of love with them. He's a statesman and that's great but their world is here and now and they are paying him to sort out their world, here and now. They know he has to do this other stuff but they want to know he cares about them, here and now. Sixth, the Third Way is fine, but it has to be a third way with liberal values. Don't just push a reform message. He has to have good old-fashioned left causes too, for the poor whatever. It's about values not reform.

It was the same argument I had been having with TB. I said so, and he said yes, but maybe he thinks you are just beating up on him. It's all about balance. He has to balance the Third Way message for his new coalition with the liberal message for the party. You have to balance frank advice with real support. On TB himself, he said he had to rediscover his joy in politics. He needed new stimuli without throwing everything out. He had to keep change with continuity. He came to the point about me not beating up on Tony. He could see for example why I thought Carole [Caplin] was a problem, but other people's emotions and psychology are not always the same. 'My brother was a cocaine addict and the word to remember for addicts is HALT. Yes, it means stop. But it also means I'm Hungry, I'm Angry, Lonely and Tired. You usually find the reason in one of those.' Clearly talking now about Monica Lewinsky [White House intern with whom he had had an affair], he said, 'I wasn't hungry but I was angry, lonely and tired. I was being beaten up by everyone. Ken Starr [Independent Counsel, prosecutor] was trying to put me in jail. Friends were leaving me and enemies were killing me. Hillary was angry with me. This ball of fire came at me as I felt H, A, L, T.'

He said he sometimes thought Tony wanted a blue ribbon and a gold badge for the work he does, 'but the ribbon and the badge are the JOB. It's a privilege. It's a great job he's got and yes it's tough but who says it shouldn't be? Get his juices flowing again.' So he summed up. Keep the Tories weak. Get back credibility with the press, remembering that you are the best and that's why they judge you so harshly. It's the same with Tony. You've got to show you're real. Get your troops back in shape by loving them a bit. Reconnect with the public by

howing it's about them. Get TB to rediscover his joy in politics. He told a story
bout the first woman he ever loved, how he left her and drove her into the arms
of a friend and she ended up hating both of them and it always bugged him. Years
ater when he was president he made contact with her and they talked it over, and
e felt happy that he had resolved an important thread in his life. Another story
bout a friend he fell out with but then when he became president they rediscov-
red that friendship. So keep your friends, get some joy back into your politics,
get a left liberal cause.

Philip then asked him what he thought I should do, whether he thought I
hould leave the job. Again, he was terrific on the analysis. A long pause, then said
hese are the factors: 1. Is it hurting you more than you're getting out of it, especially for Fiona and the family? 2. Is it hurting Tony more than you are putting
n? 3. Can anyone else do it? 4. If you stay can you deliver a new strategy? Only
ou know, but remember it's a great job and I don't like to think what could have
happened if you had not been there. He also thought in some ways Fiona would
blame herself for having let Carole take Cherie over, but she shouldn't. Really
warm and friendly. He took me to the door and said, 'Hang in. There are three
centres of power in your politics. You guys, the Tories, the press. You have an
affirmative programme. The others don't. Their job is to stop you doing your job.
Don't let them. Raise your eyes above them, and stay with it.'

As we left, both Philip and I observed that he was about as near to being a
political strategic genius as we knew. Philip asked if it made me want to stay and
t did but I wondered if TB was up for the change needed. I told TB later what
Bill's analysis had been and he agreed with most of it, apart from some of the
liberal stuff.

Monday, July 21

[Lord] Hutton* was announcing his plans at 10.30 and it was clear he would go
as wide as he wanted and do most of it in public.1 He looked far too Tory for me,
though as Fiona said, that might mean he was pro war whereas a left-wing judge
almost certainly would not be.

---

* Lord Hutton, former Lord Chief Justice of Northern Ireland, would chair what was
formally known as the 'Inquiry into the Circumstances Surrounding the Death of Dr
David Kelly CMG'.

In to finish my various notes to send to the Hutton Inquiry. There were mixed reports of what Hutton was like. Jonathan said Adams and Trimble were united for once – in saying he was dreadful. Scarlett said he was an Ulster puritan, but nobody knew if that helped or hindered. He was a conservative with a small c. It was a fairly sober meeting, because the truth was none of us knew where or how this would end, and it was fraught with risk. We went over all the background material we would need, and the areas we would need to prepare on. I called Ann Taylor* as she was about to board a ferry in Newhaven and told her in confidence I was going to leave. I was thinking about when, and felt that if the ISC [Intelligence and Security Committee] report was going to clear me, that might be the time to do it.

I got home and Fiona was walking down the stairs as I walked through the door. 'I've been fired,' she said. 'What?' She said CB had called and said she felt she ought to leave soon. She accused Fiona of briefing against her, which Fiona said was ridiculous though she accepted there had been a breakdown of trust between them. Fiona said she did believe Carole was a menace but it was not true that she had ever briefed against her, let alone against Cherie. She was really upset that CB could think as she did. She was due to go out to the ballet and I said just try not to worry about it,

I went in and told TB about CB's call and said it was unforgivable that she spoke to Fiona like that after all she'd done for her. He said people were too fraught at the moment and Cherie was feeling under pressure. I said she needed to apologize, otherwise there would be badness between them that helped nobody. He said the problem at the moment is that the public will begin to wonder whether we are governing the country. All they hear is all this stuff about personalities, process and the rest and they start to wonder if that's all we do.

---

* Taylor would chair the Commons Intelligence and Security Committee Inquiry into the published intelligence assessments of Iraqi WMD capacity, including the claim made in the September 2002 dossier that WMD could be launched within forty-five minutes. The committee's eventual report would describe the 45-minute claim as 'unhelpful', lacking context and assessment. Though the ISC would conclude editorial changes had been made within Number 10, Campbell would be exonerated from Gilligan's charge of having 'sexed up' the document.

336   JULY '03: PREPARING FOR THE HUTTON INQUIRY

I slept in a bit, having had a bit of asthma through the night. In to finalize my statement. TB didn't want any sense in there that he kept persuading me to stay. He thought it would be weakening. He wanted to write his own words about me, that there are two ACs, the one he knows and the one the media likes to portray.

Once I finished my statement I got Alison to send out a message that I wanted to see all my team and anyone else in the building who was around. They knew what was coming so they weren't exactly shocked, but there was a lot of sadness in there. I said they knew I had been thinking about going and today was the day. I had had a great time and it had been an amazing privilege and one of the things that meant most to me was the team I had built up. I could not have done any of it without them and certainly in recent weeks I could not have asked for more by way of support. I said everyone was replaceable, I would leave with nothing but good memories of them, but Fiona and I desperately wanted to get a life back for ourselves and the children. The announcement re Fiona was in there though buried in all the avalanche of coverage re my leaving. It was a real sadness to me that she was leaving on bad terms with CB and with Tony too. But she was clearly happy we were on the way, and maybe surprised I had brought it to a head so quickly.

I cleared my desk. Went on a last walk round the building to say a few thank-yous and goodbyes, met Fiona and then we walked out together. I didn't look at the hacks and I didn't bother to listen, let alone answer. I just wanted to get out, and get home. My asthma was bad though, partly the air, partly the current stress, also maybe a bit of anxiety about the total lack of certainty about what I would now do with myself. People were telling me I could make a fortune on the lecture circuit, but I can't say it held that much appeal. The most important thing was to try to get things at home on a better keel, rest, and then take stock. As I left, TB had said 'You do realize I will phone you every day, don't you?' I said yes, and I hope you realize sometimes I won't be there.

If that plane ride from Belfast after TB, BA and others had signed the Good Friday Agreement produced the highest, happiest moment of my time in politics and government, the lowest came at the end of a flight from Washington to London, and the news that David Kelly's body had been found. As I wrote at the time, I felt like a juggernaut was coming my way. It came amid a period of almost unremitting misery in which my natural tendency towards depression, a huge workload, dreadful relations with the media, and real pressure at home, combined to make me want to get out.

As it happened, Dr Kelly's death, the subsequent public inquiry and my determination to fight to clear my name of serious allegations meant that I stayed in the job longer than I had intended. But I knew it was time to go. A part of me wanted to stay to the end, and respects Jonathan Powell all the more for the fact that he did. He came under similar pressures at home, from a partner even more hostile to our Iraq policy than mine. But he did not have the profile I had, and the pressure that brought, caused by a mixture of my personality, and my role on the frontline with the media 24/7. Jonathan had become much more than a chief of staff to TB; on Northern Ireland, he was Tony's main fixer and negotiator, and he did a brilliant job.

What is clear from these diaries is that from our days in Opposition, TB was fascinated by, and determined to do something about improving the political scene in Northern Ireland. Lesser men would have given up when faced with the many setbacks along the way. But here Tony's essential optimism was important. He could see good in characters in whom others only saw bad. He could see hope where others saw reasons only for despair. And once he had tasted the success of a deal between the parties, he was never going to let it go. The peace was by no means secure by the autumn of 2003. There would be many more ups and downs, many more setbacks, many more flights to the Province for talks that went on through the night. And eventually there would be a headline none of us ever dared to imagine – Paisley and McGuinness unite for peace. For those two to become colleagues, enjoying the nickname 'the Chuckle Brothers', really did underline how far things had moved. Just as Good Friday 1998 had a touch of the miraculous about it, so did that.

Northern Ireland still has the capacity to be in the news for the wrong reasons – violence over the removal of the Union flag from Belfast City Hall came shortly before the time of writing, for example. But when I go to Ireland now, as I do regularly, for most of the time security forces north and south are dealing with the same crime issues as other police forces around the world – muggings, drugs, road traffic accidents. They know there will be flare-ups linked to the politics and sectarianism of the past. But they know there has been progress. And they know too that as far as the vast majority of people are concerned, there is no going back.

Index

Abbs, Wendy 154
ABC 54, 56 91
Abdullah, King of Jordan 195
Adair, Johnny 275
Adams, Gerry (GA) xv, xxi; under pressure 14–15; invited to launch book at Commons (1996) 29; and TB's offer of talks 44; presses case for facilities in House of Commons 45 *and n*; attacked by Bruton 51; his 'stupid response' to IRA killings 52; and Hume 57; invited to Lancaster House by CS 57; and problem of handshake with TB 71, 72, 74; talks with TB (1997) in NI 72–4, in Downing St 75, 76–9; and UUs' Maze visit 82; further talks with TB 84, 85–6, 89; and IRA killings 95, 98, 99, 100–1; at talks leading to Good Friday Agreement (1998) 105, 106–7, 111, 113, 114, 115, 116, 118; vulnerable 120; and bugging of SF negotiator 123; and IRA decommissioning 124, 126, 163; and release of prisoners 126, 127, 129, 144; and Balcombe Street Gang 128; invited to Hillsborough garden party 142; and IRA violence 143; wants meeting with DT 143; and NI elections 146; and Drumcree march 148, 149; and Omagh bombing 155, 156; TB convinced of his sincerity 158; and DT 159, 160, 163, 165*n*, 165–6, 167, 170; TB positive about 164, 165; announces that violence must be a thing of the past 165 *and n*; and BC's

visit to NI 168, 169; called 'Gerry' by TB 169; meeting with DT 171; provocative at Labour Conference 177; further problems with decommissioning 177, 180, 182, 184, 185, 198, 199–200, 201, 202, 203; too busy to speak to BC 203; taught to skateboard by Blair children 208; further talks with TB 208, 214, 217, 218, 220, 221, BA 218, DT 220, 222, and BC 221; demands explanations from AC 217; under pressure 224; and amendments to NI bill 227; further meetings and talks with TB 229, 230, 231, 239, 241; and NI devolution 243; relaxed about car bugging 244–5; talks with BA 254; has a go at PM 255; warns of 'slippery road back to conflict' 256; puts out statement on IRA 257; 'surly' with TB 260; has 'stuck his neck out' 260; 'thuggish' with PM 262; as gardener 263; sees JoP 265; talks with BA 266; gets IRA to agree statement on decommissioning 266, 267, 268; and PM's approach 269; meeting with BC 280; talks with TB 281, 285, 286, 310; calls on IRA to disarm (2001) 305, 311; gives TB a history lesson 319; believed by TB to be genuinely trying to move towards non-violence 319–20; and Bush's visit (2003) 328; and TB's request to meet IRA 332; his opinion of Lord Hutton 336
Adonis, Anthony 318
Ahern, Bertie, Taoiseach (BA) viii, ix–xi,

strategy with DT 68, 69; nervy about Labour Party Conference 70; sees UUP/SF talks as an amazing achievement 70; and transfer of Rangers thug to NI jail 70–71; meeting with SF leaders and possibility of handshake 71–4; and trouble on Belfast walkabout 74; warns GB, PM and AC to work out differences 74–5; agrees with BA on removing NI troops 75; has 'turn' 76; and Downing St meeting with SF 75–9; visits Belfast 80

1998 tries to get Heads of Agreement tabled with UUP and SDLP 81–2; and Mo's visit to the Maze 82–3; in Japan 84–5; and GB 85, 87; and Bloody Sunday apology 85, 86, 89–91; meeting with SF 85–6; and UFF killings 86–7; supports BC over Lewinsky affair 87, 88, 91; furious with Mo 88, 89; and UU rudeness at Lancaster House talks 88–9; and Iraq 90, 91; successful US trip 91–4; supports BC 93; and further IRA killings and SF expulsion from talks 95, 96, 97, 98, 99; at *Guardian* lunch 97; further difficulties with GB 98–9; seen in Westminster Cathedral 99; fed up with Cabinet leaks 100; jokes about gifts received 100; has good meeting with GA 100–1; critical of his key people 101; at Asia–Europe Meeting 102–3; furious with Mitchell and NIO 103–4; feels 'hand of history' on shoulder 104; negotiations and signing of Good Friday Agreement 104–17, 118, 122; in Spain 119; feels confident over NI 120; in 'superman mode' on Middle East trip 121; and Parades Commission 121–2, 125; praises Mo 122; has long meeting with GA and McG 123; and AC's problems with FM 123; irritated by Hattersley 123; angry with GA over decommissioning 124; chairs EU summit 124–5; does joint Q&A with JM in Belfast 125; gets cool reception from RUC 125; worried at Mo's lack of sensitivity to UUs 125; realizes he will have to campaign for GFA 126, 127, 128; livid at Mo's handling of prisoner release 128–30; his Ireland speech (May

1998) 130, 131–2; chairs Birmingham G8 132, 133–4, 136; 'obsesses' over Ireland 134; Frost interview with BC 134–5; with BC at Chequers 136, 137; bumps into Castro 138; NI speeches 139–41; and GFA referendum 141; Des O'Connor interview 142; suspicious of Cranborne 142, 143; problems with Prince Charles 142; in Dublin 142–3; meeting with IRA men in Belfast 143; and Prisoners Bill 144, 145; gloomy over NI elections 145, 146; problems with Paisley 146; gives 'worst sound bite in history' 147; in NI again 147–8; and Drumcree march 147, 148, 149–50, 151, 152, 153; attacked by JM 148–9; wants JoP more involved 150; loses his voice 154; and Omagh bombing 154–7, 159–60, 161, 162; problems with Mo 150, 158–9; recalls Parliament 162; has talks with DT and SF 162–3; with BA at Knock 163–4; and BC's visit 164; works on getting GA to say something DT can welcome 164, 165–6, 167; with BC in Belfast 167–9, and Omagh 169–70; supportive of BC 171, 172, 173; on 'day trip from hell' to New York 174–5; works on Conference speech 176, 177; difficult meeting with GA 177; at *Mirror* lunch 177–8; talks with Chinese president 178; wins Nobel Peace Prize 179, 183–4; further talks with McG and DT 179–80; at Austrian summit 180; no progress with GA 180; problems with McG 181; and tension between DT and Mallon 181–2; gives speech at the Dáil 181, 182; works well with BA; blames DT and Taylor for NI problems 183–4; a gloomy meeting with BA 185; and Iraq 185, 186; and PM's resignation over Robinson loan 187, 188, 189–90

1999–2000 thinks Hague is in trouble 193; and Tory bipartisanship 193; and Gore's visit 194; at King Hussein's funeral with BC 194–5; at JH's farewell dinner 195; and decommissioning 195; and Kosovo 197, 198, 201, 205, 211, 213; another gloomy meeting with BA 197; and de Chastelain 198–9; hatred of Brendan McKenna 199;

and fruitless SF/UUP meeting 199–200; worried re leaving Mo in charge of talks 201; and meetings on decommissioning 201–4; sees a depressed BA in Brussels 205; further meetings 206; hopeful 206–7; difficult calls with BC over Kosovo 207–8, 209; at FA Cup Final 208–9; in NI 209–10; meeting with Bono and Geldof 210; angry with DT 210, 211; uses *Times* article to kickstart process 211, 212; and further talks 212–18; gets de Chastelain to delay report 218; and DT 218, 219–20; puts pressure on SF and UU 220–24; and UUs' rejection of deal 224; wants to press on 224, 225; and NI Executive suspension bill 226–7; further talks with DT 227–8; asks Mallon not to resign 228; and Mo 229; unsuccessful meeting with SF 229–32; hates reshuffles 233, 234, 236–7; wants PM for NI post 232, 233, 236, 237–8; sees Patten about policing report 235; on GB 235; and Cherie's pregnancy 236; at Tampere summit 239; meeting with George Mitchell 239; and Mo's book idea 240; at Commonwealth summit 241; asked by BC to get more involved in Cyprus and Kashmir 242; and NI devolution 243; visits Manchester with Mo 244; relaxed about bugging of GA 244–5; worried about Mo 245; at BIIGC 246; and *Star* picture of son snogging 246; and GB's cancellation of Third World debt 246–7; relations with GB 247–8, 250–51, 256, 260; and London Mayoral election 251–3, 256–7, 259, 260–61, 266; and stalled progress on decommissioning 254–6, 257–8; not sleeping well 256; further meetings with BA, SF, UUs and SDLP 259–60; sees AC as a problem 262; at Lisbon European Council meeting 262; calls NHS meeting 263; tries to get new IRA statement out of GA and McG 263–4; attacked by Paisley 264; meeting in with BA 264; 'antsy' about Cockerell documentary 264, 270; less optimistic than BA re IRA 264; publicly mocked by PM 265; fed up with Mo

266, 269; meetings and possible progress 267; lines up arms dump verifiers 267; and title of new police service 267, 268, 270; and NI breakthrough 268, 269; gives *Times* interview 269; at *Observer* lunch 270; and 'bloody flags issue' 270; low ratings in poll 271; and Leo's birth 271–2; tells MO she is not being briefed against 273; reliant on AC 274; and Cockerell film 274; further problems with Mo 275–6; on DT 277; and MEPP 277; and IRA statement 278; wants AC to stay after election 278, 283; at Nice EU summit 279, 280; and SF 'normalization agenda' 279–80; exasperated with PM 280; and BC's valedictory visit to NI 280–81, 282; meetings more convivial than usual 281; speaks to Bush 282

2001–2003 and hunting ban 284; worried that Labour has peaked 284; meetings with SDLP and SF 284; speaks to BC 284–5; worried about UUs 284, 285; spends hours with SF 285; meets Flanagan and Irwin 286; feels progress with GA is being made 286–7; has surreal dinner at Chequers 287; and PM's resignation over Hinduja passport application 288–93, 294; does not want AC to leave 293, 294–5; irritates CB with his guitar playing 295; attacked by FM 295–6; with Bush in Washington 296; no clothes sense 296–7; and progress on NI talks 297–8; and PM's menacing mood 298; and foot-and-mouth epidemic 297, 299; and election victory (2001) 299, 300; holds talks with UUP, SDLP and SF 300 *and n*, 301; and DT's resignation and suspension of NI Assembly 301 *and n*; at Weston Park talks 301, 302, 303; not told by GB of wife's pregnancy 303–4; and Bush's visit 304; his dream for NI 305–6; and 9/11 306–9; clashes with GB 310; his Oman visit reported by BBC 310; in Washington 311; and IRA decommissioning 311*n*; criticized by Mo in Cockerell documentary 311–12; discusses with AC whether he should stay or go 314–15;

compares AC to Roy Keane 315; further problems with DT 316; plans not to fight a third election 316; raises the bar on ceasefire judgement 316; at monthly press conference 317; and Iraq 317, 318, 323; wants more formality in government 317; more worried about NI 317; compared with BC 318; PG's opinion of 319; given deadline for SF expulsion by DT 319 *and n*; given history lesson by GA 319; still hopes for progress from SF and IRA 319–20; gives major speech in Belfast 320, 321; strong at PMQs 321; intends to sack GB 322; has Jamie Oliver lunch with BA 323; talks with DT and SF 323; and RC's resignation 323; dismissive of AC's problems with FM 324; on GB as next leader 324; accepts that AC will leave 326; with Bush at Hillsborough 325, 326–8; meeting with Fiona 328; and IRA non-delivery 328–9; wants AC to go to Germany 331; worried about GB 331; worried that SF will not 'deliver' 331; asks to meet IRA 332; BC's views on 333, 334–5; and CB's firing of FM 336; and AC's departure 337
Blix, Hans 333
'Bloody Sunday' (1972) 71, 73, 85, 86, 89–91
Blumenthal, Sidney 175
Blunkett, David (DB) xix, 38, 144, 172, 184, 185, 277, 300*n*, 307, 328
Bono 210, 287
Booth, Gale 5, 117
Boothroyd, Betty xxiii, 29, 90, 130
Bosnia 21, 25, 49
Bostock, David 197
Bostock, Dr Tom 236
Boulton, Adam xxiii, 52, 194, 210, 251
Bradshaw, David 37
Bradshaw, Kerry 37
Braithwaite, Julian xx, 198, 268
Breakfast with Frost 68, 84, 128, 134—5, 142, 145, 269
Brenton, Tony 311
British–Irish Council (BIC) 246, 316
British–Irish Inter-governmental Conference (BIIGC) 246

Brittan, Leon 102, 314
Brown, Gordon xix; relations with TB 6, 26, 247–8, 256, 260; and battle with TB over leadership 3*n*, 128, 237, 283, 289, 304, 316; TB's views on 4, 10, 67, 85, 214, 235, 274, 278; and 'Clause 4' 10, 13; and TB's piece on God 23; appointed Chancellor of the Exchequer 38; sees Governor of Bank of England 39; refuses to move into No. 10 45; sees Mrs Thatcher at No. 10 46; and BC's visit 48; AC turns light out at his Denver press conference 54; friendlier than usual 58; his 'psychological flaws' 85, 86, 98–9, 235; feels undermined by TB 87; livid at not going on US trip 91; 'impossible' 95; TB wants a 'coming together' with 98, 100, 101; does economic package for NI 122, 127, 128; rift with TB is made public 149, 150; 'the root of all evil' (PM) 152; opposed to trailing summit 171; has teeth capped 172; tries to 'neuter' TB's NYSE speech 174; and PM 188, 189, 190, 233, 237, 270, 277, 290, 291; 'up to no good' 211, 213; in a 'foul mood' 243; writes off Third World debt to UK 246–7; embarrassing behaviour 250–51; Ken Livingstone's comment on 267; feels Labour is lacking a forward agenda 284; his angry doodles 302–3; monosyllabic 309, 310; clashes with TB 310; BC asks AC about 318; TB decides to sack 322; more co-operative 324; as a possible Foreign Secretary 328; TB decides to wage war against 331
Brown, Nick xix, 180*n*, 300*n*
Brown, Sarah 98, 303–4
Brown, Tina 24
Brún, Bairbre de 163, 246, 281, 319*n*
Brunson, Michael xxiii, 52, 109, 112, 116, 117, 167, 217
Bruton, John, Taoiseach xxi, 12, 14, 15, 19*n*, 22, 27*n*, 39, 40, 51, 55, 58
Burnley FC: vs Crystal Palace 31; vs York 68; vs Bournemouth 122, 258; vs Luton 171; vs Bristol Rovers 234; vs Gillingham 264; vs Scunthorpe 266, 267, 268—9; vs Nottingham Forest 277

Burnside, David 267
Burton, John 36
Bush, George W, President xxii; PM's gaffe about 279; elected President 281–2, 287; telephones TB 282; involvement with NI 286; and TB's US visit 296; in UK 304; after 9/11 308, 309; visits NI 325, 326–8; as marathon runner 330; BC's views on 332, 333
Butler, Eddie 128*n*
Butler, Richard 185–6
Butler, Sir Robin xx, 37, 38, 42, 70
Butler, Trevor 36, 74
Byers, Stephen xix, 86, 274, 310
Byrne, Patrick, Garda Commissioner 157, 158

Caborn, Richard 191
Callaghan, James (Jim) xxiii, 8
Cameron, David 46, 91
Campbell, Betty 8, 37, 195, 265
Campbell, Brendan 95
Campbell, Calum 37, 66, 68, 76, 122, 160, 166, 176, 184, 208, 234, 255, 258, 266, 268–9, 290, 299, 330
Campbell, Donald (AC's father) 8, 195, 265
Campbell, Grace 37, 124, 160, 184, 207, 264, 329, 330
Campbell, Jason 70, 71
Campbell, Rory 20, 37, 66, 68, 122, 123, 147, 158, 160, 166, 176, 184, 206, 208, 258, 290, 299, 311, 315, 330, 332
Canary Wharf: IRA bomb (1996) 19
Cantona, Eric 332
Caplin, Carole xxiv, 6, 16, 35, 36, 324, 334, 335, 336
Card, Andy 326
Carey, George, Archbishop of Canterbury 88
Carville, James 31
Casey, Louise 245
Castro, Fidel 138
Celtic fan, murder of 70, 71
Channel 4 269
Charles, Prince 142, 143, 157, 160, 189, 190
Chequers 40, 45, 60, 70, 176, 285, 286
Chilcot, John xxi, 9

Chirac, Jacques 54, 100, 102, 133–4, 136, 153, 280, 308, 309, 327
Christopher, Warren 24
Churchill, Winston 45, 60
Çiller, Tansu 134
CIRA *see* Continuity Irish Republican Army
Clark, Alan xxiii, 75, 76
Clark, General Wesley 210
Clarke, Charles 300*n*
Clarke, Ken 322
Clarke, Liam, and Johnston, Kathryn: *Martin McGuinness…* 331*n*
Clarke, Martin 196
'Clause 4' 5 *and n*, 10, 13
Cleaver, Magi xx, 41, 43, 55, 174, 304, 327
Clinton, Bill, President (BC) xxii; visits UK (1995) 17–18; overdoes praise of JM 17, 18; 'special chemistry' with TB 17, 18, 50; and TB's visit to US (1996) 23, 24–5, 26; rehearses before interviews 31; and sexual harassment case 47; visits UK (1997) 41–2, 45, 47–50; at Denver G8 summit 51–5; backs TB in putting pressure on SF 52–3, 54; has unscheduled meeting with TB at Madrid NATO summit 59–60; and NATO 60; suggests AC come and work for him 66; and Monica Lewinsky affair 87, 88, 92, 94, 161, 166–7, 168, 173, 334; and bombing of Iraq 88, 90; and TB's US visit (1998) 91, 92–4; offers help re NI 94, 96; and Good Friday Agreement 112, 113, 114–15, 116, 118, 129; UUs opposed to his involvement 126, 135; at Birmingham G7–8 meeting 133–6; on *Frost* 134–5; at Chequers with TB 137; his *Mirror* article goes to the *Sun* 137, 138; on fear and hope 140; in Russia 165; NI visit (1998) 154, 155, 163–4, 165, 167–70; at Omagh 169, 170; attacked by Lieberman in Dublin 170–71; lack of support in US 171, 172; and Starr Report 172, 173; and TB's NY visit 174, 175; TB on 176, 178, 179; speaks to TB on Iraq 185, 186; and US press 187; meets with TB at King Hussein's funeral 194–5; clear on IRA decommissioning 195; wins impeachment battle 195; offers to do whatever it takes in NI 198; and

DT 210; and Drumcree march (1999) 213; his 'flip' way 217; gives up on black humour 219; tries to keep TB's spirits up 223; against cancelling TB's meeting with DT and GA 229; lightens the mood 231; and Jack Cunningham 236; and Mo 238; against AC's soundbite at NI devolution 243; in touch with the Irish 254; criticized by PM 265; sees GA and McG at Irish Embassy 265; told by GA of imminent IRA statement 268; 'the Downing Street poisoner' 269; in Dublin 270; says nothing to journalists 273; holidays in France near AC 275; and BC's visit (2000) 279, 282; FM wants him given more responsibilities 295, 296; and PM/Hinduja affair 297; at meeting with FM and CB 299; at Weston Park talks 303; on Bush after 9/11 309; and TB's thoughts of departure 316; at meeting re arrest of SF members 318; PG recognizes his role 319; stays in NI to try to finalize deal 328–9; and MI5 transcripts of calls with McG and Mo 331; stays to the end of NI negotiations 338; runs charity dedicated to peace processes 117; mentioned 16, 42, 55, 83, 96, 123, 211, 222, 227, 242, 293, 307, 336

Prescott, John (JP) xx, 4, 247; and Clause 4 10; at TB's dinner with Eddie George 13; narrowly misses Aldwych bomb 19; can't bring himself to say 'New' before Labour 19; and TB 26; and PMQs 30, 302; and TB's arrival at Downing St 37; appointed Deputy Prime Minister 38; and BC's visit 48; at TB's UN speech 55; TB on 85, 91; and CS 87; visits Midlands flood areas 119; on news re Channel Tunnel rail link 144; and Omagh bombing 155, 156, 160, 161; and PM's book idea 191; and Gore 194; feeling bruised 233; and Ken Livingstone 265; 'mega-supportive' 269; and Mo 279, 312; and election campaign 299; and GB 324

Prescott, Mike 161, 268

Press Association (PA) 37, 52, 69, 90, 99, 150, 181, 256, 259, 273, 303

Preston, Peter 97

Preston, Roz 41

Prevention of Terrorism Act 14

Price, Lance 150, 189

Primakov, Yevgeny 172, 173

Prodi, Romano 60, 175

Progressive Unionist Party (PUP) 61–2, 89 110, 202, 203

Provisional IRA (PIRA) 96, 159

Public Administration Select Committee (PASC) 130

PUP *see* Progressive Unionist Party

Putin, Vladimir 308

Puttnam, David 31

Quinn, Christine 152*n*

Quinn, Jason, Mark and Richard 152–3

Quinn, Lee 152*n*

Quinn, Ruairí xxii, 30, 182

Ramaphosa, Cyril 267

Rangers FC: murder of Celtic fan 70

Rawnsley, Andrew 85, 248

Rayner, Terry 36, 43

Reagan, Ronald 17, 326

Real IRA (RIRA) 154*n*, 156, 157*n*, 160, 169 171, 180, 181, 183, 201, 280

Rebuck, Gail xxiv, 142, 151, 232, 275, 309 314

Red Hand Defenders 196*n*

Reid, John (JR) xxii, 274, 290, 298, 320, 321

Reynolds, Albert 47

Rice, Condoleezza xxiii, 326, 327, 328

Rich, Marc 332–3

Richard, Ivor 100

Richards, Steve 250

Riddell, Mary 28

Riddell, Peter xxiv, 24, 269

RIRA *see* Real IRA

Roberts, Sir Ivor 226, 266

Robertson, George xx, 90, 198, 229, 237

Robertson, Sandra 229

Robinson, Geoffrey xxi, 149, 184, 186–8 313; *The Unconventional Minister* 277

Robinson, Mary, President of Ireland 30 206

Robinson, Peter xv, xxii, 30, 122, 143

Rosenthal, Jim 208–9